7/1

An Enchanted Modern

PRINCETON STUDIES IN MUSLIM POLITICS

DALE F. EICKELMAN AND AUGUSTUS RICHARD NORTON, *EDITORS*

Diane Singerman, *Avenues of Participation: Family, Politics, and Networks in Urban Quarters of Cairo*

Tone Bringa, *Being Muslim the Bosnian Way: Identity and Community in a Central Bosnian Village*

Dale F. Eickelman and James Piscatori, *Muslim Politics*

Bruce B. Lawrence, *Shattering the Myth: Islam beyond Violence*

Ziba Mir-Hosseini, *Islam and Gender: The Religious Debate in Contemporary Iran*

Robert W. Hefner, *Civil Islam: Muslims and Democratization in Indonesia*

Muhammad Qasim Zaman, *The Ulama in Contemporary Islam: Custodians of Change*

Michael G. Peletz, *Islamic Modern: Religious Courts and Cultural Politics in Malaysia*

Oskar Verkaaik, *Migrants and Militants:* Fun, *Islam, and Urban Violence in Pakistan*

Laetitia Bucaille, *Growing up Palestinian: Israeli Occupation and the Intifada Generation*

Robert W. Hefner, editor, *Remaking Muslim Politics: Pluralism, Contestation, Democratization*

Lara Deeb, *An Enchanted Modern: Gender and Public Piety in Shi'i Lebanon*

An Enchanted Modern

GENDER AND PUBLIC PIETY
IN SHI`I LEBANON

Lara Deeb

PRINCETON UNIVERSITY PRESS

PRINCETON AND OXFORD

Published by Princeton University Press, 41 William Street, Princeton, New Jersey 08540

In the United Kingdom: Princeton University Press, 3 Market Place, Woodstock, Oxfordshire OX20 1SY

LIBRARY OF CONGRESS CATALOGING-IN-PUBLICATION DATA

Deeb, Lara, 1974–
   An enchanted modern : gender and public piety in Shi'i Lebanon / Lara Deeb.
      p.   cm.—(Princeton studies in Muslim politics)
   Includes bibliographical references and index.
   ISBN 0-691-12420-5 (alk. paper)—ISBN 0-691-12421-3 (pbk. : alk. paper)
   1. Shiites—Lebanon—Beirut.   2. Islam and politics—Lebanon—Beirut.   3. Women
in Islam—Lebanon—Beirut.   I. Title.   II. Series.
   BP192.7.L4D44 2006
   305.48'69782'0956925—dc22   2005048753

British Library Cataloging-in-Publication Data is available

This book has been composed in Sabon

Printed on acid-free paper. ∞

pup.princeton.edu

Printed in the United States of America

10 9 8 7 6 5 4

ISBN-13: 978-0-691-12421-6 (pbk.)

ISBN-10: 0-691-12421-3 (pbk.)

Contents

Acknowledgments   vii

Note on Language   xi

PART ONE: *Encounters, Approaches, Spaces, Moments*

INTRODUCTION
Pious and/as/is Modern   3

CHAPTER ONE
Al-Dahiyya: Sight, Sound, Season   42

CHAPTER TWO
From Marginalization to Institutionalization   67

PART TWO: *Living an Enchanted Modern*

CHAPTER THREE
The Visibility of Religion in Daily Life   99

CHAPTER FOUR
Ashura: Authentication and Sacrifice   129

CHAPTER FIVE
Community Commitment   165

CHAPTER SIX
Public Piety as Women's *Jihād*   204

CHAPTER SEVEN
The Pious Modern Ideal and Its Gaps   220

Glossary   233

References   235

Index   251

Acknowledgments

THIS BOOK is the culmination of a voyage that forms only part of my lifelong relationship with Lebanon. I am greatly indebted in myriad ways to the many people who have helped and supported me along the way, and grateful for the various forms of institutional support from which this project has benefited.

The field research for this project was made possible by a Social Science Research Council International Dissertation Research Fellowship, a National Science Foundation Dissertation Fellowship, a grant from Emory University's Internationalization Fund, and a P.E.O. International Scholar Award. The Center for Behavioral Research at the American University of Beirut (AUB), under Samir Khalaf, provided an academic home in Beirut. This version of the manuscript was written during a year at the Harvard Academy for International and Area Studies.

Many organizations in the southern suburbs of Beirut kindly facilitated my research, including al-Mabarrat Charitable Association, the Martyrs' Association, the Islamic Charitable Emdad Committee, the Imam al-Sadr Foundation, the Consulting Center for Studies and Documentation, and the media relations office of Hizbullah. I owe an especial debt of gratitude to the Social Advancement Association for including me in their activities and embracing me as a volunteer with them.

My field research experience was greatly enhanced by conversations with Mona Harb, Diane Riskedahl, Rola Husseini, Randa Serhan, and many colleagues at AUB; Diane's always good-humored comradeship in fieldwork; e-mail discussions with fellow fieldworking Emory students Daniel Lende and Donna Murdock; Hussein Nabulsi's consistent willingness to answer yet another question; and Hajjeh Umm Muhammad's warm hospitality and delicious malfouf. Lebanon would have been a much colder place without my extended family, who provided refuge, entertainment, and company whenever I needed a break. My family and friends outside the southern suburbs supported me in my research endeavors even as they doubted my sanity, and often provided unwitting fodder for thought and contrast.

I am most grateful to the teachers I have been privileged to work with, and who have shaped and supported this project from its inception. Donald Donham read draft upon draft, in various forms over the past several years. His astute guidance, inspiring scholarship, provocative questions, and unfailing encouragement pushed my thinking throughout this project, and continue to do so today. Corinne Kratz patiently read and provided insightful feedback on far too many drafts and stream-of-consciousness e-mails from the field. Bruce Knauft's reflections reminded me to keep broader contexts in mind. Suad Joseph and Debra Spitulnik provided incisive interventions for several chapters. My teachers and friends Kristen Brustad and Mahmoud al-Batal were a constant source of support, quelling my language anxieties and providing a home in Atlanta on several occasions.

Colleagues and friends in various academic locales have provided helpful comments and thoughts on pieces of this book or its arguments in one form or another. I especially thank Tom Boellstorff, Houchang Chehabi, Inderpal Grewal, Mary Alice Haddad, Sondra Hale, Robert Hefner, Mary Hegland, Carla Jones, Mark LeVine, Henry Munson, Nadine Naber, Conor O'Dwyer, Armando Salvatore, Chris Stone, Sherrill Stroschein, Jenny White, Patricia Wood, and Sherifa Zuhur for their insights. I have benefited from close readings of the entire manuscript by Donna Murdock, whose academic camaraderie has kept me sane for years, and, in the eleventh hour, by Esra Özyürek, with whom I only wish my conversation had begun sooner. I also thank reviewers Nadje al-Ali and A. Richard Norton. I am especially indebted to Richard for his encouragement throughout this process and his astute readings of Lebanese politics. Audiences at a number of academic venues including the AAA and MESA meetings, and AUB, Emory, Harvard, University of California–Irvine, and Boston University have asked questions that prompted new ideas.

My new colleagues at UC Irvine—especially Inderpal Grewal, Kavita Philip, and Jennifer Terry—have provided the sort of mentoring through the process of finalizing a manuscript that a junior faculty member can only hope for. I greatly appreciate the interest and support of Fred Appel at Princeton University Press, as well as Jennifer Nippins's patience and diligence.

I also feel grateful for the many friends and colleagues who have been a constant source of encouragement and motivation, and with whom conversations have often inspired me to think through knotty issues, particularly Katie Carson, Leila Farsakh, Maysoun Freij, Elaine Hagopian, Yamila Hussein, Amira Jarmakani, Gloria and Haitham Khoury, Michelle Mavissakalian, Dorothy McLaughlin, Nadine Naber, Wendy Pearlman, Gayatri Reddy, Nadine Samara, Sarah Saxer, Nadya Sbaiti, Rebecca Seligman, Lucia Volk, and Zeina Zaatari.

My deepest gratitude is reserved for my parents, for initiating my interest in Lebanon and always supporting all my endeavors; my brother Hadi, for inspiring me every single day with his courage and for those moments of incredible clarity and hilarious fun; my partner, Qutayba

Abdullatif, for being the sunshine that sustains me, standing by me throughout this project, and always pushing me to say what I mean; and for the people in al-Dahiyya who shared such an important part of their lives with me, especially the women volunteers who taught me, laughed with me, and moved me with their faith and steadfastness. Above all my thanks go to my "sister," "Aziza," and her family, who, despite clichés, truly gave me a home away from home. It is to her that I dedicate this book.

Note on Language

QUOTATIONS from both written and spoken sources are transliterated using a simplified version of the *International Journal of Middle East Studies (IJMES)* system. All translations are my own. Speakers used Modern Standard Arabic, Lebanese dialect, English, and French. In transliterating dialect, a few modifications, based on Brustad (2000), were necessary in order to preserve its phonemic differences (e.g., *tā marbūta* is indicated by /eh/ in colloquial, rather than /a/). For the sake of simplicity for the nonspecialist, I indicate which form of Arabic was spoken only where necessary. Also for the sake of simplicity, commonly used Arabic plurals are indicated by adding *s* (e.g., *ḥijāb*s, *jamʿiyya*s), except in those cases where that would involve the doubling of an *s*, in which case the broken plural is indicated (e.g., *majālis* rather than *majliss*). Proper nouns and terms with common English spellings are preserved as such (e.g., Nasrallah).

PART ONE

Encounters, Approaches, Spaces, Moments

I.1. An orphan sign in front of a mosque in al-Dahiyya.

Pious and/as/is Modern

HAJJEH UMM ZEIN shook her hand at the television and said emphatically, "I can't believe this! What is this backwardness?!"[1] Her daughter and I were sitting across the living room, talking about a charity event we had recently attended. "What, Mama?" "Look at this! Where in Islam does it tell them to waste their time on something empty/useless (*shī fāḍī*) like this? This is not Islam!" We turned toward the muted television. An image of the Taliban regime in Afghanistan destroying two large statues of the Buddha filled the screen, the CNN logo at the bottom. I picked up the remote and raised the volume to hear and translate the accompanying commentary, which was expressing the dismay of the world, and especially the West, at this act of destruction. The Taliban were described as Islamic fundamentalists, a characterization with which my companions took issue in a particular way. As they explained to me, the CNN reporter was correct to label them "extremists" (*mutaṭarrifīn*), but was wrong to associate them with Islam, because "this backwardness is not true Islam."[2]

These two women are pious Shi'i Muslims who live in the southern suburbs of Beirut,[3] an area known as al-Dahiyya, where I conducted field research for twenty-two months between 1999 and 2001.[4] They are loosely associated with Hizbullah (literally, Party of God), a Lebanese Shi'i Islamic political party. In the eyes of many North Americans and in the U.S. media, my friends in al-Dahiyya fell into the same general category as the Taliban: religious fundamentalists who are staunchly antimodern. This characterization reflects two of the assumptions I aim

---

[1] "Hajjeh" is a term of address for women who have completed the *hajj*, the female counterpart to "Hajj." Both "Hajjeh" and "Hajj" are also used as generic terms of respectful address for elders. All interlocutor names are pseudonyms. I have also altered incidental details of people's lives to protect their identities. In cases where people will still be identifiable to others in the community, I have discussed that situation with them.

[2] Pious Shi'is have been staunchly anti–al Qaeda and anti-Taliban since long before 9/11 and continue to distance themselves from those groups' understandings of Islam and the world.

[3] To maintain consistency, I use "Shi'i" as an adjective, "Shi'is" as a plural (e.g., "42 Shi'is") and "Shi'a" as a collective noun (e.g., "the Lebanese Shi'a").

[4] The bulk of my research was conducted between October 1999 and August 2001, with several shorter visits in 1998, 2002, and 2004.

to dislodge in the chapters that follow: that Islamism is static and monolithic, and that Islam and modernity are incompatible.

The contemporary moment is one during which public religiosities have emerged across the globe: Christian fundamentalists in the United States,[5] liberation theologies in Latin America, Hindu fundamentalisms in India, and ultraorthodox Judaism in Israel are but a few of the more prominent non-Islamic examples. Such publicly engaged religiosities have contributed to the collapse of the notion that religion and modernity are incompatible. Yet that notion persists in relation to Islam and was exacerbated after the events of September 11, 2001 and their aftermath. Various formations of "political Islam" or "Islamism" have come to represent the quintessential other, the antimodern antithesis to a supposedly secular West.[6] Yet many public Islams are part of this contemporary moment, when it has become eminently possible to imagine various modernities (including Christian ones within the United States) as enchanted in the Weberian sense, and as compatible with and potentially even dependent on pieties.[7] The pages that follow explore the multiple intersections between ideas and practices of modernity and of piety in a Shi'i Muslim community in al-Dahiyya.

My goals in this book are twofold. First, I aim to unravel the complexity around how pious Shi'i Muslims understand "being modern"[8] and how they engage with and deploy various discourses and ideas about modern-ness.[9] These include discourses that they associate with a singular Western modernity,[10] as well as those rooted in their own emphasis on pious or enchanted ways of being modern. Two major points

---

[5] Here I mean the "born-again" Christianity that Susan Harding (2000) characterizes as Christian fundamentalists' return from exile into public life in the United States, also referred to as "neo-evangelicalism."

[6] See also Moallem 2002, and, in relation to gender, Ahmed 1992. This is not a new othering; Edward Said described its basis in *Orientalism.* In today's allegedly postcolonial world, the Middle East stands out as still undergoing colonization and imperialism in various forms, with their accompanying processes of othering. See for example, Shafir's discussion of Israel as a settler-colony built on various models of European colonization (1989).

[7] Hence my choice of "An Enchanted Modern" rather than "Enchanted Modern" for this book's title.

[8] Note that I use "pious Shi'i Muslims" or "pious Shi'is" as a gloss to indicate the particular community where I worked, a community that is itself bounded by specific ideas about piety.

[9] Despite the awkward nature of the term, I use "modern-ness" rather than modernity for two reasons. First, because the latter has come to carry larger epochal meanings from which I wish to distance my discussion, and, second, because I want to emphasize that by "modern-ness" I mean the state of being modern as "modern" is understood in a particular context.

[10] Clearly, the notion of a singular essentialized "Western modernity" is problematic. When I use "Western modernity," unless otherwise explained, I am indicating my interlocutors' usage as they position "the West" as an essentialized "other" analytic category.

of confrontation emerge: the opposition between secularity and religiosity and the struggle to define gender roles and ideal womanhood. Rather than points of challenge or rejection, these are points of ambivalence and negotiation, though always in the context of the power of Western discourses and the political stakes of being modern in the contemporary world.

As we will see, the core of this enchanted modern is a dual emphasis on both material and spiritual progress as necessary to modern-ness. Spiritual progress in particular is viewed by pious Shi'is as the necessary component in providing a viable alternative to the perceived emptiness of modernity as manifested in the West. I suggest that when religiosity is incorporated into modern-ness in this way, the stakes of being pious change. The dualistic notion of progress and the global political context in which it has emerged have consequences for faith and morality on the personal level, on people's quotidian expressions and experiences of piety. These consequences are related to the notion of spiritual progress as a move "forward," away from "tradition" and into a new kind of religiosity, one that involves conscious and conscientious commitment.

This brings me to my second goal: to explore the new forms of piety—especially publicly performed piety—that have taken root in this community over the past three decades, and the ways that the normativization of public piety affects people's—especially women's—lives. It is perhaps no surprise that it is women who claim center stage in this process, as women's practices and morality have often been constructed as necessary to collective identities.[11] In al-Dahiyya, women's public piety has been incorporated as both necessary to and evidence of the enchanted modern. For this reason, as I depict the daily and seasonal dynamics of public piety, I am especially concerned with the ways that engagement with the question of how to be modern has significant effects for understandings and expressions of women's piety.

We need ethnography in order to understand the local dynamics of what has been variously called "Islamization," "Islamic fundamentalism," "Islamism," and so on.[12] Much has been made of these terms and

[11] Anticolonial nationalisms have often used women's behavior to construct collective identities that were both modern *and* culturally authentic. See Chatterjee 1993; Abu-Lughod 1998b.

[12] I use the term "Islamist" to describe Hizbullah only where it either reflects a translation of *"Islāmiyyīn"* or fits Jenny White's definition of Islamists as "Muslims who, rather than accept an inherited Muslim tradition, have developed their own self-conscious vision of Islam, which is then brought to bear on social and political events within a particular national context" (2002: 23). I understand this definition to mean Muslims who deploy an "Islamic politics" rather than a "political Islam." The latter is predicated on Islam becoming political, while the former describes a particular politics as informed by Islam in some, relatively explicit, way. In Hizbullah's case, it is politics that took on the adjective "Islamic."

movements with regard to their effects on national and international politics. This literature is broad in scope, covering large swaths of time and space, and official political and religious discourses. With the glaring exception of work on women and especially the veil,[13] less attention has been given to the everyday, to the different ways that new understandings of Islam are a part of people's lives, and to changes in the ways people pray, interact, mourn, and give—the ways that they practice and perform piety.[14] By maintaining an ethnographic focus on the ways notions of modern-ness and piety are lived, debated, and shaped by "everyday Islamists," I hope to demonstrate the complexity of those engagements and underscore the inseparability of religion and politics in the lives of pious Muslims. By looking at these complex daily enmeshments of piety and politics, we will see that Islam is not in the service of politics, nor are politics determined solely by Islam. Only by holding both in view—undoing their separation into discrete categories (a separation characteristic of secular notions of the modern)—can we come to a more complete understanding of the pious modern.

The chapters that follow constitute an ethnography of a pious Shi'i community in Beirut, and the discourses, practices, and understandings that underpin daily entanglements of piety and modernity. In chapter 1, I depict al-Dahiyya, the area of Beirut where the urban heart of the Shi'i pious modern lies, in order to excavate the visual, aural, and seasonal transformation of this public space into one of piety. Through this introduction to al-Dahiyya we see the ways the pious modern saturates the area, evidence of its visibility on the national stage. I then step back in chapter 2, and provide some crucial history and background, especially concerning the institutionalization of the Lebanese Shi'i Islamic movement over the past three decades. We will see how religion emerged as a mobilizing factor for Lebanese Shi'is in response to the failures of the left, the success of the Islamic Revolution in Iran, and the Israeli invasions and occupation of Lebanon.

The focus of chapter 3 is how religious practices and discourses—in particular those of what I term "authenticated" Islam—permeate daily life in ways that are considered new. I consider embodied and discursive forms of piety, as they emerge as both public markers of personal faith and markers of the spiritual progress of the community. In chapter 4 I take a closer look at one religious season, known as Ashura—the annual commemoration of the martyrdom of Imam Husayn, grandson of the Prophet Muhammad and one of the most important figures in Shi'ism.

---

[13] The literature is vast; I list here only a few key examples: Ahmed 1992, El Guindi 1999, MacLeod 1991, Göle 1996, Hale 1996, Zuhur 1992.

[14] A notable exception is White 2002.

The transformation that has occurred in Ashura and the commemoration's importance as a contemporary narrative framework for living public piety provides a case study through which to explore the shift to authenticated Islam in all its complexity.

In chapter 5, I take up women's volunteerism as the vehicle through which women's piety is most clearly brought into the public realm. Women's community service activities are discussed as crucial to both material and spiritual progress. I also consider the ways that piety and politics, as well as humanitarian sentiment and historical models like those of Ashura, merge to motivate women's public participation. Chapter 6 builds on this discussion with an emphasis on the ways gender is implicated in public piety and the pious modern. I explore how public piety is cast as women's *jihād* and the implications of its imperative on women's lives, as well as the relationship between women's visibility and ideas about modern-ness. Generational differences and the concomitant gaps in public piety are the subject of the final chapter, which concludes with a revisiting of the pious modern ideal in the contemporary context.

In the remainder of this introduction, I provide the setting for the chapters that follow—not in terms of the spatial or temporal terrain, but in terms of a conceptual geography, the methodological, theoretical and positional grounds on which this book rests. It goes without saying that readers bring different backgrounds and desires to texts. While this book can be read as a depiction of life in an Islamist community, it is the conceptual deployments around the notion of being pious and modern that most interest me. Indeed, it is those deployments that constitute the boundaries of the community itself.

A "Community" Bound(ed) by Piety

One of the complexities of urban fieldwork is that the research population is often defined in nongeographical and rather imprecise ways. The Shi'i pious modern is not a community clearly bounded by space. My interlocutors could generally be described based on residence or work in al-Dahiyya; however, that characterization erases the diversity of that area of Beirut. "Al-Dahiyya" also encompasses many neighborhoods in the southern suburbs of Beirut, and my research was especially concentrated in four of them. As such, it is not accurate or useful to characterize this study as one of "al-Dahiyya" as such.

Other Lebanese often refer to pious Shi'i Muslims—or all Shi'i Muslims for that matter—as a "community." In the latter case, this denotes a sectarian group in the country, while in the former it frequently involves inaccurate generalizations about the political party Hizbullah as representative of all pious Lebanese Shi'i Muslims. Although some of the people I spoke with over the course of my research were members of the party and/or volunteered in party-affiliated organizations, this gloss is misleading. Many had no direct relationship to the party whatsoever. Rather, their imaginations of themselves as a community (and their exclusions of others) were based upon their shared religious, social, and political values, which I gather under the rubric of "public piety."[15] Public piety is the public practice of faith based upon an interpretation of Islam that I term "authenticated Islam." This notion of "authentication" is built on my interlocutors' sense of a shift that has occurred in their religious understandings and practices, a shift that is a key aspect of how they conceptualize social change and the dynamics of Shi'i identity in the contemporary world.

As we will see, the values of public piety include understanding and practicing Islam "correctly"; sacrificing one's time, money, and life to help others; and supporting the Resistance against Israeli occupation. Underlying all these values is a strong belief in the necessity of both spiritual and material progress. The primacy of this notion of progress, of a continued effort toward change from what existed before, suggests that rather than "community," the term "movement" might be more appropriate. Yet neither "Shi'i Islamic community" nor "Shi'i Islamic movement" quite captures either the diversity or the porosity of this group of people.

Most people referred to their self-identified community of pious Shi'i Muslims simply as "our community"—using the Arabic term *mujtama'*. From the root [*j – m – '*], *mujtama'* carries numerous connotations, ranging from "a gathering place" to "the whole of human society." In pious Shi'i usage, it captured the meanings of both "community" and "society"—*Gemeinschaft* and *Gesellschaft*. In a sense, the inseparability of the two in their speech speaks to their refusal of the assumption that modernization leads to an impersonal society and their embrace of a modern that prioritizes face-to-face human relationships.

The phrase "our community" shifted meaning according to context. A volunteer bemoaning Shi'i poverty might use "our community" to refer to Lebanese Shi'is in general, calling upon their collective history of marginalization in the country. Or she might be referring specifically to the poor in al-Dahiyya. Another conversation might find her talking about the latest Resistance operation in the south, using "community" to mean

---

[15] As such, this account should not be read as representative of all Lebanese Shi'is but as a particular imagination of community—to extrapolate from Benedict Anderson (1983)—where the "community" is based upon a relatively simultaneous performance of public piety.

Resistance supporters. On yet another occasion, perhaps discussing the greater understanding she has attained regarding a religious principle, the volunteer might use "our community" to denote the community of the Shiʻi pious modern. It is this last sense that best describes my interlocutors as a group.

I use "the community" as the people I spoke with did, clarifying the phrase's meaning in context. When discussing elements linked to the Shiʻi Islamic movement as a process of transformation, I refer to it as such. Most frequently, I refer to the people I worked with as pious Shiʻis or pious Shiʻi Muslims. My usage of all these phrases is contingent upon the understanding that these are glosses that do not necessarily encompass all pious Shiʻi Muslims in Lebanon nor all aspects of the Shiʻi Islamic movement. Indeed, as my discussion unfolds, it will become clear that how pious a person is or appears to be plays a major role in whether she is perceived to fall within the bounds of the Shiʻi pious modern community, or whether she is instead included in a broader notion of "our community" based solely on Shiʻi sectarian identity.

THE BETWIXT AND BETWEEN OF FAITH AND IDENTITY IN LEBANON

No doubt some of those I spoke with will not agree with all that I have written here, whether because I do not limit myself to sources of information they agree are "proper," or because of what ultimately is the most difficult divide between us, faith.[16] I made an effort to answer honestly my Shiʻi friends' direct questions about my religious identity and practice—or lack thereof—but at the same time, I avoided the subject as much as possible. I do not know what many of them thought of me in that regard. My impression is that people I spent a significant amount of time with assumed a certain level of faith on my part, an assumption that stemmed from their belief that good will and faith must naturally accompany one another. Very few ever tried to convert me, and those who did generally went about it by drawing on elements shared by Christianity and Islam, while emphasizing the "correct" versions, something that indicated to me their assumptions about my beliefs.

> After the *majlis* [ritual mourning gathering] ended, our hostess came and said with a slight smile, "Lara, Hajjeh——wants to meet you," so I went and sat next to her on the sofa. With no introduction, she launched into a lecture, speaking loudly enough for the women around us to hear: "Ya *ḥabībtī*, all you need to do is accept that God is one, a whole, and that Jesus is a prophet,

---

[16] Here I do not mean type of faith or identity, but simply the existence of religious faith.

a very important prophet, but not the son of God. Because how can any person be God's son? Think about it, it is not rational! Jesus was a great prophet, and when they tried to kill him, God saved him. The Qur'an tells us this, God saved him and he continued preaching for several years before he died. But that is not what is important. What is important is that you admit that it is impossible for God to have a son because God is one and whole. And the holy spirit, what you [plural] call the holy spirit, we call that Gabriel, who came to Mary and told her in advance about Jesus' birth. Accept this and you will be a Muslim, and then you will put on the *ḥijāb* [headscarf], because always, when someone becomes a Muslim later in life, they want to wear the *ḥijāb* quickly because they are choosing the faith, so they are more committed to it than our girls are." Caught off guard, I listened steadily, saying *"insha'allah"* [a noncommittal "God willing"] once in a while. At the last sentence, Aziza walked into the room, looking apologetic. Her aunt had gone to find her when I first sat down. Aziza grabbed my hand and said that I was needed in the kitchen, as the Hajjeh concluded: "You might even wear the *ḥijāb* before Aziza does." Clearly suppressing a smile, Aziza whispered, "now Lara, just say *insha'allah*," which I obediently did before she spirited me away. (from my fieldnotes)

It is difficult to be an atheist in Lebanon, or rather, it is impossible to refuse a religious identity.[17] Everyone I met immediately tried to place me into a category. In Lebanon, the question, "Where are you from?" is a not-so-subtle way of trying to identify a person's sect.[18]

—You are American?
—I have American citizenship, but I was born in Lebanon.[19]
—Your Arabic is "heavy."

[17] These are not the same thing. Religion is used in Lebanon, as in many other places, as a marker of identity and various social distinctions.

[18] I usually follow the secularist "rule" of responding with the generic "Beirut" in an attempt to circumvent—or at least register my resistance to—the question. However, during field research I answered these queries openly. The difficulty here was that those who embraced Shi'ism as both faith and identity often assumed I harbored similar sentiments. People I did not know very well threw comments about "good Christians" or commonalities between Christianity and Islam into various discussions. As my relationships developed, this tendency wore off.

[19] The hyphen in "Arab-American" represents a negation of both identities, an impossible oxymoronic combination. Over time, the hyphenation collapsed and people accepted that I was both. As with any identity, this presented both advantages and disadvantages for research. As Abu-Lughod describes (1986), there were aspects of my life that I felt especially unable to share in al-Dahiyya because of my Lebanese identity. On the other hand, my extended family in Beirut provided me with a level of respectability that I doubt would have existed otherwise. I also faced situations where people expected me to know more than I did, especially about local politics. In this regard my family's Christian background proved helpful, as people took care to explain religious matters without assuming that I had any prior knowledge.

—Yes, I was raised in the United States and have lived there most of my life. And my mother is Armenian.[20]

—[Laughs] Yeah. . . . So you are more American than Lebanese. Where in Lebanon are you from?

—My father is from Hamat, and my mother is from Aanjar.

—Right, you said she was Armenian. Where exactly is Hamat? Somewhere in the north?

—Yes, it's north of Beirut, just past the tunnel near Batroun.

—So you're Christian?

—My father's family is Orthodox Christian.

In general, I found that sectarian identity had been solidified for many Lebanese as a result of the civil war, including for many Shiʿis I met. Yet felt and perceived sectarian divisions were fluid and contextual. A Shiʿi friend told me that while living in Europe he felt more comfortable with Lebanese of all religions than with Muslims from other Arab countries, and quite atypically, a Christian Lebanese woman told her daughter that it would be better to marry a Lebanese Muslim than a foreign Christian.

I want to emphasize that this is not a study of "the Shiʿa in Lebanon," but rather, of a particular "community" defined by forms of piety that reflect a specific Shiʿi identity. There are many people in Beirut and Lebanon who identify as Shiʿi but not with this movement,[21] and there are many who are labeled Shiʿi Muslim as I was labeled Orthodox Christian, but who do not embrace that term with regard to faith and/or identity. As anywhere else, the dynamics of identity are complex—an apt example is an acquaintance of mine who insists on being identified as a "secular Shiʿi" because he wants to "annoy the religious and identify with the underdog." This sense of "the Shiʿa" as "underdog" in Lebanon reverberates throughout this book, and is reflected in public piety, as the reclaiming and reconstruction of a stigmatized identity.

There is a *ḥadīth* from Imam Ali,[22] peace be upon him, that says that you should be considerate of the person next to you, he may be your brother by blood, and if he's not your brother by blood then he may be your brother in

[20] Armenians are stereotyped as mixing up gendered grammatical constructions when they speak Arabic. This stereotype was often invoked by others to explain my tendency to make this sort of grammatical mistake. I adopted the explanation, as it infused humor into my initial meetings with people.

[21] And there are many Shiʿis who do not support or identify with Hizbullah, but who live in Hizbullah-dominant areas quietly, without registering their dissent, whether because of social pressures or the institutional hegemony of the party in their neighborhoods. These perspectives are beyond the boundaries of this project.

[22] Shiʿis believe that Muhammad left the leadership of the Muslim community to his son-in-law Ali and his descendents, called Imams. Capitalized "Imam" should be distinguished from lowercase "imam," the prayer leader at a mosque.

Islam, and if he's not your brother in Islam, he is your brother in humanity. These are the three ties. This should be our identity. (a pious Shi'i volunteer)

In many ways I was not an anomaly in al-Dahiyya. Many Lebanese families have members who emigrate, whether permanently or for short periods of time. I spoke with people who had lived in Michigan, Morocco, Florida, France, Senegal, Quebec, Italy, Saudi Arabia, or the Ivory Coast, among other places. Many had family in North America, Europe, West Africa, or the Gulf. Moreover, the identities and identifications of Lebanon and Lebanese themselves, including pious Shi'is, shift radically by context, moment, and interaction, rendering categories like West, East, modern, nonmodern, Arab, and not Arab highly contingent. There was a sense that people felt perpetually betwixt and between.

The notion that identities and subjectivities are fluid and contextually defined is not an unusual one. Yet in Lebanon at this particular historical moment, identity seemed particularly complex and particularly fascinating, to Lebanese and non-Lebanese alike. On one lazy Beirut afternoon, an anthropologist friend and I were drinking coffee, watching passersby and enjoying the break from that constant sense that comes with participant-observation of having to be recording everything. We were both feeling a bit worn down by Beirut, by the constant hum and malaise that gripped the city on August afternoons. But we were also both feeling a bit obsessed with the city. She noted how typical our obsession seemed. And we tried to identify what it was about Beirut at this particular conjuncture that made all these people we knew—and not only researchers—want to write about it. What we kept coming back to was this inability to place anyone or anything, a slipperiness of meaning and content.

"In Lebanon, there needs to be a sense of belonging to the nation, and we have to at the same time, accept the mosaic, that all members need to coexist but that we will never be a unity." (a pious Shi'i woman, speaking in English)

Another friend of mine called this the "Lebanese identity crisis." Beyond the contradictions of identity experienced and expressed by many Lebanese, her choice of phrase points in two directions. First, it captures the perplexities of "Lebanese national culture," whatever that may be. The most colorful example that comes to mind is the dance troupe Caracalla, characterized by many as "Lebanese folklore." I attended one of their performances during the summer of 2002. The performance defined "hybridity," layering myriad styles, colors, and melodies into bright movement, the *dabkeh* dance fused with modern jazz moves, an amalgamation of "culture" far removed from contemporary political realities.[23] To a certain extent, it is the lacunae left by the lack of a unified Lebanese national identity that have cultivated the exaggerations of communal identity that are performed daily through dress, language, and behavior . . . and public piety.

Second, "Lebanese identity crisis" reflects Lebanon's candidacy for the role of a state without a nation. Its recent civil war ended with a tired fizzle rather than a solution. Many of the cleavages and resentments that sparked the conflict remain, suppressed by an almost willful amnesia. There are few national rallying cries, though there was a cautious level of national support for the Resistance between the 1996 Israeli bombardment of a United Nations' shelter where over a hundred civilians had gathered for protection and liberation in 2000.[24] In general, however, reified identity categories (e.g., us/them, modern/nonmodern, and Western/non-Western) and their erasures are at work in the relationships among various Lebanese communities.

These are linked to structural inequalities, both current and historical. For most people I spoke with, this history was one of Shi'i political and economic marginalization in the Lebanese nation-state. That marginalization—along with the visible piety of my Shi'i interlocutors—contributes to assumptions within Lebanon about "the Shi'a" as "nonmodern." Lebanese I knew whom pious Shi'is would label "Westernized"—those whose speech contained more English or French than Arabic, whose style involved form-fitting clothing and plastic surgery, and whose consumption habits easily rivaled Manhattan's Upper East Side—viewed the headscarves, somber colors, and rituals of my pious Shi'i friends as representative of their "backwardness."[25] Both these labels

---

[23] See Stone (2002) on the ways this sort of amalgamation was constructed by the Rahbani family as "national culture" for certain segments of the population in pre-war Lebanon.

[24] The anti-Syria demonstrations following the assassination of Prime Minister Rafiq Hariri on February 14, 2005 have been cast by some, both in Lebanon and in the international media, as "nationalist" in character. This characterization ignores continuing deep political divisions within the country. As this book goes to press, it remains to be seen what shape Lebanon's future after the withdrawal of the Syrian military will take, and whether the purported "unity" of the anti-Syrian opposition can hold together around other issues.

[25] In her discussion of stereotypical views of Okiek in Kenya versus in the United States, Kratz (2002) cautions against collapsing different layers of stereotypes. Like the Okiek, Shi'i Lebanese face double stereotypes (in Lebanon and in the United States). However, because Lebanese stereotypes are based on Western ideologies, Shi'is are similarly labeled in both contexts. The difference is that in Lebanon people are more likely to differentiate between Shi'i and Sunni Muslims, with some Sunni Muslims also viewing Shi'is as nonmodern. In the United States, that distinction is collapsed, so that all Muslims are collectively categorized.

involve comparative evaluations—as stereotypes always do[26] —with both sides viewing themselves as superior based on a particular set of criteria. My focus is on unraveling the second image in order to undo this opposition.[27] Like other Lebanese, pious Shi'is did indeed feel caught in the "betwixt and between"—deploying multiple discourses of modern-ness and particular sorts of piety in negotiating it. Through these negotiations, the pious modern has taken root.

UNRAVELING "MODERN-NESS"

There exists a value-laden and historicist assumption in many Western academic and media discourses that views the West as the universal example for all that is modern.[28] The often cited characteristics of this universalizing ideal range from technological advance, consumerism, and late capitalism, to secularization and disenchantment, to the prioritization of individualized subjectivities. The West is positioned at the center of a universal modernity that radiates or seeps outward to the rest of the world, where its various characteristics are adopted with some local amendment. This assumption has been critiqued by a burgeoning plural modernities literature which either suggests that alternative modernities have emerged in "other" places or highlights local appropriations of modernity, variously defined.[29] The alternative modernities framework has itself been critiqued both for implying the existence of a singular (Western) modernity to which "other" modernities are alternatives and for making "modernity" so relative a concept as to erase structural inequalities in the world.[30]

In part as a result of these debates, the terms "modern" and "modernity"—in singular and plural forms—have become academic buzzwords of late, to the extent that it can be argued that for reasons of imprecision

[26] See Kratz 2002.

[27] Again, it is crucial to note that the "other" group includes Shi'i Lebanese who did not fit into the pious modern. See Volk's (2001) dissertation about the identity-negotiations of elite Lebanese youth.

[28] By historicist, following Chakrabarty, I mean the taking of the history of the West as determinant for the rest of the world. "Historicism thus posited historical time as a measure of the cultural distance that was assumed to exist between the West and the non-West (Chakrabarty 2000a: 7).

[29] A partial list includes Donham 1999, Larkin 1997, Knauft 2002a, Rofel 1999, Gaonkar 2001, Piot 1999. Rabinow (1989) prefigures much of this work.

[30] See Knauft 2002b, Rofel 2002, Donham 2002, Kelly 2002, and Mitchell 2000a. Much of this criticism has revolved around the slipperiness of the concept "modernity" itself, with some favoring a return to adjectival form (Donham 2002) and others focusing on clarification of use (Friedman 2002, Spitulnik 2002).

and overuse, it is time to bury them. Yet their prevalence is not only a matter of academic fashion. For many of our interlocutors around the world, including pious Shiʻis in Lebanon, being "modern" is a deeply salient issue, and as such, there is a strong case for continued engagement with it, especially at the level of ethnographic complexity. We need to explore not only local understandings of being modern, but also how these understandings are employed and deployed in various contexts and to what effects, and how these uses relate to dominant global and transnational discourses about modern-ness, including western ones. At the same time, it is important to remember that people can and do draw on many different discourses about being modern simultaneously. The tensions among different understandings of modern-ness exemplify some of the power relations of the contemporary world. For this reason, rather than pluralizing the concept as such, I find it more useful to recognize the plurality of experience, interpretation, and understanding of this notion, however unwieldy, with which our informants grapple, within fields of power, on a daily basis.[31]

Despite a plethora of literature about Islamism and modernit(ies),[32] less has been written about how Islamists and pious Muslims themselves grapple with what it means to be modern, without assuming the nature of the links between modern-ness and the West.[33] Instead, much of this work has held Islamism to be either a cultural resistance to a Western modernity, or only selectively modern.[34] Both these perspectives generally work from that historicist understanding of modernity as based in the West, with Islamists either written outside that universalizing project or allowed within its technological, but not its cultural, spaces.[35]

---

[31] This approach allows us to, as Mitchell suggests, "acknowledge the singularity and universalism of the *project* of modernity . . . and, at the same time, attend to a necessary feature of this universalism that repeatedly makes its realization incomplete," the "necessary feature" being the "role of the 'constitutive outside'" (2000a: xiii, emphasis added).

[32] Examples include Abu-Lughod 1998a, Adelkhah 2000, al-Azmeh 1993, Bowen 1993, Eickelman 2000, Eickelman and Piscatori 1996, Ghannam 2002, Göle 1996 and 2000, Hefner 2000, Höfert and Salvatore 2000a, Mitchell 2000b, Peletz 2002, Rahman 1982, Salvatore 1997 and 2001, Tibi 1995, Watts 1996.

[33] Among the notable exceptions to this are Abu-Lughod 1998a, Adelkhah 2000 and Ghannam 2002.

[34] See Abu-Lughod (1998b) and Brenner (1996) for key interventions, on which I build, that instead view Islamists as "striving to construct an alternative modernity" (Abu-Lughod 1998b: 4).

[35] Differences among these arguments often emerge from differences in the definitions of this universalizing modernity. In the first case (e.g., Göle 2000), modernity includes values of secularization, future-orientation, and sometimes democracy, while Islamists are defined as looking to an idealized past. Self-labeled "moderate Muslim" scholars often share this perspective concerning Islamism but work to demonstrate the compatibility of other Islams

While it would be possible to view pious Shi'is as selecting particular aspects of a universalizing Western modernity while rejecting others, this is not the approach I want to take. Nor do I find it useful to view Islam as a strategy for coping with or resisting Westernization or as somehow inherently incompatible with modern-ness. I do not believe that the questions of whether or not people are modern are the most productive ones to ask, either for our understandings of those communities or for our understandings of "modern." Instead, I focus on how people understand the terms of debate, how they approach the question of being modern, what they desire for themselves and their community—without assuming the universality of desires or that "progress" has a singular trajectory.

By taking this approach and bringing the questions generated by the plural modernities debates into this conversation, I suggest that rather than ask whether or not Islamists are modern, it is more productive to ask how and why they draw on different discourses and assessments about modern-ness in various ways. In this sense, the ethnographic object of this book is located in these conceptual frameworks and deployments. As the modern unravels, it becomes about comparison, boundaries between groups, relations of power, identity, similitude, and difference.

Distillations: "Civilized" and "Progress"

Pious Shi'is engaged with, employed, and deployed multiple discourses and ideas about modern-ness. In Arabic, "modern" is often translated as 'asrī, which emphasizes being contemporary, or as ḥadīth, which emphasizes being new. My interlocutors used neither of these terms.[36] Instead they spoke of al-ḥaḍāra (civilization); of things being mutaqaddum (progressed/advanced) versus mutakhalluf (backward); of how life was 'abl (before) as opposed to al-yawm (today/now) and of tatawwur (development), taqaddum (progress), and tamaddun (urbanization). Some used the adjective moderne with a French intonation. Here are some examples:

1. In response to a televised report showing a Shi'i ritual practice that involves self-flagellation, a pious Shi'i woman exclaimed with a flick of her

---

with modernity (e.g., Rahman 1982, al-Azmeh 1993). In the second case (e.g., Adelkhah 2000, Ghannam 2002) the focus is instead on bureaucratization, objectification of knowledge, and technological development.

[36] See Spitulnik (2002) for a strong argument for the importance of looking carefully at the local linguistic forms we use to identify local understandings of what is modern, and for an excellent model for doing so.

hand: *"shufti kīf nizil id-dam? shū hat-takhalluf!"* [Did you see how the blood was falling? What is this backwardness!]

2. When I asked the same woman if the practice still took place in her neighborhood, she shook her head and replied: *"la', al-yawm ma ba' fī 'indna hash-shaghli"* [No, today we no longer have this thing].

3. Speaking of the neighborhood in al-Dahiyya where she worked, a volunteer said: *"eh tab'an, shufna tatawwur ktīr bil-manta'a, bas ba'd fī takhalluf"* [Yeah, of course we have seen a lot of development in the area, but there is still backwardness].

4. On a tour of a facility that included a computer classroom, an administrator said, *"badnan farjīkī eddeh 'indna l-ḥaḍāra"* [We want to show you how much Civilization we have].

5. In a conversation about how the West views her community, a young woman said, using three languages: " *'indna ḥaḍāra*, we are *moderne* [Fr.]" [We have a civilization, we are modern].

6. While describing her life story, an older woman explained: *"abl, kānu ylabsu l-binit escharpe* [Fr.] *bala fahm, hayk, kān aj-jaw taqlīdī"* [Before, they used to dress a girl in a scarf without understanding, just like that; the atmosphere was traditional].

Obviously all these terms are polyvalent in meaning, shifting with context and speaker, but what holds constant is a sense of comparison. A person, community, place, or thing is always modern as compared to some other thing, an other that is defined in the comparison as not modern or less modern.[37] This sense of comparison can be distilled into two general concepts that emerge from these terms and statements: the idea of progressive change over time, and the value-judgment inherent in being viewed as "civilized." These concepts are the crux of what remains stable throughout pious Shi'i deployments of various notions of the "modern."

Beginning with the latter, in examples 4 and 5 above, the speakers used the term *ḥaḍāra* (civilization) to indicate their modern-ness. For both of them, "civilization" is a quality, not a Culture (i.e., not "the Aztec civilization"). In this context, "we have Civilization" or "we have a civilization" means "we are *civilized*" as opposed to barbaric or backward. "Civilized" underscores the value-judgment aspects of the comparison. Both these statements were made in contexts of direct comparison with the West. "Civilized" here is highlighting not only a generalized sense of value judgment, but pious Muslims' awareness of and response to Western stereotypes of them as backward or barbaric.

---

[37] Definition around a comparison is also the case for the concept "tradition." See, for example, Kratz 1993.

The two uses of *ḥaḍāra* also differ slightly, highlighting the speakers' deployments of two different discourses about modern-ness. Speaker 4 uses the definite form of the word, *al-*, indicating "Civilization" as a quality her community shares with other civilized peoples based upon some universal standard, in this case, computer technology. On the other hand, Speaker 5 uses the indefinite form, "a civilization," indicating the possibility of multiple civilizations that may all be considered modern. Their engagements with these different understandings of modern-ness typifies the multiple uses and employments of the concept within the pious Shi'i community.

The second general concept important to understanding pious Shi'is' engagements with "modern" is a sense of comparison within Lebanon linked to progressive change over time.[38] This comparison was sometimes historical and local, suggesting progress in one's own community and the contrast between a backward and/or traditional past and a modern (or more modern) present, as in examples 2, 3, and 6. Other times the comparison was spatial, positing a difference between two areas or groups in Lebanon, as in example 1. Yet even these spatial comparisons related to a notion of progress—in that the area or group cast as backward had been left behind the one that progressed. Underlying some of these spatial comparisons is the notion of *tamaddun*, or urbanization, and leaving behind village traditions.

As I have argued, it is vital to keep in mind that for pious Shi'is, progress was two-pronged: material and spiritual. Material progress, highlighted in example 3, is essentially modernization in the sense of technology, education, health care, and economic and infrastructural development. Included here are computers, new roads, and microwave ovens, as well as—less unanimously—a ready supply of Pepsi and the latest fashions from Paris. On the other hand, spiritual progress, indicated in examples 2 and 6, is manifested by increased public piety, as well as through a process of "authenticating" Islam described further below. Material and spiritual progress were viewed as parallel, as they involve drawing on different discourses about modern-ness. They are not necessarily dependent on one another, but also, as we will see, not always so clearly divided. Thinking about modern-ness as ultimately dependent on a notion of progress opens up the concept to include a wider range of the types of changes that people experience or understand as progress, including religious or spiritual change. For example, rather than view Islamists as necessarily engaged in a struggle with modernity, we can instead view spiritual progress as a potential aspect of the modern.

---

[38] See Koselleck's discussion (1985) of the necessity to modernity of a shift in understandings of time that includes the differentiation of past and present and a new emphasis on historical change and progress.

Progress and the value judgment "civilized" are closely related. No one ever expressed to me doubts that progress was good. Those who had not yet progressed were not modern/civilized.[39] Being modern was explained by notions of authenticity, organization, education, cleanliness, hygiene, social consciousness, and piety, whereas not being modern or being backward was linked to tradition, chaos, ignorance, dirtiness, and incomplete morality. It is the value judgments attached to these sets of characteristics that place them on an axis of progress. At its most basic, modern meant "better than." And this "better than" depended on particular knowledge and awareness—enlightenment, but with a critically lowercase *e*.

So what is it that pious Shi'is are leaving behind with progress? Better than what? Progress *from what*? What/where is the noncivilized, the backward, located? Clearly for my interlocutors, based on the two-pronged notion of progress, both material underdevelopment and spiritual ignorance were being left behind. They located aspects of the negative side of the comparison—backwardness—in both the near past and the contemporary "West."[40] First, as we will see in chapter 2, Lebanese Shi'is were generally marginalized politically and economically within the nation-state for most of its history. Material progress began later than in other Lebanese communities, and pious Shi'is continued to refer to the need to catch up in that regard. They also pointed to contemporary underdevelopment within al-Dahiyya and other predominately Shi'i areas, emphasizing the need for "modernization."

The near past is also one of the locations of spiritual backwardness, often discussed as "ignorance" (*jahl*) or "tradition" (*taqlīd*). Although pious Shi'is most often deployed "modern/civilized" in response to national and international judgments and stereotypes about the Shi'a as backward, they also employed the notion to distinguish themselves from practices associated with their own recent past, practices they labeled "traditional." The distinction was similarly utilized to set themselves apart from other Lebanese Shi'is who maintained those traditional practices. It is in these spaces that modern/civilized and modern/progress came together. People's efforts to develop themselves spiritually and to

[39] See Karp (2002) for a discussion of the implicit moralizing within development discourses.

[40] Another, less common, comparison cast Lebanese as more "modern" than Arabs from the Gulf States. Lebanon is a tourist destination for many wealthy Gulf Arabs, who are often pointed to as the quintessential example of how money does not necessarily make one "modern," and ridiculed for everything from their dress to their immense SUVs to their gender relations. Some pious Shi'is who had returned from the *hajj* complained about the "backwardness" of Wahabi Islam, especially regarding issues like sex segregation in restaurants.

contribute to what they conceptualized as their community's spiritual progress involved the "authentication" of Islam.

"Authentication," Moving Away from "Tradition"

The contemporary extent of public piety among Shiʻi Muslims was a relatively recent phenomenon in the eyes of many, tied to their notions of progress along a value-laden axis. They viewed it as new and different—different from what they often referred to enigmatically as "before" or "how we were" and different from what they called *al-taqālīd* (traditions). Their ways of practicing Islam and being in the world were set in clear opposition to the ways of their grandparents.[41] In lieu of practices and beliefs cast as traditional, they espoused what I refer to as "authenticated" Islam, expressed in public piety.

Pious Shiʻis did not use the Arabic term *asāla* for "authenticity" or *aslī* for "authentic." Instead they described a process of establishing the true or correct meaning, understanding, or method of various religious and social practices and beliefs (*al-maʻnā al-ḥaqīqī* or *al-fahm al-ḥaqīqī*), a process I call "authentication." Authentication is dependent on textual study and historical inquiry, as well as on a particular notion of rationality. It is a process similar to "objectification" as discussed by Dale Eickelman and James Piscatori (1996). They explain objectification as "a heightened self-consciousness" or "the systematization and explicitness of religious tradition" (39). This self-consciousness is defined as a process involving a conscious community engagement with basic questions about religion and its importance to one's life and behavior, facilitated by direct access to texts and, therefore, religious knowledge and interpretation.

I prefer the term authentication for two reasons. First, I think it better captures the nuances of "truth" important in this community. "Authentication" and its root "authentic" convey truth based upon accuracy of textual interpretation and historical research.[42] They also connote a sense of being genuine, the truth in character that, along with accuracy, is important to pious Shiʻis. Authentication is therefore a process by which those interpretations of Islam that are considered most trustworthy and legitimate are revealed. There are two other shades of truth suggested by the root "authentic" that are relevant here. One is the idea of cultural authenticity—of being true to one's community and faith. Pious Shiʻis viewed the authentication of Islam as related to their cultural authenticity

---

[41] The root of the word *taqlīd* means "to imitate."

[42] Another possible term here would be "verification," which denotes being factual. However, verification does not encompass the other meanings I want to encapsulate in "authenticate."

both to one another and communally within Lebanon. Another is the notion of personal authenticity, truth to oneself. I find that this idea resonates with pious Shi'is' insistence on using one's mind ('aql) to arrive at true meaning. Personal authenticity—in the sense of sincerity of intention—also hints at the notion that ideally, a person's public and personal piety should correspond.

Second, I find that the term "authentication" allows for greater discursive and historical fluidity than "objectification," and allows me to distance conceptualizations of this framework from the notion of a moment in a universal process at which Islam is understood as having recently arrived.[43] When I use "authenticated" to describe certain practices, I do so with the understanding that it refers to a constant process and never an end result.[44] In this sense, authentication captures the "ideal typical" nature of the Shi'i pious modern. Furthermore, after Talal Asad's (1986) critique of anthropology's approach to Islam, I hope that my insistence on the processual nature of authentication will underscore that I understand my interlocutors' contrasts between "orthodox" (read: modern) and "nonorthodox" (read: traditional) Islam to be both constructed and contextual.[45] Asad's notion of Islam as a "discursive tradition" creates a space where it is possible to consider its authentication without assuming the absolute opposition of this process to existing forms of religious practice and discourse.[46] Essentially, Asad's formulation reminds us that the "tradition" that is often opposed to "authenticated" is also historical. Practicing Muslims—those who are reading religious texts or discussing the tenets of religious practice in their daily conversations, as well as those who are not—are engaged in practices and discourses that have a history, and have been variously interpreted, debated, and authorized throughout that history. Contemporary authentication is a continuation of these discourses and practices in a particular form. Processes of conscious community engagement with religious ques-

---

[43] Cf. Mahmood's critique of the concept, along somewhat different lines (2005: 53–57).

[44] I also want to emphasize that I use "authenticated" to describe discourses and practices viewed in this way by my interlocutors; I am not advocating for one Islamic formation over another.

[45] Asad notes that the former term, "orthodox," is generally associated with "the scripturalist, puritanical faith of the towns," while the latter refers to "the saint-worshipping, ritualistic religion of the countryside" (1986: 6). More recent manifestations of this problematic division often position urban Islamists in opposition to rural tradition, or men's text-based religion in opposition to women's practice-based or folk religion.

[46] Asad's use of "tradition" is as follows: "A tradition consists essentially of discourses that seek to instruct practitioners regarding the correct form and purpose of a given practice that, precisely because it is established, has a history" (1986: 14). See Fischer and Abedi's (1990) discussion of debates in Shi'ism as a cogent example of Islam understood as a discursive tradition.

tions and concepts are no doubt affected and altered by communication technologies and educational opportunities, but they are not entirely new processes.

Having said that, I want to note that many people I spoke with expressed experiencing a disruption in the way they practice, understand, and talk about Islam: a disruption related to recent changes in access to participation in the authentication process. For this reason I think it important to highlight the contemporary moment's distinction, as it impinges on pious Shi'i Muslims' daily lives. The relative abruptness of this disruption, and the concomitant political, social, and economic changes that have occurred in the Lebanese Shi'i community only served to reinforce people's sense of a clear-cut difference between "now" and "then"—a difference that they often juxtaposed with the contrasts "authenticated" versus "traditional," and "modern" versus "backward."[47]

Pious Shi'is frequently contrasted their self-conscious efforts to incorporate specifically authenticated forms of Islam into their lives with what one woman called "'ib' al-taqālīd," "the burden of traditions."[48] We will see this contrast in myriad arenas, including the visual and seasonal rhythms of al-Dahiyya, religious practice and discourse, community service, and gender roles.[49] Authenticated forms of Islam are intimately bound with the idea of spiritual progress, and as such, are understood by pious Shi'is as both necessary to and evidence of their modern-ness.[50]

The concept of rationality is important to this relationship between authentication and modern-ness. One way of looking at this is by drawing parallels with Weberian rationalization. This works if the latter is understood broadly as a process of religious change involving the self-conscious and logical standardization of religious beliefs or practices.[51]

---

[47] This resonates with the similar processes by which nation-states mark their beginnings with a moment of rupture, giving a before-after form to temporality, see Çinar 2001.

[48] Similar self-consciousness regarding religion's role in daily life is frequently noted in discussions of the "Islamic awakening" or "Islamic revival," particularly with reference to Egypt. The "Islamic awakening" (al-sahwa al-islāmiyya) is the term used in Egypt, and has been brought into literature on Islamic movements. See Salvatore 1997: 189–216.

[49] Another common manifestation of authentication is referral to or implementation of sharī'a, usually glossed as "Islamic law." See Salvatore's (1997) argument that sharī'a became a medium of social normativity after the rise of the public sphere, again linking authentication/objectification to notions of modern communication. In Lebanon, sharī'a is most relevant for family/personal status law, the only area that falls outside the jurisdiction of state civil law. However, despite the particulars of its regulatory authority in relationship to the Lebanese state, many people were concerned with living in accordance with sharī'a, crucially understood here as a mode of moral normativity rather than as "law."

[50] A parallel can be seen here with the Calvinist notion that morality is inherent in working toward progress. See Walzer 1965.

[51] See Weber 1963.

The relatively recent emphasis of pious Shi'is on religious and charitable institutions and large public ritual gatherings—like those described in the pages that follow—are one example of such systematization of religion.[52] While in the Weberian analysis this rationalization accompanied secularization and eventually led to disenchantment, in the Shi'i pious modern rationalization is instead implicated in the tensions between personal and public piety.

Another sense of rationality is emphasized in the Shi'i pious modern via the notion of al-'aql, "reason, understanding, mind." People often explained to me that it was necessary to use one's 'aql to think about any religious knowledge or practice and make sure that it made "sense."[53] While rationality has long been a method of religious interpretation on the part of mujtahids (those who have attained a certain high level of religious training and can thereby interpret religious texts), the notion that ordinary people with no specialized religious training can and should read and think for themselves about religious texts is relatively new. Pious Shi'is emphasized that authenticated Islam was a particularly "modern" form by virtue of its reliance on accuracy of interpretation, rationality, and personal knowledge-seeking.[54] Yet there also exists a tension in the Shi'i pious modern between the imperative to use one's 'aql to understand religion and the practice of relying on a religious scholar (one's marji' al-taqlīd) for authoritative interpretation.[55] This tension is not resolved, but as we will see, it is implicated in the importance of public piety.

A Fraught Relationship

In addition to the near past of the Lebanese Shi'a, the other location for spiritual backwardness—here in the sense of ignorance, immorality, and "emptiness" rather than tradition—is the contemporary "West." "The West" (al-gharb) and "western" (gharbī) are polyvalent terms as well. In the context of spiritual ignorance or immorality, "the West" generally referred to the United States and Europe as well as Lebanese who were

---

[52] Cf. Adelkhah (2000) for a similar discussion of rationalized religious practices in Iran.

[53] This notion has a long history, but it was reemphasized to varying extents by many thinkers associated with the Islamic Revolution in Iran (e.g., Shari'ati, Motahhari, Khomeini). See Adelkhah's discussion (2000).

[54] Compare Eickelman and Piscatori (1996), who emphasize objectification's dependence on mass education and literacy, communication technologies, and publishing. In keeping with this, Rosiny found over 130 Islamist Shi'i publishing houses in Lebanon, established mainly during the past three decades (2000).

[55] To a certain extent, this is a matter of level, or the position of any one moment of understanding along the "chain of authentication"—a sequence of attestations to authenticity (see Irvine 1989: 257–58).

seen as westernized.[56] However, most people were more specific, emphasizing that it was particular values and characteristics that they attributed to the West that were the problem—including atheism, violence, capitalism, consumerism, materialism, sexual promiscuity, the objectification of women, an emphasis on the individual to the detriment of social relations,[57] and the collapse of the family. By including the West in the backwardness that must be left behind through progress, pious Shi'is inverted western valuations of the Islamic world as nonmodern.[58]

Despite their moral censure, Shi'i Lebanese were unable to escape the West in ways that complicated their relationships to certain notions of the modern. Western power, in its various forms, infused the major arenas of encounter. The "West" was palpable in their lives; felt on a daily basis through media, material goods, and military actions, as well as via family and friends who lived in North America and Europe. While in much of the postcolonial literature Europe is taken as the center of the West, for many Lebanese, this place was reserved for the United States instead. No doubt this is related to multiple factors, including the military presence of the United States in the Middle East, directly in Iraq or indirectly through Israel (which is viewed by many Lebanese as a U.S. proxy in the region); U.S. involvement during the Lebanese civil war; and U.S. cultural imperialism and economic power. The very real consequences of U.S. policy in the Middle East on human lives form a subtext of this book, because they are the backdrop within and against which pious Shi'is, like many other people around the globe, live.[59]

The meaning of "the West" was further complicated by history, politics, and differences of style within Lebanon. On the one hand, pious Shi'is contrasted themselves with westernized or "Americanized" Lebanese, a label they used to explain moral laxity as well as what was perceived as blind emulation of U.S. culture and materialism.[60] On the other hand, they did not define themselves as "eastern." "Eastern"

---

[56] Whereas some, like evangelist Franklin Graham, emphasize a binary division between Islam and the West based on a Christianity-Islam divide, for my interlocutors it was secularism (which they understood to mean the absence of religious values in daily life) and *not* Christianity that was the problem. I often heard comments along the lines of "if only Christians would apply their faith to their lives . . ."

[57] This theme often emerged in conversations with people who had lived in North America and found the comparative lack of warm relationships with neighbors and colleagues disturbing.

[58] A similar inversion can be seen in Turkish Islamists' accusations of "backwardness" directed toward secularists (Özyürek n.d., 234).

[59] Here I find apt Kelly's use of "a grotesque" (2002) to describe U.S. power since World War II. See also Shalom (2001).

[60] Such criticism was not limited to my interlocutors. A recent Lebanese rap's refrain enjoins youth to "*ḥaj til'ab(h)a amerkāneh!*" (stop acting American!).

meant traditional, a part of what was being left behind as the community progressed. Nor did they always identify as Arab, sometimes eschewing the term as too closely linked to Saudi Arabia and the Gulf States.

Pious Shiʻi Muslims' fraught relationship to the West was also confounded by consumer desires for western products, capitalist business practices, and technology. Yet in none of these areas was desire unambivalent. Active opposition to U.S. cultural imperialism coexisted uncomfortably with lifestyle practices and desires that belied that opposition.[61] Technology posed the most difficult dilemma, though attempts were made to find ways of embracing material modernization based on nonwestern models, by emphasizing the examples of Japan and Iran as alternatives.[62]

But the aspect of people's relationships to the West that most concerns me is in the discursive realm. Pious Shiʻis consciously engaged discourses about being modern that were understood as western, including perceptions about Muslims and Lebanese Shiʻis more specifically (read: Hizbullah). Despite academic disagreement on the actual unity, singularity, and definition of western modernit(ies), there is no escaping the global dominance of these ideas and judgments about what is modern. They emanate from various media and are backed by political, economic, and military power. This is what I mean by western discursive power.[63] As modern needs its other, discursive power is relational, and, as Foucault wrote, "resistances . . . can only exist in the strategic field of power relations" (1978: 96). The dominant western standards of measure for modern-ness could not be ignored, not only because of imbalances of power, but also because those standards permeated the often contradictory ways pious Shiʻis themselves thought about being modern.[64] They worked within and against dominant western discourses by self-consciously acknowledging their terms as they challenged, accepted, or ambivalently tolerated them. The pious modern would not exist in the same way without these processes.

In the end, rather than arguing that it is possible to be both Islamic/ Islamist *and* modern, pious Shiʻis asserted that their form of Islam *is* modern. Furthermore, this meant both that Islam is modern/civilized

---

[61] Boycotts of various U.S. chain restaurants take place periodically throughout Lebanon, and many people have replaced their Marlboros with Gitanes.

[62] On Japan as an alternative model, see also Abu-Lughod (1998b: 15).

[63] In the Foucauldian sense (1978).

[64] As a result of distillation through media and politics, pious Shiʻis generally encountered western ideas about modern-ness in essentialized form. To indicate this, I subsume what is in fact a more complex field of ideas about modern-ness under the label "dominant western discourses" (dominant here meaning both common and backed by power).

and modern/progressive, as well as superior in certain ways to the empty modernity of the West.[65]

It is critical not to ignore the economic, discursive, and military power behind western notions of the modern and the effects of that power on people's deployments of various and sometimes contradictory concepts of the modern. Indeed, it is in the spaces of contradiction and ambivalence where we see the workings of power on multiple levels. As Lisa Rofel put it, "The stakes in confronting modernity are about politics, in all the fullness of that term" (2002: 175).

ENTANGLED AMBIVALENCES AND DEPLOYMENTS

Writing specifically about gender and modernity in the Middle East, Lila Abu-Lughod argues for refusing "to be dragged into the binary opposition between East and West in which so many [arguments] are mired," by "fearlessly examining the processes of entanglement" of these constructed poles (1998b: 16). To that end, I turn now to the ways pious Shiʻi employments of discourses about modern-ness were both oppositional and entangled, particularly around the areas of secularization and gender roles.

An Enchanted Modern

By now, the assumption that modernity and secularism—or more accurately, modernization and secularization—go hand in hand has been thoroughly critiqued,[66] as well as established by the emergent public faces of religiosities around the globe. In keeping with this, my interlocutors imagined modern-ness without disenchantment.[67] Yet Islamisms continue to be positioned as nonmodern, often in relation to ideas about temporality and rationality.

One argument often made about Islamists is that they are antimodern because they strive to return to the ideal society of the Prophet's era. This was not the case for pious Shiʻis.[68] While they did look to models in

---

[65] This is similar to Ruth Benedict's discussion of Japanese beliefs in the superiority of their "faith in spirit" over the United States' "faith in things" (1946).

[66] See, for example, Antoun and Hegland (1987), Bowen (1993), Brenner (1996), Casanova (1994), Hefner (1998), Dorraj (1999), Eickelman (2000), Eickelman and Piscatori (1996), Meyer (1999).

[67] In the Weberian sense (1958). Also relevant is Holmes's (1989) discussion of the disenchantment of life in rural Italy via both capitalist hyperbureaucratization and the Catholic Inquisition's intellectualization of local religious belief.

[68] Hegland argues that religious "resurgence" during the Islamic Revolution in Iran was not about a "return" to Islam but rather was about "a transformation in Shiʻism" (1987: 196). While her overall argument is more instrumentalist than I believe makes sense in Lebanon, there are notable similarities. Also compare Brenner 1996.

the past, they were just that: models for moral behavior that are applicable to the contemporary world. Just as a person might look to Gandhi or Susan B. Anthony as a role model, emulating positive characteristics associated with their characters, a pious Shi'i woman might look to the Prophet's granddaughter Zaynab.

Another area where Islamic and secular notions of temporality collide is in belief in Judgment Day. As Koselleck (1985) elucidates with regard to the Protestant Reformation in Europe, the religious wars around reformation were believed to be part of a process of hastening the end of the world and the second coming of Christ. Similarly, in the 1980s American evangelist Jerry Falwell called upon millenarianism and the idea that there was little time left before Judgment Day to mobilize born-again Christians into social action.[69] Pious Shi'is shared the belief that there is a definite end point to history, and believed that the Hidden Imam would return on Judgment Day. However, they did not act to bring about that end. Nor was Judgment Day something they viewed as "just around the corner" or something that filled their existence with a constant sense of expectation. Rather, pious Shi'is simultaneously believed in a known end and understood the space between the present and that known end as an unknown and unpredictable future, with much room for progress.

The authentication process upon which the pious modern is predicated also emphasizes historical accuracy and the use of rationality.[70] While similarities to Enlightenment notions of rationality exist, *al-'aql* is premised on faith, that is, it is not a question of whether there is a God or a God-given order; rather rationality is used to ascertain the nature of that God-given order. It is a matter of starting from different foundational assumptions, though the types of reasoning that follow are comparable. So for example, the details of religious-historical events could be questioned while remaining within the framework of faith. In addition, as we will see, authentication has also accompanied a process of bureaucratization and institutionalization akin to Weberian rationalization.

This notion of a nonsecular modern rests upon a particular understanding of science within Islam, one of compatibility and even necessity. Seeking knowledge—including scientific knowledge—is an obligation, provided that the seeker's intent lies within the bounds of Islamic morality. The notion of having a moral "intent" works to separate scientific knowledge from values associated with the West. Science and Islam are especially compatible in cases where scientific knowledge can be used for

---

[69] See Harding 2000: 243.

[70] This and other themes are clearly related to various Islamic modernisms whose discourses have permeated Islamic interpretation since the nineteenth century. See Chehabi (1990) on Shi'i modernism in Iran, and Mervin (2000) on nineteenth- and early twentieth-century Shi'i reformers in Lebanon.

the community's greater good. An example of this can be taken from Ayatollah Khomeini, whose jurisprudence is a model for many pious Shi'is. Khomeini used "secondary apparent rules"—a method of jurisprudence for the application of religion to the contemporary world—to overturn previous religious injunctions forbidding the use of Muslim cadavers for anatomy study, because "the use of human bodies for scientific purposes is serving the cause of Islam by helping to train better Muslim doctors" (described in Rajaee 1993: 119).

Prominent Lebanese Shi'i *ulama* have also supported science. Sayyid[71] Musa al-Sadr—who many credit with mobilizing the Lebanese Shi'a—wrote in an Islamic journal that "the truth is that science has committed no sin save the discovery of the truth" (cited in Rajaee 1993: 115).[72] Here we are very far indeed from scenes like the Scopes Trial in Tennessee, with its fundamentalist Christian attack on science.[73] As Höfert and Salvatore have noted:

> There are routes other than the Protestant Ethic paradigm by which religious traditions might produce comparable achievements in terms of economic, bureaucratic, and even scientific rationalities. There are, for example, other views of community, other concepts of rights and obligations, virtues and vices, other models of personality, and, in particular there are views and notions where *we do not necessarily observe a disenchantment in the Weberian sense*." (2000b: 16, my emphasis)

Scientific rationalism has not replaced religious belief. Rather, the two are able to coexist in an enchanted modern.

It could be argued that disenchantment is a particularly Christian or Western phenomenon.[74] However, parts of the Christian West are also emphatically not secular and not disenchanted. Lest we forget, the United States' self-identified born-again Christian president declared that his presidency was predestined by God.[75] Even before the second Bush

---

[71] "Sayyid" is the title for a descendent of the Prophet. Many Shi'i religious scholars come from sayyid families. They are distinguished from shaykhs—religious scholars who are not sayyids—by the color of their turbans: sayyids' are black and shaykhs' white.

[72] Ajami (1986) and Halawi (1992) also discuss al-Sadr's ideas about science.

[73] See Marsden 1980; Harding 2000.

[74] This is Woodward's view (2002). He argues that Christianity and Islam are fundamentally different in their textual bases, characterizing problems in Christianity's relationship to modernity as cosmological, and Islam's as sociological. In contrast, see Meyer (1999). In her discussion about Peki Ewe African Christians' appropriations of aspects of mission Christianity she notes, "Modernity and enchantment should certainly not be conceptualized in terms of an opposition in which the latter is represented as a sign of 'backwardness'" (216).

[75] See Jackson Lears, "How a War Became a Crusade," *New York Times*, March 11, 2003.

administration took power pious Shiʻis were aware that the United States was not an entirely secular place. They sometimes asked me about Christian fundamentalism, wondering why it was so important to the West for the Islamic world to secularize when clearly middle America had not. Their framing of this question is indicative of the oppositional nature of their deployment of a nonsecular modern; an opposition was not only set up against an essentialized (and idealized) secularized western modernity, but, more importantly, against prescriptive western discourses about the Islamic world's status and nature. This dualism also underlies the second area of contention, that of gender roles.[76]

A Gendered Modern

When I began this project, I did not intend to focus primarily on the lives of women. This changed for two reasons. On a practical level, I had access to much more of women's lives than men's, though much of my participant-observation took place in mixed-sex environments. More importantly, the status and image of Muslim women was one of the most consistently arising and contentious issues that emerged during my field research, in people's passionate and often unsolicited responses to western discourses about Muslim women. Women's lives are critical because of both local and international concern, as well as local concern about international concern. And gender is a basic component of discourses about being modern, "one of the central modalities through which modernity is imagined and desired" (Rofel 1999: 20).[77]

The tendencies of both European colonizers and local elites to use the status of women as a measure of the level of modern-ness (in the related senses of modern/civilized and modern/progressive) has been noted by scholars with regard to the Middle East, South Asia, and elsewhere.[78]

---

[76] A partial list of recent work focused specifically on Islamist women includes Abu-Lughod 1998a, Afshar 1998, El Guindi 1999, Göle 1996 and 2000, Haddad and Esposito 1998, Hale 1996, Hammami 1997, Hegland 1998a, Holt 1999, Kamalkhani 1998, Mahmood 2005, Mir-Hosseini 1999, White 2002. I especially want to note el-Bizri's (1996) study of Lebanese Shiʻi Islamist (she uses "Islāmiyyīn") women activists, based upon interviews with ten, mostly elite, women. Many of the issues I discuss also emerge in her interviews. However, she argues that these women are caught between tradition and modernity, where modernity is a western concept that includes ideals of "women's liberation."

[77] Although Rofel (1999) writes with reference to the very different relationship of western feminists to China, this statement also holds for the Shiʻi pious modern. The relationship of "the woman question" to understandings of modernity in the Middle East has a long history, especially prominent at the turn of the twentieth century; see Abu-Lughod 1998a/b.

[78] See Ahmed 1992, Bernal 1997, Chatterjee 1993, Chakrabarty 2000b, Göle 1996, Abu-Lughod 1998a, and Haddad and Esposito 1998.

This pattern remains prominent in current U.S. media discourses about Muslim women.[79] Nadia Hijab has noted that by the 1970s, "the status of women seemed to have become *the major indicator* of a country's modernity" (1988: 7, my emphasis). Similarly, one woman I spoke with observed that "all these Westerners come to interview us because they are looking to see if Islam is modern, and 'how the women are treated' or 'what the women do' has become the sign of which cultures are modern."

Measuring modern-ness by the "status of women" assumes a universal standard of measure, one that is based upon a particular liberal western feminist notion of emancipation and liberation.[80] That in turn is based upon the notion that modern selves are individualized selves.[81] Stereotypes about Muslim women as backward are partially grounded in these universalizing notions. The women (and some of the men) with whom I spoke about these issues confronted such stereotypes and related assumptions about the modern-ness of their community by putting forth an alternative model for an ideal modern woman, one based in public piety. This ideal entails demonstrating knowledge and practice of authenticated Islam, being dedicated to self-improvement, and participating actively in the public life and betterment of the community. Rather than an individualized self, this modern self is embedded in social relationships. In addition to the "emancipated woman," who is imagined as selfishly abandoning her family and community, or as demanding an irrational absolute equality (understood to mean identicality) with men, this pious modern woman is set in opposition to two other ideal types in Lebanon: the "traditional" person, who practices religion improperly or without true comprehension and who believes that her only role is a domestic one; and the "empty modern" and "westernized" person, who is selfish, materialistic, and obsessed with her appearance and social status.

As these various "types" show, the pious modern alternative is not cast in absolute opposition to liberal feminist discourses about modern women but, as Abu-Lughod has argued (1998b), is rather entangled with them. First, with regard to individualism, while on the one hand, a pious embedded self challenges the idea of autonomous individuality, it also emphasizes self-improvement and self-discipline. This potential

---

[79] For excellent discussions of this and its effects, see Abu-Lughod 2002 and Hirschkind and Mahmood 2002.

[80] See Saba Mahmood's (1998, 2001, 2005) critique of the assumption that "liberation" according to such a model is a universal desire for women.

[81] Clearly this is problematic and contested within the West as well, especially through feminist scholarship; however, my focus here is on the transnational dimensions of this discourse.

contradiction is ameliorated by invoking communal end goals: self-improvement should lead a person to truly desire to contribute to her community while also better enabling her to do so effectively.

Suad Joseph's concept of "relationality" provides a cogent framework for understanding this dual emphasis.[82] Relational selves are in between individualized and collective, both embedded in social relations and possessing agentive potential. "It is productive to view persons in Arab societies as embedded in relational matrices that shape their sense of self but do not deny them their distinctive initiative and agency" (Joseph 1999a: 11). For pious Shi'is, these relational matrices not only shape their senses of self, but are crucial to their understandings of community commitment as necessary to morality. At the same time, these matrices have been reconfigured to a certain degree, so that the community of the pious—both peers and institutions—has become more imbricated in selfhood, in addition to (and sometimes more than) "traditional" extended family relationalities.

The moral imperative of community commitment—and indeed, that of public piety more generally—is in many ways particular to women. While at first glance this is comparable to those situations where women were cast as the preservers of tradition in opposition to a masculine modern,[83] it also inverts that model. Both the burden of cultural authenticity and the markers of public piety fell more heavily on the shoulders of women than men, and had specific ramifications for women's lives. Yet issues of responsibility for domestic work and women's participation in the public were actively debated, and solutions posited to facilitate women's work outside the domestic sphere. In this regard, the pious modern ideal uses a notion of modern womanhood that seems similar to western notions of "liberation." However, despite desiring women's greater participation in the public arena, as we will see, my interlocutors' underlying motives for that participation differed. Additionally, their role models for activist women were located in Islamic history.[84]

[82] Joseph posits relational selves as a concept useful for approaching a similar dilemma in literature on selfhood in the Arab world, which posits Arab selves as both highly individualized and highly collective (see Joseph 1999a).

[83] Chatterjee (1993) discusses this as a response to colonial attempts to "modernize" women, Najmabadi (1998) with regard to the Islamic Revolution in Iran and responses to cultural imperialism, and Wardlow (2002) as a response to and part of a local appropriation of modernity.

[84] Lebanese history further complicates the relationship between western and pious modern discourses about women's public participation. Khater (2001) demonstrates that the domestic ideal for women was a western model of modern middle-class womanhood that "came" to Lebanon via returnee emigrants in the early twentieth century. At the time, Lebanese feminists and others used the model of "traditional" women's labor outside the home to combat this newly isolating domesticity.

The following passage provides a taste of these issues, which will be further unpacked in later chapters of this book.

> I asked a group of three Hizbullah-affiliated volunteers—Hajjeh Umm Muhammad, an outspoken woman in her late forties with five children who is currently taking university-level courses in the hopes of someday obtaining her degree; Zahra, a talkative younger newlywed in her early twenties; and Rula, a shy woman, also in her early twenties, who lived at home with her parents and siblings[85]—who their role models were. They immediately replied in unison "Sayyida Zaynab, peace be upon her." Zahra then explained, "What Sayyida Zaynab did, that was *jihād*. Just as her brother, her husband, her son all fought for God, she also fought for God, she fought with everything she had." Rula added quietly, "She gave her spirit and she gave her self." Nodding emphatically, Umm Muhammad said, "I also want to add Sayyida Khadija, peace be upon her. Because she sacrificed her money and everything she had to help spread Islam. She gave her efforts and her resources." "She was the first one," added Rula, as Zahra spoke again, "And there is Mother Theresa, I consider her an important role model for us. She was a person who stood out, in her work and in her life. Even when her health was bad, when she was sick, she continued to fight (*tjāhid*)." There was a pause, then Hajjeh Umm Muhammad: "You realize we are mentioning only women, of course there are the Prophet and the Imams, but here we are mentioning women. Some people will say we are being extremists in mentioning only women. But I feel that sisters are closer to what we work for. I am not saying this only because I am a woman, but because I truly feel that there is an actualization of potential for women here, in this work for our community. I feel actualized, I find my potential and my personality, and my existence through this work. And I feel that only sisters can really be models for us in that way."[86]

An Entangled Modern

My interlocutors' positing of the pious modern in contrast to notions of modern-ness as involving secularization and women's "emancipation" was a knotty process. "The modern occurs only by performing the distinction between the modern and the nonmodern · · · each performance opening the possibility of what is figured as nonmodern contaminating the modern, displacing it, or disrupting its authority" (Mitchell 2000b: 26). Even as they addressed Western stereotypes of Islamic communities and women as nonmodern, they recreated the same modern/nonmodern

---

[85] Many unmarried people in Lebanon, male and female, reside with their parents until marriage.

[86] This is a reconstruction of an interview using a translated transcript.

binary among Lebanese Shi'is. Again, "modern" must always have its other. For pious Shi'is, that other was most often represented by the uneducated poor in al-Dahiyya and by those who practiced what they labeled "traditional" Islam. Both categories of people were bemoaned as "backward" and in need of progress—in both the material and spiritual senses.

Constructing the pious modern was also an ambivalent process. Perhaps the most fraught manifestation of this ambivalence lay in the contradictory deployments of multiple discourses about modern-ness simultaneously. While pious Shi'is made an effort to undermine western standards for defining modern-ness, at the same time, they used those same western standards to claim value as equally modern/civilized as the West. People took care to point to their "modern" things and practices, including internet cafés, school science labs, women who worked outside the home, childrearing practices, and the availability of Kellogg's and Kraft products. The West, along with other communities in Lebanon, was perceived as a compelling audience, one which I was asked to teach that "the Shi'a are modern." In this context, "modern" meant modern according to those dominant western standards. For example, in the pious modern, women working outside the home represented women improving themselves while contributing to the greater good of the community, in keeping with authenticated Islam. Yet when someone pointed to these women in order to demonstrate modern-ness to me, a paradigm shift occurred and they—just for that moment—represented women who were "liberated" from family and community obligations. Incompatible desires came together here—the desire to undermine dominant western discourses about being modern and the desire to be modern (or to be seen as modern)—according to those same discourses.

This was further complicated by an underlying—and historicist—discourse that said "we are still trying to catch up," in the modern/material progress sense. To paraphrase Chakrabarty's observation regarding third-world nationalisms and their modernizing ideologies, pious Shi'is in Lebanon have been complicit to a certain extent in equating a particular West with modernity (2000a: 43).

In the end, despite its messiness, the attempt to redefine the terms of discourse around being modern was really an attempt to posit a way of being that is neither West nor East, and that is both "modern" and "authentic." As a result, over the past twenty years, the community of the Shi'i pious modern has emerged and been institutionalized, in conjunction with the Shi'i Islamic mobilization in Lebanon. This has involved two parallel notions of progress: progress as increased modernization and progress as "increased" piety. Increased piety means piety that is more deeply felt, more clearly understood according to specific interpretations, and crucially, more *visible*. As both evidence and method of spiritual progress, public piety is the key to the pious modern.

PUBLIC PIETY, *VISIBLE* PIETY

Visibility as a term provides a sense of tangibility, conveying the concreteness of piety, while also highlighting the often overlooked dependence of the anthropologist on what is visible or made visible to her.[87] Beyond issues of translation and interpretation, this reminds us that to empathize with the experience of piety without shared faith is difficult.

Visibility also speaks to multiple layers of what is recent or new for the Shi'i pious modern. Here I refer to the many elements that will emerge in the following chapters: the new visibility of religion and of publicly performed piety, the increased visibility of women in public spaces and work, the visibility of new forms of ritual commemoration, and the visibility of pious Shi'is as a collectivity both within Lebanon and on the international stage. The most foundational of these elements—in that it impinges on all of the others—is public piety, a phrase which brings together the notion of piety meant to be seen with that of piety that is inextricably linked to the public good.[88]

"Public piety" is my own phrase, which I use to describe the expression of the pious Shi'i concept of *iltizām* (commitment). *Iltizām* ranges in meaning from obligations that are contractual to those that are linked to a personal sense of duty. Pious Shi'is' usage of the term included much of this range, though it is closer to the latter, internalized sense. *Iltizām*'s spectrum reflects the complexity of a human being's relationship with God, a relationship that is both contractual, in the sense that a person is God's agent on earth, and emotional, located in the nexus of faith and submission to God. There are many ways to express *iltizām*; a socially inclined person might distribute food to the poor, a politically inclined person might collect donations for Hizbullah Resistance fighters, and a religiously inclined person might pray and fast regularly. Ideally, these three strands merge in a person, forming the perfect braid of the humanitarian,

---

[87] I choose to use the term "visible" to connote perceptible, tangible, or evident, because I feel that—although other senses are crucial to processes of learning and encounter (for both the anthropologist and anyone)—sight is privileged in many ways. It is the sense most privileged in stereotyping, in identifying stigmas, in grouping people together, and, recently, it has taken a central role in cultural analysis. See Jay (1996) on the "pictorial turn."

[88] In this sense, this book can be read in part as an ethnography of an Islamicized public sphere, though elucidating public piety's imbrications with public spheres in the Habermasian sense is not its project. For that sort of analysis, see L. Deeb 2005.

the political, and the religious that is *iltizām* and that is expressed through public piety.

This image of a tightly wound braid requires further nuance, because a braid implies cords that are theoretically separable, and these three elements are so inextricably intertwined as to be one thing. The concept of "religion" as a separate and unified category of analysis did not make sense in my interlocutors' world, nor does divorcing the concepts of "humanitarian" or "social" and "political" from it.[89] Yet at the same time, pious Shiʻis used the adjectives "religious" (*dīnī/iyya*), "humanitarian" (*insānī/iyya*), "social" (*ijtimāʻī/iyya*), and "political" (*siyāsī/iyya*), saying things like "my motives for this are religious" or "our work here is not political." It would be more accurate to say that the social, the religious, and the political are at once a tight braid *and* an integrated notion of *iltizām*. I try to maintain this flexibility, treating *iltizām* as single state that includes this triad of elements while also drawing upon the three separate categories where it is most useful—both because those I spoke with did so and, perhaps more importantly, because even problematic categories are sometimes necessary to think with.

Visibility is crucial to public piety on both the personal and communal levels. There have been other moments where religiosity has undergone profound change, linked to making religion visible in new public ways. In Weber's reading of Protestantism, visibility linked success in this world to success in the next, making public the interiority of one's relationship to God. The context was a moment of uncertainty of faith due to rationalization. In Susan Harding's reading of Jerry Falwell's born-again Christianity, a moment of uncertainty where religion had lost ground to a hegemonic secularism in the United States led to a recoupment for religiosity through a visible engagement with the public sphere. For the Shiʻi pious modern, a moment of uncertainty similar in ways to both of these has contributed to the public piety imperative.

This moment emerges from a collage of factors. First, there exists an uncertainty tied to the changes authentication brings to experiences of faith. As more people are enjoined to use their rationality to understand the authenticated meanings of religious texts and practices—a charge that coexists in a tense and contradictory relationship to the role of particular *mujtahid*s in authoritatively interpreting religious texts—an instability of knowledge results. Authentication means that belief and knowledge are constantly being questioned in the community, and that "correct" belief and knowledge are highly valued. Yet authenticated belief and under-

---

[89] See Asad (1993) for elucidation of how religion itself has become a category of analysis by processes rooted in western understandings of the relationship between Christianity and the modern world. See also Salvatore 1997.

standing is an internal state, invisible unless made visible through public piety.

On a personal level, piety that is made visible, brought from the personal realm to the public, establishes a person's morality and membership in the Shiʻi pious modern through both its active performance and its existence as evidence. It was signaled by pious Shiʻis in various ways, including their dress, their activities, and the topics they chose to discuss. Especially for women, making piety visible has become an imperative, as public piety has become part of the normative model of morality in their community. To paraphrase Salvatore (1997: 48–49), Islam has become an umbrella category for a discourse that is able to convert a transcendent order into a set of socially immanent norms, at the same time as it connotes a personal commitment to a transcendent God. A parallel can be seen here to the Calvinist Saints during the English Reformation, for whom industry and diligence "*revealed* their saintliness" (Walzer 1965: 211).

Juxtaposed to this, Shiʻi experiences of political-economic marginalization, civil and international conflict, and the betwixt and between of identity in Lebanon provide another layer of uncertainty. This is accompanied by the dominance of western notions about modern-ness in the contemporary world. On a communal level, the visual imprint of public piety is part of the process of defining the pious modern—as both a community and a concept—foregrounding religion as an alternative to the West. Within Lebanon, public piety is linked to a general performance of religious identity, most obviously seen in what jewelry is worn, which clothing is chosen, or how a scarf is pinned. The sorts of holiday lights and decorations that adorn streets in different neighborhoods fulfill the same function on a different scale. For Shiʻi Lebanese in particular, this involved embracing and reclaiming what was once—and still is to a certain extent—a stigmatized identity. There are many markers of identity in Lebanon, including dress, mannerisms, and regional accent. Some Lebanese even claim that they can identify people by sect based solely on "looks." That aside, there are particularly visible markers based in public piety associated with being Shiʻi Muslim, especially, for women, wearing a *ḥijāb*.

In part, visibility is forced by a sense that Lebanon is caught in that "betwixt and between" identity crisis. The uncertainty inherent in the notion of "Lebanese-ness" is manifest in the continual performance of identities on a national stage—as various groups announce their presence and sometimes try to impose that presence as more dominant than others. Like uncertainty, this sense of being betwixt and between existed on both the personal and the communal levels, and contributed to the importance of public piety to the Shi'i pious modern. Before turning to the manifestations of public piety and the ways it has changed the stakes of being a religious person, I turn briefly to some of the dynamics of my field research, as they illuminate and impinge on these issues.

BUILDING RAPPORT, FINDING BEARINGS

My fieldwork experience was facilitated by a woman I met at a Ramadan food distribution center run by a local *jam'iyya* (community welfare organization). She was volunteering there, and I had just been invited to join them. When we first met, Aziza, as I call her here, was in her late twenties, a college graduate from a well-respected family in al-Dahiyya.

Our first conversations focused on our work, both at the center and outside. Once she and some of the other volunteers understood the nature of my project, they kept up a steady stream of explanation about the center's activities and the details of their faith. Topics for these short impromptu lessons ranged from Ramadan to charitable donations to how one should choose a *marji'*. My fourth day at the center, Aziza took me aside, and encouraged me to ask her anything I wanted without hesitation. I promptly took her up on this and asked her why, especially given that the day before she had explained the rationale behind the *ḥijāb* to me, she herself did not wear a headscarf. Smiling, she replied, "You know, Lara, I pray, and I fast, and I know God, and I know that the right thing to do is wear the *ḥijāb*, but I don't want to, not yet. Maybe someday God willing, but not now."

Aziza became both a close friend and a discreet facilitator, subtly directing conversations, accompanying me to exhibits, meetings, gatherings and events, and defending me unfailingly whenever my presence was questioned. Until I assured her that I did not mind, she tried to protect me from questions regarding my own identity and faith, as well as from conversion attempts and marriage proposals. Above all, Aziza and I had fun, whether climbing an Israeli tank in the south the day after Liberation or sitting on her balcony drinking coffee and smoking sweet flavored tobacco in an *argīleh*. Our conversations were never one-sided, and she asked me almost as many questions about myself and my views as I asked her. I never recorded a formal interview with her, but her presence and her experiences as a pious woman who does not perform piety in a "complete" way inform my project both explicitly and implicitly.

As often seems to characterize anthropologists' closest relationships in the field, in many ways Aziza was not a typical member of her community. She did not wear the *ḥijāb*, but moved in circles where most women did. She was pious in faith and practice, but felt strongly that certain aspects of her faith were intensely personal and not subject to community judgment. Her education, friendships outside al-Dahiyya, and role of responsibility in her household afforded her a mobility not necessarily shared by other Lebanese women her age. At the same time, Aziza was from a large and politically prominent extended family, with all the support and obligations that entailed.

I met many of the people in these pages through Aziza, and her presence smoothed my meetings with several others. Her general attitude was that anywhere she was welcome, I should be welcome. This was particularly crucial during the first six months of research, before I had secured official research permission from Hizbullah's media relations office. For example, she took me with her to a Hizbullah Women's Committee seminar on community participation one afternoon. Upon our arrival, it became clear that this was an "invitation-only" event, but we were welcomed nonetheless. While I cannot be certain, I suspect that had I been alone, the response would have differed.

Aside from those I met through Aziza and her family, most people I spoke with were volunteers or employees at one of four *jam'iyyas* in al-Dahiyya. The *jam'iyya* that became my primary field site is the Social Advancement Association, an independent women's organization. In addition to regular visits to their office and volunteers' homes, I worked at their food distribution center during two Ramadans; tutored two girls; attended and assisted with exhibitions, *iftārs*, fund-raisers, and other events; participated in a month-long training seminar for volunteers; and interviewed volunteers and employees at the *jam'iyya*. The other *jam'iyyas* are larger umbrella organizations with educational and health institutions located all over Lebanon. One, al-Mabarrat Association, is affiliated with renowned *marji'* Sayyid Muhammad Husayn Fadlullah, while the other two, the Islamic Charity Emdad Committee and the Martyrs' Association,[90] are both affiliated with Hizbullah.

My experience at the Hizbullah Women's Committee seminar taught me that my presence at party-affiliated *jam'iyyas* required following a hierarchy of communication and working through Hizbullah's media relations office. Their facilitation proved to be a mixed blessing. On the one hand, I was able to almost instantly make appointments that would have taken weeks and repeated phone calls to make on my own. On the other hand, having to go through the media office limited my access in particular ways and added an official quality to some interviews that I would

---

[90] The Arabic *"mu'assasat al-shahīd"* can be translated literally as either the "Martyr" Association or the "Martyr's" Association. However, I use "Martyrs' Association" in order to highlight the notion that the association is *for* martyrs and their families.

have preferred to avoid. This was balanced a bit by my "unofficial" conversations with party supporters whom I met through Aziza.[91]

It is perhaps worth emphasizing that the political climate in which I did field research differed dramatically from that during which I wrote this book. At the turn of the twentieth century, although "Islamic fundamentalism" was a commonly heard catch-phrase on the evening news, eyes were not often turned towards Lebanon. Before I left the United States to begin fieldwork, the most common question I heard was "How are they going to respond to you as an American?"

> A group I was part of that was trying to implement a park project in the area had a meeting at one of the local organizations to seek their very hesitant cooperation. To break the ice, our spokesperson went around the room introducing us. When he got to me he said, "This is Lara Deeb, she is a researcher from the American University of Beirut and another university in America. She is going to help us with our project, and (with a wink) we don't know, she might be spying on us." The ice was broken with laughter.

I began this project during what turned out to be the last eight months of the Israeli occupation of Lebanon, and a sense of constant surveillance permeated the neighborhoods where my interlocutors lived. I heard rumors of Hizbullah cameras lining major roads in the area, strict instructions never to carry a visible camera with me while walking around, and stories about spies and collaborators. One story was about how an Israeli had pretended to be the deaf friend of a Lebanese collaborator, eventually mapping out the location of the residence of an important Hizbullah figure who had been kidnapped from his village by an Israeli helicopter. In most cases, initial suspicions about me wore off quickly and, as my contacts grew to include people at local *jam'iyyas* and members of the party, ceased to be an issue for most people I met.

> The tour of the organization over, we returned to his office to discuss when I could return and begin interviewing. One of the women I had just met stuck her head in the door and said, "It's very good that you are writing this, because you are not Shi'i and there is a greater chance that people will listen to a scholar like you who is coming from outside. You will be able to teach the Americans about us, and show them that we are not terrorists."

---

[91] Nevertheless, I present the perspectives of Hizbullah volunteers and administrators with the understanding that they represent—to a certain extent—the party's "ideal type." There was a uniformity of perspective expressed by party members that cannot be attributed solely to limitations on my access. Yet it is also important to realize that the "official party line" is not necessarily so clean-cut. Alternative perspectives emerged in informal conversations, demonstrating that Hizbullah is not a simple entity and that there is disagreement and debate over various issues within the party.

More difficult were the conversations in which women would tell me how glad they were to be talking to me, because I was going to be able to explain to "the West" or to "Americans" that they were not terrorists, that they were "just defending their children" and fighting to liberate Lebanese soil from an occupying army. That was not the difficult part. What was paralyzing was that many people went on to express the hope that somehow my research was going to help change U.S. policy in the Middle East. Having completed most of the research upon which this book rests, I moved back to the United States in August 2001. Political considerations during field research soon gave way to different ones during the writing process. In the late nineties, I recall hearing Hizbullah described as "guerrilla fighters" rather than "terrorists" in U.S. news reports.[92] Today, they have been promoted by U.S. officials to the "A-team" of terrorists,[93] the U.S. juggernaut occupies Iraq, Palestinians are threatened with "transfer,"[94] and threats of violence pervade the entire region; in this context, my Shi'i friends' hopes have haunted the writing of this book.

Another expectation I encountered is typified by a colleague in Lebanon who urged me to seek out the places where what he called "the façade of faith" did not hold up, the places where water fell through the sieve, in order to explain how faith is "really" a political-economic strategy. My response is that I am working from the premise that faith is not a façade, not just a mystifying thing that we need to look past in order to understand what is "really" going on. Instead faith *is* what is going on, it is a very real thing in and of itself, located in practices, discourses, inner and outer states, relationships, and effects in the world. This is not unique to the Middle East or Islam. One only needs to drive through the "Bible Belt" in the southeastern United States to realize that faith is a very real part of the lives of many U.S. Christians. The question my colleague hinted at, about how much of faith is "true" and how much instrumental, false consciousness, whatever term we choose, is not a question I can answer, nor one that I think it is necessary to answer in order to shed light on the relationships between faith, social and political action, and positionality in the contemporary world. Rather, in Chakrabarty's words, "I · · · think from the assumption that the question of being human involves the question of being with gods and spirits" (2000a: 16).

To this end, I place my faith in ethnography, in looking at the daily

---

[92] See "Israel launches attack against Hezbollah guerrilla bases," *CNN.com*, November 28, 1998, www.cnn.com/WORLD/meast/9811/28/mideast.01/.

[93] "Hezbollah Becomes Potent Anti-U.S. Force," *New York Times*, December 24, 2002.

[94] "Transfer" is a euphemism for the forcible removal of Palestinians from the West Bank and Gaza, a "solution" popular among some in the right-wing Israeli leadership. See Avnery (2003).

practices of faith, the mundane expressions of piety in acts of charity and sacrifice, and how ritual commemorations in various forms provide paradigms and concepts that can be applied to contemporary life. The chapters that follow depict an enchanted and modern Shi'i community where the issues sketched here—issues of what it means to be modern, traditional, pious, western, authentic, and moral—intersect in powerful ways, both discursively and in the real effects that they have on people's lives in the context of their faith, community, nation, and world. It is a portrait of one possible relationship—involving multiple intersections and imaginations—between piety and modernity.

CHAPTER ONE

Al-Dahiyya: Sight, Sound, Season

RESIDENTS and outsiders alike refer to the southern suburbs of Beirut as *"al-Dahiyya"*—a word that simply means "the suburb" in Arabic,[1] but that connotes "the Shiʿi ghetto" to many in other parts of the city. More a conglomeration of multiple municipalities and neighborhoods than a single suburb, al-Dahiyya is bounded by the city to the north, Beirut International Airport to the south, the Mediterranean on the west side, and an agricultural area to the east. It used to be that due to this location al-Dahiyya was unavoidable. To get from the rest of Beirut to the airport or anywhere south of the city, you had to drive through it. Until recently, outsiders passing through caught glimpses of the area from the old airport road or from the coastal highway that leads south to Saida (Sidon) and Sour (Tyre). Today new highways, built to bypass al-Dahiyya, connect Beirut to the airport and to the south, allowing visitors and Lebanese alike to avoid acknowledging its presence.

The residents of this often ignored or maligned area of Beirut who were my interlocutors often referred to *al-bīʾa*, the milieu, of al-Dahiyya as a critical factor in their religious, social, and political understandings, identities, and practices. The visual, aural, and temporal textures[2] of this milieu are the focus of this chapter, and frame the spaces of those that follow. These textures layer religion and politics into public space, and are pointed to as evidence of the spiritual progress of the community and of its recent visibility in Lebanon.

To focus is to allow the surrounding context to blur into white. Before permitting Beirut to fade like this, a few paragraphs are necessary to capture this city that—despite its betrayals and violences—is fiercely claimed as home by Lebanese of all persuasions.

---

[1] Although the southern suburb is not Beirut's only suburb, popular usage has designated it "the suburb," while other outlying areas of the city are referred to by name (e.g., Borj Hammoud).

[2] I take the term "textures" from Tacchi's discussion of radio's creation of a "textured soundscape" (1998: 26).

Al-Dahiyya *in* Beirut

> Clarice, the glorious city, has a tormented history. Several times
> it decayed, then burgeoned again, always keeping the first
> Clarice as an unparalleled model of every splendor, compared
> to which the city's present state can only cause more sighs at
> every fading of the stars. . . . Populations and customs have
> changed several times; the name, the site, and the objects
> hardest to break remain. Each new Clarice, compact as a living
> body with its smells and its breath, shows off, like a gem, what
> remains of the ancient Clarices, fragmentary and dead.
> —Italo Calvino, *Invisible Cities*

Beirut is a balance of constant stimuli and contagious ennui. The former assaults your senses and drains your energy, the latter emerges in the
omnipresent hopelessness and a slow rhythm of bare motion. There is no
way to capture the essence of Beirut: the romance, the dirt, the reality. It
is a word the international media have turned into an epithet for destruction and that Lebanese expatriates have turned into the whimsy of a
golden past. Much has been written about Beirut,[3] its deaths, and resur-
rections, but this is not the place for me to recap that. Instead I simply
highlight three aspects of the city that begin to give a sense of its
rhythms: size, resilience, and traffic.

Lebanon, at a mere 10,400 square kilometers (roughly seven-tenths
the size of Connecticut), is tiny relative to most countries in the world.
Barring horrible traffic, you can drive its length along the coast in four
hours, and its width in less than two. Centrally located Beirut is accessible from anywhere in the country. This smallness of scale creates a density of activity and relationships that intensifies and localizes experiences. At the same time, the fact that places are within easy reach of one
another amplifies the impact of the immense psychological and ideologi-
cal distances that divide them. Many residents of areas of Beirut I trav-
eled between daily had never set foot in the "other" neighborhoods simply because they were "other."[4] Samir Khalaf, among others, has
discussed this retrenching of sectarian identities in space:[5]

---

[3] A small selection: for history of Greater Beirut, particularly the southern areas, see
Khuri 1975; for history, urban planning, postwar reconstruction see Khalaf 1993a, 1993b,
1998, 2002; Harb el-Kak 1996, 1998, 2000; and Rowe and Sarkis 1998; for a memoir
portrait of the city see Makdisi 1990.

[4] The civil war amplified the sectarianization of space in Lebanon. Prior to the war, there
existed many intersectarian social networks, especially among women (Joseph 1983).

[5] See also Khalaf 1993b, 1998, and 2001; Faour 1991; and Sennett 1993.

This compulsion to huddle in compact, homogenous enclosures further "balkanized" Lebanon's social geography. There is a curious and painful irony here. Despite the many differences that divide the Lebanese, they are all in a sense homogenized by fear, grief, and trauma. (Khalaf 2002: 247)

The smallness of Beirut and Lebanon also emerges in the threads that connect people, strung throughout the fabric of the country. Six degrees of separation are rare; two or three far more common. There is little anonymity; even corporate institutions like banks treat their customers to coffee and conversation with business.

Beirut is also a city of unbelievable resilience. Surviving years of war is the city's greatest testament to this. I witnessed a much smaller example on the morning of February 8, 2000. The night before I had awakened to the sounds of Israeli planes breaking the sound barrier and bombing infrastructure around Lebanon. They destroyed three power plants, leaving fires you could see burning from balconies in the city. Despite this, early the next morning a friend of mine picked me up for a meeting in al-Dahiyya. The only discernable differences during that day and those that followed were the dark circles underneath people's eyes, the extra sweaters worn to guard against the cold in places that would have been heated with electricity, the flashlights carried to light the way up stairwells when elevators were not running, the simmering anger in voices discussing the events, and the constant whir of generators that had sprung up overnight. After a few days of darkness, electricity was rerouted and rationed throughout the country, generally on a six-hour on-and-off cycle.

Resilience is accompanied by adaptability and a coexistence with a certain level of chaos. This is represented in the illogic of traffic, something visitors and residents alike often find frustrating. One-way streets switched direction every block or two; traffic lights sometimes worked and sometimes didn't, and were sometimes assumed to be merely suggestions; there were few marked lanes and many bottlenecks; and appropriate distance between vehicles was measured by the proximity of your neighbor's car skimming yours.

Chaotic traffic, resilience, and compactness are notions that could describe almost any area of Beirut. Yet Lebanese who do not live in al-Dahiyya often assume these general characteristics to be especially true of al-Dahiyya. I had a hard time convincing many Lebanese, especially but not only those who were not Shi'i, to accompany me to al-Dahiyya, and sometimes even to give me a ride to an organization or an acquaintance's house in the area. This reluctance sometimes stemmed from fears and false assumptions about what it meant to be in an area controlled by Hizbullah. For others, however, it was simply an unwilling-ness to navigate the narrow roads, dead ends, and one-way streets that inevitably led to a headlock situation where one driver was forced to drive backwards the way she came, hoping there would be no other traf-fic behind her. A similar reluctance was expressed by many I knew in al-Dahiyya with regard to other areas of Beirut, particularly Ashrafiyye, the mostly Maronite Christian suburb to the east. Again, for some, it was a hesitation based in fear and stereotypes, while for others it was the same unwillingness to navigate the gridlock of an unfamiliar part of the city.

The responses I encountered when I first broached the subject of my re-search with residents of other parts of Beirut were typical of this. Time and again eyes grew wide, and "You're going to do *what?*" was followed by a more cautionary "You will have to be careful." Later responses in-cluded a note of admiration, disbelief, or simply, "You're crazy." This was not confined to Lebanese who were not Shiʻi; if anything, wealthy Shiʻis who did not live in al-Dahiyya responded the most stridently. To nonresi-dents, mention of al-Dahiyya often elicits such responses of discomfort, ranging from caution mingled with curiosity to outright trepidation: re-sponses built on stereotypical associations of "al-Dahiyya" with poverty, illegal construction, refugees, armed Hizbullah security guards and secret cameras, and "the Shiʻi ghetto." Such stereotypes obscure al-Dahiyya's complexity. Before moving on, it is necessary to address this complexity in order to undo some of these common assumptions.[6]

Assumptions Undone

Al-Dahiyya Is Not Uniform

Al-Dahiyya encompasses several municipalities and a number of very dense neighborhoods, with a combined population of approximately five hundred thousand people in an area of sixteen square kilometers.[7] Mona Harb el-Kak divides al-Dahiyya into eastern and western zones, with the former made up primarily of older villages that were incorporated into the urban fabric of the city and a few illegal sectors along the edges,[8] and the latter consisting of a combination of dense illegal sectors and less urbanized areas (1998, 2000). Within these multiple municipalities and neighborhoods, there is immense variation with regard to class, length of

[6] For an excellent discussion of the complexities of "al-Dahiyya" and its neighborhoods, see Harb el-Kak 1996, 1998, 2000.

[7] See Harb el-Kak 1998. This was approximately one-third of Beirut's total population.

[8] "Illegal" is a complex label in this context, often having to do with building codes and laws, in addition to real estate ownership.

1.1. A typical street in al-Dahiyya.

residency in the area, and political leanings, as well as some religious diversity.[9]

One of the characteristics of stereotypes is that they homogenize. As a real space, al-Dahiyya was not uniform; it was not *only* "poor," "illegal," or "Hizbullah." The region signified by the term included areas where Harakat Amal[10] was the principal political party rather than Hizbullah, and there existed older legal residential districts as well as newly built illegal neighborhoods, some lingering Christian residents, "original" residents mingled in among more recent arrivals displaced by the wars, and an emerging Shi'i "middle class" living in constant contact with its poorer neighbors. During my field research, the *ra'is baladiyya* (mayor) of one municipality, Haret Hrayk, was a Maronite Christian who worked in close cooperation with Hizbullah. And on some streets, elaborate homes and the latest model BMWs indicated wealthy residents, as did the shops selling European fashions that existed alongside internet cafés, vegetable stands, and corner markets.

Al-Dahiyya Has a History

Stereotypes also belie the fact that this area has not always been predominately Shi'i or (sub)urban. Thirty years ago, much of it was semirural, its population a mix of Shi'i Muslims and Maronite Christians. A quarter century and a civil war later, this had become the second most densely populated area of the country, exceeded only by the Palestinian refugee camps, and it was predominately Shi'i Muslim.

Prior to the end of World War I and the subsequent French mandate in Lebanon, al-Dahiyya was rural and several of its current municipalities were villages. By 1970, one of these villages, Chiyah, had become two suburbs with a population of thirty thousand people and four thousand more households than had existed forty years earlier.[11] Much of this growth was due to the wave of rural to urban migration that occurred throughout Lebanon in the 1950s and '60s, though the southern areas of Beirut were mostly settled by Shi'is from the south and the Beqaa.

Writing in 1975, Fuad Khuri described the suburbs thus:

> A glance at the suburbs gives the impression that nothing is placed where it is supposed to be. The observer is immediately struck by the lack of planning,

---

[9] Lack of recent censuses made it difficult to assess levels of religious diversity in al-Dahiyya, though there were some Christian families residing there.

[10] Harakat Amal is the other major Shi'i political party in Lebanon. It did not have a major presence in the neighborhoods where I worked.

[11] See Khuri 1975.

zoning, a center to the town, straight streets, and standardized buildings. Apartment buildings of various sizes and indistinct style blotch the horizon. They are often separated by one-floor houses with concrete pillars on the roof to suggest that the unfinished part of the building will be completed soon; or by small, neglected orange or olive orchards; or by well-cultivated vegetable gardens. Goats and sheep are often seen roaming around the twisted streets, looking for garbage to feed on. Chickens are more frequently heard and are seen caged in small poultry runs in gardens, beside houses, or on house-top. (1975: 37)

Soon after, the remnants of village life vanished with the arrival of thousands of Shi'i refugees from the northeastern suburbs of Beirut, the south, and the Beqaa during the years of war. Refugees continued to pour into al-Dahiyya, as it grew southward and westward, throughout the violence, and especially in 1978, 1982, and 1993, as villagers from the south and the Beqaa fled Israeli invasions and bombardments.

These consecutive surges in migration altered the sectarian makeup of the suburbs. The original village of Chiyah had a Maronite Christian majority and a Shi'i Muslim minority, a ratio that was gradually reversed over the next few decades through both Shi'i migration to the area and Maronite emigration to South America (Khuri 1975). Before the wars began, there was still a slight Maronite majority in the southern suburbs. By the late 1990s, approximately 70–80 percent of the population was made up of Shi'is who were displaced during the wars.[12]

At the beginning of the twenty-first century, when you enter al-Dahiyya from many other areas of Beirut, there is generally no clear marker of division, but there is a palpable change. Your senses clearly indicate that you have entered an area that is dominated by a particular mix of politics and piety. The recent demographic changes that have occurred in al-Dahiyya marked a new visibility for many Shi'i Muslims as a presence in Lebanon, and especially in Beirut, inscribed on public space and time. In what follows, I render the temporal, visual, and aural textures of al-Dahiyya that contribute to the sense of community cohesion held by those located within the pious modern.

Although most of my interlocutors resided in al-Dahiyya and it was their shared values that dominated public space in the area, al-Dahiyya was not coterminous with Shi'i "Islamism" or piety in Lebanon. On the one hand, while urban Lebanese Shi'i Islamism was concentrated in this suburb, its roots and reach extended throughout the country, and especially into the south and the Beqaa Valley. On the other hand, there

---

[12] See Harb el-Kak 1998. Faour (1991) notes that by 1988 the population of al-Dahiyya was mostly Shi'i Muslim.

existed within al-Dahiyya other political perspectives, religious beliefs and identities, and lifestyles. Yet my focus lies with those who both claimed a particular religious identity based in authenticated Islam and were active participants in shaping their social landscape in accordance with that religious identity.

As I move to describing what pious Shiʻis called *al-bīʼa* (the milieu), I want to emphasize that the forms I discuss are those that were both ubiquitous and hegemonic,[13] both at first glance to an outsider *and* to the particular public of the pious modern. So, for example, in describing the plethora of signs that papered al-Dahiyya's streets, I focus on images of orphans, religious leaders, and Resistance martyrs.[14] There were also pictures of other political figures and candidates, especially around election times. And there were other sorts of images—building names, signs advertising commodities and services—but these were not what were perceived to set the cityscape apart from other areas of Beirut. Nor were these images the ones people pointed out to me when describing the positive changes that had occurred around them over the past few decades. As Susan Ossman notes, understanding the meanings of particular portraits and their place in the hierarchy of images that dot the urban landscape "depends on a personal and collective narrative" that leads to specific interpretations (1994: 144). The dominant collective narrative that framed images of orphans, religious leaders, and Resistance martyrs is that which unfolds throughout this book.

Additionally, the rapid growth, shifts in population, and surges in building that have come to characterize al-Dahiyya were experienced by many residents as the making of an area of Beirut that was explicitly Shiʻi—essentially as the creation of a place for the religious-political-social movement they were working to forge.[15] For them, the various textures of al-Dahiyya's milieu that I describe in this chapter were significant

[13] I use "hegemonic" here to highlight the relationship between cultural dominance of these particular images and the political dominance of Hizbullah in these neighborhoods, and to note the relationship between this particular milieu and the social order of the pious modern.

[14] While martyrdom was originally linked to "witnessing," in the contemporary meaning to be martyred is to be killed for a belief or principle. In the United States the term is used more narrowly to mean to be killed for one's religious beliefs. In Lebanon, one can also be martyred for one's nation. Indeed, all political parties and militias in Lebanon use "martyr" to indicate members who died during the civil war (AbuKhalil 1991). The concept of national martyrs is equally important in the United States though the term itself is rarely used. I use "martyred" rather than "killed" in order to convey my interlocutors' emphasis on the sacrifice made by those killed for religion and/or nation.

[15] See Houston's discussion of Islamicized public space as a space connoting "empirical presentations of an imagined social order even as they constitute it" but whose meanings can also be subverted by different consumptions of those same spaces (2001: 82).

because they represented the rooting of the uprooted, and because they were evidence of the "rise" of "the Shi'a" as a critical community in Lebanon. As we will see in the next chapter, many experienced this as movement from a position of deprivation and marginalization relative to other groups in Lebanon, to one of visibility and influence within the city and nation-state. I now turn to the details of this visibility.

TEXTURES OF AL-DAHIYYA

Sight

The first time I entered al-Dahiyya, I went by taxi. My luck was with me that day, as my driver was both loquacious and from one of the neighborhoods that would eventually become part of my field site. After I explained that I would be working with the *jam'iyya* (social welfare organization) where I had an appointment that day, he began to point out landmarks to help me get my bearings. As we turned off the old airport road, we joined a slow stream of traffic, with men pushing vegetable carts wandering between the cars, and pedestrians crossing at will. *Servīces*—ubiquitous shared taxis that are always old Mercedeses—held up the flow, and young men on motorbikes whizzed loudly around weaving closely between cars. The buildings looked taller, something I immediately attributed to less regulated construction, and there seemed to be a lot of billboards with pictures of children on them. Similar pictures dotted many of the electrical poles, alongside posters of Nasrallah, another sayyid who looked a lot like him to me, and Khomeini. When the driver saw me looking at a huge canvas painting of Khomeini that leaned against the side of a building, he gestured to it and said simply, "*qa'idna*" (our leader).

Several months later, I was driving myself around al-Dahiyya with relative ease, though I still dreaded parking and frequently had to ask for directions. I had learned that that other sayyid who had looked a lot like Nasrallah was in fact Sayyid Abbas al-Musawi, the previous Secretary General of Hizbullah who had been assassinated by Israel along with his wife and five-year-old son. And I now knew that those children's faces were the faces of need, of orphans representing the many charitable organizations that worked in the area.

I had also learned that, contrary to what some people from other Beirut neighborhoods had indicated, in certain ways al-Dahiyya looked a lot like many other regions of the city. Some of the buildings were indeed taller and more closely spaced, and that did have to do with unregulated building. But this was not unique to al-Dahiyya. Nor was the high level of pedestrian traffic in the streets unique to this particular part of

Beirut, although the especially high population density was probably reflected here to a certain extent. Yet in other ways, there was something that set al-Dahiyya apart. This was the presence of a particular politics of piety, a sense of publicly displayed and claimed piety: what my friends at the American University of Beirut glossed as "Hizbullah" but what was in fact far more complicated than a political party.

This public piety appeared in the higher prevalence of women who wore Islamic dress and the *ḥijāb* than in perhaps any other part of the country, and certainly in the numbers of women in Iranian style *'abāyas.*[16] It was also manifested in the ease with which I and other women could walk through the streets. Al-Dahiyya was the only area of Beirut where I was never subject to a single catcall. The only comment ever made to me by a strange man was a singular occasion when someone said *"Allah yahdīkī"* (May God give you guidance), apparently in reference to my modest but unveiled appearance, something that my (at the time) new Shi'i acquaintances found quite amusing. Another area where public piety appeared was in the pervasiveness of certain images: portraits of orphans, religious leaders, and martyrs.[17]

As I noted above, these were not the only signs in al-Dahiyya. Billboards and posters advertising products were also common, as were political signs during elections. These specific portraits also existed in other areas of Beirut, especially during *jam'iyya* Ramadan fund-raising campaigns or when Hizbullah and Harakat Amal were competing for visual dominance in a neighborhood or at a prominent intersection. But unlike in other areas of the city, these particular portraits were commonplace in al-Dahiyya, accepted by many as a natural and comfortable part of the cityscape. Some residents of other areas responded negatively to the explicit presence of Shi'i public piety in their neighborhoods as an encroachment. For example, when one woman saw the poster of a Resistance martyr plastered on a wall near her home she said, "See, al-Dahiyya is creeping up on us."

In contrast, within al-Dahiyya, a person would sometimes point to a poster of a martyr while describing her solidarity with the Resistance, or to a portrait of a religious figure while explaining "how far the

---

[16] *Abāya* is the Arabic term for the full-length loose black outer garment worn by women in Iran (where it is called a *chador*) and some Shi'i women in Iraq.

[17] Kratz identifies three—often overlapping—genres of portraiture common to the United States, Africa and Europe: personal, governmental, and journalistic (2002: 119). In the Middle Eastern context we might add political or public portraiture to that taxonomy. Berger lists three types of public photography: scientific, political, and media/communicative (Berger and Mohr 1982: 98). The portraits I discuss here are both political *and* communicative—part of a mass media of images that inscribe a political community and identity.

1.2. Image of an orphan.

community had come." For many, the iconographic salience of orphans, martyrs, and religious leaders lay in the ways these images claimed and defined the space of al-Dahiyya as belonging to their community.[18] Through these visual signifiers, al-Dahiyya was claimed as a place for the Shi'i Islamic movement and a place within which (a particular) piety would be nurtured. At the same time, the presence of these particular portrait images exemplified the freedom pious Shi'is felt within al-Dahiyya to claim this piety publicly. As will be discussed later, many felt strongly that they were part of a communal group that had always been dispossessed in the Lebanese polity. The images that filled al-Dahiyya were evidence to them of the progress their community had made within the nation-state. Increased piety—visible spiritual progress—was linked to political success.

Images of orphans, martyrs, and religious leaders were read differently by those who felt a part of the Shi'i Islamic pious modern than by

[18] This mirrors at least one of the intentions behind the display of these portraits. As Mona Harb related to me, when she asked a Hizbullah representative why they put up pictures of martyrs, he answered that it was so that when you entered the area, "You would know where you are" (personal communication).

those who did not. Outsiders sometimes saw photographs of orphans as children being used for fund-raising purposes. Depending on one's political leanings, portraits of sayyids and shaykhs might be read as frightening evidence of an insistence on an Islamic state, or as a distressing reminder of the failures of the secular left, or as elements in an internal iconographic war among Shi'i political parties. Responses to the renderings of martyrs often seemed to vary with the political climate and latest events; in the months leading up to and following Israeli withdrawal in 2000, they were regarded by many as national heroes who liberated the south.

Obviously these meanings and valences change when the spectator identifies with the images and their collective narrative. In the case of orphans, the differences relate to a different set of values through which images are interpreted. So within the community, the power of orphans in fund-raising did not stem merely from their embodied innocence as children, but also from the shared assumptions of viewers that orphans were the children of Resistance martyrs.[19] On the other hand, in many ways the salience of portraits of religious leaders emerges from a set of meanings shared with other communities in Lebanon. Here what differs is not understandings of what images represent, but responses to those representations.

Portraits of sayyids and shaykhs are not solely religious images, rather they are part of the plastering of public surfaces with the images of prominent political figures that is common to all of Lebanon and much of the Middle East. In Jordan, posters and large paintings of the late King Husayn and the current King Abdullah fill public space. In Syria one finds omnipresent images of late President Hafez al-Asad and his successor and son, President Bashar.[20] Similarly in Morocco images of the king are mandatory in all public buildings and often appear in homes and offices as well.[21] The lack of one dominant political persona in Lebanon, the lack of a singular face confronting spectators at every turn, reflects the sectarian political system in the country and underscores the usage of portrait images as weapons in a continuous turf war. The prominence of particular leaders declares political loyalties and produces the effect of territorial claims that may, whether intentionally or not, influence the fears and resegregation of Lebanon's various communities. In

[19] During Ramadan 2004, this was highlighted in Martyrs' Association billboards juxtaposing images of orphans with an image of Nasrallah.
[20] See Wedeen's discussion of what she calls "the Asad cult" in Syria (1999). See also Özyürek (n.d.) on images of Ataturk in Turkey.
[21] As described in Ossman 1994.

1.3. Image of martyred Shaykh Raghib Harb.

al-Dahiyya, the dominant faces were those of Hizbullah political leaders, with competition in some areas from Harakat Amal.

The political, rather than religious, significance of these images is reinforced by who was not represented among them, namely Sayyid Muhammad Husayn Fadlullah. Those who were represented were all religious leaders who had clear political roles: Ayatollah Khomeini and his successor Ayatollah Khamenei; Secretary General of Hizbullah Sayyid Hasan Nasrallah; his martyred predecessor Sayyid Abbas al-Musawi; Shaykh Raghib Harb, another martyred Hizbullah leader; Sayyid Musa al-Sadr, the original mobilizer of the Lebanese Shi'a; and even Shaykh Subhi Tufayli, whose movement split from Hizbullah during an internal conflict in the early 1990s. But there were no posters of Fadlullah hanging from electrical poles or balconies. Many of his followers had framed photographs of him in their offices or homes, but this was a personal statement of religious allegiance and admiration, rather than part of the political iconography of the area. Indeed, when I asked people why Fadlullah's picture was not prominently displayed, given his clear importance as perhaps the most influential Shi'i religious leader in Lebanon, the response occasionally indicated that it would be somehow polluting to his role in the religious realm to treat him as a political leader, especially as he has staunchly refused to affiliate with any one political party, calling instead for unity among all believers and coexistence among all Lebanese.

A similar negative association was expressed to me by a close relative of Sayyid Musa al-Sadr, perhaps the religious leader most frequently pictured in posters and paintings in the country:

> He said that it really upsets him, "the whole thing with the pictures," and tears welled up in his eyes. He continued, saying that he has thought about this a lot and that it is clear to him that these pictures are being used for political goals, to help people win elections, because they always put a picture of Berri [Amal's political leader], of the exact same size, next to al-Sadr's image. He then added that he thinks some people just put the pictures up everywhere out of ignorance, because they loved [al-Sadr] and think this is a good way to show it: "It's an ignorant expression of love."

This man resented both the political uses to which al-Sadr was being put and what he perceived as the misplacing of admiration in political postering. Indeed, al-Sadr is perhaps one of the most contested faces in al-Dahiyya. The turf wars expressed through these portraits are often strongest among political parties affiliated with the same sect. In al-Dahiyya, as well as some other areas of Beirut and Lebanon, the political and territorial battles between Hizbullah and rival party Harakat Amal have been played out in images since the end of the civil war.[22] Amal has always claimed al-Sadr, yet Hizbullah also utilizes his image, as they claim descent from the same origins. Each party believes itself the true heir to al-Sadr's movement and political goals. Few other crossover associations take place, although I did see at least one painting of Khomeini with Amal symbols around it.

Turf wars also emerge in less sanctioned images. In a few streets in al-Dahiyya, small spray-painted stencil images of renegade Shaykh Subhi Tufayli covered the cement walls of buildings. This was not official postering associated with a party, but an expression of loyalty to the shaykh and his movement by area residents. Again, it is the political leadership

---

[22] During the civil war, especially in the late 1980s, these battles over territory were fought in street-by-street violence throughout al-Dahiyya.

1.4. Image of a martyr; it reads "The martyred fighter [so-and-so]."

of the shaykh that is emphasized through his representation, rather than his religious position.

Like pictures of religious leaders, portraits of martyrs work to indicate political loyalties and claim territorial space. Yet these images also carry a duality that emerges from their memorializing aspect. This duality is related to "the tension between personal identity and social identity, individual and type, a tension integral to portraiture" (Kratz 2002: 119). In contrast to the sayyid pictures, images of martyrs are invested with an intensity of personal meaning. As photographs of individual martyrs, these images work as expressions of grief; they play a role in memorializing particular loss. Even though martyr images were displayed publicly, on streetlights and electrical poles, the smallness of al-Dahiyya and the few degrees of separation among members of the community guaranteed that some of those who passed the photographs on a daily basis would know one of the martyrs or his family, or at least be familiar with them. Just as there was little anonymity in life, there was even less in death.

But just as martyr photographs are individualized and localized, at the same time they facilitate mourning on the community level, and promote and declare community solidarity and political loyalties. Any display of martyr photographs in al-Dahiyya contained an element of homogenization of form. Take, for example, the signs placed by Hizbullah's media and art department on electrical poles and streetlights along many of the main streets (illustration 1.5). Each sign showed the head and shoulders of a martyr against a bright pastel background, with the yellow Hizbullah flag flanked by pink at the top and blue at the bottom. Written in white along the blue at the lower edge was the name of the martyr, with a caption "The martyred fighter so-and-so" or "The martyred brother so-and-so." These signs followed you down many of these roads, different faces gracing streetlight after streetlight. Or are they different? The uniformity of the signs has the effect of rendering the martyrs themselves faceless, like indistinguishable masks. They become both metonymic pieces of a collective and the whole itself—each in itself representative of the Resistance, and simultaneously each part of the inseparable whole that is the Resistance, along with all who have sacrificed for it, past, present or future. In martyr portraits, this duality links to the binary function of memorial photography: to remember death and to remember the life that has ended.[23] Public portraits of martyrs did exactly this: they memorialized the deaths of individuals while representing solidarity with the community epitomized by the lives that were sacrificed.[24]

The duality inherent in the tension between the personal and the collective in martyr photographs is present to a lesser degree in images of religious leaders and orphans. It is the duality common to all photographs that Roland Barthes describes in his contrast between the *punctum* and the *studium*, the two aspects of looking at a photograph, the former a private emotional experience and the latter based in culturally mediated and shared experience and meaning. "To recognize the *studium* is inevitably to encounter the photographer's intentions, to enter into harmony with them, to approve or disapprove of them, but always to understand them, to argue them within myself, for culture (from which

[23] See Ruby 1995.

[24] This tension is also related to the temporal disruption created when any photograph is taken and later looked at, the gap in time between its taking and viewing (Berger and Mohr 1982). Kratz notes that this temporal difference links a portrait to the life changes that have taken place since its capture (2002: 119). With regard to martyr portraits, this effect is intensified because the image "seems to confirm, prophetically, the later discontinuity created by the absence or death" (Berger and Mohr 1982: 87).

studium derives) is a contract arrived at between creators and con-sumers" (Barthes 1981: 27). In relation to portrait images in al-Dahiyya, the *studium* captured the intentions of the displayer as well as the pho-tographer, and the communal solidarities expressed and provoked by the act of displaying these particular images. The *punctum*, in contrast, dis-turbed (punctuated) the *studium:* "it is this element which rises from the scene, shoots out of it like an arrow, and pierces me" (26). It emerged from the personal relationships a member of the community may have had with a martyr, an orphan (whether the one pictured or not), or a sayyid or shaykh, one's own feelings of faith, doubt, oppression, or soli-darity.

In this regard, these portraits fall into a space between private and pub-lic photographs, between the affective and the collective. This distinction is linked to the relationship between the context in which the images are taken and the context in which they are read.[25] For personal photo-graphs, these contexts are generally similar, so their meaning remains in-tact in ways that are not possible for public photographs that "offer information severed from all living experience" (Berger 1980: 55). Dislo-cation between the contexts of creation and consumption allow public photographs to be used chaotically, by anyone who provides narrative context. But narrative context itself can bridge this gap, as in the 1955 photographic exhibition "The Family of Man" where images from around the world were presented as though part of "a universal family al-bum" (961).[26] In that case, the globe rather than the family became the context for the "family" photo. Similarly, in al-Dahiyya, the Shi'i Islamic movement and the community of the pious modern stood in for "family."

One did not have to have a personal relationship with a martyr, reli-gious leader, or orphan to understand his image as part of one's "fam-ily." The smallness of social scale that heightened the chances that one would actually have such a personal relationship served to intensify a sense of community solidarity, but that sense was there nonetheless. At the same time these portrait images were public: displayed in such a way as to provide an iconography of community, incorporated into a narra-tive of collective identity, one in which leaders, ideal participants, and those in need were all represented.

Like images anywhere, martyr, religious leader, and orphan portraits in al-Dahiyya did not possess inherent meanings. Nor were meanings solely determined by the production and display of these images, which

---

[25] See Berger 1980.

[26] In contrast, Sandeen (1995) argues that "The Family of Man" contained a political narrative based in an antinuclear stance and constructed around a politics of human com-monality that emerged from the historical moment in which the exhibition was constructed.

frequently was controlled by *jam'iyyas*, political parties, and other institutions. Instead, the meanings carried by these photographs and paintings were situated in a wider social and narrative framework. In al-Dahiyya, the particular iconography associated with the Shi'i Islamic movement dominated the visual landscape, facilitated by the hegemonic character of its narrative framework in the area. It emerged from a complex context that included social welfare and political institutions, the residents of al-Dahiyya, Lebanese national polity and public(s), and the global order. Spectators played a crucial role in this process. Through the meanings they brought to the images around them—whether personal mourning, solidarity, a sense of belonging in a place, or something else—pious Shi'is were participating in the creation and maintenance of the context within which the images carried meaning: the framework of the pious modern. I now turn to another key element in its manifestation, moving from the visual to the aural.

Sound

Along with images, the cityscape of al-Dahiyya is textured with sound. This soundscape had regular features. Most prominent, after the din of the streets, were sacred sounds, again reinforcing the sense of public piety that characterized this area of the capital. Perhaps the most constant feature of the soundscape were the regular calls to prayer, the *adhān*, projected five times a day over loudspeakers from each of the many mosques in the area. One effect of the *adhān* is to sacralize space. In al-Dahiyya, this transformation was acknowledged through gesture: even if she was not going to pray at the time, a person would often shift her posture, uncrossing crossed legs, and straightening her back, and would touch her hand to her head quickly when the *adhān* began.

The *adhān* also marked time in al-Dahiyya. Rather than, "I'll meet you there after lunch," or "I'll meet you at 12:30," I was often told, "I'll meet you there right after the noon prayer." The significance of the *adhān* to the daily rhythms of life was highlighted for me when we set our clocks back an hour in the fall for daylight savings time. I had noticed, as I always do, darkness creeping in earlier, but for Aziza the change was even more striking: "I can't believe it's only 11:35 a.m. but it's already *al-dhuhr* (time for the noon prayer)!" she exclaimed upon hearing the call to prayer. The sound of the *adhān* is what divided morning from afternoon and afternoon from evening. Because the *adhān* is set by the path of the sun, and not the clock, daylight savings had the jarring effect of abruptly bringing afternoon an hour earlier, shifting the divisions of the day. For Aziza, afternoon began shortly after 11:35 a.m. that day.

In addition to marking space and time in al-Dahiyya, *adhān* in Lebanon marks sectarian space and identity.[27] There are areas of Beirut where it has always been typical to hear churchbells and *adhān* sharing the soundscape,[28] but most neighborhoods of al-Dahiyya did not fit this description. Moreover, in Lebanon, the details of the *adhān* declare the sect of the mosque. Shi'i mosques are distinguishable by an added line bearing witness that Ali is the *walī* (deputy) of God.

Other related sounds do not mark daily time, but are instead weekly, like the sermons, Qur'anic recitations, and noontime prayers that emanated from many mosques on Fridays. This mosque-based soundscape also included seasonal elements, discussed further below. Also important are occasional manifestations of sound that can be read by residents, such as the Qur'anic recitations that took place when someone had died. On several occasions I would be visiting someone in al-Dahiyya when the recitation slipping in the window prompted her to wonder aloud who in the area had passed away. Ears would then strain to hear the announcement that would follow, informing the community of who had died and when the burial would take place.

Sound in al-Dahiyya marked time, transmitted religious and community knowledge, and engendered or facilitated emotion. Most crucially, elements of the soundscape underscored the indissolubility of religion from everyday life, linking the mundane to the sacred. These sacred sounds were everyday sounds, part and parcel of the spaces where people live.

In the contemporary moment, the mosque is not the only source for pietistic sound in al-Dahiyya. It has been joined by cassette tapes of sermons and Qur'anic recitation,[29] as well as two major radio stations and a television station. The radio stations—al-Bashā'ir (the Messenger or Herald) affiliated with Fadlullah, and al-Nūr (the Light) affiliated with Hizbullah—broadcast a variety of programming, the former primarily religious and social, and the latter a mix of religion, politics and current events/news updates. The television station, Al-Manār (the Lighthouse), is affiliated with Hizbullah, and also has a wide variety of programming, ranging from news updates and in-depth current events discussions,

[27] On the *adhān* as a marker of spatial boundaries and community identity, see Khan (2001) on colonial India, and Lee (1999) on Singapore.

[28] This is not to say that people *necessarily* find "other" religious sounds upsetting; rather, on a few occasions I caught older Christian residents of Beirut humming along with the *adhān*.

[29] Cassettes of sermons, especially Fadlullah's, are readily available at stores throughout al-Dahiyya. The importance of religious cassettes in Islamic movements has been discussed by Eickelman and Anderson 1999b, Hirschkind 2001, Larkin 2000, and Sreberny-Mohammadi and Mohammadi 1994.

interviews, and debates, to children's shows and fictional serials, often based on religio-historical events.

All these media pause their programming in order to sound the call to prayer, and to broadcast Friday sermons and prayers. Many commented on the importance of these media, emphasizing their contribution to the religious milieu as well as their educational value. Religious radio and television were also contrasted positively with past practices of playing nonreligious music, like the classic Egyptian singer Umm Kulthum, in public spaces like shops. There was a sense that these particular media represented progress for al-Dahiyya: a sense related to the feeling that these media provided an outlet, a voice, for the pious modern in Lebanon.

Neither the soundscape nor the visual cityscape were uniform throughout the year in al-Dahiyya. It is to the cycle of seasons and the related shifts in texture that this chapter now turns.

Season

The standard visual and aural textures of al-Dahiyya were supplemented by seasonal additions, following the ritual cycle of the Hijri, or Islamic calendar. The first month of the year is Muharram. For Sunni Muslims, 1 Muharram is celebrated as the beginning of the New Year. Yet for Shiʻi Muslims, the year begins in tragedy. The first ten days of Muharram are commemorated as days of hardship for the Shiʻi leader Imam Husayn and his followers, leading to their martyrdom on 10 Muharram.

Imam Husayn was the grandson of the Prophet, the son of his daughter Sayyida Fatima and his cousin and son-in-law Imam Ali. In 680 CE, Husayn was killed in battle by an army sent by the Caliph, Yazid, on the plain of Karbala, now in Iraq. This was perhaps the most major of a series of conflicts over succession to the leadership of the Islamic community that divided Shiʻi and Sunni Muslims. A group of Shiʻis in Kufa, also in Iraq, had called upon Husayn to lead them in revolt against Yazid. He agreed and set out on the first of Muharram, taking with him armed guards and his family. They were intercepted and besieged at Karbala. The battle began on the tenth of Muharram, and by the end, all the men except one of the Imam's sons had been killed and the women and children taken captive.[30] The entire ten-day period that culminates in the commemoration of the battle and martyrdom on the tenth of Muharram is referred to metonymically in Lebanon as "Ashura."[31]

[30] For more on this history see Ayoub 1978, Jafri 1979, Momen 1985, and Pinault 1992.

[31] "Ashura" (from the Arabic root meaning "ten") technically denotes the tenth of Muharram, the day on which the battle took place, but Lebanese Shiʻis use "Ashura" to refer to the entire ten-day commemoration period.

For Shi'i Muslims, Ashura ushers in a season of mourning and darkness. The details of Ashura commemorations and their meanings are discussed in depth in chapter 4, but for now it is important to note the general atmosphere of solemnity that pervaded al-Dahiyya during Ashura and for several weeks following it. People generally dressed in somber clothing—black, perhaps navy after the tenth of the month. Celebrations, such as weddings or birthday parties, were frowned upon. Ritual mourning gatherings were held throughout the season, continuing for forty days after the day of the martyrdom, and many in al-Dahiyya considered the second month of the calendar, Safar, to be a time of year as sober, if not more sober, than Muharram itself.

The religious seasons in al-Dahiyya were reflected in the imagery and soundscape of the area. During this period of solemnity, it was common to hear the lamentative strains of at least one *majlis 'aza* (mourning gathering, plural, *majālis*) radiating from a mosque, *husayniyya*,[32] street corner, or private home. The recent use of microphones in privately held *majālis* has increased this in the past decade. Many pious individuals listened to tapes of *majālis* or *nudbas*, which are like dirges, mourning songs commemorating the events around the martyrdom. Radio and television programming on the Fadlullah and Hizbullah frequencies also reflected this mood, broadcasting *nudbas* or educational programming about the life of Husayn and the meanings of Ashura.

The standard portrait imagery was supplemented with black banners hung from buildings and balconies, strung across roads, and attached to streetlights and electrical poles. Written on these banners were texts commemorating Husayn's martyrdom: sayings of the Prophet, verses from the Qur'an, or quotes from Khomeini and other important figures, all of which highlight Ashura's importance to the contemporary era. While some of these carried no political insignia, and were erected by mosques or religious organizations, others were clearly linked to territoriality and political affiliation. In 2000, two black bridgelike structures spanned a highway south of Beirut a short distance apart, one clearly marked with Amal signs and the other Hizbullah. In Hizbullah territory, the standard yellow flags of the party are usually replaced by red and black ones.

After the season of mourning, the rest of the year is one of neutrality marked with joy. Some people insisted that Shi'i Muslims exist in perpetual shadow, in a state of constant sadness. However, they were

---

[32] Named after and built in honor of Husayn, *husayniyyas* are buildings used primarily for mourning gatherings, but also for other religious, family, political, and community events.

1.5. Ashura banner; it reads "Hussein's choice is our choice, Khamenei is our leader, and the Resistance is our Karbala."

rare individuals whose piety approached asceticism. Two other major commemorative times mark the Hijri calendar: Ramadan and the *hajj*, both of which are shared by Shi'i and Sunni Muslims alike. Before turning to them, however, I want to touch upon the smaller celebratory moments, the *mawlids*. During the last week of the month Safar one year, I was at a *jam'iyya* while some volunteers were planning a fund-raiser. They had wanted to hold this event for some time, but were waiting for "*mawsim al-mawālid*," the season of *mawlids* (birth celebrations), as one woman put it, to do so. When I asked why, she responded: "Just as

God gave us Ashura which is a sad occasion, he gave us the *mawlid*, the happy occasion of the Prophet's birth."

A *mawlid* commemorates the Prophet Muhammad's birth (in Rabi I) in a celebratory event that often includes professional religious singing in his honor. Shi'i Muslims also hold *mawlid*s to mark other occasions, like the birthdays of Imam Husayn (in Rabi II), Imam Ali (in Rajab), and Imam al-Mahdi, the twelfth Imam (in Shaban). The fund-raiser this particular *jam'iyya* was planning was to coincide with the anniversary of Imam Ali's marriage to Sayyida Fatima, the Prophet's daughter, one of the numerous annual commemorative dates that are noted in al-Dahiyya. *Mawlids* generally did not affect the public sound or cityscape in al-Dahiyya, because they were usually held as private gatherings.

The next major moment in the religious calendar is the month of Ramadan, the ninth month of the year and one whose importance is emphasized by all Muslims. Ramadan is the month in which the Qur'an was revealed to Muhammad. The night on which this is believed to have occurred, the twenty-seventh of the month, is commemorated as *laylat al-qadr* with special prayers.[33] For all Muslims, observing Ramadan involves prayer and fasting—meaning abstaining from food, drink, smoking, and sex—between sunrise and sunset throughout the month. At sunset, the fast breaking meal, or *iftār*, has become a lavish undertaking for many, though this has been criticized by those who fear that Ramadan is losing its religious significance. The end of Ramadan is celebrated as Eid al-Fitr, also called Eid al-Saghir (the minor holiday).

Because Ramadan is a month of reflection and generosity, many *jam'iyyas* conducted their primary fund-raising activities during this time. Some held large banquet *iftārs*, placing an envelope underneath each plate for donations. Others placed advertisements asking for donations, and reminding pious individuals of their religious duty to help the less fortunate. Ramadan fund-raising made use of a wide variety of media, and contributed to the particular textures associated with the month. This is the season during which the orphan as icon took center stage. Billboards and signs showing forlorn yet happy orphans sprouted up all around al-Dahiyya as well as other parts of Beirut, often accompanied by a verse from the Qur'an or a *ḥadīth* enjoining passersby to remember the orphans during the month of generosity, or reminding them that those who help orphans will secure their place in heaven. The radio waves were not immune to this either, as various *jam'iyyas* placed ads that combined children singing with requests for donations.

The other seasonal markers that appeared with Ramadan were

---

[33] There is debate as to whether *laylat al-qadr* is always on 27 Ramadan or on another of the odd-numbered days during the month's final ten days.

celebratory lights and decorations reminiscent of Christmas in the suburban United States. Strings with colorful lanterns, lightbulbs, and paper decorations hung across intersections in al-Dahiyya, and neon lights, including some of the Hizbullah symbol, lined many roads. In 1999 and 2000, the coincidence of Ramadan and Christmas prompted the trimming of Hamra Street—a major road outside al-Dahiyya in Ras Beirut—with neon blue and pink signs alternating *"Ramaḍan karīm"* with "Merry Christmas" and "Happy New Year." Those same years, Hizbullah constructed a large nativity scene in an al-Dahiyya neighborhood.

The two months following Ramadan are relatively quiet, as people resume their normal schedules. Around this time a flurry of banners began to appear, advertising different *ḥajj* organizers, called *ḥamlāt*.[34] The *ḥajj*—the pilgrimage to Mecca required for Muslims who are able to go once in their lifetime—takes place during the first ten days of the last month, Dhu al-Hijjah. At the end of the pilgrimage is Eid al-Adha (the holiday of sacrifice), also called Eid al-Kabīr (the major holiday), during which families slaughter a sheep or other animal and distribute the meat to the poor, in commemoration of Abraham's willingness to sacrifice his son Ishmael at God's command and God's mercy in substituting a lamb for Ishmael. During these festivities, which like most holidays include feasting and visiting, the houses of people on the *ḥajj* were decorated with streamers, often extending across the street or over balconies. Driving through al-Dahiyya, one could easily identify many of the households who had a member on the *ḥajj*. When family members returned, dressed in white to signify their completion of this sacred duty, they were welcomed by celebratory crowds at the airport. Visiting then commenced for weeks, as friends, family and acquaintances came to greet the new Hajj or Hajjeh, who had brought tokens of the voyage to distribute, including prayer beads, Qur'ans, jewelry, and *may al-zumzum* (water from the sacred Zumzum well in Saudi Arabia).

For Sunni Muslims, this Eid and the close of the *ḥajj* season marks the last major moment in the Hijri calendar until the new year a couple of weeks later. Shi'i Muslims, however, mark one more day, the eighteenth of Dhu al-Hijja, or Eid al-Ghadir, on which they quietly acknowledge the moment Muhammad made Ali his successor. From that point, the calendar begins its shift from the seasons of joy to the season of mourning, as Muharram and Ashura approach once again and black returns to shroud al-Dahiyya.

The creation and claiming of a place for the Shi'i Islamic movement and its constituents in al-Dahiyya, a place where the milieu is established

---

[34] *Ḥamla* literally means "campaign," but the term is used for the groups that travel together on the *ḥajj*.

in part through the various textures of piety and politics described in this chapter, is crucial to the totality of progress. Yet places and communities are not claimed or created through texture alone, but also through a shared sense of history and shared practices and meanings. The latter are the subject of the bulk of what follows, but first, it is necessary to backtrack a bit, to provide some of that shared sense of history. To that end, I now turn to a brief summary of some of the basic tenets of Shi'ism and the history and institutionalization of the Shi'i community and Shi'i Islamic movement in Lebanon.

CHAPTER TWO

From Marginalization to Institutionalization

> History always constitutes the relation between a present and
> its past. Consequently fear of the present leads to mystification
> of the past.
>
> —JOHN BERGER, *Ways of Seeing*

THE TEXTURES depicted in the previous chapter are relatively new to
Beirut, just as the community of the Shi'i pious modern is relatively new
to the Lebanese national scene. In order to understand where all this
came from, it is necessary to glance through recent Shi'i Lebanese history, culminating in the institutionalization of the Shi'i Islamic movement. The public visibility of religiosity, and, more importantly, the accompanying changes in understandings of what it means to be a pious
person, are rooted in a historical trajectory that took Lebanese Shi'is
from a marginalized position to one of institutionalized influence. This
trajectory also allows us a glimpse of what pious Shi'is sought to leave
behind via progress.

All history is fraught and contested, but the events of the past thirty or
so years in Lebanon seem particularly precarious. Taking the work of
remembering beyond the mystification Berger points to in the epigraph
above, Lebanon suffers from a case of national amnesia, a willful and
perhaps psychologically necessary burial of much of the past several
decades—specifically of the (un)civil wars.[1] Not that reams haven't been
written about "the events," as people still refer to them, *al-aḥdāth*. Foot-
notes will point to sources,[2] but with the caveat that history writing is
often subject to the same tensions and divisions that plagued the nation
into violence. Many historians are deeply embedded in the history they

---

[1] See also Khalaf (2001) on Lebanese "collective amnesia" and Henderson (2003) on the
lack of civil war memorials. I use "(un)civil wars" to highlight (a) the international aspects
of Lebanon's wars, and (b) that no war is civil.

[2] There are many understandings of what the wars were "about," including political-
economic marginalization along sectarian lines, and conflicts over the Palestinian resistance's presence in Lebanon. For an excellent account of the war see Fisk 1990. See also
Cobban 1985, Picard 1996, Salibi 1988, Hanf 1993, O'Ballance 1998, Hiro 1993, and
Khalaf 2001 and 2002. Sayigh (1994) describes the Palestinian perspective, and Khazen
(2000) and Salibi (1976) focus on failures of the Lebanese state up to 1975.

seek to elucidate.[3] All history is suspect. There is no agreement on a Lebanese national history textbook.

To describe the (un)civil wars in a sentence: what began as an altercation between a few armed groups in Lebanon quickly exploded into a series of wars spanning a decade and a half, and involving, over the course of its ebb and flow, over twenty-five Lebanese militias; Palestinian liberation groups; the state armies of Israel and Syria; troops from the United States, France, Italy, and Iran; and agents from Iraq, Libya, and who knows where else. In a word: hell.

> Just when one thinks that the war is over, that, for better or worse, one has understood what it was all about, that one knows, to borrow the vulgar Lebanese phrase, on which stake one has been impaled; just as one gets one's political bearings after emerging from the bomb shelter in the latest battle, and, looking around, blaming this or that faction for its arrogance, shortsightedness, cruelty, and treacherous alliance with this or that foreign power; just then the whole picture changes again. A new battle erupts, and new political realities appear. It is like looking through a kaleidoscope: Shake it, and a design appears; shake it again, and an altogether different one replaces it. Shifts happen so often that one wonders if they will ever end, or, if they do, if one will recognize the end, having long ago despaired of reaching it. (Makdisi 1990: 30)

Below, I sketch only those events directly related to my interlocutors' lives and the chapters that follow. Although the Lebanese wars technically ended with the Ta'if Accord in 1989,[4] it is the gash in history/memory that forms the background for these details of community formation. Much of the trajectory of Lebanese Shi'i mobilization is tied up with the war years, their events, actors, and catalysts. And while for most of the country the experience of war ended in 1990 when oppositional General Aoun was ousted, for many Shi'is in al-Dahiyya, along with those living under Israeli occupation, war did not end until Israeli troops left Lebanese soil in May 2000, after initially invading the country in 1978. The rapid sketch I provide here is not sharp; I intentionally allow edges that are ragged to overlap, gaps to claim their space. I draw on secondary source materials and on interviews, depending on the latter more heavily as I move toward the specifics of the pious Shi'i community. As such, this is a history that reflects my interlocutors' concerns and understandings. On the way I take the opportunity to explain basic

---

[3] For an eloquent critique of the possibility of writing histories of the wars see Raad's visual essay (1999).

[4] Named after the place it was signed: Ta'if, Saudi Arabia.

tenets particular to Shi'ism that are important to understanding this history.[5]

ON THE MARGINS

Origins and the Marji'iyya

From the initial division between Sunni and Shi'i Islam, the latter has—with few exceptions, most recently the Islamic Republic of Iran—existed on the margins of political power and the larger Muslim community. That initial split was at first political, based in conflict over succession to the Prophet Muhammad after his death. Simply put, a small group of Muslims believed that Muhammad had chosen his cousin and son-in-law Ali to succeed him, and that community leadership should be hereditary—through Imams descended from the Prophet through his daughter Fatima and Ali. When the Prophet died in 632 CE, another group chose one of his companions, Abu Bakr, to lead the community as Caliph. Those Muslims who supported Ali instead were known as *shī'at 'Ali*—a phrase meaning "the partisans of Ali" from which the name "Shi'a" is derived. Ali eventually became the fourth Caliph as recognized by Sunni Muslims, while remaining the first Imam to Shi'i Muslims.

Over time, this initial division—solidified by the continued assassinations and martyrdoms of many Shi'i Imams, most prominently Husayn—led to doctrinal differences with Sunni schools of Islam. During this process, several groups split from the main body of Shi'ism, including the Isma'ilis and the Zaydis. The majority of Shi'is today, including those in Lebanon, follow what is known as "Twelver" (*ithna-'ashari*) Shi'ism. This designation refers to their belief that the twelfth and last Imam, Muhammad al-Mahdi, is in occultation—that is, he has been hidden from humanity until his reappearance just before Judgment Day. This poses a problem with regard to Shi'i spiritual and political leadership, the details of which are beyond this study.[6] For our purposes, what is important is that each Shi'i Muslim looks to one established religious scholar—known as a *marji' al-taqlīd* (henceforth *marji'*)—as the Imam's deputy, and emulates him with regard to religious practices.[7]

---

[5] For discussion of the origins, history, development, and doctrines of Shi'ism, I point the reader especially to Momen 1985 and Halm 1997.

[6] See Momen 1985, Richard 1995, Abdul-Jabar 2002 on this issue. This is important to the notion of *wilāyat al-faqīh*—see note 41 later in this chapter.

[7] "*Marji' al-taqlīd*" literally means "source of emulation." See Moussavi 1985, Momen 1985, Halm 1997, and Abdul-Jabar 2002 on the *marji'iyya* (the term for the institution of this practice).

A cleric who has attained the status of *marji'* is at the apex of the hierarchy of theological rank, and is often called *ayatullah al-'uzma*, or Grand Ayatollah, by his followers.[8] In addition to religious interpretation, a *marji'* is responsible for collecting and distributing religious taxes, *khums* and *zakāt*.[9] At times in history there has been one *marji'* for all Shi'is, while at other times there are several, and each individual may choose whom to emulate. Hajjeh Umm Ali explained her relationship to her *marji'* to me:

> Look, like you now when you do research, you want to review the sources, it's the same thing. I'm not going to take information from anywhere, no, I want to go to the *marji'* [source]. The *marji'* interprets. His work is to understand the *hadīth*, the Qur'an. The good thing is that we have the door of interpretation [*bāb al-ijtihād*] open, so you can continue to develop, you keep reading, the world is progressing, religion didn't come to restrict you, to say, really, Lara, this is this and that's it. Of course, there is something absolute, you have been given a line, *ya'ni*, prayer, fasting, etc., but there are issues, social issues, worshiping issues, that aren't set, so these are about interpretation. So on those issues, each believer looks to his own interpreter [*mujtahid*] for understanding. . . . If there was going to be only one opinion, there wouldn't be a need for something called interpretation. *Khalas* [that's it], one person speaks and all else are silenced, there is no progress in the world, but because the door is open, you read and I read, you understand and I understand, and so on, each does what makes him comfortable . . .

Of the many points included in Hajjeh Umm Ali's explanation, I want to reiterate and link two: the notion that in Shi'ism, the door of interpretation is open (*bāb al-ijtihād maftūh*),[10] and the idea that the existence of multiple *marji'*s is good for progress. The phrase "the door of interpretation is open," came up almost every time anyone—regardless of sect—explained the difference between Shi'i and Sunni Islam to me. The word *ijtihād* literally means "exertion," from the same root as *jihād*, which denotes "effort." In our context, *ijtihād*, which I gloss as "interpretation" is the process qualified religious scholars, called *mujtahid*s, use to

---

[8] "Ayatollah" literally means "sign of God." "Grand Ayatollah" is a relatively new term, originating as recently as sixty years ago in an inflation of titles by followers of competing religious scholars (Houchang Chehabi, personal communication, May 5, 2004). See Momen (1985: 205–6) for more on clerical rankings.

[9] This ties the *marji'iyya* to control of large sums of money. *Khums* is a Shi'i tithe of one-fifth of the increase in one's income minus living expenses annually.

[10] "The door" is open because human beings—other than the infallibles (Muhammad, Fatima, and the twelve Imams)—are fallible. God gave humans the faculty of reason (*'aql*) to be used to understand God's will, but human fallibility means that no person's interpretation can ever be absolute.

make judgments about issues pertaining to religious law and practice. What Hajjeh Umm Ali and others who used this phrase meant was that religious law was constantly open to reinterpretation by *mujtahid*s, allowing for greater flexibility in applying it to the contemporary world. Her last sentence opens the door even wider, to include all literate people as potential interpreters. This both points to the uncertainty generated by the tension between authentication's emphasis on individual rationality and the *marji'iyya* as an institution,[11] and signals that Hajjeh Umm Ali follows Fadlullah, as she highlights his distinctive emphasis on individual interpretation.

Differences among interpretations allow for debate and the continual development of doctrine, a sign of progress. One example is the issue of Khomeini ruling in favor of using cadavers for medical study noted in the introduction. Another example arose when I wanted to go to the mosque with Aziza. Some *mujtahid*s have judged that non-Muslims may not enter mosques, which would have presented a problem in my case. Aziza, however, followed Fadlullah as her *marji'*, so she called his office to ask about his view. It ended up being acceptable for me to accompany her.[12]

Like many pious Shi'is, both Hajjeh Umm Ali and Aziza followed Fadlullah, whose status as *marji'* is relatively recent and somewhat contested. Many Lebanese Shi'is followed Khomeini until his death in 1989, while others emulated Khu'i, who was perhaps the *marji'* with the widest influence in recent years, until his death in 1992. Fadlullah had been one of Khu'i's *wakīl*s (deputies) in Lebanon since 1976, and only after his death took on the role of *marji'*. He is the most prominent *mujtahid* in Lebanon today, and is also internationally renowned, with followers throughout the world, especially in the Arab Gulf states. Today there are also several prominent *marji'*s in Iran and Iraq, including Khamenei and Ruhani in Iran and Sistani in Iraq. Most pious Shi'is I knew followed either Fadlullah or Khamenei (Nasrallah is one of his deputies), with a few choosing Sistani, and some continuing to emulate Khomeini or Khu'i postmortem instead.[13] Many of these religious figures

---

[11] This tension is amplified by the fact that both authentication and the *marji'iyya* are dependent on similar facilitating processes. For example, in Lebanon, *marji'* authority was generally irrelevant, especially in rural areas, until communication technology and literacy facilitated access to their interpretations in the 1960s.

[12] Fadlullah has written, "I rule on the purity (*taharah*) of every human being, regardless of whether he is a non-believer or a Muslim, for there is no impure (*najis*) person in his essence" (1998: 218). This view is crucial to his support of sectarian coexistence in Lebanon.

[13] Debate exists about the permissibility of emulating a deceased *marji'*. Fadlullah holds that it is only permissible if a person began following that *marji'* while he was still alive.

have played important roles in the movement of Lebanese Shi'is out of the margins, a history to which I now turn.

Shi'a in Lebanon

Twelver Shi'is have resided in areas that are today part of Lebanon since the ninth century, primarily in the south, in a region called Jabal 'Amil,[14] and in the Beqaa Valley, with another small community north of Beirut near Jbeil. Under Sunni Ottoman rule, because Shi'ism was considered a "delinquent" sect, they were often persecuted.[15] Some people I spoke with noted that their ancestors had practiced *taqiyya*, or religious dissimulation, permissible in situations of danger.

In 1920, the French mandate established the existing borders of the Lebanese nation-state, by combining the Christian-majority Ottoman province of Mount Lebanon with surrounding areas, including the Beqaa Valley and the south. According to the 1932 census,[16] the last census ever taken in Lebanon, Shi'i Muslims were 17 percent of the population, making them the third largest minority in a nation with no clear majority and sixteen recognized religious groups.[17] A decade later, an unwritten National Pact was established among the major communities in Lebanon, especially the Sunni Muslims and Maronite Christians. Among other things, the Pact laid the groundwork for a confessional political system, distributing government positions according to the 1932 census's proportions. As such, Shi'i Muslims received ten seats in the fifty-five member Parliament.[18] Additionally, the Pact stipulated that the cabinet would be divided equally between Christians and Muslims, with equal numbers of Maronite and Sunni members, a move that ensured Shi'i underrepresentation. Finally, with independence in 1943, it was understood that the President would always be Maronite, the Prime Minister always Sunni, and the relatively powerless speaker of Parliament, Shi'i.

The confessional nature of this system was structurally stagnant. Throughout later decades, it would fail to take into consideration population changes, exacerbating Shi'i underrepresentation. Furthermore, the

---

[14] See Abisaab (1999) for an early history of the Shi'a in what is today Lebanon.

[15] For more about Shi'i experience under Ottoman rule see Cole 2002.

[16] Maktabi (1999) argues that even the 1932 census was highly politicized and undertaken so as to ensure a Christian majority in order to establish "a Christian nation." Picard (1997) notes that many Shi'is in the Beqaa were not counted by this census.

[17] Today there are eighteen recognized groups.

[18] The ratio of Christians to Muslims in Parliament was 6:5. Christian seats were primarily allocated to Maronites. Sunni Muslims received eleven of the twenty-five Muslim seats and the Druze four.

institutionalization of sectarianism in Lebanon was accompanied by a more subtle process by which the category of sect became increasingly necessary to the groups themselves. A sectarian political leadership supported the establishment of sectarian social institutions (e.g., schools, hospitals) rather than common ones, so that sect became a means of accessing resources.[19] Here underrepresentation contributed directly to poverty as government funds were routed into other communities. Aggravating this was the fact that Shi'i seats in Parliament were usually filled by feudal landowners and other elites—men detached from the realities of life in rural Shi'i regions of the country.

Postindependence economic and structural development in Lebanon was concentrated mainly in Beirut. The Maronites and urban Sunni were tied into a network of western capital inaccessible to the relatively isolated Shi'a, who were by far the most rural of Lebanon's communities.[20] Living conditions in Shi'i villages did not approach the standards of the rest of the nation. For example, at independence, the Southern Lebanon district—consisting of three hundred mostly Shi'i villages—contained no hospitals and no irrigation schemes. Poverty and illiteracy were the norm among the Shi'i peasantry.[21]

After a brief civil war in 1958, the new president, Shihab, began a program of nationwide development and "modernization"—known as Shihabism—seeking to raise the standards of the rural infrastructure to those of Beirut. At that time, transportation routes were built tying villages into the road network, and schools were established in rural areas. The new government also began hiring more Shi'is in military and civil service positions and introduced "export-based agro-capitalism," which replaced earlier economic bases with cash crops like tobacco.[22] These new policies and infrastructures prompted a mass migration of rural Shi'is to Beirut.[23] Many of these migrants settled in a ring of suburbs around the capital, known as the "misery belt" (Khuri 1975).

By this time Beirut had become the undisputed center of the financial network linking the industrial world with the oil-producing nations of the Gulf.[24] But the rapid urbanization that came with incorporation into

---

[19] See Joseph 1975, 1978, 1997b.

[20] Picard (1997) notes that in 1948, Shi'is made up 70–85 percent of the population of the rural south and Beqaa, and only 3.5 percent of the population of Beirut.

[21] See Ajami 1986, Cobban 1985, Picard 1997, Norton 1987.

[22] See Picard 1997 and Halawi 1992 on these economic shifts.

[23] By 1973, only 40 percent of Shi'is remained rural, and Shi'is constituted 29 percent of Beirut's population (Picard 1997).

[24] Lebanon's location, geography, probusiness government policies, and banking secrecy laws facilitated this, along with the closures of Haifa and the Suez Canal due to the Arab-Israeli conflicts.

the capitalist world economy further exacerbated economic, social and regional disparities within Lebanon.[25] Again it was the rural and recently urbanizing Shi'is who suffered disproportionately. If Beirut in the 1960s and '70s was the Paris of the Middle East—as is commonly quipped by reminiscing expats—then Shi'i villages were in Limousin and urban Shi'is lived in Vitry sur Seine.

Much of this newly urban population consisted of young Shi'i men seeking their fortunes in Beirut. Upon arrival in the city, these young men often found themselves trapped in wage-labor at a level substantially below that of their educations. Some worked in factories, although many remained unemployed or self-employed as peddlers, because the service sector was saturated by the mid-sixties.[26] In addition to producing a discontented youth, the new accessibility of Beirut exposed blatantly the uneven distribution of resources across sectarian groups. Arenas for intersectarian competition for resources, employment, and services were created.

Unequal modernization and an ever-growing sense of disenfranchisement were factors that would contribute to the eventual political mobilization of the Shi'a. In addition, Beirut was a space of contact for Shi'is from different regions of Lebanon. Equally important, the road networks facilitated constant movement between village and city. Migrants returned to their villages to marry, visit family, and vote. Rather than an urbanized population, what emerged was a connected population.[27]

The initial mobilization of the Shi'a was not along sectarian lines. As the state became tangible in the city, political parties on both ends of the spectrum competed for Shi'i loyalties. In the 1960s and early '70s, Shi'is made up much of the rank-and-file membership of the Lebanese Communist Party and the Syrian Social Nationalist Party. They also participated in the early days of the Palestinian liberation movement in Lebanon, though that connection did not last long. This environment— combining political awareness and discontent with the desire for modernization—provided the ground for a Shi'i sectarian mobilization.

This sectarian mobilization, described in the next section, is often cast as instrumental, a response solely to poverty and disenfranchisement within the Lebanese state. Because the system is sectarian, Shi'i clerical leadership and especially that of Sayyid Musa al-Sadr, discussed below, are viewed as cleverly giving the Shi'a what everyone else already had: a

---

[25] See Diab 1999 and Kubursi 1993.

[26] See Halawi 1992.

[27] In addition, by the mid-fifties, many Shi'is had emigrated to West Africa, including Senegal, the Ivory Coast, Sierra Leone, Liberia, and Ghana. They maintained ties to Lebanon and had a high rate of return, contributing to an even broader network of connection.

sectarian political movement.[28] While this is no doubt part of the picture, this perspective does not give either faith or political contingency enough credit, nor does it take into consideration differences within the movement. On the one hand, as we will see, the years of Shi'i mobilization were years of intense political and military strife in Lebanon, during which Israel, a power backed by the West, invaded the country twice. On the other hand, the success of the Islamic Revolution in Iran proved that Islam was a powerful worldview able to act as a counternarrative to ideas about western modernity. The Shi'i mobilization did not merely respond to frustrated desires, it restructured desire to include the spiritual along with the material.

For many pious Shi'is, hindsight has cast their history of dispossession and marginalization as a moment of perceived spiritual ignorance. Evidence of spiritual backwardness was found in the membership of Shi'i youth in secular parties, the corruption of village clergy and their support for the elite landowning class, and the ways that particular religious practices and rituals were carried out. The framework of progress out of spiritual backwardness provides the link through which global politics have consequences for how people understand themselves as moral on a micro-level.

Both spiritual and material backwardness were to be left behind through mobilization. As it developed over time, this mobilization became a Shi'i Islamic movement. Its aims were shifting and multiple, but broadly speaking included political representation, education toward authenticated Islam, and improved education, health care, and other social services, especially in the absence of government-supported public services. In the next section, I describe the political development of this movement. I touch upon the accompanying details of religious reform only briefly, as they are the primary focus of the following chapters.

LEAVING THE MARGINS: MOBILIZATIONS AROUND RELIGION

A Personal Perspective on Change: Hajjeh Khadija Hammoud

When I first began community work [al-'amal al-ijtimā'ī], I wasn't muhajjaba [veiled], but then I became muhajjaba and committed [multazima]. I became committed to the path of Islam from its beginning, perhaps twenty years ago. It has been a long path.

The truth is, it was a difficult situation; there was a big struggle between different political movements [tayyār]. There was a communist side, and a

[28] As presented in Ajami 1986.

capitalist side, and then the Islamic side began to appear. In the beginning we were mostly members of secular groups, and very attached to the things that some people consider descriptive of modernity/civilization [ḥaḍāra], like short clothing and sports. Also education, because at that time girls didn't have their educational rights. So these political movements opened our horizons and taught us that we should learn. Even though if we go back further, the truth is that it is Islam that gave us the right to education, before anyone else. Islam gave rights to women before any other movement, whether communist or capitalist.

So we were, you know, the generation of the sixties; we thought women's liberation was progress. Our parents were of a generation that was very conservative and had many traditions that they wanted to preserve, and we were a generation that came to change these traditions. But when I arrived at a point where I was in school, obtaining my education, and I was dressing the way I wanted, casually, short skirts and tank tops, with the fashion, once I obtained those things and realized those freedoms, then what? I began, perhaps because I wanted to be free so strongly, I began to feel that I was missing something, that I had a spiritual emptiness. This spiritual emptiness was something I needed to fill, so I began to think about that and to read the Qur'an. Even though we used to consider this something that just sat at home. We had a Qur'an just sitting on the side; no one used to read it. And it began to bother me, that I was stuck between the issues that I worked for and the religious motivations I had that pushed me towards God. I lived in the midst of a very intense struggle, and then I came to the Qur'an and tried to learn how to pray.

And at the time there were religious leaders who were beginning to work in our area, so I said, OK, I'll go and see what this one says. His name was Sayyid Faisal al-Amin, he's dead now. He had a very modern style [style ktīr moderne (Fr.)], a style that made sense to us, and in truth he was able to tolerate us. He used to answer all my questions openly, but he used to tell me that I was very difficult, and I was, just because I would ask him every possible question. But he tried to answer all of our questions, because we believe in Islam that there are answers to all questions, just that some of them may not exist for us right now, but in the end we will have the answers to all questions. And we appreciated this, especially those of us who had the revolutionary spirit.

It was at this point that my true work began, with a group of women who built the Cultural Committee. We were all young women, sixteen, seventeen, eighteen years old. I was still in secondary school. There were only three of us who were *muḥajjaba* in secondary school. We three were of the same mindset, we all had been very sporty [*sport* (Fr.)], and modern [*moderne* (Fr.)], and then we all became committed. And everyone was surprised when we put on the *ḥijāb*, because our mindsets were very liberated. But we believed that it was through our commitment that we truly became liberated from all limitations. We then had freedom, freedom in that we were able to respect others and be respected, freedom of behavior because we knew that we were acting the right way, in ways that wouldn't hurt others. And thanks be to God all three of us were fighters from the beginning of our movement.

We also did very well in school, especially in things like math and science, things that they used to say "those Muslims, of course they can't learn that, they are stupid, they won't accomplish anything." We even had a mathematics teacher—she was a Communist party organizer—she used to debate us. We had many discussions with her, and thanks be to God, even though she was much older than us, we were able to debate with her. Even though she didn't share our convictions, we respected her very much. Because she was defending her path and that is her right; we respect the opinions of others. And then she also began to respect us; after our discussions, she realized that we weren't committed just like that, but that our commitment to our religion was from understanding and awareness, and not merely a blind traditional thing.

And thanks be to God there truly has been change, change from traditions, and the deep ignorance that we had had as Muslims, towards the freedom of truth, and the knowledge of our religion, and the application of this truth in our lives, our work, our interactions, in addition to our worship of God.

Beginnings: The Movement of the Deprived and Hizb al-Daʿwa

The man most often credited by scholars with uniting many Lebanese Shiʿis into a separate nonsecular political movement of their own is Sayyid Musa al-Sadr.[29] He was an Iranian Shiʿi cleric with Lebanese family ties who came to Lebanon in 1959 to replace the late clerical leader in the southern Lebanese city of Tyre.[30] A charismatic orator, al-Sadr challenged the leftist parties for the loyalty of Shiʿi youth, offering in their stead an infusion of religion into the political world. Halawi puts it thus: "[Sayyid Musa] was ready to defend the faith . . . to revitalize Islam and counterpose it to radical ideologies as an appropriate vehicle for change" (1992: 114). He was instrumental in establishing the Supreme Islamic Shiʿi Council—a body created to articulate Shiʿi needs to the state—in 1969. In 1970, he led the first general Shiʿi strike in Lebanon, calling on the government to assist those displaced by Israeli attacks in the south.[31] Four years later, al-Sadr established *ḥarakat al-maḥrūmīn*—the Movement

---

[29] See Ajami 1986, Halawi 1992, and especially Norton 1987.

[30] The links between south Lebanon, especially Jabal ʿAmil, and Iran, especially Qom, reach back to the Safavid Empire.

[31] Many Shiʿis initially supported Fatah, the military wing of what became the PLO. But in the 1970s, when Israeli retaliations began to affect Shiʿi villages, many turned against the Palestinians. The first Shiʿi militia, Amal, was initially trained by Fatah (Norton 1987) but this relationship disintegrated into violence during the 1980s "Camp Wars."

of the Deprived, a political movement dedicated to attaining rights for the deprived, which essentially meant the Shi'a. When war began the next year, a militia branch was founded: Amal.[32] However, at this point the movement was still small and many Shi'i youth fought with secular party militias during the first few years of war (1975–76).[33]

Yet despite academic focus on al-Sadr's role, and despite an almost universal acknowledgment of his importance to Shi'i mobilization, when they explained their movement's history many pious Shi'is did not attribute sole credit to him. While they noted that they all "stood on his foundation," and often claimed to be his "true heirs," they also described another stream of Shi'i political, social, and religious activism that had begun to take shape in Lebanon in the 1960s and '70s.

While al-Sadr's roots were in Iran, many other activist Shi'i religious leaders came from Iraq, and especially the religious schools (hawzas) of Najaf. Among them were Fadlullah and Sayyid Hasan Nasrallah, who is the current Secretary General of Hizbullah.[34] Najaf was the center of hizb al-da'wa al-islāmiyya, (literally, the Party of the Islamic Call), which had a branch in Lebanon at this time. Hizb al-Da'wa is an Iraqi Shi'i Islamist party established in the late 1950s.[35]

At the beginning of the wars in 1976, the eastern suburb of Beirut—Nab'a—where many Shi'is lived and where Fadlullah worked, fell to the Phalangists (a Maronite Christian militia) and the Shi'i population fled to al-Dahiyya. With them went Fadlullah, who, in keeping with the ideals of Najaf, began teaching and establishing social institutions in the area. He emerged in the early 1980s as one of the key figures in the Islamist Shi'i community. Some of my Shi'i friends were active in the Lebanese Union of Muslim Students (ittihād al-lubnānī li-al-ṭullāb al-muslimīn) which had been established as early as 1973 by Najaf-trained clerics. One of them compared Musa al-Sadr with Hizb al-Da'wa:[36]

---

[32] "Amal" means "hope" in Arabic and is also an acronym for afwāj al-muqāwama al-lubnāniyya (the Lebanese Resistance Brigades).

[33] Musa al-Sadr's success in uniting the Shi'a under a sectarian banner has been variously evaluated, with some (Ajami 1986) attributing him greater success than others (Norton 1987).

[34] Also among them were the late Shaykh Muhammad Mehdi Shamseddin (head of the Supreme Shi'i Council during my field research), Shaykh Subhi Tufayli (former Hizbullah leader, removed from the party during a dispute in 1998), and the martyred Sayyid Abbas al-Musawi (Secretary General of Hizbullah until Israel assassinated him in 1992). While Shamseddin had ties to the state and was acknowledged by my interlocutors as an important Islamic thinker, most of them found him either obtuse or politically suspect.

[35] See al-Ruhaimi 2002.

[36] AbuKhalil (1991) observes that Fadlullah and al-Sadr were working from different perspectives as early as the 1960s.

Hizb al-Da'wa was the more religious of the two. The party thought that the best way to contest power [in Iraq] was to withdraw from it and to build and grow and develop in secret. This heritage [*irth*] came to Lebanon with them. This is still before the war, they believed that they could build Shi'i power by working quietly through culture and education. The main premise was that the first step towards political work in Lebanon was cultural work. Sayyid Musa [al-Sadr] came from a different world; it wasn't religious in this way. He came from Iran, and began the work of raising the Shi'a up from their position, but from within the system, dealing directly with politics.

The basic place where these two paths differed was in their approach to politics: one worked from outside the system and the other from within. Al-Sadr was intent on establishing institutions that would provide Shi'i Lebanese with the sort of government leverage that other sects in Lebanon had (e.g., the Shi'i Islamic High Council). Yet despite these differences, they agreed on the importance of Shi'i mobilization in combatting Shi'i marginalization.

A Catalytic Moment: Al-Sadr Disappears, Israel Invades, the Left Fails, and Iran Succeeds

Between 1978 and 1982 a number of events propelled the nascent Shi'i mobilization forward and further divorced it from the leftist parties: two Israeli invasions of Lebanon, the unexplained disappearance of Musa al-Sadr, and the Islamic Revolution in Iran. In 1978, while on a visit to Libya, al-Sadr mysteriously disappeared, catapulting him directly into the narrative of the Hidden Twelfth Imam, and initiating a surge in his popularity. Suddenly, al-Sadr's face was postered all over the south, the Beqaa, and parts of Beirut. That same year, Israel invaded south Lebanon, displacing 250,000 people.[37] The initial consequence of these two events was Amal's revitalization, as it grew and entered the fray of war.[38] Another factor here was Shi'i perceptions that the Lebanese left had failed, both in securing greater rights for the poor and in protecting the south.[39] Then came Iran.[40]

> Now honestly, I can tell you, before the victory of the Iranian revolution none of this meant anything to us. We didn't know that it needed to. (Rasha)

[37] See Yahya 1993.

[38] See Norton 1987.

[39] For more on the failures of the Lebanese left, see AbuKhalil 1988. Other contributing factors include a general mistrust of atheism and the end of the Nasser era.

[40] Much has been written about the Islamic Revolution in Iran and its reformulations of Shi'ism. See Aghaie 2001, Cole and Keddie 1986, Halm 1997, Hegland 1983 and 1987, Fischer 1980, Keddie 1995, Rajaee 1993, Yousefi 1995.

Now, you really began to see *iltizām* after the victory of the Islamic Revolution in Iran. It revived the principles of the Holy Qur'an, saying that our religion is modern/civilized [*ḥaḍārī*] and it advances through all eras, all times. (Dalal)

It [the Islamic Revolution] demonstrated that it was possible for a people to overcome and be victorious, that it was possible for a people to challenge oppressors. And people saw that this worked, and that the Iranians were able to successfully overthrow the biggest imperial power in the world. No one thought it was possible to overthrow the strongest empire in the world with just a group of simple everyday modest people. A person living in a small poor simple room was able to change society and the world. And where did this come from? It wouldn't be possible for a person to do this if he didn't have the power that comes from Islam. (Hajjeh Khadija)

The interview over, I switched off the tape recorder. As I began to thank him, Hajj Qasim interrupted, tapping an index finger forcefully on the framed photograph of Khomeini that sat on his desk. "You want to know where all this came from? This," he said, "This is it." (fieldnotes, June 22, 2000)

The 1979 Islamic Revolution in Iran is one of those events that reverberated around the world. Those reverberations were particularly loud in Lebanon. Without fail, pious Shi'is pointed to the revolution as one of those historical moments people hold in awe, and as the ultimate locus of their inspiration. By embracing revolution directly and calling on the notion of *wilāyat al-faqīh*,[41] Khomeini's path differed from those of both Musa al-Sadr and Hizb al-Da'wa, setting a new sort of example for the mobilizing Shi'is. It also provided an alternative counternarrative to the West from that espoused by the political left, at precisely the moment when the Lebanese left lost the faith of many of its Shi'i constituents. Not only did the Islamism that emerged from Iran speak to historical redemption and the rise of the oppressed, but it did so *successfully*. This success proved that the best path to progress was one that included the spiritual along with the material.

The last ingredient in this cauldron of events was the second Israeli invasion of Lebanon in June 1982, during which another 450,000 people were displaced. This time Israeli troops marched north and laid siege to West Beirut. Tens of thousands of Lebanese were killed and injured during the invasion and siege, many of them Shi'i Muslims. It was during this time that the Sabra and Shatila massacres took place. Between September 16 and 18, 1982, under the protection of the Israeli military and then Israeli Defense Minister Ariel Sharon, a Lebanese Phalangist militia

---

[41] Meaning "guidance of the jurisprudent," this is the basis of the Islamic state in Iran: spiritual and political authority reside in the same institution, headed by a cleric who is the Hidden Imam's representative on earth.

2.1. Larger-than-life Khomeini.

unit entered the Sabra and Shatila refugee camps in Beirut, and raped, killed, and maimed thousands of civilian refugees.[42] Approximately one quarter of those refugees were Shiʻi Lebanese who had fled the violence in the south. Further fuel was provided in October 1983, when an Israeli

[42] There is some debate as to whether it was a Phalangist or Lebanese Forces militia. Casualty figures range from 800 to 3,500, and are most likely in the vicinity of 2,000. Several hundred people also "disappeared." The 1983 Israeli Kahan Commission Report attributed "personal responsibility" for the massacres to Sharon (Harik 2004). For reports and

occupation force convoy disrupted the Ashura commemorations in Nabatieh, leading to violence in which two Shi'i Muslims were killed and a number injured. The second Israeli invasion was perhaps the most essential catalyst in the eventual formation—from many of the existing strands of Shi'i mobilization—of Hizbullah.

Hizbullah

Following the events of 1982, many prominent members of Amal left the organization.[43] Many of them, along with Nasrallah, went on to form the leadership of Hizbullah. A number of small Islam-based resistance groups emerged in the south, the Beqaa, and al-Dahiyya. By this time, there were also Iranian revolutionary guards in the Beqaa, beginning to train Shi'i fighters. Over time, these groups, which included many of Fadlullah's followers, former Amal members, Islamic Amal (a splinter group), the Lebanese Union of Muslim Students, Hizb al-Da'wa, and a group called the "Committee Supporting the Islamic Revolution" that had existed since 1979, among others, coalesced into a single organization: Hizbullah.[44]

With the Iranian revolution, support for Hizb al-Da'wa and its methods had faded in Lebanon, and many of its members were absorbed into Hizbullah, but the popularity of Fadlullah did not fade and only grew with time. In much of the literature and media, Fadlullah is inaccurately characterized as "the spiritual leader" of Hizbullah. In keeping with his belief that a *mujtahid* should not be affiliated with any single political party, Fadlullah has always held that Islamic work should occur through multiple institutions and has always denied having any official role in the party.[45] Yet as a major scholar and eventually *marji'*, and as one of the most prominent figures in the Lebanese Shi'i community, Fadlullah's teachings and sermons have influenced many Hizbullah members. This relationship will be further explored below.

---

documentation of these massacres, see Fisk 1990, Kapeliouk 1982, Siegel 2001, the reports of the Kahan Commission 1983 and the MacBride Commission 1983. See also Harik 2004: 35–36 and 64–65.

[43] This was related to a shift in Amal's leadership after al-Sadr disappeared; since 1980 it has been led by Nabih Berri, who angered many by participating in U.S.-brokered negotiations in 1982. Today, Amal remains one of the two major Shi'i political parties in Lebanon, with strength in parts of the south and a few al-Dahiyya neighborhoods—and Berri is Speaker of the Lebanese Parliament.

[44] There is a plethora of literature detailing Hizbullah's origins, history, relations with Iran and Syria, and military and political activities. See especially AbuKhalil 1991, M. Deeb 1988, Hamzeh 2000a and 2000b, Harik 2004, Norton 1999 and 2000, Jaber 1997, and Saad-Ghorayeb 2002.

[45] See Mallat 1988: 28.

Although its foundations were laid throughout the late 1970s and especially between 1979 and 1982, Hizbullah did not formally declare itself until 1985.[46] Its military branch at first consisted of small independent groups of resistance fighters in the south, with no clear leadership. By 1984, clashes over political and territorial power between a more organized Hizbullah and Amal had begun, and in 1985, Hizbullah announced its Islamic Resistance (*al-muqāwama al-islāmiyya*), which eventually came to dominate the resistance movement in the south. The men I spoke with who were among the early resistance fighters always expressed their surprise and appreciation at how the organization had grown to a large political party with multiple branches and institutions. They often noted with pride, "I have been on this path from the beginning. I am of them."

In 1988, tensions between Hizbullah and Amal escalated to all-out warfare, in the south as well as in Beirut. In al-Dahiyya, this often meant street-by-street fighting, which some people described as turf battles. This intra-Shi'i fighting ended with a Syria- and Iran-brokered agreement in 1989.[47] Today, influence among Shi'i Muslims remains split, though in al-Dahiyya, Hizbullah's presence is the stronger one.

In the United States, Hizbullah is generally associated with the 1983 bombings of the U.S. embassy, Marine barracks,[48] and French MNF headquarters in Beirut, as well as with the 1985 hijacking of a TWA flight to Beirut. They are also cited by the U.S. State Department in connection to the kidnappings of westerners in Lebanon and to the hostage crisis that led to the Iran-Contra affair, as well as to two bomb attacks against Israeli targets in Argentina in the early 1990s. However, Hizbullah's involvement in these attacks remains unclear.[49] These associations are the purported reason for the party's listing on the U.S. State Department's list of terrorist organizations, and for the current characterization of Hizbullah as on the "A-list" of terrorism.[50] Yet, as Norton (1999 and 2000) and others have argued, "Hizballah may not simply be dismissed as an extremist or terrorist group" (1999: 2).

---

[46] In a February 1985 "Open Letter" or manifesto.

[47] See Norton 1999 and 2000. Harb el-Kak (2001) notes that subtle political conflict between the parties continues, with Hizbullah holding more grassroots support and Amal more governmental legitimacy.

[48] While attacks on civilians and the taking of civilian hostages—no matter who the responsible parties—are clearly acts of terrorism, the bombing of the Marines was an attack on a military force that had engaged in battle in Lebanon, and can be seen as an act of war.

[49] See Blanford (2003) and Harik (2004: 65) on the lack of direct evidence linking Hizbullah to these attacks.

[50] Aside from the United States, only Israel and Canada list Hizbullah as a "terrorist organization;" Canada's listing came under legal pressure from pro-Israel groups in 2002.

There are two reasons for this. First, Hizbullah's military activity has been committed and confined to one major (and legal) goal: ending the Israeli occupation of southern Lebanon. In 1985, Israel withdrew from most of Lebanon, but continued to occupy the southern zone of the country, controlling approximately 10 percent of Lebanon using both Israeli soldiers and a proxy Lebanese militia, the Southern Lebanese Army (SLA). Hizbullah's Islamic Resistance, along with other resistance contingents,[51] fought that occupation until it won the liberation of the south in May 2000. Secondly, as we will see, Hizbullah has developed into a legitimate Lebanese political party and an umbrella organization for myriad social welfare institutions.[52]

Hizbullah since Ta'if: A Legitimate Political Party

The Lebanese wars came to a spluttering and unresolved end with the signing of the Ta'if Accords in 1989. Basically all Ta'if did was reassert the balance of religious interests in Lebanon. The National Pact arrangements were shifted slightly so that Parliament would now be divided equally among Christians and Muslims, and some of the President's powers were moved to the Prime Minister. This did not reflect actual population shifts, as by then Lebanon was estimated to be around 60 to 70 percent Muslim.[53] Furthermore, while actual numbers for different groups in Lebanon are highly contested—because high political stakes ride on them—there is general agreement that by the end of the wars, Shi'is made up at least one-third of the national population, making them the largest confessional community and the one that gained the least at Ta'if.

Nevertheless, when the first postwar elections were held in Lebanon in 1992, Hizbullah decided to participate and work within the existing Lebanese political system.[54] In that first election, Hizbullah won eight seats, giving them the largest single bloc in the 128-member Parliament, and its allies won an additional four seats. From that point on,

---

[51] Among these were *al-sirāya al-lubnāniya lil-muqāwama*, a multi-confessional group affiliated with (funded, armed, and trained by) the party.

[52] Hizbullah also established a weekly newspaper (*al-'Ahd/al-Intiqād*) in 1984, al-Nūr radio station in 1988, and al-Manār television in 1989.

[53] Faour (1991) estimated Muslims to be 65 percent in 1988. Nasr (1993) estimated Christians at 35 to 38 percent.

[54] Reasons cited for this shift include the end of the Lebanese wars and the reestablishment of the state, the end of the cold war and Syria's integration into the international community, the possibility of imagining an end to the Arab-Israeli conflict, and changes underway in Iran (Picard 1997, Norton 2000, Hamzeh 2000a).

Hizbullah developed a reputation—among Muslims and Christians alike—for being a reputable political party on both the national and local levels.[55] This reputation is especially important in Lebanon, where governmental corruption is assumed, clientelism is the norm,[56] political positions are often inherited, and, in terms of its members' personal wealth, the Parliament is the wealthiest legislative body in the world.

While Hizbullah's parliamentary politics were generally respected as legitimate, even by those who disagreed with their positions, levels of national support for its Islamic Resistance in the south fluctuated over the years.[57] Israeli attacks on Lebanese civilians and infrastructure—including the destruction of power plants in Beirut in 1996, 1999, and 2000—generally contributed to increases in national support for the Resistance. This was especially true after Israel bombed a UN bunker where civilians had taken refuge in Qana on April 18, 1996, killing over one hundred people.[58] During my field research, most Lebanese with whom I spoke, including many Christians, expressed their support for the Resistance, and I sometimes saw Hizbullah collecting donations in unexpected areas of Beirut.[59]

The occupation of south Lebanon was costly for Israel. Israeli prime minister Ehud Barak made withdrawal a campaign promise, and later announced that it would take place by July 2000. A month and a half before this deadline, in the wake of the collapse of potential talks with Syria and SLA desertions,[60] a chaotic withdrawal from Lebanon ensued, taking many by surprise. At three a.m. on May 24, 2000, the last Israeli soldier stepped off Lebanese soil and locked the gate at the Fatima border

[55] For more on Hizbullah parliamentary politics from 1992 to 1996, see el-Bizri 1999. For more on the 1998 municipal elections, see Hamzeh 2000a and Harik 2004: 95–110. Harik (1996) and Norton (1999) note that Hizbullah's diverse constituency includes secular and middle-class people. This acceptance of the party as a legitimate and major player in Lebanese politics was confirmed by its role in the discussions and dialogues that took place during the mobilizations against the Syrian presence in Lebanon in spring 2005.

[56] See Hamzeh (2001) for a discussion of clientelism in Lebanon.

[57] See Norton (2000) for a detailed discussion of the development of Hizbullah's Islamic Resistance.

[58] See the UN Report on this incident, dated May 1, 1996. It states that, contrary to Israeli claims, "it is unlikely that the shelling of the United Nations compound was the result of gross technical and/or procedural errors."

[59] For more on support of Hizbullah and the Resistance, see Jaber (1997: 196–200) and Harik (2004: 73–79).

[60] See Norton 2000. He notes "unilateral withdrawal was a *default strategy*" for Israel, which would have preferred withdrawal to take place in conjunction with an Israeli-Syrian agreement (31).

crossing behind him. Many predicted that lawlessness, sectarian violence, and chaos would fill the void left by the Israeli occupation forces and the Southern Lebanese Army (SLA), which rapidly collapsed in Israel's wake. Those predictions proved false.[61]

From my fieldnotes, Thursday, May 25, 2000:

Today is the first annual "Day of Liberation and Resistance in Lebanon." The past few days have been a whirlwind. The war in Lebanon is over. Never mind that most people refer to the end of the war as having been in 1990. Never mind that there are still Syrian military checkpoints scattered around the country.[62] For those in and from the south and the Western Beqaa, and for those who supported the Resistance, the war ended yesterday.

A few days ago, on Sunday evening, Israeli troops began to leave outposts in Lebanon. The news really hit on Monday, as residents of newly freed villages called their relatives in Beirut and reports started coming up on Al-Manār [Hizbullah TV station]. Suddenly it seemed like all of al-Dahiyya started flooding south. There was literally a wave of people pushing the SLA farther and farther back; like dominos, Israel would pull back, the SLA behind them, and this human wave following—except that you couldn't really tell where the impetus to motion was coming from. Everyone has been glued to Al-Manār since. Today al-Dahiyya is relatively quiet, as people have gone south, to be reunited with family they haven't seen in twenty-two years, tour former Israeli and SLA sites, or just share in the general atmosphere of celebration.

Aziza, her mother, and I got in the car yesterday to go see for ourselves. All along the way we passed deserted Israeli tanks, adorned with Hizbullah flags and piles of young boys climbing all over them. Hizbullah security was directing traffic. We eventually made it to Khiam and were among the first people to enter the notorious Khiam Prison. Less than twenty-four hours earlier the townspeople had stormed the prison and freed the 145 prisoners. The rooms were exactly as they had been when the prisoners left: tiny, dark, a horrible stench. A book one prisoner had been reading lay on the bed, blankets, clothing, cans of food. Writing on the walls of the cells. A former prisoner who had been released some years earlier was guiding journalists and the curious through the detention rooms, describing in painful detail the torture methods used in each. In one room you could see the electrical wires attached to a chair where they were tortured. There was still an Israeli flag in a pile at the entrance; a group of young boys began ripping it up.

---

[61] SLA members either fled or surrendered; most of the latter were given short jail sentences. See Norton 2000 and 2002, and L. Deeb 2000.

[62] Syria's military forces did not withdraw from Lebanon until the spring of 2005.

2.2. View of the south, looking out from Khiam Prison.

Despite withdrawal, a territorial dispute continues over a fifteen-square-mile border region called the Shebaa Farms that remains under Israeli occupation. The eventual outcome depends in great part on Syria and eventual Syrian-Israeli negotiations.[63] Yet even if Hizbullah someday disarms their military branch, the political party and the vast social-welfare network associated with it will continue to work for its constituents in Lebanon.

That social network is one element in a more general institutionalization that emerged from Shi'i Islamic trends in Lebanon. Institution building was a key step in bringing Shi'i Lebanese out of the margins. These institutions provided and continue to provide structures within which pious Shi'is work toward material and spiritual progress.

[63] Israel claims the area belongs to Syria, not Lebanon. Hizbullah has continued to operate within the Shebaa Farms. For more on this dispute and its "rules of engagement," see Norton 2002, Alagha 2001, Saad-Ghorayeb 2002, Roumani 2004, Sobelman 2004, and Blanford 2003.

ISLAMIC INSTITUTIONALIZATIONS

Islamic Social Welfare Organizations

Like politics, most social welfare organizations, or *jam'iyyas*, in Lebanon are sectarian in orientation. Among the consequences of the wars were economic stagnancy, government corruption, and a widening gap between the ever-shrinking middle class and the ever-expanding poor.[64] Shi'i areas of Beirut must also cope with massive displacements from the south and the Beqaa. In this economic climate, sectarian clientelism has become a necessary survival tool. "Lebanon may have its charms, but the government has no social conscience and provides no safety net for the poor. One turns to the family and a variety of sectarian charities for assistance" (Norton 2002: 44).[65]

Prior to the war, as noted above, one of the consequences of Shi'i marginalization was a lack of resources being funneled into Shi'i areas. Before the 1960s, there were only a few scattered Shi'i organizations, including the "Charity and Benevolence Society" established in the south by Musa al-Sadr's father-in-law in 1948.[66] Beginning in 1963, al-Sadr added to this organization, building institutions in Beirut as well as in Tyre. Two of the major ones were the Imam al-Khu'i Orphanage in Beirut, founded in conjunction with Fadlullah and Shamseddin, and the Zahra Cultural and Vocational Complex for orphan girls in the south.

Following al-Sadr's disappearance, his *irth*, or inheritance, was divided among the major players in the Shi'i Islamic movement. In that division,[67] the Imam al-Khu'i Orphanage came to Fadlullah. From that starting point, he established al-Mabarrat Charitable Association (*jam'iyyat al-mabarrāt al-khayriyya*, henceforth, al-Mabarrat) in 1978. In 1987, Fadlullah began actively expanding al-Mabarrat into the large umbrella association it is today. Much of the money for this expansion

---

[64] See Norton (2002) and Kubursi (1993) on the postwar economy. Per capita income went from $1,800 in 1974 to less than $250 in 1989 (Kubursi 1993). Severe inflation sent the value of a U.S. dollar in Lebanese lira rocketing from the single digits to 2,000 in the span of a few years. Today the lira is fixed at 1,507 to US $1, and both currencies are used interchangeably.

[65] See also Joseph 1975 and Yahya 1993.

[66] el Khazen (2000) lists social service associations by sect in 1965 and 1977–78. In 1965, there were 13 Shi'i organizations, as compared to 28 Maronite, 42 Greek Orthodox, and 26 Sunni. In 1977–78, there were 38 Shi'i organizations, as compared to 70 Maronite, 44 Greek Orthodox, and 66 Sunni (67). These differences are magnified by differential populations (e.g., there were many more Orthodox institutions *per capita*).

[67] Amal was led by Nabih Berri and Shamseddin inherited leadership of the Shi'i High Council. Musa al-Sadr's sister, Sayyida Rabab al-Sadr Charafeddin, took over the Zahra Complex and established the Imam al-Sadr Foundation in 1984.

has come from wealthy Shi'is who followed Khu'i and/or follow Fadlullah as their *marji'*, especially in the Gulf States. For example, the Bah-
man Hospital, which opened in al-Dahiyya just before I arrived in the
field, was built with a donation of US $60 million by its Kuwaiti name-
sake.

Al-Mabarrat has grown into one of the most respected charitable associations in Lebanon. Its institutions span the country and include at
least fourteen schools and six orphanages, as well as hospitals, cultural
centers, and institutions for the blind, deaf, and physically disabled. In
2000, the *jam'iyya* supported over 3,250 orphans and thirteen thousand
students. In addition to one-time major donations, other funds come
from Ramadan fund-raising events that sometimes include over fifty
thousand guests and amass over two million dollars in one evening,
khums paid to Fadlullah by his followers, and orphan sponsorships.
There are also a series of businesses from which the organization profits,
including gas stations, a publishing house, a copying store, a factory for
halal foods, and a computer company. Of all the *jam'iyyas* whose employees or volunteers I interviewed, al-Mabarrat was the one least dependent on volunteer labor.

I made several visits to an al-Mabarrat school in al-Dahiyya. On one
occasion, the principal gave me, and another Lebanese education professional whom we both knew well, a tour. Here is an excerpt from my
notes from that day:

> The school seemed huge. They currently have around 2,300 students (full ca-
> pacity is 2,700), mostly in the first primary section. The principal told us that
> she essentially had to build the entire school system from scratch, from writ-
> ing a mission statement to establishing a registration office to picking out uni-
> forms and blinds. She dealt with every little detail. The school was built with
> *khums* given by two wealthy men—a Lebanese guy living in Africa and a
> Kuwaiti. It basically runs at cost, with fees at US $1,000 a year. Public schools
> in Lebanon cost US $133 and are generally, especially in al-Dahiyya, under-
> staffed, underequipped, and extremely crowded. Other private schools gener-
> ally cost between six and twelve thousand dollars. This school runs both
> French and English sections and teaches the Lebanese national curriculum
> plus religion classes. We saw new computer labs for all ages, well-equipped
> science labs, play areas, a working child-sized kitchen, exercise rooms, and a
> wood-paneled room for Qur'anic recitation. Jeanne [the educator] said after-
> wards that she was both surprised by and impressed with the quality of the
> facilities, and that they surpassed many of the schools she had seen in the
> country.

In addition to al-Mabarrat, Fadlullah opened another *jam'iyya* in
1983, called *maktab al-khadamāt al-ijtimā'iyya*, the Social Services

Office. This organization was founded to address social needs and poverty more holistically and to distribute religious taxes. The *jam'iyyas* founded and guided by Fadlullah are among the largest in al-Dahiyya. The other major group of large-scale Shi'i Islamic *jam'iyyas* in the area are those affiliated with Hizbullah. These include the Islamic Charity Emdad Committee (ICEC), the Martyrs' Association, *Jihād al-Binā'* Development Organization, the Hizbullah Women's Committee, the Association for the Wounded, and the Islamic Health Committee. I focused on the first two of these.

An ICEC administrator who has been with the organization since its beginnings shared its story with me. In 1986, a group of young people decided to confront the poverty in the area. So they began to collect food and money from businesses and distribute it to the poor. Soon afterwards, representatives from an organization in Iran came to al-Dahiyya to establish a sister association.[68] The two groups agreed to work together, and founded the Lebanese ICEC in 1987. The fledgling *jam'iyya* set two criteria for the families it would assist: the provider/father of the family had to be unable to provide and the family could not be covered by any other Hizbullah *jam'iyya*. This included families where the father was deceased (but not a Resistance martyr), in prison (again, not in Israel or in the south), physically disabled (but not injured fighting with the Resistance), or absent. They chose to support the orphaned children of these men—today numbering over four thousand—by helping their mothers or extended families raise them at home with monthly support and supplemental nutritional, educational, housing, and health assistance.

In 2000, the ICEC budget came mainly from donations, religious taxes, Ramadan fund-raisers, almost three thousand full sponsorships for orphans, and the ubiquitous collection boxes that are scattered all over Lebanon. The *jam'iyya* is heavily dependent on volunteer labor, with only around ninety employees but over three hundred and fifty volunteers. It includes five financially self-sufficient schools, a school for children who have Down's Syndrome, and a summer camp.

The basic difference between the ICEC and the Martyrs' Association is their constituencies. The families of those men who are specifically not covered by the ICEC—namely the martyrs, prisoners, and injured of the Islamic Resistance—are supported by *jam'iyyas* specific to those cases. The Lebanese Martyrs' Association was established in 1982 by Khomeini as a sister organization of the Iranian Martyrs' Foundation. With six hundred volunteers and even more employees, the *jam'iyya* tries to fill the "provider" role for martyrs' families. Again, they provide financial,

---

[68] See Adelkhah on social organizations in Iran (2000: 53).

housing, educational, health, and nutritional support, as well as employment assistance for widows and orphans, and youth activities like scouts and camps. The Martyrs' Association also runs a primary school and a major hospital in al-Dahiyya, whose services are free to the families of martyrs and detainees, and low cost to others.

In addition to those affiliated with Hizbullah and Fadlullah, there are a number of small *jam'iyyas* throughout al-Dahiyya, including family-based organizations, charitable groups, and women's groups. I spent a good deal of time volunteering with one of these organizations, the SAA, a small Islamic women's charitable association. While I was in Beirut, they had approximately seventy-five official members, perhaps a third of whom were active volunteers. Their activities included a campaign to end child labor by providing public school fees, a Ramadan food distribution center, and general aid for about 250 families in al-Dahiyya. They also ran a low-cost daycare that facilitated women's employment, summer camps, and an exercise facility for girls and young women. Donations provided the bulk of their budget, though they also held fund-raising events.[69]

Like the resistance fighters who were with the initial mobilization that eventually became Hizbullah, many women volunteers began their work during the war, before there was an institutional structure to facilitate it. One of them, Suha, explained this to me:

> Let me tell you something. We, a long time ago, we began through the *husayniyya* [Shi'i ritual gathering hall]. You would see what people trapped in the shelters needed: cleaning stuff, medicines, food, drink, supplies. You would be in charge of a shelter, and there were no kitchens in them so everything happened in the *husayniyya*. Or sometimes in a school, or in our homes. Now, no. Now you feel that there has been a lot of development in this work: now the martyrs have a center, orphans have a center, there are many different *jam'iyyas*, each one is by itself. There is now a system. Before, there was work and giving, but now there is a division of labor: each one has a particular role and takes on that role. The work has been organized, there is a system, there are institutions and organizations, there is now a secretary, a treasurer. Before you had to do every little thing with your own hands. Now, no. Now there is a computer, there is technology, so that you are able in far less time to accomplish things that took you days and nights to do before. You see?

The transformation Suha describes epitomizes the institutionalization and bureaucratization of the Shi'i Islamic movement in Lebanon. From small origins, multiple threads, and charismatic leaders emerged a number

---

[69] For example, tickets to one breakfast fund-raiser were $35 and many women made additional donations.

of institutional—social and political—structures that facilitated, encouraged, and oriented the social, political, and religious trajectories of the movement. While there were and are differences and divisions within the movement, shared values provide a common framework for work on the ground. The four *jam'iyyas* within which most of my interlocutors worked or volunteered—the SAA, ICEC, Martyrs' Association, and al-Mabarrat—all shared a basic Islamic outlook and dedication to the poor, orphaned, and otherwise needy in their community. In general, relationships among them were excellent, and they actively cooperated with one another in assessing need and providing for poor families. So for example, the same family might receive aid from multiple institutions: Fadlullah's Social Services Office might provide them with a monthly food ration, the ICEC might assist with the medical costs, the SAA might pay the public school tuitions for two of the family's four children, and the other two children might live at an al-Mabarrat orphanage and attend school there. Yet despite this cooperation, differences among the various branches of the Shi'i Islamic movement could be seen in some of the relationships among them and their volunteers. In closing this chapter, I want to touch upon some of these differences and the attitudes of the various branches of the movement toward one another, in order to highlight and remind us of the variation within the movement and among pious Shi'is.

Dynamics of the Shi'i Islamic Movement Today

In al-Dahiyya, the Shi'i Islamic movement at the turn of the twenty-first century was centered around and in between Fadlullah and Hizbullah. Others in Lebanon may instead cite Amal, or the Imam al-Sadr Foundation in the south as the "true" inheritors of the movement. People I spoke with generally viewed the Sadr Foundation as more Lebanese "old school" (meaning built around personal relationships with elites) than the al-Dahiyya-centered *jam'iyyas* of Fadlullah and Hizbullah. For their part, people affiliated with the Sadr Foundation said they felt that Hizbullah was not dedicated to working within the Lebanese polity. They spoke more positively of Fadlullah, and to my surprise several people told me that they followed him as their *marji'*. This may reflect the shift in Fadlullah's position that occurred throughout the 1990s, away from a position calling for revolution and toward one that emphasizes communication, coexistence and cooperation among religious groups in Lebanon, a position closer to that of al-Sadr.

This respect for Fadlullah is also reflective of the general attitude toward him in Lebanon. Everyone I spoke with in the country—Christians and Muslims alike—spoke highly of Fadlullah as a religious leader who was rational, clear-thinking, and dedicated to modernizing his community. For example, an Orthodox Christian man raved about him to me, explaining that he was the reason the Shi'a were modern (he said "modern" in English) today. He went on to give me examples of some of Fadlullah's "modern" interpretations that he had read about in the newspaper, including one about how technology can be used to establish when the lunar month will begin and therefore set the Islamic calendar in advance.

Many Shi'is who were not particularly devout also spoke highly of Fadlullah, more than one indicating that "if" she were going to be religious (*mutadayyina*), he was the person whom she would choose as her *marji'*. I asked one friend who had expressed this view why that was, and she explained that it was because Fadlullah was the most "open-minded" *marji'*, and that she especially liked the way "he realizes that the Shi'a have to modernize along with the rest of the world" so he brings science and religion together and also makes religion more logical, "you know, so all that religious stuff actually makes sense."

I also asked a shaykh at Fadlullah's *marji'iyya* office about his popularity. He explained that the *fatwa*s Fadlullah issues are based on the practical reality in which people live, and that is why many people follow him.[70] The shaykh then brought up another *marji'*, the late Sayyid Muhsin al-Hakim, who said, "If I have followers who have a problem from the *sharī'a* and I can solve that problem, why shouldn't I, as long as I am following the *sharī'a*?" Fadlullah follows this principle, in the shaykh's words, "If something can be changed to better fit today's lifestyle but still be within the proper interpretation of the *sharī'a* then that is a good thing. The Sayyid is realistic; he works with reality."

Among the pious who follow Fadlullah, his emphasis on al-'aql and using one's mind is often the primary reason they cited as to why they choose him as their *marji'*. One woman who became committed to Islam during the war credited this emphasis: "Sayyid Muhammad Husayn said,[71] 'Think! Challenge what you hear, don't take it for granted, don't let anyone lead you except your mind!' And I remember one time when he said, 'I don't want followers, I want partners.' He likes and encourages people to ask questions, to debate him on ideas." The ideas about personal interpretation expressed by Hajjeh Umm Ali earlier in this chapter also reflect this emphasis, and underscore Fadlullah's especial appeal to the educated. In this sense, Fadlullah adds weight to the public piety imperative. Multiple possibilities for interpretation mean that

---

[70] See Messick (1996) on *fatwas'* relatively recent relationship to daily life issues.

[71] Pious Shi'is referred to Fadlullah as "Sayyid Muhammad Husayn," indicating both respect and familiarity.

uniformity of belief cannot be taken for granted, making an external demonstration of piety necessary to the community.

Fadlullah's followers also appreciated his reformist views on Shi'i religious history and on gender. In interpreting religious history, he aims toward "questioning metaphysical beliefs by rational reasoning and overcoming the provocative aspects of Shia dogmas" (Rosiny 2001). The latter is important in the context of sectarian coexistence in Lebanon. With regard to gender, as we will see, Fadlullah emphasizes the necessity of women participating actively in their community. He has also stated that women may become *mujtahida*s and even *marji'*s.[72] For all these reasons, in many ways Fadlullah epitomizes the Shi'i pious modern.

Fadlullah and Hizbullah each have a sphere of followers/supporters in al-Dahiyya, with those spheres overlapping partially. While Hizbullah officially follows Khamenei as the party's *marji'*, individual members are free to choose any *marji'* they want, and many I spoke with chose Fadlullah. At the same time, there are limits to the overlap. While many of Fadlullah's followers supported Hizbullah politically, not all did. Political allegiance and religious emulation are two separate issues that may or may not overlap for any single person.

At various moments over the past decade, there have been differing levels of tension between Fadlullah's and Hizbullah's spheres.[73] Most people understood these differences to be centered around a disagreement over the concept of *wilāyat al-faqīh* (guidance of the jurisprudent). In Fadlullah's view, the notion of a single and united spiritual and political authority (which is the essence of *wilāyat al-faqīh*) is impossible until the Hidden Imam's return. Hizbullah, on the other hand, supports and looks to the institution of *wilāyat al-faqīh* for ultimate guidance in both spiritual and political matters. These differences were usually downplayed, hearkening back to the space Shi'ism provided for differences of interpretation. And in practice, most of Fadlullah's followers supported Hizbullah's political goals even if they did not agree with all the party's tenets, and most party members held Fadlullah in high esteem.

In the end, the ultimate goal of the Shi'i Islamic movement described in this chapter—in *all* its strains—is progress, in both the senses outlined in the introduction: spiritual *and* material. Each of the *jam'iyyas* to emerge from that movement—whether associated with Fadlullah, Hizbullah, or neither—is dedicated to developing their community mate-

---

[72] See Rosiny 2001.

[73] After Khomeini and Khu'i died, Fadlullah did not recognize Khamenei as *marji'*, but instead looked to Sistani, who has been critical of the Iranian regime, until Fadlullah eventually began to establish himself as a *marji'*. These dynamics are related to Iranian politics as well as struggles around the *marji'iyya*.

rially and spiritually, and dedicated to the enchanted modern. Their existence as institutions itself speaks to how far from the margins their community has come.

Through these institutions, it becomes apparent that the Shiʻi mobilization via religion has had consequences for faith and morality on the personal level. Institutionalization both facilitates public expressions of piety and the infusion of religious discourses into a broader public arena and insists on them. The methods and discourses of the *jamʻiyyas*—especially as they promote the values of public piety in their volunteers and the constituents they support—will be taken up in the second part of this book. First, I begin part 2 with a discussion of public piety and religion on that personal level—in the practices and discourses of daily life.

PART TWO

Living an Enchanted Modern

3.1. Young girls participating in an authenticated Ashura *masīra* (chapter 4).

CHAPTER THREE

The Visibility of Religion in Daily Life

visible: 1) capable of being seen; perceptible; 2) noticeable,
apparent, open, conspicuous
—*Webster's Revised Unabridged Dictionary*

ONE AFTERNOON in May, I stopped in to see my friend Aziza. She led me
through the formal living room onto the balcony, where I was met by the
mingling aromas of coffee and apple-flavored tobacco, faint hints of
roasting meat and exhaust from the street far below, and occasional
whiffs of gardenia brought from the balcony's other end by the breeze.
Three other women were seated there, enjoying the spring weather. I had
met them all over the past six months, either through Aziza, or at one of
the *jam'iyyas*. Ghada, a neighbor in her late teens, often sought refuge
from her housework and young siblings on Aziza's balcony. I had met
Noor, a distant cousin of Aziza's who was studying at a local university,
at a *jam'iyya*, and only recently made the connection between her and
my friend. Sanaa' was from another *jam'iyya*; she was slightly older, a
loquacious divorced woman in her early thirties. As I greeted them,
Noor teased, "Ah, Aziza, you invited your friend so you'd outnumber
us!" (*shū 'azīza, jibti rfi'tik litkūnu aktar minna!*).

I must have appeared as puzzled as I felt, because Noor then looked at
me and gestured at the scarves covering her and Ghada's heads. She
wore a long beige skirt with a matching long jacket. Her scarf, printed in
pastel hues of rose and blue, was pinned at the side of her head, falling
across her shoulders so that only her face was visible. Ghada wore an
ankle-length flowing navy blue dress, with a navy and white paisley
scarf. Her scarf was pinned underneath her chin, also showing only her
face, and periodically, she ran an absentminded hand along her hairline,
tucking in stray hairs that had slipped out from under it. My entrance, in
jeans and a short-sleeved shirt, hair pulled back in a barrette—along
with Aziza's casual lime-green sundress and dark curls, and Sanaa's
stretchy red capri pants and t-shirt, her dark blonde hair loose down her
back and her face done in the fashion-plate make-up typical of Beirut:
lip-liner, mascara, the works—had created a situation that was relatively
unusual for this neighborhood where *muḥajjaba* women usually out-
numbered non-*muḥajjabas*.

Aziza never responded to Noor's comment, as she had hurried inside to bring another coffee cup for me. When she returned, bearing not only the cup, but another *argīleh* and a carefully balanced platter of sour green plums, strawberries, fresh green almonds, and a small plate of salt, she said, "Yalla, why did you change the subject? Lara doesn't mind." Turning to me, she added, "Noor was telling us about this Druze guy in her class." Noor concluded the story I had interrupted, and slowly I gathered that she had just spoken to this person for the first time, and discovered that he knew nothing about his religion. "Every time I meet a person who is Druze I ask him, but they never know." "Yeah, because it's forbidden to know until you turn forty." "It's a huge problem; how can you wait that long?" "And what if you don't live to be forty? A person must know his religion; it is necessary. That's how God made us, to know our religion."

"Yes, but we can't say that people in our community know their religion either." This was Sanaa' speaking, and the other three immediately retorted: "What do you mean?" "Look around you, you can see how much better things are here than they used to be!" And Aziza: "Yeah, I'm not *muḥajjaba*, but I pray and I fast and I know my religion! (*bṣalli w bṣūm w ba'rif dīnī!*)" "Yes, but you know what I'm talking about, like all those people who think the point of Ramadan is to fast all day so they can gorge themselves at night, and then they throw away the leftovers! They don't feed the poor, they're rude, they don't understand its true meaning, but they think they are being good Muslims just because they fast," and gesturing rapidly to the world beyond the balcony, Sanaa' concluded, "99 percent of Lebanese are like this!" Ghada and Aziza immediately disagreed with the extent of it, but concurred that, "Unfortunately, there are still people who don't understand the true meaning of religion." But Noor remained unconvinced: "I don't think that is such a big problem here these days, but what is a problem is these people who will drink [alcohol] during the year, and then during Ramadan suddenly they stop." It was Sanaa's turn to take issue: "What's wrong with that? Ramadan is supposed to be the month people make the most effort, because God knows that people are too weak to behave correctly all year." Ghada interjected, "You know during the time of the Prophet, people fasted for eleven months of the year. Because God knew that humans were too weak to commit to that, it was reversed." "Yes," contributed Aziza, "and I learned last Ramadan that the Sayyid [Fadlullah] says that it's wrong (*ḥarām*) to give a drunk person, or a person who drinks, food during Ramadan." Taking advantage of a slight lull in the conversation, I asked Noor, "Why do you think that this is a problem?" Shaking her head slightly, she replied, "It shouldn't matter, Ramadan or not, they shouldn't drink; today they shouldn't drink and tomorrow they shouldn't drink. But there are some people who think that it becomes 'OK' as long as they behave properly during Ramadan."

• • •

The conversation that May afternoon was typical. There had been moments over the past months when I suspected that shifts in conversation to topics around the tenets or practice of religion happened for my benefit, as a non-Muslim Arab-American researcher in the community. And indeed, on occasion someone would express her hope that through my research I would come to an understanding of Islam that would lead naturally to my conversion. But later that week, as I reflected back on that afternoon and on the previous months of conversation I had shared with these, and other pious Shi'i women and men, I realized that I often walked into discussions of religion already in progress. Certainly there were times when something particular was explained to me specifically, as when Aziza once turned to me in the middle of dinner and out of nowhere asked, "Lara, do you understand the difference between things that are pure (*tāhir*) and things that are impure/dirty (*nijis*)?" But just as often, perhaps more often, people would explain details of belief or practice to one another, or debate the most correct way to interpret an event or injunction, as happened at a breakfast gathering I attended where the guests talked at length about what happened to Jesus after the attempt to kill him failed (they agreed that his body had been switched with another while he was on the cross, but could not come to any agreement beyond that point).[1]

Conversations like the one described above repeated themselves time and time again—similar not only in content, but more importantly, in their demonstration of the constant and very natural presence of religion in daily life.[2] In anticipating field research, I knew religion would be a crucial aspect of peoples' lives, but I was unprepared for its thick tangibility. Religion simply permeated everything. It was a palpable, yet unobtrusive, presence in streets, on balconies, in cafés, kitchens and *jam'iyyas*, at women's morning visits and men's evening conversations, and with

---

[1] In this case, my presence as a "Christian" may have influenced the particular topic, but that does not detract from my point that religious issues are a constant element in daily conversation.

[2] Rather than the visibility of religion, the visibility of *Islam* might be a more accurate phrase. "Religion" as a category used to translate the Arabic word "*dīn*" is problematic (see Asad 1993 and Salvatore 1997). Islam is better described as a mode of being in the world. At the same time, the authentication process contributes to the construction of Islam as "a religion," and my interlocutors spoke of Islam as "a religion" in English as well as Arabic.

families sitting around the television at night. It was visible in the way people spoke, in their greetings, negotiations, and farewells. "How are you today?"—"Thanks be to God" (*kīfik al-yawm?—al-ḥamdullah*). "Will we see you later this evening?"—"God willing" (*ḥan shūfkun il-layleh?—inshallah*). References to the interpretations of *marjiʿ*s and to holy texts—the Qur'an, *ḥadīth*, and sayings of the Imams—dotted speech, particularly during moments of argument or explanation. It was visible in daily conversation. Lunchtime gossip about a man cheating on his wife might lead to a discussion of in what ways he was and was not violating the *sharīʿa*. Rumors of who had recently become *muḥajjaba* and what difficulties she was having with her *ḥijāb* might be spoken softly during exercise walks along the unfinished highway that bisected the neighborhood. And more, religion was visible in people's habits and motions, in the discreet flow of women through the streets, in the postures bodies fell easily into during prayer, in nicotine addicts' automatic cessation of smoking during the Ramadan fast, in the weeping that swelled and subsided during Ashura commemorations. Religion as visible, manifest, concrete, and inseparable from daily life is the subject of this chapter.[3]

Over time I came to learn that many people I spoke with viewed the form that this indissolubility of religion from daily life took as something new and different. Public piety and the continuing authentication of Islam were considered among the accomplishments of the Shiʿi Islamic movement, a manifestation of spiritual progress and the pious modern. A clear break was perceived between the past "then" and the current "now" with regard to religious practice and understanding. "Then," no one fasted properly, no one understood why the *ḥijāb* was important, no one knew why it was important to pray, no one understood that Islam teaches that women have an active role to play in the community, no one knew the true meaning of religious concepts or practices. It was all "only tradition." Religious practices done as a part of one's heritage did not "count" as truly pious acts; instead piety was to stem from an understanding of the "correct" interpretation of Islam.

This chapter focuses on the contemporary visibility of personal expressions and acts of *iltizām* according to that "correct" authenticated Islam. These personal practices of piety take public forms and carry public meaning in two senses. They are read by other devout Shiʿis, often as markers of a person's morality, signaling membership in the community of the pious modern. They are also read by others (those who are not pious, not Shiʿi, and/or not Lebanese), usually as demonstrations of the new national and international political presence of the Lebanese Shiʿa.

[3] This is *not* unique to Islam. For example, Christianity structures and imbues daily life in many communities in the United States.

I consider both embodied and discursive practices of piety in what follows. While on the one hand, I hope to convey a sense of the visibility of religion and the perceived newness of authenticated Islam, on the other hand, I also wish to trouble that sensibility, by pointing to contestations over the details, definitions, and delimitations of both personal and public religiosities. To that end, this chapter concludes with a discussion of the ways that "correct" religious knowledge is accessed, obtained, and constructed through communication. But first, I turn to embodied piety.

EMBODIED PIETY

Just as religion was inscribed in the spaces and sounds of al-Dahiyya, it was inscribed on the bodies of the devout. Bodies form a canvas on which personal piety can be transformed into a subtle public demonstration of faith and/or a louder demonstration of collective identity.

Many people in the community believed that piety should infuse one's entire life. In their view, each person has "an account" (*ḥisāb*) with God that would gain and lose points and be tallied upon death, determining the course of one's afterlife. Of course, the extent to which this belief was applied in a believer's life varied widely: there were those who lived almost ascetically, devoting their lives to the fulfillment of religious duties, while others "just" completed what they considered to be the necessary minimum—prayer, fasting, alms-giving, and the avoidance of major sin. However, for most people, fulfilling these "minimum" requirements was not sufficient according to the "correct" understanding of authenticated Islam. To foreshadow chapter 5, this understanding incorporates social and community relationships in key ways not satisfied by the "five pillars" or by the sorts of embodied piety discussed here.

Embodied piety appeared in many ways in al-Dahiyya, but three areas stood out most strikingly on a daily basis. The most visible of these, in both my fieldwork and current scholarship on Islam, was dress. But before turning to dress, and its major signifier, the headscarf, I want to discuss two other practices that signaled *iltizām*. The first, prayer, is one of the duties of an individual Muslim, and the second, not shaking hands with members of the opposite sex, is a marker used to indicate religiosity.

Prayer

Prayer (*ṣalāt*) is one of the most basic requirements for a practicing Muslim—so essential that I only met two people who professed to be believers yet would admit to not praying. Muslim prayers have a formal structure: phrases must be pronounced correctly, movements are uniform. There are five obligatory prayer times—early morning, noon, afternoon, sunset, and evening—that include seventeen prostrations. Shi'i Muslims may choose to combine the noon and afternoon prayers and the sunset and evening prayers, completing their daily prayer in three sets, rather than five.[4] Girls' obligation to pray begins at age nine, and boys at age ten, though many children begin emulating their parents at much younger ages, and are praised for doing so. From that age on, prayers that are missed must be made up at a later time, though their value is believed to lessen. A woman who begins to pray at age forty has thirty-one years of outstanding prayer to complete.

If a person dies before completing all her prayer, her eldest son may pray the remainder for her, or, alternately, someone may be paid a set fee to do so (this works for fasting as well). After the death of one man who had never prayed, his family hired someone to pray for him. At the time I spoke to them, it had cost them over four thousand dollars. When I asked why they had done this, the man's nephew explained that the payment of prayer on behalf of the deceased's soul would alleviate his guilt before God to a certain extent. A niece immediately disagreed with this, interjecting that no matter what the circumstance, a person cannot "get out of" prayer, "even if he does good deeds and lives a good life, it doesn't matter, it doesn't help, nothing can replace prayer, nothing!"

> ISSUE #275: I work in an area that is not our area, and I cannot pray, so I do so in the evening. And if I leave this job and work in our area, I will not receive the same salary, and I need this salary. What is the solution?
>
> ANSWER: It is necessary to find/plan a way to pray at the correct time, and it is not permissible to keep this job, in this situation, if it is possible for you to live with less, especially if it is possible to find other work. *Wa man yatawakal 'alā allāh fa huwa ḥasbuhu* [God provides for those who depend on God]. (Fadlullah 1996b: 109)[5]

The importance of prayer was frequently highlighted in interviews and conversations, no matter what the topic. For example, on a tour of a local school, my guide noted that prayer "is a practice that maintains constant communication with God." A volunteer at a Hizbullah *jam'iyya* described the "key to the movement" as prayer, "because prayer is the

---

[4] Other small differences between Shi'i and Sunni prayer include variations in preprayer ablutions, in the position of the arms, and in the small clay tablet to which Shi'is touch their foreheads instead of the ground.

[5] These excerpts in question-answer form are taken from Fadlullah's published collections of jurisprudence.

basis, every time a person prays that is five minutes he spends with God, five minutes where that person sees God instead of the world."

In these instances, prayer's importance hinges on the development and maintenance of a person's relationship with God; prayer is the practice of spending time with God. Not only does prayer stem from *iltizām*, but it also leads to it. Talal Asad has argued that medieval Christian monks constructed virtuous selves through daily monastic practices (1993: 143). Similarly, prayer, with its regularity and ritual qualities, contributed to the manifestation of *iltizām* in practicing Muslims in al-Dahiyya.[6] As one woman told me, "No religion in the world can ensure *iltizām* the way Islam is able to, because it is practical, it is inherent in the details of how things work."[7]

In addition, prayer holds public importance. People do not pray only at the mosque and in their homes, but may pray wherever they happen to be at the time. As a result, prayer is a highly visible practice. In the *jam'iyyas*, groups of volunteers often prayed together, laying out a carpet in a quiet room, and during visits it was common for someone to leave the room to pray. Before Nasrallah's victory speech in Bint Jbeil after Israeli withdrawal from south Lebanon, many people prayed the noon prayer on the ground before entering the stadium where the event was held. And during the annual Ashura procession in al-Dahiyya, hundreds of thousands of Lebanese Shi'is prayed the noon prayers on the street behind Nasrallah.

The power of prayer as a group ritual was most apparent in these public settings, but whether one prayed alone or in a group, there was always a sense of engaging in an activity that indicated and fostered membership in a community of believers.[8] Group prayer incorporates persons into a single undifferentiated body of belief, utterance, motion and intent. As Maliha, a young volunteer, put it: "Why is prayer in a group? Because you find everyone, poor, rich, educated, uneducated, all are standing in a single line praying together. They've forgotten the whole world and are thinking only of God, so you find that this world no longer has these problems; the rich sit next to the poor."

Furthermore, praying in a public setting effectively demonstrated one's *iltizām* to others. Put simply, seeing a person pray, especially if they interrupted a social visit or their work in order to pray at the proper time,

---

[6] See Mahmood (2005: 122–34) on prayer as a means to cultivating a pious self.

[7] This does not mean that Islam prioritizes orthopraxy over orthodoxy. See Asad 1986: 15.

[8] Knowing that others are praying simultaneously extends a transnational imagined religious community in a parallel to Anderson's (1983) argument about national communities.

said a lot about that person's piety. In al-Dahiyya, where piety was highly valued, public prayer carried social capital.[9] This does not mean that those who prayed in public had ulterior motives beyond communion with God, but rather that whatever one's motives, public prayer was read by others. Additionally, because prayer was believed to contribute to *iltizām*, it demonstrated one's desire to attain piety. In contexts like the *jam'iyyas*, where praying might go unnoticed, *not* praying was a resonating act that could generate comment from one's sister volunteers. Yet, again anticipating chapter 5, I want to emphasize that prayer was not considered "enough" by the devout. Prayer had to be accompanied by other aspects of comportment, as discussed here, and most importantly, by social responsibility.

Finally, public prayer also conveys meaning to those who are not part of the Shi'i pious modern. Especially during mass events like the Ashura gatherings, the force of hundreds of thousands of men and women praying together was harnessed effectively as a display of political strength, within the Lebanese polity and internationally. Hizbullah's (and others') Ashura commemorations were televised and understood by non-Shi'i Lebanese in ways that varied by political climate and the perspective of the viewer. Just before the liberation of the south, for example, many Lebanese viewed Hizbullah favorably, a view which extended to the commemorations. Some, however, saw instead the 1980s Hizbullah and reacted to the televised mass prayer with shudders.[10] As a key aspect of public piety, prayer contributes to multiple levels of visibility of and within the Shi'i pious modern.

(Not) Handshaking

Unlike prayer, the second practice that I consider is not a basic religious duty. Rather, it is an act of restraint, one that signals modest comportment in interactions with members of the opposite sex: refraining from shaking hands in greeting. As in the United States, physical contact during greetings is taken for granted by most Lebanese. Depending on the level of familiarity, persons greeting one another will shake hands, indicating unfamiliarity, or embrace lightly, kissing alternate cheeks two or

---

[9] See Soares (2002) for an interesting discussion of the social capital of prayer as a public sign of piety in Mali—where the marks purportedly left by prayer stand in for the act itself, as opposed to al-Dahiyya, where it is the visible act that carries public meaning.

[10] Take for example, CNN's coverage of commemorations of Imam Husayn's fortieth memorial, just after the U.S. invasion of Iraq. Interpretations ranged from hailing the freedom of religion the commemorations represented to apprehensively speculating that they indicated an organizing Shi'i resistance to U.S. occupation.

three times. When an unrelated man and woman greet, they often do not kiss, but shake hands lightly instead.

Yet devout Muslims refrained from any physical contact with members of the opposite sex other than those who are *maḥram*, meaning anyone other than one's spouse or close relatives.[11] Handshaking itself is specifically discussed by many Shi'i *mujtahid*s, and there is general agreement that unrelated women and men should not shake hands because sexual feelings, no matter how slight, could potentially arise during skin-on-skin contact.[12] Rather than shake hands, pious Muslims either nodded while saying hello, or, especially in more formal situations, placed their right hand on their chest.[13] While whether or not a person shakes hands with members of the opposite sex may seem trivial, handshaking (or not) has taken on meaning in al-Dahiyya, beyond the inevitably awkward situations that result when one person extends a hand only to realize that it is inappropriate. In fact, handshaking was used by some as a gloss to indicate *iltizām*. This was particularly true for men, as they did not have the headscarf as a blatant signifier of religiosity. Every so often, while someone was describing another person, she would say, "he doesn't shake" (*huwi mā bisallim*). I once asked Noor why that was important, and she replied simply, "because that means he is religious."

As is often true of unspoken social "rules," the unexpected power of (not) handshaking was most frequently seen in two situations: when one person in an interaction was assumed to be unfamiliar with the "rule" or when the "rule" was violated. In the first instance, for example, when a devout Muslim met a non-Muslim for the first time, care was taken to explain why a hand was not extended, both in order to teach appropriate behavior and to ensure that the outsider would not take offense at what might be perceived as rudeness. In situations in al-Dahiyya where one or both individuals did not know how the other would react, those who would normally shake hands often hesitated, waiting to gauge the other's response, or simply made the safer assumption of religiosity. It was generally assumed (correctly) that women who were *muḥajjaba* did not shake hands with unrelated men, and women who were not *muḥajjaba* did. This formula did not always work, however, as there were non-*muḥajjaba* women who refrained from handshaking, or did so

---

[11] A woman's spouse, father, father-in-law, uncles, sons, and nephews are *maḥram* to her, as are a man's spouse, mother, mother-in-law, aunts, daughters, and nieces to him. Everyone else, essentially anyone a person could legally marry, are *ḥarām* to her or him.

[12] See for example, Fadlullah 1997: 162–64.

[13] This alternate form of greeting represents a new way in which unrelated people may enter the public and recognize one another as participants in its activities and discourses.

selectively depending on who else was present. For example, one of my non- *muhajjaba* friends shook hands with men unless one of her particularly pious uncles was present. Women who did shake hands with men often had a difficult time gauging when it was appropriate. As Aziza replied when I asked her how I was supposed to know what to do when meeting people, "You just have to know." She then went on to list a number of men she knew who had stopped shaking hands with women at seemingly random moments over the past few years.

> ISSUE #979: Is it allowed to shake the hands of women in European countries when there is an interest-related/business relationship [*maṣlaḥa aw maṣāliḥ*] with them? Especially when they do not understand the reasons for not shaking their hands and are extending their hands to be shaken? And when there could be embarrassment or confusion if one does not shake hands?
>
> ANSWER: It is not allowed except in cases of extreme embarrassment that could lead to material or spiritual damage [*al-ḍarar*], or to unbearable confusion in relation to general social norms. Note also that one should not go to places that might require this of him except in cases of necessity. (Fadlullah 1996b: 414)

During my first few months in al-Dahiyya, men who did not shake my hand upon meeting me often provided lengthy explanations of how they could not shake hands with women because of the danger of "electricity" and the chaos (*fitna*) in society that would therefore ensue.[14] Many of my women friends encouraged me not to shake hands with men, because "while shaking your hand they might touch it too much, or have other intentions or thoughts in their mind." Others related feeling that they had to explain their refusal to shake hands in order to prevent misunderstandings. Hajjeh Khadija Hammoud recounted an awkward moment at a reception with a prominent diplomat who was a close acquaintance of her family:

> We were at a reception for Mr. ——, he was about to leave the country for another post, and he came, and in front of everyone he said that he wanted to tell me something that had been bothering him from the beginning. So I said to him, "Go ahead, I'm listening." And in front of everyone, you know how they are, all these elite capitalists, he said, "Everyone shakes my hand except for the wife of Ali Hammoud [her husband], why is that?" So I said to him, "Look, I respect you and I appreciate you. Everyone else greets you with their hand, which is something material. I am greeting you with my heart. Would

---

[14] *Fitna* is understood to be caused by extramarital sexual relationships. Rather unusually, my interlocutors placed responsibility for avoiding *fitna* on both women and men.

you prefer the meaningful and spiritual greeting or do you want the material one?"

The second and more prominent situation in which the meaning and importance of (not) handshaking emerged was whenever this "rule" was violated, whether intentionally or not. Unintentional violations were simply instances where people accidentally brushed up against one another, perhaps if two people were trying to open a door at the same time. This generally resulted in a slight jumping back, blushing, an apology muttered under the breath. The intentional violations I witnessed and experienced were rare but pointed moments. On one occasion, I was a few minutes early for an interview with a school principal, and was shown into his office while he saw a student. Before the student entered, the principal explained that this was a minor discipline case, a girl in her early teens who had been caught in the schoolyard without her *ḥijāb*. When the student entered the office the principal stood and extended his hand to her. She immediately jumped back with a shocked look on her face, indicating that she did not shake hands with members of the opposite sex. He then explained to her that he had just treated her like a woman who was not *muḥajjaba*, because that was what he assumed she wanted to be. His point made, the student indicated that she understood and promised not to remove her *ḥijāb* again.

My position as a non-Muslim, albeit one who dressed modestly, seemed to provoke intentional violations as well. On several occasions, men at *jamʿiyyas* who did not shake hands with women extended their hands to me in greeting, but only when no one else was present. When I told Aziza this, she was horrified, and instructed me to place my hand on my chest in greeting when this happened. Soon after, one of these men joked *"shū, sirtī mtdayyini?"* (what, you've become religious?). When I explained that I felt more comfortable not shaking hands, he expressed dismay that "we've affected you" and said that he had hoped my presence would provoke more openness in the organization, especially around "these silly rules" like not shaking hands.

These men were considered pious in the community. They prayed and fasted, and several of them had been on the *ḥajj*. Moreover, they had chosen employment in *jamʿiyyas*, often over more lucrative career possibilities. This intentional violation did not necessarily reflect a lack of piety. Rather, it highlighted disagreement over whether handshaking should be a measure of piety in the first place, and underscored the variation in definitions and understandings of piety itself, even among those who identified with the Shiʿi pious modern.

Contestation came from outside the community as well. Refraining from shaking hands with those of the opposite sex was interpreted by some devout Shi'is outside al-Dahiyya as an inappropriate delineation of religiosity. This was illustrated most clearly when I visited the Imam al-Sadr Foundation in south Lebanon. Almost everyone there shook my hand, even when I automatically lifted mine to my chest instead. My surprise when a well-known religious scholar extended his hand to me in greeting was so apparent that another woman in the room chuckled, "Oh yes, he shakes." She herself was *muhajjaba*, but she pulled the sleeve of her sweater over her hand like a glove, in order to shake his hand.[15] Later, when I asked the scholar why he shook hands with women, he responded, "There are those who think that religiosity (*tadayyun*) shows in these little things, that if you regulate everything, you will build a religious society, but I am not one of those people."

In both cases, contestation over (not) shaking hands is related to disagreements over how to be modern. Handshaking was viewed by many as a western practice. For some, it represented the moral decay of the West—especially with regard to sexuality—and was therefore something to be eliminated from daily practice as part of the Shi'i Islamic movement's two-pronged model of progress. The less common view in al-Dahiyya was that handshaking is an act that should instead be embraced as part of that progress. Those who held the latter view saw handshaking as an issue around which religious interpretation should facilitate the participation of pious Shi'is in the contemporary world. The final area of embodied piety to which I now turn is perhaps the most contested arena—transnationally—of Muslim gender politics: veiling.

Veiling

Not all women—nor even all pious women—in al-Dahiyya wore Islamic dress, and variations in dress and style existed among those who did. The term *muhajjaba* shares its root with that used to denote the most common form of Islamic dress: the *hijab*. The *hijab* is a headscarf, worn so as to cover a woman's head, hair, and neck, sometimes falling over her shoulders. There are myriad ways to pin a *hijab*; some styles are associated with particular political parties, age groups, or trends. Some Shi'i women tucked their *hijabs* into their collars; others tied them under their chins, tossing the ends over their shoulders, and many who were affiliated with Hizbullah pulled one side under their chin to just below their other ear, pinning it there so that the remaining fabric hung down loosely in front. A woman's *hijab* could be silk, cotton, or synthetic, and fabrics spoke to socioeconomic class. Colors and prints varied; older and

---

[15] According to most Shi'i *mujtahids*, handshaking between sexes is permissible if there is no skin-to-skin contact.

"more pious" women tended towards muted, simpler, and darker shades, while the fashion conscious matched their *ḥijābs* to their outfits.

A *ḥijāb* could be worn over jeans or pants and a loose shirt, or over a suit with a long jacket. Most commonly, women wore long, loose-fitting solid-colored dresses or tailored overcoats in beiges, navy, or blacks, known as *libs sharʿī* (*sharīʿa* or Islamic dress). For some people, only a woman who wore full Islamic dress with her *ḥijāb* was properly *muḥajjaba*, and the term *muḥajjaba* itself was then used as a gloss for one who did. While Islamic dress went further to erase class lines, again, wealth (or its display) was indicated by fabric quality and accessories such as purses, shoes, bracelets, and rings. Some members of Hizbullah, as well as women related to religious scholars through blood or marriage, wore an *ʿabāya* over their clothing and *ḥijāb* when out in public. This is a black wrap that covers a woman from head to toe, revealing only her face, hands, and feet and concealing her form. It was extremely rare for a woman in al-Dahiyya to cover her face. The few who did wore a thin not-quite-opaque piece of black cloth called a *fīsh* over their faces, along with gloves.

Once a woman becomes *muḥajjaba*, ideally she should remain so throughout her life, though there were some who began wearing the *ḥijāb* at a young age and later removed it. As with (not) shaking hands, a *muḥajjaba* woman wears her *ḥijāb* in front of all men who are *ḥarām* to her, that is, men other than her spouse, father, father-in-law, uncles, sons, and nephews.

> Freedom [*al-ḥurriyya*] in Islam means that a person has control of himself [*yamluk nafsahu*] and his movements, within the domain of the legal limits [*al-ḥudūd al-sharʿiyya*] that God requires him to respect. Thus the *ḥijāb* to which women commit does not eliminate their freedom. I do not think that the addition of a piece or two, or a meter or two, of clothing could change the issue of freedom, for freedom is defined by the freedom of women in work/activity [*al-ʿamal*], and this is not incompatible with the *ḥijāb*. (Fadlullah 1997: 137)

Women's dress is perhaps the most visible embodied expression of piety in al-Dahiyya, as well as in the Muslim world more generally. The veil is also one of the most common symbols used in the West to gloss the "oppression" or, alternately, the "resistance," of Arab or Muslim women.[16] Recently, especial attention has been paid to the "re-veiling" of young, educated, urban women. This "re-veiling" is generally discussed as either a symptom of Islamism or as an instrument of political

---

[16] For a thorough explication of the veil's history, contexts, and meanings, see El Guindi 1999.

resistance.[17] Strikingly, it is rare to see piety included in these discussions of veiling.[18] Instead, women are often assumed to veil for one of three reasons: because they have no choice or have known nothing else (e.g., it is law or it is "tradition"), because they are making a political statement (e.g., during the Iranian revolution), or because it facilitates movement in public spaces (e.g., it is easier for family/society to accept a woman working if she is veiled). The dominant assumption seems to be that if given the option, women would naturally choose not to veil. Yet however true these assumptions and arguments may be for some women in some contexts,[19] they neglect and negate the critical factor of faith. In other words, they neglect to take piety seriously.

> Today at the SAA's volunteer training seminar, our instructor told us that the *ḥijāb* feeds the poor by saving money, it kills the beauty competition that many women get caught up in and spend money on, and it creates a cleaner society because people spend the time they would spend sinning helping others instead. Immediately one of the younger girls sitting across the table from me responded under her breath, "Yeah, but now they compete over scarves [*escharpes* (Fr.)]. The instructor heard her and answered, "This is because people are lying in their religion." (fieldnotes, July 6, 2000)

The question of why many pious Shi'i women veil is one whose answer threads throughout this book. I do not intend to prioritize piety above all else exclusively, but I want to incorporate piety into a broader understanding of what both Islamic dress and *iltizām* more generally mean to practicing Shi'is in al-Dahiyya. The increase in veiling that has occurred in al-Dahiyya since the 1980s has coincided with the Shi'i mobilization detailed in the last chapter and paralleled its trajectory. It is important to reiterate, however, that this mobilization has had consequences for how faith plays out in people's lives, and no less with regard to dress.

It is also important to note that pious women's dress has taken on public meaning beyond the community of the pious modern in ways similar to prayer, marking the public arena as Islamic. This view was

---

[17] These arguments tend to fall into two categories. The first is exemplified by MacLeod's (1991) argument that veiling represents "accommodating protest," a means by which women can work outside the home while maintaining their respectability (see also Zuhur 1992). The second posits veiling as a strategy of resistance to colonial and neocolonial repression, sometimes involving coercion from nationalist movements. The most common examples are Iran and Palestine (e.g., Hammami 1997, Hegland 1987, Sullivan 1998).

[18] Notable exceptions include Brenner 1996, El-Guindi 1999, Kamalkhani 1998, and Mahmood 2005.

[19] Instrumentalist arguments regarding why women veil are frequently made in reference to Egypt.

especially prevalent among outsiders to this community, who often commented to me about the visible increase in numbers of *muhajjaba* women in public spaces. *Muhajjaba* women were often assumed to represent "the Shi'a" or "Hizbullah"—whether the speaker viewed their visibility as an encroachment, a threat, or simply a change in the political dynamics of the country. The headscarf also figured into the stereotyping of Shi'is as backward and nonmodern, reflecting the discourses that link modern-ness with secularism discussed in the introduction. I will return to this broader visibility and its relationship to the pious modern in chapter 6, and focus here on the meanings the *hijāb* carries with regard to piety.

The relationship between piety and the headscarf is neither always nor necessarily straightforward. Most practicing Muslim women and men agreed that the proper practice was for women to veil, and, when asked why, provided a relatively standard religious argument, stating that it is a woman's responsibility to "hide her charms" so as to preserve order in society and so that she will be treated with respect and not as a sexual object. These arguments were sometimes presented by non-*muhajjaba* women, who would then explain that they were not yet fully convinced of their own arguments, and hoped that God would someday bring them to a point of conviction so that they too would put on the *hijāb*.

Devout Shi'i women in Lebanon wore Islamic dress for a wide range of reasons involving combinations of piety, personal experiences, instrumentality, social pressures, and politics.[20] Women's increased veiling has been accompanied by a similar increase in women's public participation. However, rather than ordering these emphases and arguing that women veil in order to facilitate their participation, I would argue that in this case, veiling and public participation have been simultaneously emphasized as two facets of spiritual progress through authenticated Islam.[21] As Aziza retorted when I commented that it was interesting that a local woman preacher's sermons had changed over the past ten years to include both the importance of the *hijāb* and the importance of women's role outside the home, "*shū* (what?) It's completely natural that the two go together."

---

[20] See also el-Bizri 1996. An explication of Shi'i religious reasoning on the veil is outside the scope of this project. Fadlullah's interpretations are well explicated in Fadlullah 1997. Iranian *mujtahid* Murtaza Mutahhari was also cited by my interlocutors. See Mutahhari n.d. and Jam'iyyat al-ma'ārif al-islāmiyya al-thaqāfiyya 2001.

[21] Being *muhajjaba* may actually hinder a woman's chances of employment outside al-Dahiyya. Within the area many businesses do hire *muhajjaba* women; Islamic organizations often hire them exclusively.

Women who advocated Islamic dress linked piety and practicality in other ways as well. On one occasion, Hajjeh Zahra expounded:

> Why have women been so manipulated by the media? It's exploitation, this objectification, they are being used to sell things to men, to dirty people! When is a woman more dignified, when she wears the *ḥijāb* or this alternative? If we have no rules, then my son can come and say that he is free to be a drug addict and I can say nothing to him. Whenever I feel at all restricted, I remember the alternative for women, and I remember that God loves us, and that he can see these things more clearly that we can, so he puts these restrictions to protect us from ourselves. Because there is abuse of women! Women are measured by their bodies or appearances, beauty, and sex, having to sell themselves. If this is the price we pay for being feminine, the *ḥijāb* is needed. Because I wear the *ḥijāb*, I know that whenever I am accepted it is because I am capable. There is no other factor, I know that I am accepted for my abilities. I have more self-acceptance this way, more self-worth. In the *ḥijāb*, when a woman is accepted, it is because of her merit. This is why I can speak my mind in any situation, because I know that because of my *ḥijāb*, I am seen as a person, not a female.

Hajjeh Zahra's positing of the *ḥijāb* as a solution to the objectification of women—an argument I heard frequently—is particularly interesting in the Lebanese context. Lebanese women are generally stereotyped in the Middle East as being beautiful, resilient, and promiscuous.[22] Lebanon is also notorious for high rates of cosmetic surgery—especially nose jobs, breast enhancements, and collagen lip injections.

> [QUESTION]: What is the pragmatic representation of the correct/true/authentic [*ḥaqīqī*] *ḥijāb* in Islam?
>
> [ANSWER]: The true *ḥijāb* is represented first of all by a woman veiling/covering [*satr*] all parts of her body except her face and palms, and not going out while displaying her charms ['adam al-khurūj mutabarija]. So the *ḥijāb* has a material aspect manifest in the covering of the body, and also a symbolic aspect represented by a woman entering society as a human being, without trying to attract attention. In this way it is possible for the *ḥijāb* to be manifest in speech: "then be not soft in speech, lest he in whose heart is a disease" (Al-Ahzāb 32)[23] and in all other behaviors. (Fadlullah 1997: 32)

---

[22] This stereotype emerges in jokes about Lebanese women and in "observations" about the "real" work of Lebanese female television personalities who travel to Arab Gulf states.

[23] This is from the Qur'an, the full verse reads: "O wives of the Prophet! You are not like any other women. If you keep your duty, then be not soft in speech lest he whose heart is diseased should be moved with desire, but speak in an honorable manner." (Al-Ahzāb 32).

While no one I spoke with argued against the *ḥijāb* in principle, the issue of whether it should be required in public buildings other than mosques was hotly contested. Many people understood the logic of asking non-*muḥajjaba* women to wear a *ḥijāb* when entering Islamic schools, so as to maintain a proper example for the students. However, strong disagreement existed over the Martyrs' Association's policy requiring women to wear a *ḥijāb* inside Al-Rassoul al-'Azam Hospital. This disagreement hinged on the belief that veiling was only meaningful when done through free and conscious choice. This begins to explain the perspective of those pious non-*muḥajjaba* women who characterized themselves as not yet "convinced" (*muqtani'a*) of their own arguments for veiling. In contrast to the argument described above linking the act of prayer to the cultivation of *iltizām*, this view contends that *iltizām* must come first with regard to the *ḥijāb*.

The prioritization of *iltizām* in this case is linked to the powerful visibility of the *ḥijāb* as a symbol of a woman's morality. One of the issues that arose in these debates concerns whether the *ḥijāb* necessarily represents an inner state of true piety. This is illustrated by a conversation that took place one evening as I was relaxing in a café with a group of friends that spanned Lebanese diversity. One friend remarked that she wished she had asked her cousin to join us, and was immediately told by another that it would have been inappropriate, because the cousin was *muḥajjaba* and therefore should not be in a place that served alcohol and played popular Arabic music. I countered: "Why would it matter, as long as she doesn't drink?" The friend who had objected explained that a *muḥajjaba* woman must live according to proper religious morals and not even enter a place that challenges that morality, because the *ḥijāb* is "not just a piece of cloth," but something that carries responsibility. In her view, the *ḥijāb* represents a choice to uphold morality, and a public declaration of that choice.

I heard this notion of the *ḥijāb* as both material and moral again and again in lectures and sermons, as well as in arguments against enforced veiling. To paraphrase a sermon given by Fadlullah's son, Sayyid Ali Fadlullah, the *ḥijāb* is not merely a cover for one's head and hair, but for one's heart and morals and life as well. People who argue that *iltizām* must come first note that without *iltizām*, a woman's *ḥijāb* loses meaning. However, the notion that a woman must be "convinced" (*muqtani'a*) and "committed" (*multazima*) before she adopts the headscarf was contested, and furthermore, social pressures and norms affected the possibilities for choice in the matter. This debate is related to the importance of the headscarf as a public marker of piety, the emphasis placed on understanding the reasons for the *ḥijāb*, and the sense that such understanding was a relatively recent phenomenon.

"Then" versus "Now": A Processual Interlude

Over and over again, people would say to me, "Lara, twenty years ago you would not see *muhajjaba* women like this," or, "Lara, twenty years ago people did not pray like this." The perceived changes in religious practice and understanding from "then" to "now" are changes from "tradition" that was cast as unaware and rote to a purposeful and knowledgeable Islam. This transformation paralleled the trajectory of the Shi'i mobilization outlined in the last chapter, and similarly, the 1979 revolution in Iran and Khomeini's rise to international prominence played a major role in catalyzing reforms in religious practice. Occasionally, a woman who remembered the revolution would declare proudly, "I was one of the first in the community to *hajjab*" (adopt the *hijāb*). Rasha was one such woman:

> RASHA: I was eight years old when I decided to wear the *hijāb*, and my entire family except my sister was against it. At the time, I was a student at a Catholic school. Each morning I would leave the house, put my scarf on to walk in the street, then remove it when I arrived at school. And that was OK, because the school was all girls and nuns, except for once a week when a priest came to lead mass. On those days, I used to hide under my desk so that he would not see me.
> LARA: How did you know that was what you wanted to do?
> RASHA: I learned from a friend, she was also eight, she convinced me about the *hijāb*. We were in scouts together, and we used to go to the mosque together on Fridays.

The vanguard of religious reform, particularly those who were women, often faced parental disapproval or objections to their newly conceptualized and implemented religious practice.

Others instead faced what they considered their family's "ignorance." Dalal fell into the latter group. When I asked her if she had been raised in a religious family, her rather wry response clearly delineated her understanding of the difference between being "religious" and being "traditional":

> No, I became aware of religion on my own. My family was traditional [*taqlīdiyya*]; it was all tradition, they practiced religion as tradition, but not because of awareness [*wā'ī*] or knowledge [*'ilm*]. I am from a traditional Lebanese family, in the traditions [*taqālīd*] and the customs [*'adāt*] and even the religious observances. They inherit them; it is heritage [*turāth*], but it has nothing to do with awareness or having studied and understood authentic/true religion.

In the "now" of contemporary al-Dahiyya, for many pious Shiʻis, "tradition" has been replaced with "authenticated" practice rooted in knowledge and understanding. Yet despite the prevalence of the embodied practices of piety depicted above—viewed as evidence of spiritual progress in the decades following the Shiʻi Islamic mobilization—few people articulated a sense that they or their community were "religious" (*mutadayyin/a*). As one woman told me: "We still need more change, we need more consciousness."

Even for those who seemed devout, "becoming religious" was a continual process that required constant effort. I first realized this when it was pointed out to me that I was taking the term "religious" for granted. I had casually said to an acquaintance, "You consider yourself religious, don't you?" and he replied that actually, no, he didn't, but rather that he considers himself a "practicing Muslim." When I asked why, he explained that to consider himself religious implied much more than he felt he could live up to, and that it carried too much responsibility. There were "things that religious people had to do," like not sitting at a table with someone who is drinking alcohol, things he felt not yet able to do.

I decided to take my question to someone who I knew did those "things that religious people had to do" so one morning, over coffee and cookies, I asked Hajjeh Khadija if she considered herself religious. I had known her for almost a year at the time, and knew that she worked and volunteered at Islamic schools, prayed regularly, fasted during Ramadan, and held Ashura gatherings at her home. Furthermore, she was someone who was clearly respected as devout by others. Hajjeh Khadija's initial response was simply "*inshallah* (God willing) someday I will be religious." At that point we were interrupted by a neighbor needing a favor, so later I asked her again: "Hajjeh, I don't understand why you said *inshallah* you will be religious; you pray, you fast, you volunteer, you know so much about the Qur'an, you do all the things religious people are supposed to do, don't you?" Smiling mysteriously, she replied:

> *Layki habībtī*, I say *inshallah* I will be religious. I must never stop climbing the ladder of faith, you know it is a ladder, and at the top, the last thing, there is what we call *taqwā* [absolute faith and piety],[24] and that is something we must all walk towards. You know, *habībtī*, we have fundamentals of religion that a person should practice: faith in God, in Judgment Day, in God's Prophet. These are the basics for someone to be a Muslim. And of course there are the

[24] The best definition of *al-taqwā* I heard was Hajjeh Umm Hadi's, as she paraphrased Imam Ali: "It's not seeing anything without seeing God before it and after it and in the thing itself. This is *al-taqwā*, this absorption, this fusion."

practices of prayer, fasting, *zakāt* [religious taxes]. And, *il-ḥamdillah* [thanks be to God], I try also to apply/manifest the other things, the things we call *muʿamalāt* [mutual reciprocal social relations] and *fiqh* [religious jurisprudence]. On the level of *fiqh*, we should try to understand as much as we can, for example, with regard to issues like purity, things like that, personal things, and to apply those things. And with regard to *muʿamalāt*, a person tries to live correctly, and *inshallah* I will be able to.

As Hajjeh Khadija noted, "becoming religious" involved more than faith in the fundaments of religion, and more than the fulfillment of practices like prayer and fasting. It included both social relations and religious understanding and knowledge. The latter was both necessary in order to practice Islam correctly and an essential part of authenticated Islam in its own right. The importance of religious understanding also had to do with pious Shiʿi notions of what it means to be a modern person. One aspect of a pious modern self is cultivated piety—the piety of a person who uses her rational capacities to understand and practice authenticated Islam in an effort at continual self-betterment.[25] Such a person stood in sharp contrast to the traditional person who might veil or pray without understanding correctly why she did so, or who might do so improperly.

There were numerous routes by which the pious could gain religious understanding and knowledge, all of which shared the key element of communication. Beyond "becoming religious" on a personal level, discourses about religious practices and meanings are crucial to the construction of what is considered authenticated Islam. Indeed, the process of authentication itself occurs in large part through processes of communication and community discourses. As such, this chapter now turns to its final focus: a consideration of the ways pious Shiʿis constructed, learned, and practiced authenticated Islam through discursive piety.

DISCURSIVE PIETY

Religion permeated most talk in al-Dahiyya, in part because Lebanese speech conventions include liberal doses of phrases like *al-hamdullah, insha'allah, allah rād, twakila'allah* (thanks be to God, God willing, God willing, depend on God). For example, *insha'allah* is often used as an all-purpose answer to questions, and can range in meaning from "yes," to "maybe," to "we'll see," to "probably not," to "no way," depending on tone and context. Devout people also recited verses from the Qur'an or

---

[25] In Egypt a similar concern with self-cultivation is encouraged by sermons and women's mosque lessons (Abu-Lughod 2000, Mahmood 2005).

sayings of the Prophet or Imams, using quotations like proverbs, to illustrate or underscore a point.[26] While the phrases and interjections were not necessarily associated with religiosity, quotations generally indexed at least a certain level of familiarity with religious texts. They are speech acts that carry the pragmatic function of indicating piety.[27] Indeed, prayer itself, in addition to being an act of embodied piety, is also one of discursive piety. Rather than these speech acts, however, what I want to focus on in this section is the inclusion of religion as a topic of conversation in daily talk.

Piety was not only embodied in acts like praying, veiling, and Qur'anic quotation, it was also talked about. It was both a factor in what was being discussed by the pious, and in how they spoke about various matters. The visibility of religion and of religiosity in al-Dahiyya was inscribed in these discourses. They ranged from daily talk about how to be properly pious to debates about the correct meaning of religious rituals or events, and engrossed not only religious leaders, but importantly, the wider community of devout Muslims.[28] Religious talk works both pragmatically, establishing the speaker's piety via her stated concern for or expertise in understanding authenticated Islam, and metadiscursively, as discourse about the Discourse (in the Foucauldian sense) of piety.[29]

Debating Authenticated Islam in Daily Talk

Performing religious practices correctly entails knowing how to do so. In al-Dahiyya, such knowledge had multiple sources, often glossed as "the Islamic milieu" (al-bī'a al-islāmiyya or al-jaw al-islāmī). For some, this concept included the notion of fiṭra, or innate disposition, so that a person born Muslim was believed to instinctively know aspects of her religion. Fiṭra alone was not thought sufficient, however, as those aspects might still need to be awakened. More commonly, al-bī'a encompassed the atmosphere of the home, family, and perhaps school as well. As many put it: kil shakhs ibn bī'tu (every person is a child of his milieu).

---

[26] Devout Christians and missionaries quote the Bible profusely in similar ways.

[27] I take this notion from Spitulnik's separation of language use that is pragmatic— "performing or signifying a social identity"—from that which is denotative—"referring to a local concept" (2002: 194).

[28] In al-Dahiyya, new Islamic schools and publishing houses have no doubt contributed to the abilities of younger generation pious Muslims to participate in religious debates.

[29] Here again I follow Spitulnik in her use of capitalized "Discourse" to mean a body of knowledge that is "organized, legitimated, stabilized, experienced, and even contested in large part through concrete events and patterns of speaking—that is, discourse writ small" (2002: 197).

Aziza's response when I asked her how she knew so much detail about her religion was typical:

> Sitting and listening, all my life, I learned. There are always conversations about different situations. And all my life I've been listening. Whenever I don't understand something, I ask about it. Maybe not right then, but it sits in my mind and I think about it and later I will ask about it. The same way that you are always asking questions that come into your mind, I do the same thing. And I always keep on asking until I am convinced [*muqtani'a*] of the answer, until the right answer is in my mind [colloquially, *bālī*] and I am convinced of it.

And indeed, during the time I spent in al-Dahiyya, the details of religious practice were frequently a part of daily conversation. While this was sometimes directly related to my presence, just as often I found myself walking into these conversations, or merely witnessing them as they occurred around me, the participants seemingly oblivious of my ignorance of the topic being discussed. This was the case one fall afternoon while I was visiting with Hajjeh Umm Zein (a relative of Aziza's), her cousin Hajjeh Widad, and two other women I had just met. The cool weather had us sitting inside, wondering when the electricity would return so that we could turn on the heater in the room. Ramadan was approaching, and the conversation turned to how little time remained to complete one's fasting from the year before if a person had not yet done so. This made sense to me, as I knew that during menstruation a woman does not fast, yet she is expected to fast the days she missed before the following Ramadan. Hajjeh Widad noted disapprovingly that she expected that her daughter would be fasting extra days after Ramadan had passed instead. One of the younger women with us replied curiously, "Isn't it true that if you don't complete your fast before Ramadan you must either pay or give wheat to the poor?"[30] Hajjeh Widad clarified, "Yes, but you also can fast three days for every one that you missed instead." This was further corrected by Hajjeh Umm Zein, "Yes, but don't forget that it is three days added to each day you missed, so it becomes four instead of one."

Another afternoon Aziza was trying to convince me that Shi'i interpretations were far more sensible than their Sunni counterparts. She had begun with the practicality of temporary marriage (*mut'a*) contracts,[31] and with differences in divorce (Shi'is must have a judge certify a divorce). At

---

[30] For each day of fasting that is missed, a person may pay a set amount, believed to be enough to feed sixty poor people, or give a set amount of a staple food (e.g., wheat) to the poor.

[31] Her argument was that temporary liaisons occur in both Shi'i and Sunni contexts, but that only Shi'ism provided a religious contract that protected women and any resulting children. For more on temporary marriage in Shi'ism, see Haeri (1989).

this point, the doorbell rang, and we were joined by Hajjeh Widad and a teenaged relative of Aziza's, who had met on the stairs. After the standard inquiries about health and family, we picked up the conversation. "Did you tell her about traveling during Ramadan?" the younger woman asked. Aziza shook her head, "I'm not sure about that, you explain it." "For us, if you travel outside Beirut and leave before the noon call to prayer, you don't fast that day, and you don't have to do it later." Aziza: "But if you leave after the noon prayer?" "Then you have to fast. But the Sunni don't have these rules to make things like travel more practical."

Daily religious talk was not limited to the details of correct practice. Nor were women only the recipients of religious knowledge. Debates during women's social gatherings often took up the meaning of events, texts, and beliefs. Through these discussions, religious knowledge and meaning was sometimes reinforced and sometimes reinterpreted. These processes—involving women producing religious discourses that both reflect and impinge on their *iltizām*—are an important component of the ongoing authentication of Islam.

> After the *majlis* [mourning gathering] ended and most of the guests had left, we sat outside in the courtyard eating grapes and sweets and drinking coffee. Only about eight of us remained, including our hostesses (Randa, Hajjeh Umm Muhammad, and Noha), myself, Hajjeh Umm Zein, Noor, and two others whose names I didn't catch. At one point, someone passed around a bowl of apples, and just then Randa's husband entered the courtyard to ask her a question. As he left a moment later, she offered him an apple and, chuckling, he made a comment about Hawa [Eve] tempting Adam. Randa commented that it had all been Adam's fault anyway, since he was the one who insisted on covering up with a leaf after eating the apple. That led into a discussion about how there had been no *tahāra* [purity] or *najāsa* [impurity] in the garden of Eden, so Adam and Hawa hadn't had to cover themselves. Someone asked, "But then how did sex happen? Did they enjoy it?" More laughter. This then led somehow to a more serious side conversation about Mariam's [the Virgin Mary's] pregnancy, and how everyone had cast her out and accused her of adultery, but God told her to come and sit under a date tree, and whenever she was hungry, dates fell down to her and provided her with all the nutrition she needed. Hajjeh Umm Muhammad was narrating this, with some of the others interjecting comments here and there. (fieldnotes, April 11, 2000)

This shifting conversation was not directed at anyone specifically, though no doubt Hajjeh Umm Muhammad felt that some of the women present were not familiar enough with the details of this religious history. Beyond demonstrating how religious knowledge was reinforced, the conversation highlights the presence and prevalence of religious issues in people's minds. Associations with religious events and texts arose easily as asides in conversations that seemed to begin in unrelated ways. Everything could be brought to religion at some point, and often was.

Some of these conversations took the form of vehement debates. One of the most commonly debated topics revolved around superstition and the involvement of *jinn* (spirits) in the human world. Women exchanged stories about experiences with the evil eye and with being "written on"—a euphemism for being cursed by another—and argued about the truth of such stories, and about what religious texts say about them. At one gathering, Hajjeh Umm Hadi asserted strongly that she believed in *jinn* because of a personal experience. A post-childbirth illness had left her bedridden for several weeks, until a wise older woman visited her. The older woman told Hajjeh Umm Hadi that there was a *jinn* involved, and began to read the Qur'an and speak under her breath until she eventually began speaking in a male voice, presumably that of the *jinn*. She then fell silent and a small piece of paper dropped from the ceiling. Written on the paper was a message saying that the *jinn* had left Hajjeh Umm Hadi. She immediately recovered and began going about her normal daily activities.

Hajjeh Umm Hadi's audience was divided on both how believable such occurrences were and on whether it was religiously acceptable to seek remedies for them. Quotations from the Qur'an and *ḥadīth* flew back and forth across the room. Some women argued that there are people who work with *malāk al-jinn* (good spirits) whose role it is to counter the *jinn* (bad spirits). Others argued that it was all nonsense, and that it was illogical (*ghayr 'aqlī*) to believe in *jinn* and improper to seek superstitious remedies for nonexistent curses. Most of the latter did concede that remedies that included only verses from the Qur'an were acceptable, if only because holy words could do no harm.

This debate about *jinn* and curses is an example of the visibility of religion in the everyday lives of pious Shi'is, and also of their participation in the continual process of authenticating Islam. In other words, it is an example of women's participation in the metadiscourse on piety. This participation subverts two stereotypes about women's religious knowledge and practice: that women's belief is "folk" as opposed to men's "orthodox" belief and that women's religion is "practice-based" as opposed to men's "text-based" religion. In these debates about *jinn*, it was women who were arguing clearly on both sides, and drawing on religious texts in order to form their arguments. Those women who were critical of belief in curses were advocating for authenticated Islam.

Another common topic of discussion was the history surrounding the commemoration of Ashura. This is one of the most prominent paradigms in Shi'ism. Yet it also is a history whose interpretation and meaning has changed over the past few decades, and continues to be debated today. Pious Shi'is were expected to know the history of Ashura in detail, and frequently shared new information they learned through sermons, readings, conversations, and commemorations with one another. Ashura was so important that asking a question that revealed ignorance about the history often led to a response of surprise and disapproval. Rather than an indication of piety, in this case seeking basic knowledge was seen as a sign of ignorance.

A detailed case study of the transformation of Ashura into its authenticated form is the subject of the next chapter, but I want to give a brief example here, in order to underscore the prevalence of discussion of Ashura, and the importance placed on understanding religious history. Several weeks after Ashura had ended in 2001, as I was sitting with Aziza and her mother in their kitchen, drinking tea and eating *mana'īsh kishik*,[32] her mother began to tell me the story of what happened to Imam Husayn's head. She related that after Husayn's martyrdom, Yazid (the corrupt caliph who had him killed) was parading about the Arab world with the head, bragging about his feat. "And then a good Christian man bought Husayn's head from Yazid and gave it a proper burial." At this Aziza chimed in, reminding her mother that despite this being the "traditionally" told version of events, there was no agreement nor any proper evidence as to where Husayn's head is buried. She then related a different story that she had heard at a *majlis* a few weeks before. In this version, Husayn's head was thrown onto the grounds of a monastery in Syria, where it began to speak. It identified itself as Husayn's head and reminded the monastery priest of the sufferings of Christ, prompting the priest to convert to Islam and then give the head a proper burial. While Aziza told her story, her cousin walked in to get a glass of water, and stood listening to her. When she finished, he added that he had asked his uncle—a man reputed to know a great deal about religious matters—about this, and he had confirmed that Husayn's head had been buried in Syria by a priest, but had doubted that the head spoke. The cousin then added another layer of detail about how the head came to the monastery in the first place.

For my companions, each addition to this conversation brought the story of what happened to the Imam's head closer to credible evidence. Aziza's mother's version was the "traditional" story she had always known. This was corrected by Aziza and replaced with a more detailed

[32] A round bread baked with a layer of reconstituted dried yogurt, meat, and spices.

version, one learned at a recent *majlis*. Authentication culminated in her cousin's confirming and disputing various details based on the knowledge of his uncle, a person accepted by all three as an authority on such matters. In part, it was through conversations like these that particular discourses were authenticated, and canonized into a dominant discursive form.

Such conversations reinscribed the importance of correct knowledge, demonstrated the piety of the speakers, provided an informal space where questions could be asked and points clarified, and conveyed crucial information to younger people or those who have recently become committed. Yet for many who sought religious knowledge, daily conversations with their peers were not enough. This was particularly, though not exclusively, true for older women, those who espoused religious commitment in spite of their traditional families, and for women who volunteered at one of the Hizbullah *jam'iyyas*.[33] These women emphasized that actively seeking correct knowledge is an important part of piety itself. To obtain greater religious understanding they turned to a wide range of sources offering official discourses on authenticated Islam and piety.

Actively Seeking Knowledge through Authoritative Discourses

> Learning is also religious work. Islam encourages us to learn about our religion. It's a duty [*wājib*]. It is necessary to learn, it's not just something that is looked upon favorably [*mustaḥabb*]. Education and learning is a duty for all Muslims.
> —A Volunteer at the ICEC

A volunteer at the Martyrs' Association expanded upon this thought, emphasizing that seeking knowledge was not only important to one's own piety, but was crucial for educating others in authenticated Islam:

Islam encourages us to learn; the Prophet said to seek knowledge throughout one's life. We also have a *hadith*: "*al-mu'min al-qawī khayrun min al-mu'min al-da'īf*" [the strong believer is better than the weak believer]. The strong one isn't strong in physique, he is strong in competence and evidence. If I believe in something, I should have the ability to convince others of it. Because "*lā khayran bi-dīn lā 'ilman fīhi*" [there is no good in religion that has no knowledge]. If I believe in Islam and I am not conversant in it, in social situations, for example if my neighbor asks me why I am committed to the *hijāb*, if I don't

---

[33] I would speculate that this is related to Hizbullah's emphasis on religious education, as well as to these women's more pronounced tendencies towards evangelism.

have a verse to support my *ḥijāb*, I will appear weak in front of her. Or, "Why are you committed to community work [*al-ʿamal al-ijtimāʿī*]?" If I don't have a verse or a *ḥadīth* to demonstrate the necessity of social work I won't be able to teach you about its importance. The strong believer is strong in evidence.

There existed numerous means by which religious knowledge could be obtained and answers to questions about particular tenets or practices sought. In general, what was sought was a correct understanding of the interpretations of one's *marjiʿ* on a specific issue. In other words, people looked to religious discourses that were sanctioned as official and that carried a certain authority. To access these discourses and find out how her *marjiʿ* interprets a particular issue, a person might turn to books, sermons, radio, television, websites, and/or the telephone.

One of the women who worked at the *jamʿiyya* had recently had surgery, and was confined to her bed at home. She called in several times today, asking another volunteer to call the office of Sayyid Khamenei, her *marjiʿ*, in order to find out for her how she should pray, given that she couldn't get out of bed. The volunteer did so immediately, and called her back with a complex answer detailing exactly how she should place a pillow in front of herself, how she should sit and lean, and in what direction she should look as she said each part of the prayer. (fieldnotes, February 21, 2001)

Each *marjiʿ* has numerous books elucidating his interpretations and answering common questions, as well as expositions on particular topics. For example, as of June 2001, Fadlullah had published over sixty-five volumes. The best-selling ones are his books of jurisprudence (*kutub al-fiqhiyya*), followed by his books on youth and women. There are also *marjiʿ* offices in al-Dahiyya where people could go or telephone to ask questions. Fadlullah held open hours during which people could meet with him. Many of his followers expressed appreciation for his accessibility, with regard to the time he spent with them, the organization of his office, and the clarity of his language in sermons and writings:

LARA: So how do you know what your *marjiʿ* says?
HAJJEH UMM ALI: From everywhere. There are writings. There is a book for each *marjiʿ*. Now, what I am able to understand from it, I understand, and when I don't understand, I ask those who have knowledge. Any shaykh close to the Sayyid, or the Sayyid himself, will explain it to me. It's not a complicated thing. Especially these days, on the Internet you can press a key and get the information. It is no longer like in the beginning with the *marjiʿ* sitting who knows where and you needing who knows what to reach him. We even call him on the telephone with our questions.

Most women began their search for information about a specific topic by reading what their *marji'* had written on it. Some favored this method, noting that reading also extended their religious knowledge more generally, and citing Fadlullah's own emphasis on the importance of textual study and interpretation for all, men *and* women. Others, who did not read much or at all, preferred to ask directly, either by phoning or going to their *marji'*'s office. With regard to issues other than the details of religious practice, people often sought multiple interpretations, and then formed their own conclusions. This is one way that the tension between personal interpretation and asking an authority was resolved.

Sermons, radio, and television programming provided additional sources of authoritative religious knowledge, from a variety of perspectives.[34] Many people listened to the Friday sermon of at least one sayyid or shaykh, if not at a mosque, then on the radio or later via cassette. They also listened to the Hizbullah- and Fadlullah-affiliated radio stations and watched Al-Manār, Hizbullah's television station. Programming on all three stations included numerous shows about religious matters, especially programs where listeners/viewers could call in to have questions answered by a religious scholar. For example, many women listened to the radio call-in program hosted by Fadlullah's son, Sayyid Ali, at 9:00 a.m. each morning on al-Bashā'ir.

Some women attended classes at mosques, *ḥusayniyyas*, or the local *ḥawza* (religious school). Lessons were taught about religious texts, and in *fiqh*, as well as in various life skills, such as child rearing. Finally, as noted by Hajjeh Umm Ali above, Shi'is who live outside Lebanon can access information through the Internet and other media.[35] In addition, the radio stations and Al-Manār are accessible through the Internet and Al-Manār is available via satellite.

Today I went to the Internet office of Sayyid Muhammad Husayn [Fadlullah], run by his son Najib, and met with him [Najib] and the web programmer. Najib told me that the website has been up since June 1997, and that they are currently receiving between 1.5 and 2 million hits a month. According to their records, between mid-1997 and the first four months of 2001, the Sayyid received 2,118 questions via e-mail, 421 via fax, and 424 by mail. An exponential increase over time is also apparent, as the questions from the second half of 1997 filled one binder, those from 1998 filled three, those from 1999 filled

---

[34] Several scholars have noted the role of modern media technology (e.g., cassettes, radio, television, and the Internet) in facilitating access to religious discourses (see, for example, Eickelman and Anderson 1999a, Larkin 2000).

[35] Fadlullah's website—www.bayynat.org—includes the texts (and some audio) of his Friday sermons and other lectures, interviews, and seminars; his views and rulings on various issues; a biography; and a link through which people may e-mail him questions.

four, and those from 2000 filled eight. The most e-mails had been received from Bahrain, followed closely by the United States, with Lebanon coming in third.[36] The web programmer noted that the most popular question topics are about the *marji'iyya* and issues of *taqlīd*, *khums*, work issues (like whether you can sell pork in a restaurant to non-Muslims—it turns out this one is complicated because you can sell pork, but it is *ḥarām* to buy pork, so you can't actually get pork to sell), cigarette smoking (the Sayyid recently completely prohibited smoking as *ḥarām*), temporary marriages (a newer trend), and Ashura.[37] When an e-mail question is received, the programmer translates it into Arabic if necessary and passes it on to a shaykh. The shaykh handwrites an answer on the paper, and passes that onto the Sayyid. The Sayyid reads and revises the answer and sends it back to the programmer, who types it up and sends the final typed version back to the Sayyid. He looks it over and if he approves, he stamps the paper. The answer is then e-mailed to the person who asked the question, and the stamped paper filed. This process used to take an average of seventeen days; it now takes an average of four. (fieldnotes, June 18, 2001)

Whether by asking questions, reading books, listening to sermons, or attending classes, many devout Shi'is placed great importance on actively seeking religious knowledge through authoritative or official discourses. The continual process of "becoming religious" depended on this knowledge, which they applied in their practices of embodied piety, and drew upon in their conversations and debates. Demonstrating an understanding of authenticated Islam was an essential part of making one's own piety visible while underscoring and facilitating the spiritual progress of the community of the pious modern as a whole.

• • •

To be visible does not only connote being able to be seen in the sense of existing, but also, crucially, it involves standing out from the surroundings enough to be seen, not blending too much, not losing too much texture. In my interlocutors' world, religion was on the one hand omnipresent, common, and normalized, and on the other, it was conspicuous. This quality of conspicuousness stemmed from the recent processes of authentication and change that took place with the institutionalization of the Shi'i Islamic movement in Lebanon.

---

[36] E-mails had also been received from almost every other Arab and European country as well as Iran, India, Malaysia, Pakistan, Canada, Nigeria, Australia, New Zealand, the Philippines, and Brazil, among others.

[37] Other topics included food and drink; the lives of the Prophet, his family, and the Imams; Qur'anic interpretation; music and dancing; sexual relations; marital difficulties; lotteries and gambling; finances; pregnancy; purity and impurity; and traveling.

Pious Muslims were constantly engaged in defining, reinforcing, and prioritizing certain religious discourses and practices over others, constantly distancing themselves from those considered traditional. These processes of authentication have contributed to shifts in the atmosphere of al-Dahiyya over the past several decades, from a traditional milieu to an "Islamic" one. In the latter, value is not placed on the completion of religious practices merely as an end in itself, but rather on the completion of religious practices as the end result of correct religious understanding. Beyond fulfilling one's religious obligations correctly, it is also important to seek the knowledge necessary to obtain this correct understanding, and to contribute to the authentication process itself.

Piety hinged on both embodied and discursive religiosity; it was constituted by and stemmed from both words and actions. Those who cultivated both contributed to their own spiritual progress and to that of the pious modern more generally. Through their words and actions, authenticated Islam has taken root. In this way, piety is not only personal, it spills out from individuals into the public realm, bringing others to share authenticated interpretations of Islam and erecting the boundaries of what the devout often called "our community." Piety also served as a public marker of morality, a marker that imbued a person with moral status in that community. And public piety carried meaning outside the circles of the devout in the national and international political arenas as well. Perhaps the most visible annual moment of public piety—important both for reasons of personal faith and for its political interpretations—takes place during Ashura. Ashura provides a perfect case through which to consider more closely the processes of authentication, the relationship between personal and public piety, and the Shi'i Islamic movement's notions of the pious modern. It is to this ritual commemoration of the martyrdom of Imam Husayn that this book now turns.

CHAPTER FOUR

Ashura: Authentication and Sacrifice

Min'īsh bil-ḥuzn [We live in sadness].
—*Rasha, a pious Shi'i volunteer*

All that we have accomplished is from Karbala.
—*Khomeini*

If you look at the history of the Shi'a in the modern era, no heroes were born except in the *ḥusayniyyas* and the mosques. No one struck back at Israel except the children of the *ḥusayniyyas* and mosques. They learned about the spirit of Husayn and they said, if Husayn did so much, why don't we do this little to free our land?
—*Hajj Muhammad*

As Hajjeh Rula began to narrate the final moments Husayn spent with his eldest son, Ali al-Akbar, sobs rose heavily around us, filling the room with palpable grief. Her voice cracked as she lamented poetry into her microphone, describing how Husayn looked upon his son, who had come to him for his blessing before riding into battle, with the knowledge that the next time he saw Ali, the latter would be a corpse. This mournful parting was followed by an all-too-vivid description of the son's death, his body mutilated by the enemy's swords, Hajjeh Rula repeating the details of swords cutting flesh over and over, weaving in foreshadowings of Husayn's death that was soon to follow, bringing the weeping in the room to a crescendo. Then she paused. After waiting a moment for the sobs to subside, she began to lecture, explaining very clearly what the Qur'an, *ḥadīth*, and *ḥadīth* of Imam Ali teach about love and responsibility in parent-child relationships. Another pause, and the tears returned to their place in her voice. Returning to her poetic narration, she depicted the love of Ali's parents, Husayn and Layla, for their son, and then devoted the final piece of her lamentation to Zaynab. Zaynab, the aunt who looked upon Ali al-Akbar's devastated corpse with all the horrific grief of a mother looking upon her martyred son, a grief far too real for many in the room (fieldnotes, April 10, 2000/Muharram 5).

• • •

Ashura—the commemoration of the martyrdom of Imam Husayn—is frequently taken as an essential cultural paradigm for Shi'ism, by both scholars and Shi'i Muslims themselves, including my interlocutors.[1] It is the commemoration of both a battle of righteousness against corruption and evil and a key moment in Shi'i history—a moment so powerful that subsequent moments were characterized by an "overriding paradigm of persecution, exclusion, and suffering" (Pinault 1992: 56). To recap, Husayn, the Prophet's grandson and the third Shi'i Imam, was called upon by residents of Kufa to lead a revolt against Caliph Yazid's corrupt regime. He and his party were intercepted at Karbala. Several days later on the tenth of Muharram, a battle began, during which Husayn and all his men were killed. The survivors—women, children, and Husayn's only surviving son, who was too ill to fight—were captured and paraded to Yazid in Damascus. Among them was Sayyida Zaynab, Husayn's sister, who led the group in captivity.

As a cultural paradigm, Ashura is heavily dependent on and constitutive of public piety. The shared narratives, practices, and meanings associated with its commemoration have been a focal point of the authentication process and are crucial to the construction of the Shi'i pious modern.[2] As such, Ashura provides an apt example through which to explore the transformations precipitated by the Lebanese Shi'i Islamic mobilization and institutionalization. We will see that a key element in this shift involves the reinterpretation of Zaynab's behavior at Karbala, a reinterpretation bearing consequences for Lebanese Shi'i women.

In this chapter, I first consider the changes that have occurred in the details and meanings of the commemoration itself as an illustration of the authentication process. I then move to a discussion of the ways Ashura has become a critical presence in al-Dahiyya, the ideal models for public piety that are provided by Husayn and Zaynab, and how

---

[1] Fischer (1980) calls this the "Karbala paradigm." Discussions of Shi'ism often focus on Muharram/Ashura. Iran has been a major focus (Chelkowski 1979b, Fischer 1980, Good and Good 1988, Hegland 1983 and 1987, Loeffler 1988, Thaiss 1972); followed by South Asia (Hegland 1998a and 1998b, Pinault 1992 and 2001, Schubel 1993), Lebanon (Mazzaoui 1979, Norton and Safa 2000, Peters 1956, Riskallah 1997, Sharara 1968), Iraq (Fernea and Fernea 1972, Fernea 1965, Waugh 1977), and North America (Schubel 1991).

[2] Drama—especially that associated with specific calendrical dates with salient historical value—is important in mobilizing collective identities at specific moments (Donham n.d., Tambiah 1996). Historical tragedy also contributes to collective identity—for example, the Armenian genocide has been a focal point for Armenian ethnic identity in diaspora.

those ideals and the Ashura paradigm are lived by pious Shi'i men and women today.

COMMEMORATIONS TRANSFORMED

Commemorating Ashura in Lebanon involves holding and attending both private and public *majālis*, or mourning gatherings in which the history of the martyrdom is retold, and tenth-day *masīras*, or lamentation processions, during which men often perform *laṭam*, a ritualized striking of one's body in grief.[3] Both the structure and meaning of Ashura and these lamentation events have always been historically fluid, incorporating different elements in different locales and reflecting the changing political and social status of Lebanese Shi'is. However, a particularly dramatic transformation has accompanied the institutionalization of the Shi'i Islamic movement.

Ashura commemorations similar to contemporary commemorations that my interlocutors label "traditional" (*taqlīdī*) have occurred in rural Lebanon and in what is today al-Dahiyya since at least the early twentieth century.[4] As we will see, several elements characterize these traditional commemorations, including *laṭam* that draws blood and a focus on grief (expressed in weeping by both sexes)[5] and regret, rather than activism. According to Ende (1978), the earliest written evidence of a clerical effort to reform these practices—especially self-injurious *laṭam*—dates from the late 1920s. At that time Sayyid Muhsin al-Amin, a religious scholar from Jabal 'Amil (south Lebanon) who lived in Damascus, criticized self-injurious *laṭam* as unlawful.[6] This set off a controversial and virulent debate between al-Amin and the few scholars who agreed

---

[3] Some people held *majālis* for three days after the tenth, and others observed a forty-day mourning period. Nakash (1993) identifies five major Muharram rituals in Shi'ism: the *majālis*, *masīras*, and *laṭam* I discuss, along with pilgrimage to Karbala and passion plays. The earliest documented *masīras* took place during Persian Buyid rule in Baghdad in the tenth century (Chelkowski 1979b: 3). For history of Muharram rituals, see Ayoub 1978, Nakash 1993, and Halm 1997.

[4] The practice of self-injurious *laṭam* was brought to south Lebanon from Iran in the early twentieth or late nineteenth century (Ende 1978; Hasan al-Amin, personal communication). It is thought that this practice originated with Shi'i converts in the Caucasus, perhaps reflecting the incorporation of Christian elements (see Nakash 1993).

[5] The prevalence of weeping among men and women alike contrasts with Abu-Lughod's (1993b) observations about gender differences in lamentation among the (Sunni) Awlad Ali Bedouin.

[6] Ende (1978) notes that others put forth similar views around the same time. See Mervin (2000) on these various arguments for reform.

with him, and the major sayyid families of Jabal 'Amil who formed a religious and landowning elite. In the end, the elite sayyid families succeeded in rallying most of the uneducated villagers against al-Amin's calls for reform.[7]

The important point here for our purposes is that while the lawfulness of self-injurious *latam* became a major debate among Shi'i religious scholars in Jabal 'Amil, Damascus, and Najaf in the 1920s, the issue did not garner popular interest at that time. Decades later, as Shi'i Muslims began to move to Beirut, they brought traditional forms of commemoration with them. The urban visibility of Ashura grew in tandem with these population shifts. Traditional commemorations were viewed by many nonparticipants as a frightening display of Shi'i "backwardness," and cited as one of the differences marking the marginalized Shi'is as less modern and developed than other Lebanese.[8]

Despite the earlier attempts at reform and the stigmatization of the commemorations in the urban milieu, it was not until the 1980s that strong opposition to traditional forms of Ashura appeared among Shi'is who were not religious scholars. The first signs of this came in 1974, just after Musa al-Sadr founded the "Movement of the Deprived." Norton notes that "Under Imam Musa's considerable influence, religious commemorations became vehicles for building communal solidarity and political consciousness" (1987: 41).[9] However, while al-Sadr was among the first to link contemporary Shi'i mobilization in Lebanon with Ashura, large-scale transformation of its rituals with regard to both practice and meaning did not take root for another decade.

---

[7] Ende (1978) suggests that sayyid families were invested in maintaining Ashura commemorations as they were because they reinforced the peasantry's allegiance to them and also brought in crowds (and money) from surrounding areas.

[8] It is difficult to ascertain who participated in these commemorations. Nonparticipants included non-Shi'i Lebanese, though political leaders sometimes attended *majalis* held by elites, and Peters (1956) suggests Christian participation in a village in the 1950s. Nonparticipants also included nonpracticing Shi'is. Khuri (1975) relates how al-Hajj Khansa—a migrant from the Beqaa—established the first *husayniyya* in al-Dahiyya and began holding large public Ashura commemorations there in 1939. This provoked opposition from local residents (some of whom were also Shi'is) who feared the commemorations would damage their relationships with other sectarian communities, especially Sunni Muslims (1975: 183–86).

[9] Ajami quotes Musa al-Sadr as saying, "The revolution did not die in the sands of Kerbala; it flowed into the life stream of the Islamic world, and passed from generation to generation, even to our day. It is a deposit placed in our hands so that we may profit from it, that we draw out of it a new source of reform, a new position, a new movement, a new revolution, to repel the darkness, to stop tyranny, and to pulverize evil" (Ajami 1986: 143). This is particularly interesting as Musa al-Sadr is descended from two of the major sayyid families of Jabal 'Amil (al-Sadr and Sharafeddin).

Around that time, after the catalyzations of the movement discussed in chapter 2, Shi'i opposition to traditional commemorations increased. This opposition reflected trends in Iran, where reformist and Islamic intellectuals had promoted Ashura discourses linking the commemorations to an alternative and revolutionary Shi'ism, in contrast to a politically quietist one.[10]

Crucially, this time the debates were not confined to the clerical leadership. Debate among religious scholars is not enough to create actual changes in practice of the scale seen in Ashura commemorations over the past few decades. Such transformation requires the active participation of a wider community. Literacy, education, and urbanization, as well as political mobilization against both injustice within Lebanon and Israeli aggression, facilitated the mass participation of Shi'is in discussions about the reforms and in their practical implementation, resulting in a shift from what pious Shi'is called traditional forms to authenticated ones. In many ways it is this mass participation that exemplifies the continual process of authentication.

The shift from traditional to authenticated Ashura is especially apparent with regard to three areas: the *masīras*, the *majālis*, and most crucially, the meaning attributed to the events of Muharram. The importance of Ashura has not changed; rather, the transformation involves the details of commemorative practices and a reordering of their two primary emphases, with the soteriological that dominates traditional commemorations sharing primary ground with the revolutionary in authenticated ones.

Masīras

A TRADITIONAL *MASĪRA*: 10 MUHARRAM IN NABATIEH (2000)

Each year on the tenth of Muharram, people pour into the southern Lebanese town of Nabatieh; some to participate in the Ashura passion play and traditional mourning *masīras*, others to watch what has become a spectacle, drawing tourists and journalists from Beirut and other parts of the country.[11]

The sunrise call to prayer woke us early. Soon after, the shaykh's voice exploded into every corner of town. Facilitated by loudspeakers, he began the day's lamentation. By 7:30 a.m. we could hear the crowd beginning to gather outside. All I could see from the balcony was a sea of black—spectators waiting for the day's events to begin. They had carefully left the road framing the

[10] See Aghaie 2001, Hegland 1983 and 1987, Keddie 1995, and Fischer 1980.
[11] For another description of Ashura in Nabatieh, see Norton and Safa 2000.

town center clear for groups of mourners to pass. People claimed spots on balconies, ledges, and rooftops, and a group of young men climbed the mosque at the corner of the square. Those whose homes overlook the center opened their doors to guests, serving coffee and food throughout the day.

The sea of black was dotted here and there with white and red—the men who were "hitting *ḥaydar*."[12] They began in the early hours of the morning and continued through the end of the reenactment.[13] A group of between six and twenty men or boys would move quickly along the road, blood flowing from self-inflicted wounds on their heads and staining their white shirts or bare chests draped with white cloth (representing shrouds) a bright red. Throughout the morning, group after group passed beneath the balcony, almost at a jog. Their chants were punctuated by the sounds of their hands hitting their heads and the stomps of their feet. One or two sometimes held the razor blades or knives that had been used to cut a small incision at each man's hairline (though I was told that these cuts were usually made by a town butcher or barber). As each hit his wound in rhythm with the group, their blood flowed down their faces and chests.

Each group chanted "Haydar," "Ali," "Husayn," or "With spirit, with blood, we support you, Oh Husayn" in unison. They stuck close together, sometimes holding on to one another. Friends or relatives sometimes walked alongside them, restraining those who lost themselves in their fervor and began to injure themselves too much. In each group there were a few who staggered a little, or were held up by a friend or paramedic as they continued to hit their bleeding heads. Red Cross or Islamic Health Committee paramedics carrying stretchers flanked the mourners, both to contain them and to care for those who passed out.[14]

The majority of those "hitting *ḥaydar*" were youth, though there were boys as young as ten or twelve and older men as well. Younger boys seemed to be out earlier in the day, before the sun became too hot and the crowd too large. Some fathers carried their young sons—some who looked as young as two or three years old—on their shoulders, the children hitting their uncut heads along with the others in the group. A few men had cut their sons' heads lightly and were helping them to gently tap the cuts so a little blood would flow.

---

[12] "Hitting *ḥaydar*" is the colloquial term for this particular form of *laṭam*. "*Ḥaydar*" is another name for Imam Ali.

[13] Several people insisted that one should not begin to "hit *ḥaydar*" until Imam Husayn has been martyred in the play, but as far as I could tell, very few people waited.

[14] I heard reports of up to twenty thousand participants a year in Nabatieh alone. It is this scene that has contributed to the sensationalization of Ashura in Nabatieh, exemplified in the opening sentence of a Lebanese English-language newspaper's article: "The Shiites of Nabatieh commemorated the 10th day of Ashura in traditionally gruesome fashion Wednesday, with thousands of chanting, blood-soaked mourners thronging the town square" (Blanford 2001).

None of the children were crying. I was told that these were usually children who had been ill, and whose parents had vowed that they would "hit *ḥaydar*" if God helped them recover.

By the time the reenactment began,[15] everywhere, including the balcony where I stood, was packed with spectators and mourners. . . . Even during the reenactment, every so often a group "hitting *ḥaydar*" or, more rarely, a car draped in Hizbullah flags with an elegy blaring from its speakers, passed by.[16] By noon there were streams of blood in the street, and groups of men and boys walking around with their faces and chests soaked red and bandages wrapped around their foreheads.

The most obvious change that has occurred in *masīras* concerns the style of *laṭam* that men perform. As the Shi'i Islamic movement grew in popularity, the shedding of blood during *laṭam* was criticized as un-Islamic because it involves purposely injuring oneself. This echoed the criticisms put forth by al-Amin in the 1920s, and interestingly, al-Amin's work was republished in Beirut in the early 1970s (Ende 1978). A few people I spoke with knew about those writings, and referred to them as "finally" being implemented. Eventually, following the lead of Iran,[17] Lebanese Shi'i clerics issued *fatwas* condemning the practice, and Hizbullah banned it outright in the mid-1990s.[18]

This was accompanied by calls for those who feel the need to shed their blood during Ashura to do so for the community good, by instead donating blood to local bloodbanks. Indeed, the Islamic Health Committee's offices in al-Dahiyya reported receiving so many blood donations during Ashura in recent years that they had a large surplus each year immediately after the commemoration. In Nabatieh itself, Hizbullah began setting up a blood donation center on the tenth of Muharram in 1998, attracting over five hundred donors in 2000.

Part of the opposition to traditional *laṭam* may represent a response to

---

[15] Those "hitting *ḥaydar*" are not the only attraction. The day's main event is a passion play reenacting the battle during the *majlis* narration. Because this reenactment is specific to Nabatieh and outside my comparative framework, I do not go into detail here.

[16] Tensions were often high between Hizbullah and Amal during Ashura, occasionally resulting in violence. Those performing traditional *laṭam* sometimes wear Amal symbols. My local hosts in Nabatieh in 2000 expressed frustration at how "Ashura has been taken out of our hands; it has been made so political." That year the reenactment went overtime and Hizbullah began its *masīra* before it ended, blocking the actors from exiting the field. Since 2003, political symbols and parties have been banned from the Nabatieh commemorations, which are now organized by an independent local association.

[17] Khomeini frowned upon the practice before his death in 1989, and Khamenei officially condemned it in a 1994 *fatwa* (Chehabi 1997; Pinault 2001).

[18] Each year just before Ashura religious and community leaders reiterate their opposition to traditional *laṭam*. But there also remain many who support the practice.

4.1. Traditional *laṭam* in Nabatieh.

stereotypes linking Ashura to Shi'i "backwardness." Such stereotypes persist today: when I returned to my office at the American University of Beirut after attending Ashura in Nabatieh, several people expressed shock that I had gone, and one woman bemoaned the television broadcasting of traditional Ashura, saying, "Look what a horrible picture this gives of Lebanon; now we'll all be associated with such barbarism." Similarly, many pious Shi'is in al-Dahiyya were astounded that I would

4.2. Traditional *laṭam* in Nabatieh.

want to attend the event in Nabatieh, often expressing their disgust at *"kull ḥa-dam"* (all that blood).

A sharp contrast to traditional *masīras* and *laṭam* is presented by Hizbullah's *masīras*, that take place each year in several areas of Lebanon, including al-Dahiyya, Nabatieh, and Baalbek in the Beqaa.

AN AUTHENTICATED *MASĪRA*: IO MUHARRAM IN AL-DAHIYYA (2001)

Each year on the tenth of Muharram, people pour out of their homes into the streets of al-Dahiyya to attend *majālis* and participate in the Ashura *masīra*. They gather at public tents that are set up across roads and parking lots, and at mosques and *ḥusayniyyas*.

> When Aziza and I finally made it through the crowd and arrived at the over-flowing tent a few blocks from her home, it was nearly 9 a.m., about an hour into the *majlis*. People sat on every available inch of curb and ground, listening attentively to the narration being broadcast from the tent's speakers. We found a spot under the overpass near the women's entrance to the tent . . .
>
> There were children everywhere, babies in strollers and kids running around or trying to wipe away their mothers' tears. They too were dressed in black, some with t-shirts or headbands that said "oh Husayn" or "oh Abbas."

Many little girls—including a friend's five-year-old daughter—wore *ḥijābs* or *'abāyas* even if they were too young to normally wear them. When the *majlis* ended, everyone walked towards the upper road to join the *masīra*. Thanks to our Hizbullah press passes, Aziza and I were able to skirt crowd control and take a shortcut down to the highway so that we could watch the entire *masīra* from the beginning.

The *masīra* was highly organized. It began with four huge portraits of Khomeini, Khamenei, Nasrallah, and Musa al-Sadr. These were followed by many groups of boys, scouts, youth, and men, organized by increasing age. They were either dressed uniformly as scouts or entirely in black, "Husayn" written on their colored arm- or headbands. Each group marched in three neat rows behind a microphone-bearing leader, who initiated *nudbas* [elegies] and chants, and ensured that everyone performed *laṭam* in perfect unison. This *laṭam* did not involve blood.[19] Instead, those performing it swung both arms downwards, then up, then out away from their bodies, and finally in to strike their chests with their hands.[20] It was done to a four-count rhythm so that on every fourth beat the sound of hands striking chests resonated loudly, providing a percussive accompaniment. The organized groups were followed by a large group of men marching in solidarity, some hitting their chests lightly, and by a group of shaykhs and sayyids, surrounded by security, walking quietly.

Then the women's part of the *masīra* began, with colored panels of Ashura scenes. These were followed by female scouts and students, again in orderly rows organized by age, all dressed in full *'abāyas*. The girls chanted in response to a leader or sang *nudbas* but did not perform *laṭam*. One group wore *fishs*—full face veils—and were chained together, representing the women who were taken captive by Yazid's men. Some marchers carried photographs of young Resistance martyrs, assumed to be their relatives. Again, the organized women were followed by a large group of female supporters walking en masse, not necessarily wearing *'abāyas* but all *muḥajjaba*. Many pushed young children in carriages.[21]

As the *masīra* arrived at the field designated as its end point, men went to one side and women to the other. Nasrallah spoke, then everyone prayed together behind him . . .

---

[19] Some who disapproved of self-injurious *laṭam* only used *"laṭam"* to refer to the authenticated form described here, in order to further distinguish between forms. They called self-injurious *laṭam* "hitting *ḥaydar*." The verb root *nadab* (to mourn or lament) was also sometimes used for either form, with context indicating the specific act it connotes (e.g., *laṭam* versus singing an elegy).

[20] This style of *laṭam* is a hybrid of faster-paced Iranian and slower Iraqi styles, and seems to have become the dominant form for Hizbullah as well as Fadlullah's followers since the mid-1990s. Different styles are encountered by pilgrims at Shi'i shrines, most commonly at Sayyida Zaynab's shrine in Damascus.

[21] If a child is ill, a woman may vow to march with him if her supplications for his health are answered.

4.3. Scouts in the Hizbullah *masīra*.

While the most striking and commonly discussed difference between these two *masīras* is the style of *laṭam*, two other crucial differences are the level of organization and the role of women. First, authenticated *masīras* were highly ordered, and worked to demonstrate Hizbullah's strength while also demonstrating the organizational capacities of the pious modern.[22] Second, while women were generally spectators in traditional *masīras*,[23] watching from curbs, balconies and rooftops,[24] in authenticated *masīras*, they were no longer relegated to an observational role. In typical fashion,[25] the Shi'i Islamic mobilization called upon

[22] See Özyürek's discussion of Turkish state-organized parades as demonstrations of power (n.d.)

[23] In Nabatieh in 2000, I counted six women "hitting *ḥaydar*." My hosts were as surprised as I was to see this, and speculated that these women had participated to fulfill vows they had made.

[24] Given the strict gender segregation in many Shi'i communities during religious rituals (e.g., Fernea 1965, Fernea and Fernea 1972, Hegland 1998a and 1998b, Pinault 2001, Torab 1996), it is worth making the small point that the less strict gendering of Lebanese society is reflected in Lebanese Shi'i ritual. While *majālis* were either held separately or with divided seating, men and women mixed relatively freely outside while watching *masīras*.

[25] The classic examples of women's mobilization as part of broader national or religious movements are Iran and Algeria. See also Peteet (1991) on the Palestinian national resistance.

4.4. A girl in the *masīra* carrying a martyr's photograph.

women to participate actively and publicly in Ashura commemorations. As we will see, this paralleled a greater emphasis on women's participation more generally. Both the new style of *laṭam* and women's visibility in the *masīras* were viewed by many pious Shi'is as indications of both progress and authenticity. I will return to this point below, after a comparison of the *majālis*.

4.5. Young women representing the captives. Their face veils (rare in Lebanon) indicate that they are representing women of the Prophet's family.

Majālis

During a *majlis*,[26] no matter where it fell along the traditional-authenticated spectrum, a recitor (*qāri'*)[27] narrated a part of the events of the first ten days of Muharram in a lamentation style reminiscent of a liturgy, detailing graphically the suffering and martyrdom of the Imam and those with him. Some recitors included a sermon explaining lessons to be learned from Ashura. The affect of the audience paralleled these shifts in tone, the lamentation evoking intense crying that quieted to pensive concentration during the sermon.

While all *majālis* included the lamentative narration of the *masā'ib*, the tragic events of Karbala, recitors that were considered "traditional" dwelled on the details of suffering, in order to elicit maximum emotionality from the audience. Many also embellished the dialogue among

---

[26] *Majlis* is used to refer to both *majālis 'aza* (mourning gatherings) and to the text that is read/recited during them.

[27] The word *qāri'* can be translated as "recitor" (especially of religious texts) or "reader." Most recitors had a text to which they referred, often a notebook filled with handwritten notes, but they seemed to move fluidly between reading and recitation.

4.6. Women supporters marching en masse.

Husayn, Zaynab, and others with them. The ultimate goal for traditional recitors was to move people to cry as much as possible for the
martyrs and captives. Mourning for 'ahl al-bayt (the Prophet's family)
was believed to have salvatory effects, as those who shed true tears on
their behalf may appeal to them for intercession in the afterlife. A
shaykh at Fadlullah's office criticized this emphasis on mourning:

> Our problem is that many recitors do not go to school to learn to recite. . . .
> Anyone with a good voice can decide, "I want to become a recitor." There is
> no organization to forbid incorrect recitations. There are some who are very
> traditional and backward and others who are cultured.[28] The backward ones
> read only to make people cry, but the cultured ones teach lessons in their
> recitations.

As the shaykh implies, authenticated *majālis* were characterized by
longer sermons and a more restrained lamentation. Eliciting an emotional

---

[28] Advocates of authentication commonly used the opposition "backward" (*mutakhal-
lif*) versus "cultured" (*muthaqqaf*) to structure contrasts between traditional and authenticated commemorations. Another common framework was "then" versus "now" (despite
the existence of a spectrum of Ashura practices today).

response became a secondary goal. These *majālis* were primarily intended to teach religious, social, and political lessons, and to elucidate the authenticated meanings of Ashura and link it to the present. Recitors who strove for authenticity were concerned with historical accuracy and avoided including exaggerations that they saw as being "merely" to heighten emotions. Pious Shi'is often described these changes—particularly the promotion of "scientific" (*'ilmī*), textually based, and therefore "accurate" (*ṣaḥīḥ*), histories over exaggerations viewed as "myth"—as evidence of spiritual progress.

From the perspective of a recitor:

> Today, now, there is more awareness. Before, crying was the purpose, people cried about Imam Husayn, but they did not know him. The kind, sad voice reminded them of things, and they would cry, but they would not understand why the revolution happened. Of course, there is an emotional side to the recitations. . . . This is necessary because it is human nature that if one is sad for someone he loves, he will sacrifice for him more readily. . . . But Imam Husayn did not want us to cry.

Emotion remains important for this recitor, yet emotion is given contemporary purpose in its revision from an end to a means.

Those who have attended *majālis* over the past three decades articulated the shift as well, noting that today's *majālis* are "more accepted by our minds." Dalal explained:

> They recite the same story about Husayn. But the lecture differs. It depends on the audience and the recitor and the topic and his own relationship to Ashura. But they are better than before, because they are being tied into our daily lives, this linking of the past to the present and the future, this is better. Before we used to just go and listen to the story. Now, we are not just going to cry for Imam Husayn, we are going to learn from his school. The lecture is important, it is clarifying why you are crying, and why Imam Husayn was martyred.

The following juxtaposition of two women's *majālis* provides a more nuanced depiction of these differences. The *majālis* share a basic structure: The recitor opens the *majlis* with a quiet group recitation of *sūrat al-fātiḥa*, the Qur'an's opening verses. Along with the salutations that may follow, this establishes a sacred context and brings participants into a contemplative mindset. The recitor may then insert a *nudba* (elegy), though these are usually left to the end. The lamentative narration follows, interrupted by a sermon of varying length. At the end, the recitor usually leads at least one *nudba*, with those who know the words singing along. If held in a private home, the *majlis* may be dedicated to the hostess's family. Finally, *majālis* often conclude with everyone standing and reciting *ziyārat al-ḥusayn*, a supplicatory prayer to the Imam. Hospitality always follows privately held *majālis*. Coffee and sweets are routinely offered, though some women serve their guests a light lunch.

A TRADITIONAL WOMEN'S *MAJLIS:* 7 MUHARRAM 1422 AH/2001 CE

This *majlis* took place in a *ḥusayniyya*, a building dedicated to Shiʿi commemorations. It was large enough to hold around 150 people, with chairs arranged in rows and benches lining the walls. A podium at one end was draped in black, and black banners hung along the walls with salutations printed on them, including *"al-salāmu ʿalaykum yā sayyid al-shuhadā'"* (peace be upon you, lord of martyrs). When the room was full, Hajjeh Fatima walked to the podium, turned on the microphone, and began:

> After we recited *sūrat al-fātiḥa*, Hajjeh Fatima broke into a series of salutations: *"al-salāmu ʿalaykum yā ḥusayn, al-salāmu ʿalaykum yā . . .* [etc.]," including Husayn's children, friends, brother Abbas, and finally, with especial emphasis and emotion entering her voice, Zaynab. After a short *nudba*, she segued into her narration, focusing on Husayn and Zaynab's half-brother Abbas. She first related how Zaynab had chosen Abbas as her *kāfil* [supporter]. After about ten minutes, Hajjeh Fatima paused, took a few deep breaths, and then gave a short ten-minute lecture about how Abbas's character demonstrates the qualities of a good Muslim. She then returned to the lamentation, and, this time using mostly Iraqi poetry, vividly described Abbas's death. She described the children's thirst and cries, and Abbas's decision to bring them water from the Euphrates. How, on his first attempt, he was wounded and the water spilt. And how, despite his wounds, he tried again, but was killed, his hands cut off, leaving bloody stumps. How his handless corpse returned to the camp draped over his horse, and how Zaynab cried out, "What were you doing leaving us like that? How can you leave us, you who are responsible for us?" And most of all, how Zaynab cried.
>
> This was the longest lamentation I have heard so far. The instant Hajjeh Fatima's voice broke into lament, the women listening began to weep loudly. The emotion in the room was overwhelming; sobs filled the air. Some women cried out or spoke under their breath as they wept. These were mostly older women, though this entire audience seemed older than others. Even Aziza, who usually sat calmly and cried silently at *majālis*, had pulled her knees to her chest and wrapped herself around them, her body shaking as she wept. Hajjeh Fatima threw her head back as she lamented, tears streaming down her face, her voice rising and breaking as she cried out the words, sometimes screaming into the microphone *"yā* Zaynab" or *"yā* Husayn." At one point she stopped articulating altogether, buried her head in her arms on the podium, and wept for several minutes. Eventually, someone took her some

water, and she slowly lifted her head and resumed her lamentation where she had left off.

When the lamentation ended, everyone dried their eyes and slowly began singing two *nudba*s, joining in at the choruses if they didn't know all the words: *ramz al-'atā', rūḥ al-shuhadā', lī-man bakayt huwa al-ḥusayn fī karbalā'* [symbol of giving, spirit of martyrs, I cried for Husayn at Karbala] and *dammī mū 'aghlā min dammak yā ḥusayn, jismī mū 'aghlā min jismak yā ḥusayn* [my blood is not more precious than yours, oh Husayn, my body is not more precious than yours, oh Husayn]. Many women struck their chests with their hands keeping a slow percussive accompaniment to the *nudba*s. One little girl was hitting her chest so hard she left a red welt. A woman sitting near me noticed this favorably, saying it was obvious how moved the little girl was. At the conclusion of the *nudba*, several young women brought coffee and *rāḥa* and *bascot* [biscuits with a sweet resembling "Turkish delight," eaten "for Husayn's soul"].

AN AUTHENTICATED WOMEN'S *MAJLIS*: 11 MUHARRAM 1422 AH/2001 CE

The following *majlis* was held at a private home. Chairs filled the formal living room in three concentric circles, spilling into the hallway and onto an adjacent balcony. About forty women attended, ranging from great-grandmothers to young brides. Soon after we arrived, one of our hostesses distributed tissues to everyone present. On that cue, Layla, the young recitor, picked up her microphone and began in a clear voice, leading the recitation of *sūrat al-fātiḥa*, then "*ṣalli 'alā muḥammad wa āli muḥammad*" thrice.[29] She then spoke a few sentences about Ashura's importance, segueing into her recitation:

> Layla's tone shifted as she began to detail the *masā'ib*, but she remained clear relative to others I've heard and used only Lebanese dialect. Her focus was the young women, especially Zaynab, after the battle: how they coped with the deaths and how they were paraded through the desert as prisoners, even though they were 'ahl al-bayt. As soon as her voice made the shift to lamentation, several older women in the room began to weep loudly. Others buried their faces in their tissues; a few just lowered their heads, tears streaming silently from their eyes.
>
> After around ten minutes, Layla abruptly broke her lamentation and returned to her speaking voice. The sobs in the room subsided, backs were straightened, heads lifted, and tears wiped. Layla then began a long lecture about Yazid's corruption and Zaynab's strength in confronting him with his crimes. She then turned to the *ḥadīth* "*ḥusayn minni wa 'anā min ḥusayn*"

---

[29] This phrase is an element of prayer—used here as a salutation or salvo of benediction that assists in the shift to a sacred framework. It is also commonly invoked at intervals during sermons or speeches given by religious/political leaders.

[Husayn is from/of me and I am from/of Husayn], explaining that this meant that anyone who loves Husayn is in turn loved by the Prophet and by God.

Layla's voice then began to shake again and she returned to her narration. The audience immediately resumed weeping, as Layla detailed Zaynab's entrance into the prison of Yazid's palace. Another prisoner inquired, "How are 'ahl al-bayt?" and Zaynab responded that they were dead, but continued in a strong voice, "I, I am of 'ahl al-bayt, I am Zaynab, granddaughter of the Prophet Muhammad, sister of Imam Husayn, 'anā Zaynab!" This affirmation brought the weeping to a crescendo, after which Layla quietly ended her recitation. Faces were dried and tissues discarded as she blessed the house where we had gathered.

Then she instructed us to stand, face the direction of Husayn's tomb, and recite ziyārat al-ḥusayn. Layla then introduced a nudba, reciting its chorus twice so everyone could sing along. That marked the end, and Umm Ali's daughters were waiting with trays of coffee, rice pudding, fresh fruit juice, macaroons, and dates. Most women socialized before beginning to leave, commenting quietly on Layla's voice. One older woman noted that it wasn't very moving, to which her daughter responded, "Yes, but she was very clear."

The first discernable difference between these majālis is that of generation. Attendees at traditional majālis tended to be older, though privately held majālis often had a wider age spectrum as women invited relatives, friends, colleagues, and neighbors. Public majālis varied: in contrast to the ḥusayniyya described here, the nightly Hizbullah majlis in al-Dahiyya tended to attract younger women.[30]

Additionally, the responses of participants often varied by generation, with older women prone to more intense emotionality. In part this reflects differing attitudes towards Ashura, with authenticated majālis appealing to younger and more educated women. Some of the younger women I spoke with questioned older women's tears: "Some of them just go to cry, but they don't know why they are supposed to be crying. It's just tradition and habit. They go from majlis to majlis all day long crying. The recitor begins, you begin to cry; this is how it is for them. And worse, some of them are crying about ones they have lost, not Imam

---

[30] Crowds at different authenticated majālis differed as well: for example, Fadlullah majālis tended to attract slightly older and more intellectually oriented people, while Hizbullah majālis appealed to younger and more "revolutionary" attendees—in one woman's words "intifāḍa akthar" (more "intifada"). This also related to the more overt politics of Hizbullah majālis, as well as the difficulty older women had sitting on the ground for hours—Hizbullah majālis were long and so crowded that it was impossible to stretch one's legs once seated. Since I left Beirut, Hizbullah has built a new auditorium where majālis are now held.

Husayn." When I asked her how one should participate, she explained, "You should think about what the recitor is saying, and understand it, and then it will affect you and you will cry for the right reasons, because you understand the true meaning of it." Contrast an older woman's response: "During the *majlis*, I feel as though I am with them, in the same situation; in every moment, in every suffering, it's an internal feeling." I will return to the different experiences of temporality expressed here below.

The age difference between recitors is also significant along a traditional-authenticated spectrum. In addition to emphasizing the didactic elements, younger recitors were more likely to have formal training. For example, while both Hajjeh Fatima and Layla explained that they recite in order to express their love for 'ahl al-bayt, Hajjeh Fatima began reciting after seeing them in her dreams, while Layla began through her seminary studies.

Related to the difference in didactic emphasis is a common tension between clarity (*wuḍūḥ*) and tenderness/compassion (*ḥanān*) in recitations. Traditional recitors were generally praised for their ability to move people with the tone of their voices, sacrificing clarity for emotionality. For this reason, they sometimes used Iraqi poetry during their lamentations. Listeners may not have understood every word, but the style, tone, and symbolism alone were moving, as Iraqi was often characterized as the dialect of compassion and longing and the Iraqi tradition of Karbala poetry as richer than the Lebanese. In contrast, recitors who were concerned that their audiences understand every word of the recitation and its lessons preferred to use only the Lebanese dialect to ensure comprehensibility.

In both these *majālis*, indeed, in all *majālis*, powerful emotion is generated, but its extent and intensity varies. Women take emotional cues from the recitor though ultimately, the differences are individual ones. Generally, participants in authenticated *majālis* were inclined to more tempered expressions of sorrow.[31] These differences were reflected in the relative time recitors spent on the lamentation versus the sermon, and in the affect of the recitor herself. Every recitor I saw was clearly engaged emotionally in her recitation, yet older recitors often seemed to enter a trancelike state, where their grief emanated from them to wrap itself around the other participants. The narrations themselves also vary; each recitor chooses the poetry she will include, and traditional ones often

---

[31] In about half the *majālis* I attended, at least one older woman would shriek or faint, bringing quick attention from others, who attempted to comfort her. This was explained by saying the *majlis* "ghat 'ā 'alb[h]ā" (it hit her heart). Some people assumed she had lost someone in the Resistance or wars.

included bloodier descriptions of death and prolonged dramatic dialogue. As noted above, ultimately it is the order in which the two goals of *majālis* are prioritized that differs; one emphasizing mourning for *'ahl al-bayt* and its soteriological effects, and the other focusing on lessons to be learnt from their example and applied to life today. These life applications will be taken up in a moment, but first I turn briefly to the most striking difference in *majlis* content: the reinterpretation of Zaynab's behavior at Karbala.

REINTERPRETING SAYYIDA ZAYNAB

For many women the root of Ashura's lesson—as emphasized in authenticated *majālis*—lay in the reinterpretation of Zaynab's behavior during and following the battle:

> Before they would present Sayyida Zaynab as crying, screaming, wailing, but, no, Zaynab set the stage . . . for revolution against tyranny. She didn't mourn Husayn but thought how to save the rest and how to keep his message going. She was imprisoned, and yet she stood up with all confidence and spoke her point of view instead of feeling defeated. This changed our lives, we are now ashamed to feel weak, or to feel sorrow. Whenever we are faced with a problem, we remember the words, and feel shamed if we complain. No, we instead feel strong and deal with it and move on. (Hajjeh Umm Hadi)

Traditional narrations often portrayed Zaynab as buried in grief, pulling at her hair and shedding copious tears over the dead and dying. Advocates of authenticated *majālis* criticized these portrayals for their exaggerated emphasis on her tears. "Before, they would describe Sayyida Zaynab as crying and tearing her clothing. Now, the shaykhs, of course the ones who know, said that this is incorrect, and isn't mentioned at all. In fact, it's the opposite, she was in control of herself and wasn't affected emotionally in this way" (Suha).

Through authentication, representations that had depicted Zaynab as a plaintive mourner were transformed to renderings that accentuated her courage, strength, and resilience.[32] Zaynab became the person who "stood up in the face of the oppressor" and "told him that she was the victor." Her role as the Shi'i leader in captivity, and afterwards until Zayn al-'Abidin took his place as Imam, is highlighted in these accounts.

---

[32] Another interesting shift is that Zaynab is emphasized more than Fatima, who is often considered the paramount female model of piety in Shi'ism. This prioritization was particular to my interlocutors and not to the religious leadership. Fadlullah, for example, emphasizes *both* women as models for women's participation in the community's religious, political, and social life. See Rosiny (2001) for Fadlullah's views on Fatima. See also Pinault on representations of Zaynab as "defiant in defeat" (1998: 82–83).

It is Zaynab who carries the history of Ashura forward to future generations of Shi'i Muslims. As Hajjeh Umm Hadi's shifting tenses above indicate, as she described history's direct effect on contemporary lives, this reinterpretation has had major ramifications for the participation of pious women in the public arena. We have already seen these effects in women's visibility in authenticated Ashura masīras. Other effects—on women's participation in public discourse as well as in community service—will be taken up further below and in the following chapters. Suha's statement above also reveals the role of authoritative textual and historical interpretation in the authentication process: "the shaykhs, of course, the ones who know . . . said that this . . . isn't mentioned at all." Religious scholars reinterpreted the Ashura history to promote an activist stance in the present, shifting the dominant meaning of Ashura from mourning to revolution.

Meaning: From Mourning to Revolution

As can be inferred from these descriptions of majālis and masīras, grief and regret dominated "traditional" Ashura commemorations. Tears shed for 'ahl al-bayt are mustahabb, or religiously commendable. Both evoking these tears and shedding them are acts believed to impart 'ajr (divine reward), potentially increasing one's chances of entering heaven.[33] Blood spilled in memory of Karbala is similarly an embodiment of grief and an empathetic expression of solidarity with the Imam's pain and sorrow. Yet it can also express regret or remorse. Some people who defended self-injurious latam explained that it demonstrated their regret for not being at Karbala with the Imam—a reference to those Shi'is who originally asked Husayn to lead their revolution but then failed to arrive in time to either protect him or die with him. This can also represent a generalized remorse for all the times in one's life when one did not live up to Husayn's example.

In the context of pre-1970s Lebanon, when Shi'i Muslims were the least politically organized group in the country, all of these meanings can be seen as stemming from Shi'i political quietism. Even al-Amin's early reform efforts did not criticize weeping, and in fact encouraged it as fostering Shi'i identity and promoting salvation.[34] The emphasis during Ashura was on personal and embodied religious experiences of mourning, as well as on the reinforcement of community identity built around shared sorrow and suffering rather than political activism. While at first

[33] See Aghaie 2001, Ayoub 1978, Pinault 1992 and 2001, and Schubel 1993 on the redemptive and intercessory importance of mourning the Karbala events.
[34] See Nakash 1993.

glance the association of blood with quietism may seem contradictory, in this instance, violence is directed at the self, not outwards, implying a personal expression of grief, an internal struggle with regret, and the potential for individual salvation, rather than collective political or social action.[35]

It is less clear whether traditional commemorations since the Shi'i mobilization connote a similar quietism—certainly for some participants they did, while for others tears and blood demonstrated their readiness for self-sacrifice for the community. In Nabatieh in 2000, many of the people watching and weeping around me commented that the display of self-injurious *laṭam* demonstrated their youths' readiness to defend the community and resist the Israeli occupation.

Yet from the perspective of those who advocated for "authenticated" meanings and practices, blood and too many tears are un-Islamic and passive: "Too much crying leads to personalities who cry. The Shi'a will take on crying as a cultural trait, and this is wrong. Emotions are necessary, but they should be understood as a way to learn Husayn's lesson. The heart should be used to reach the head, not as an end point in and of itself" (a shaykh). This is a reflection of Fadlullah's views on the matter. His campaign to reform Ashura—as explicated by this shaykh—involves several issues: First, he emphasizes choosing "appropriate" (meaning educated and "cultured" [*muthaqqaf*]) recitors and appropriate (meaning logical and unexaggerated) material for *majālis*. He also suggests incorporating alternate forms into commemoration, such as plays and art. Basic to Fadlullah's reforms is the discouragement of *shawā'ib* (defects or impurities) in Ashura, especially self-injurious *laṭam*. The final element—one that few religious leaders espouse—is criticism of the act of crying itself, as reflected in the shaykh's statement above.

Fadlullah's perspective is located toward the far end of the authentication spectrum and was seen as too extreme by some.[36] Hizbullah members, who often cited Nasrallah's viewpoint in contrast, sometimes criticized Fadlullah for overintellectualizing Ashura and placing too much emphasis on knowledge, understanding, and application: "It's not just a philosophy, it's not just knowledge, it's not just a phenomenon, it is a feeling, an emotion, the embodiment (*tajsīd*) of meaning. It's not just mind (*'aql*) it is also emotion (*'āṭif*). People have to *feel* with Husayn." But Fadlullah's critics also noted that the difference was one of relative

---

[35] Contrast Hegland's (1987) observation that in the community where she did research in Iran self-injurious flagellation was revived during the revolution as a form of political resistance.

[36] See also Fadlullah's sermons and lectures, available in Arabic and sometimes English via www.bayynat.org.

emphasis, that Hizbullah also valued knowledge and understanding more than those who espoused traditional commemorative forms. In their view, however, they sought a balance between mind and emotion. As we will see below, this may relate to the very practical links between Ashura and Hizbullah's Islamic Resistance.

Accompanying the discouragement of traditional practices and emphases was a redirection of Ashura's message outwards, away from personal meaning. This is not to say that notions of *'ajr* and salvation have been stripped from Ashura, but rather that the primary tone of the commemorations has been altered. Indeed, those who champion authentication insisted that *'ajr* comes from attending or holding *majālis* and from remembrance, but *not* from the act of crying itself. The affective and the collective coexist in all Ashura commemorations—the former located in private emotional experiences of piety, and the latter bridging shared experiences and meanings—but their proportion and ordering are being rearranged.

In the context of war and deprivation, as Lebanese Shi'is mobilized socially and militarily, the message of revolution in the events of Muharram was highlighted.[37] The energy and emotive power contained in the commemorations was redirected and focused onto a shared set of goals. Emphasizing historical accuracy and evidence was crucial to this process: when myth was stripped away, the "authentic" historical record revealed that Husayn's martyrdom took place in a context of revolution.

As understood in al-Dahiyya, this revolution was a moral one.[38] Many Shi'is do not believe that Husayn went to Karbala intending to overthrow Yazid's regime, but rather, that he went with foreknowledge of his own death. His victory is rooted in this conscious self-sacrifice. As a young volunteer at the SAA explained to me: "Gandhi used to say, 'I

---

[37] Fischer describes this process for the Iranian revolution, which he characterizes as "the ultimate passion play of the Karbala paradigm" (1980: 183). That success and what Hegland (1983) calls the " 'Imam Husain as Example' framework" fueled this reinterpretation in Lebanon. See also Aghaie 2001, Momen 1985, Mottahedeh 1985, Peters 1956, and Thaiss 1972 on the political meanings of Ashura in various contexts. See Shryock 1997 and Gilsenan 1996 on the practical uses of historical narratives in other Middle Eastern contexts.

[38] Here "revolution" or *thawra* (it is used in both languages) refers to rebelling against a situation of oppression, and attempting to reorder the world in order to make it a better place. This meaning differs subtly from the post–French Revolution notion of "revolution" as "an attempt rationally to design a new political order" (Donham 1999: 1; see also Koselleck 1985). Yet there are also links to this second notion—especially via Iran, and no doubt related to Shari'ati and others who were influenced by Marxism. See also AbuKhalil's cogent comparison of Hizbullah with Leninist groups; he writes that Hizbullah is "an Islamic adaptation to the era of Leninist revolutionary organizations" (1991: 394).

learned from Husayn how to be oppressed and be victorious.' It's true that Imam Husayn was oppressed and was killed, yet he was victorious. After he was killed, people became aware by way of his death. His death was wisdom for people. After he died, people learned, they saw the truth."

The revolution's fundamental lesson was that one must always stand up to one's oppressor, because only through resistance is freedom possible. This lesson was explained to me again and again, often in terms that exploded spatial and temporal boundaries. In the words of a recitor:

> In every era there is an oppressor and an oppressed. And this history always repeats itself, throughout all eras. Ashura reminds us of this, so we will never forget that there is a Yazid and a Husayn in every time, in every nation, in every government, and people should always have the spirit of revolution against oppression, in all its faces, no matter what its identity. . . . Oppression doesn't have a specific identity; it is general, it exists all over the world, in all confessions, in all religions. People should have this spirit of revolution against oppression because time repeats itself, history repeats itself, and in every age there is injustice.

Every single pious Shi'i Muslim with whom I spoke emphasized the universality and importance of this message. *"Ab'ād karbalā' tārīkhiyya"* (the dimensions of Karbala are historical), one Hizbullah member said passionately, "Without Karbala there would be no revolution! Karbala is for all the world, what Husayn did was stand against oppression!"

This shift in Ashura's meaning from the soteriological to the revolutionary suggests a parallel shift in understandings of time. Traditional Ashura commemorations involve reexperiencing the battle each year, as though one were there with the Imam; in a sense, time is captured at this essential and essentializing moment in Shi'i history. In contrast, authenticated commemorations' emphasis on the revolutionary implies linear temporal change, lessons to be learned from history but applied towards the future, reflecting a commitment to progress. Yet temporality also reveals a peculiarity of the spiritual aspect of the two-pronged notion of progress. While pious Shi'is advocated working towards revolutionary change in the near future, they also believed that the far future is not unknown, and will eventually bring the return of Hidden Imam on Judgment Day. In this case, as discussed in the introduction, secular linear time has its limits.

A Juxtaposition of Moderns

Pious Shi'is viewed authenticated Ashura meanings and practices as distinctly modern. To some, this may seem paradoxical, because it insists that religion can be modern.[39] Yet this concern dissipates when we recall that it is the dominance of particular discourses of the modern itself that pious Shi'is called into question. By linking specific religious interpretations to modern-ness, they constructed an alternate discourse through which "modern" is defined. Within this alternate discourse—the discourse of the pious modern—authenticated Ashura represents spiritual progress.

Rather than a paradox, what we have here is an illustration of the complexity surrounding notions of modern-ness. By constructing the pious modern in part through a constructed distinction between "traditional" and "authenticated" forms, pious Shi'is reified a new binary. What is now categorized as traditional is set "behind" what is understood to be authentic, creating forward movement, or spiritual progress. Adding to this complexity are the ways people deployed multiple discourses of the modern simultaneously in order to highlight their community's progress. The key elements that differentiate authenticated from traditional commemorations—condemning self-injurious *laṭam*, removing myth and exaggeration from *majālis*, de-emphasizing Zaynab's tears, and prioritizing revolutionary meaning over soteriological—were established as modern within multiple frameworks. On the one hand, they were cited to emphasize an enchanted modern: Historical and textual accuracy leads to greater religious understanding, which leads to spiritual progress. Revolutionary meaning leads to communal solidarity and activism. And Zaynab—pious, caring, strong, and outspoken—is a role model for women in the Shi'i Islamic movement.

Yet on the other hand, the modern-ness of these same elements was claimed through a definitional framework that was understood to be western. Attempts were made to establish the community as equally modern/civilized as the West according to local perceptions of western standards of judgment. The global field of power relations impinged upon the reformulation of Ashura commemorations. For example, when Khamenei issued his 1994 *fatwa* condemning self-injurious *laṭam*, he did not cite only the un-Islamic nature of the practice, but also the negative image of Islam that rituals involving blood project both within and outside the Islamic community.[40] This speaks directly to stereotypes among

[39] Conflicts over what constitutes authentic or "real" tradition frequently involve the use, sometimes counterintuitively, of discourses of modernity by one or more of the parties involved. Cf. Donham's discussion of the initial interpretation of the Ethiopian Marxist revolution in Maale as a vindication of tradition (1999: 59–81).

[40] See Pinault 2001. Similar notions may have partly motivated al-Amin in the 1920s. Ende (1978) notes that his critique included reference to mockery and criticism from other religious communities.

non-Shi'i Lebanese associating traditional *laṭam* with "backwardness" and "barbarism."

For most of my interlocutors most of the time, however, the authentication of Ashura commemorations represented their progress away from both the "backwardness" they saw in tradition and the immorality they saw in the West. Authenticated Ashura was the continuation of the community through tradition,[41] but in a new form, a form perceived by its adherents as more coherent and apropos to the contemporary world.

In the second part of this chapter, I discuss the relationship between authenticated forms of Ashura and public piety. I first consider the emergence of Ashura in public spaces and the role of public discourses in the authentication process. Then I conclude with a discussion of how authenticated Ashura, with its emphasis on activism, provides role models for pious men and women in martyrdom and community service, respectively.

LIVING AUTHENTICATED ASHURA

> The slogans of Karbala are the slogans of life in its entirety. . . .
> Living Ashura is standing against oppression. Such a stand
> should fill our hearts and minds each time we face the
> oppressors and arrogant powers, whether in Muslim countries
> or in the whole world. It is not living in a tragedy of tears and
> hitting ourselves with swords or chains . . . for swords should
> be raised against the enemy as we were taught by the Imam
> (pbuh).
>
> — Sayyid Muhammad Husayn Fadlullah,
> sermon commemorating Imam Husayn, 2003

Ashura in Public Spaces and Discourses

Authenticated forms of Ashura commemoration were the standard in al-Dahiyya, especially among those who followed Fadlullah and/or supported Hizbullah. Concomitant with the transformations of practice and

---

[41] The importance of temporal continuity to identity cross-culturally is discussed by Kratz (1993). She notes that what may be perceived by the external observer as change in tradition is understood by Okiek as continuity in the *process* of change in tradition. Certain arenas may be simultaneously domains of continuity and change depending on one's point of observation. With regard to Ashura, I would posit that Lebanese Shi'is held the notions of continuity and change in mind simultaneously, switching between them depending on how broad a notion of history was being discussed.

meaning discussed above, the relationship between Ashura and public space has changed. This is especially apparent with regard to *majālis*. While *majālis* continued to be held in homes, loudspeakers and microphones guaranteed that they would be heard throughout buildings, streets, and neighborhoods. Public *majālis* themselves are not new—as evidenced by the long history of Nabatieh's annual commemorations, and the *majālis* held in the al-Khansa' family *husayniyya* in al-Dahiyya since the 1930s. Yet the numbers of both private and public *majālis*—and the levels of attendance at them—have increased dramatically.

In addition to public *majālis* at mosques, *husayniyyas*, and more recently, *jam'iyyas*, since the mid-1990s *majālis* have been held in tents constructed by Hizbullah and Amal in parking lots and other empty spaces around Beirut. Most prominent among them is the main Hizbullah "tent" in al-Dahiyya, from which the party televised *majālis* from 1995 until a new hall was constructed in 2002,[42] and where Nasrallah spoke on alternate nights. In 2000 and 2001, construction of this "tent"—really a huge enclosed structure that incorporated a major road and adjacent lots—started over a week before Muharram. Security guards lined the roofs of nearby buildings and patrolled adjoining streets and alleyways. The *majālis* began on the eve of 1 Muharram, and as the tenth of the month approached, the growing crowd of approximately ten thousand attendees a night spilled beyond the tent onto curbs and sidewalks. Additionally, no less than fifty-one Hizbullah-sponsored *majālis* were held in Beirut alone in 2001.[43] While it is difficult to estimate attendance at these *majālis*, major Lebanese newspapers agree that "several hundred thousand" people participated in the 2000 and 2001 *masīras*, while Al-Manār television estimated two hundred thousand marchers in 2001.

The visual environment was markedly altered during Ashura as well, as described in chapter 1. The black banners hanging over streets read "Husayn is from/of me and I am from/of Husayn" (*husayn minnī wa 'anā min husayn*); "Every day is Ashura, every place is Karbala"; "All that we have is from Karbala"; "The Resistance is our Karbala and Khamenei is our leader." An aura of mourning was palpable; people spoke quietly, laughter was frowned upon in the *jam'iyyas*. Many made an effort to dress in black or other somber colors; indeed, the preponderance of black everywhere strikingly distinguished al-Dahiyya from the rest of Beirut during Muharram. This was considered a positive development because it expressed respect for Husayn through "public sadness."

[42] Hizbullah held their first public *majlis* in 1993 at a *jam'iyya*, later moving it to the "tent."

[43] Based on the announcements in *Al-'Ahd*.

Ashura's expansion indicates a broader public exposure to and participation in the articulation and use of authenticated Ashura discourses as well as in the production of authenticity itself. One aspect of this involves new religious and political mass media. While these media provide wider access to the officially produced discourses of sayyids and shaykhs, they also afford wider participation in the production of Ashura discourses, through a plethora of call-in radio shows for both adults and children and television ranging from Karbala-inspired serials to documentaries about Ashura-inspired poetry. One radio program addressed to children posed questions about the Ashura history, for example, "How many people went with Imam Husayn to Karbala?" Children then called in and received prizes for correct answers.[44]

Ashura discourses are also constructed through informal conversations—the daily talk among pious women and men discussed in the previous chapter. Quite a few of these conversations—principally during and immediately after Ashura—contributed to the authentication of particular Ashura narratives. For women in particular, participation in the authentication process was in keeping with Zaynab's reformulated role at Karbala—as the bearer of the message of revolution to others. Whether over coffee in a neighbor's kitchen, or en route to or from a *majlis*, women often debated the historical accuracy of details of the events of Karbala.[45] For example, Aziza and her neighbor once discussed at length whether it could be corroborated that Husayn had given his young daughter Ruqayya a cup before his death, telling her that it would turn black inside if he were killed. Some of these conversations were sparked by skepticism toward a specific recitor, others triggered by discord between the version of an episode recited in a *majlis* just attended and the version broadcast over the radio in the car on the way home.

Women's debates about the authenticity of particular narratives and details also reflect the tension that exists between "traditional" and "authenticated," and the constant reformulations and renegotiations that ensue. This was demonstrated in a conversation I had with three women at Aziza's one afternoon during Ashura about changes in a local *ḥusayniyya*'s

[44] As Eickelman and Anderson discuss, these media become more participatory as the asymmetries between producers and consumers are reduced, and "the boundaries between public and private communication that once seemed clear become blurred" (1999b: 4). Here, blurring occurred as telephone calls brought conversations that were once privately held into the public arena via radio.

[45] While some of these conversations no doubt were prompted by the necessity of assuring that the anthropologist present recorded the "correct" version of the Imam's martyrdom, as indeed I was urged to do, heated conversations during which I was not present were frequently related to me after the fact, and on several occasions I joined discussions of *majālis* details already in progress.

presentation of the *majlis* about Husayn's nephew Qasim. The conversation began with Aziza relating how the *husayniyya* had stopped including Qasim's wedding in the *majlis* devoted to him for a period of two years, because it had been found to be "inaccurate." During those two years, two members of the family that owned the *husayniyya* had died, leading their relatives superstitiously to reinstate the wedding. At this point I announced that I had no idea what Aziza was talking about by *'urs qāsim* (Qasim's wedding), provoking a long and contested explanation that continued through the next afternoon when Rasha took me aside to insist that the details she had provided were the most accurate.

In sum, Qasim was betrothed to Husayn's daughter.[46] "Before," in traditional *majālis*, just before Qasim's martyrdom is narrated, their wedding was enacted, and flowers and sweets passed around the *husayniyya*. The juxtaposition of the wedding with death, not only Qasim's death almost immediately afterwards, but also that of the bride's brother Ali al-Akbar just before, served to significantly heighten emotionality. However, Hajjeh Umm Zein asserted that reformers had criticized the wedding reenactment on the grounds that it is illogical that the marriage would have actually taken place during such sadness and war. Aziza corrected this, explaining that no one believed the marriage actually happened at all, but that because Qasim died while engaged, during Ashura people would enact a wedding for him, as a tribute to what should have come to pass but did not. Then Rasha chimed in, saying that this had also been criticized by some advocates of authentication, who think that the wedding enactments constitute a false addition to the narrative, and as such should be avoided. She eventually concluded: *"bas nās baddun l-'urs, li'annū hay at-taqlīd, fa-ba'dun byamlū bil-husayniyyeh"* (but people want the wedding, because this is the tradition, so they still do it at the *husayniyya*).

In their long debate, the three women's constant corrections of one another confirmed the continual process by which authenticated Ashura narratives are being shaped. Researching and understanding the most accurate history of Karbala was not a task left only to religious scholars, but was one in which lay persons participated actively. Here we again see the difference between contemporary authentication and al-Amin's reform efforts in the 1920s. Crucially, the current authentication of Ashura meanings and commemorations was included by many people as part of the revolution itself. In the words of one woman:

> Those who killed Imam Husayn were victorious in battle. He died, didn't he? And the women suffered? But if we look over history, he was victorious. Who

---

[46] For a detailed description of an Iranian version of the *majlis* (and "wedding") of Qasim, see Humayuni 1979.

is mentioned? It is rare that history will mention those who killed him. But Imam Husayn is the hero. And this is increasing. Why? Because the understanding is being more deeply rooted. For example, in some places they read the *majlis* in a way that we call backward, reactionary, we don't accept this. We are trying to develop it to truly manifest the truth of Ashura and maintain it as a historically understood event, a liberatory event, an event about the continuity of humanity.

This participation in the authentication process is one way in which not only revolutionary activism, but public piety (as discursive piety) can also be manifested. Public piety is additionally linked to Ashura through the translation of the message and values taught in the commemorations into models for contemporary daily life.[47] The Karbala paradigm "provides models for living and a mnemonic for thinking about how to live" (Fischer 1980: 21). While traditional forms of commemoration involve embodying emotion in blood and tears, authenticated forms involve embodiment through realized activism. In Ashura "the world as lived and the world as imagined are fused together" (Nakash 1993: 162). The final section of this chapter explores that fusion.

Sacrificing Blood, Sacrificing Sweat

The most obvious parallels between Ashura and currently lived experience for many pious Shi'is were with the Islamic Resistance. Indeed, the battle of Karbala was explicitly linked to contemporary instances of injustice and oppression in Lebanon, especially the Israeli occupation.[48] This association was unequivocally articulated in one woman's description of her experience of the moment when Hizbullah leader Sayyid Abbas al-Musawi and his wife and five-year-old son were martyred in 1992:

> I was in the south, and it was a beautiful day, cold and sunny, like today. My son was a baby, and they told me it was good to walk him in the sunshine, so I went outside to walk with him. Then I saw a plane. It was normal in that area; the Israelis flew over us many times a day, and they were bombing regularly. But this plane flew out towards the coast, and, I don't know why, or what was different about it, but suddenly, suddenly, it occurred to me that this

---

[47] Fischer notes the emphasis, within the Karbala paradigm, on the Prophet's family as models for behavior (1980: 13).

[48] Another highly relevant parallel is made with the current U.S. occupation of Iraq. In his speech on the fortieth-day commemoration of Husayn's martyrdom in 2003, Nasrallah stated, "Why are these millions going to Karbala? To be inspired by Hussein's spirit of revolution to fight injustice" (quoted in the *Daily Star*, April 23, 2003).

plane was from Yazid! That this was Yazid, and Yazid didn't care about children; he killed Sayyida Zaynab's young child without caring. And when this occurred to me, I held my son close and ran back into the house quickly with him. I felt so scared for him, as though this plane was going to kill my son. And later that day I learned that that same plane, the plane that I had seen, was the plane that killed Sayyid Abbas and his son.

Just as Yazid was equated with Israel—an association underscored in 1983 when the Israeli army disrupted the Ashura commemorations in Nabatieh—the Islamic Resistance was equated with Husayn. Hizbullah nurtured these associations directly. For example, at the end of a play about the captives of Karbala—performed by students at a Hizbullah school and sponsored by the party's Women's Committee—segments were shown from Al-Manār television. Aside from clips of the *masīra* and Nasrallah's speeches, there were scenes of Resistance operations, with a booming voice-over: "This is our Karbala, this is our Husayn, we live on, Karbala lives on in the Lebanese Resistance."

A Hizbullah *jam'iyya* administrator tied the authentication process to Liberation:

> Every year there is progress. This is the greatness of Imam Husayn and his revolution. One thousand and four hundred years ago, imagine that, and today someone says "Imam Husayn" and begins to cry. This is the spirit. It needs someone to embody it. There are those who say "I have my faith in my heart." Faith in the heart is not enough; faith is in the heart and in work. Feelings without work are not enough. In the end, embodiment is in work. This is the revolution of Imam Husayn. Truly, who thought that the Islamic Resistance would be victorious? The day the Zionists left, they didn't leave by themselves, and they didn't leave voluntarily, they withdrew defeated. Who thought that would happen?

Those who were not in Hizbullah also linked Ashura and the Resistance. One man related an anecdote about his response to a radio journalist:

> In that way, a skeptic, he asked me, "What did Husayn do?" I was silent for a while, I said, let's finish our coffee first. And I said to him after we finished our coffee, "If I tell you on the air what I know about Husayn, it will take hours, and if I go and do some more research and then tell you, it will take three months. But you are asking what Husayn did?" I said, "He made Jabal Safi and the Western Beqaa, he is sitting up there." And he shut up.

The two places this man mentions—Jabal Safi and the Western Beqaa— were Israeli outposts in Lebanon that were retaken by the Resistance. All the parallels drawn between the battle of Karbala and the Resistance

4.7. Ashura banner; it reads "Historical Karbala changes the face of history today."

blur Husayn with the Resistance fighters. In this context, Imam Husayn was the ideal role model for pious Shi'i men. In Lebanon since the early 1980s, that has clearly translated to participation in the Resistance. This participation may be either military or supportive—working in a *jam'iyya*, rebuilding homes destroyed in Israeli attacks, or teaching in a *hawza*, just to cite a few examples—depending on one's age, abilities, and disposition.

My field research did not include participation-observation of Resistance activities and none of my interlocutors—to my knowledge—were currently fighters with the Resistance. The perspective I am able to provide here is rather that of the wider community in al-Dahiyya. Pious Shi'is held martyrs and their families in the highest esteem and frequently credited them with making the greatest possible sacrifice for the freedom and integrity of their community. Martyrs' names were announced and known. They were memorialized in the photographs that line the streets, in newspapers, and on radio and television. Every day Hizbullah's radio station listed those who died on that day in past years. Al-Manār television interviewed martyrs' families—who always spoke of their pride and faith—and broadcast video messages taped by martyrs before death.[49] Exhibits displayed writings and other "martyr artifacts" (athār al-shuhadā'), which are being collected by a special department at the Martyrs' Association until a museum is built to house them.[50]

None of this is very different from the esteem in which members of the U.S. armed forces are held when they give their lives for their country. The names and photographs of soldiers killed in action are broadcast on local television, and their families are sometimes interviewed, also speaking of them with pride and frequently with faith. Local memorials are held, as well as national ceremonies in Washington, DC. On March 17, 2003, in a speech about the imminent invasion of Iraq, President George W. Bush stated, "War has no certainty except the certainty of sacrifice." Because the wars fought by the United States take place in far away places, and because of the scale of the United States more generally, it is easy to forget how personal that sacrifice is. In al-Dahiyya, and Lebanon more generally, the places seen on television are familiar and the faces are often recognized.

Two small differences that could be suggested are the definitions of the communities, and the motivations underlying soldiers' sacrifices. In the first case, it could be argued that the community the U.S. armed forces serves is a nation-state, while that of the Islamic Resistance should instead be defined on either a local or transnational level. However, the ultimate goal of the Resistance has been the liberation of an occupied

---

[49] Al-Manār also broadcasted video of Resistance military operations. These videos are replete with video noise and a black-and-white grittiness that serves to underscore the "truth and reality" of the images. When I asked a Hizbullah representative why they videotaped their operations, he said that it was to counter Israeli claims that denied the effects of the Resistance on their outposts.

[50] This department was filled with binders holding martyrs' last statements, letters, essays, journal entries, philosophical writings, and poetry. Most of the documents were handwritten, some were typed, and a few had been published. One martyr had written a play.

nation-state, and especially in recent years it has cast itself—and been cast by the Lebanese state—as a *national* resistance movement.[51]

The other potential difference, and the one emphasized most often by the U.S. media, involves the underlying motivations for self-sacrifice and the notion of going willingly to one's death. This is not the place for a detailed comparison of soldiers who die in wars and those who die in martyrdom operations,[52] so I limit myself to two brief points. First, only twelve Resistance martyrs died in martyrdom operations. Most were "killed in action" as are members of military forces anywhere. Second, the issue of motivation is complex. For fighters with the Islamic Resistance, Husayn's model provided inspiration—because he went to his death knowingly, unafraid, and with faith that his death was part of a greater victory. Pious Shi'i men who chose to sacrifice themselves in martyrdom operations are understood as having had absolute faith in the value of their deaths and in the afterlife. I do not know about faith in the U.S. armed forces, though I imagine that it varies widely. However, it is important to note that within Lebanon, Islamic Resistance fighters are not the only people who have undertaken martyrdom operations. As we are seeing in Palestine today, resistance fighters with secular organizations also sacrifice themselves for their nation. In Lebanon, martyrdom operations against Israeli Occupation Force targets were carried out by Palestinian resistance groups, the Syrian Social National Party, the Lebanese Communist Party, the Arab Socialist Ba'ath Party, and the Progressive Socialist Party, in addition to Hizbullah and Amal.[53]

While some martyrs in both the Lebanese—and as highlighted in recent news reports—the Palestinian resistances have been women, the translation of Husayn's martyrdom into a model for military participation was directed exclusively at men.[54] This is not to say that Husayn did not also provide a model for women with regard to general self-sacrifice for one's community. However, for women, the paragon of piety and sacrifice that emerges from Ashura was embodied instead in Sayyida Zaynab.

In the reformulation of Zaynab's behavior at Karbala described above, three characteristics are emphasized: her strength of mind, her

---

[51] See Munson (2003) on nationalism and Islamic movements.

[52] Martyrdom operations, *'amaliyāt istishhādiyya*, are military operations where a fighter's death is a planned aspect of the operation, what the U.S. media often refers to as "suicide attacks." Another possible translation is "self-sacrifice operations."

[53] See AbuKhalil 1991.

[54] Lebanese women martyrs were from secular parties. Recently, Fadlullah has stated, in reference to the Palestinian struggle, that there are situations in which women can carry out martyrdom operations.

compassion and dedication to others, and her courage to speak. The first of these was especially important to women's expected role as the mothers, wives, or sisters of martyrs. Women who had lost loved ones to the occupation frequently pointed to Zaynab's ability to endure similar loss. They explained that they coped with their grief by emulating Zaynab's equanimity during and after Karbala. They compared their losses to hers, and in so doing, expressed feeling that they had lost little in comparison: "We didn't lose everyone, like Sayyida Zaynab did. We have to say, if she could go on, why can't we? And we at least have role models; there is acknowledgment in society for the mothers of martyrs, the Sayyida had none of that."

Being the mother—or the wife or sister—of a martyr was valued among pious Shi'is, and many whose family members had been martyred carried their loss as an honor:

> I am the wife of a martyr. He left me two children and I am responsible for them. When he was martyred, my son was one year and two months old and my daughter five days old. And of course sometimes it's difficult; of course, life is difficult, but I say to myself, once in a while, thanks be to God that God honored me by allowing me to be a martyr's wife and to raise a martyr's children, and to carry the message of Imam Husayn and Sayyida Zaynab. (a volunteer)

Although Zaynab's model provided strength for women who had lost loved ones, this was not the area in which her positive qualities were most frequently stressed. Significantly, the model of Zaynab—particularly her compassion and outspokenness—was understood to be a model for public activism, an important addition to the relatively passive role of "mother of a martyr" often delegated to women in nationalist and religious struggles.[55] One arena where this new emphasis can be seen is in the Ashura commemorations. As described above, women participated actively in authenticated *masīras*. They also contributed to the authentication process itself through daily conversations and debates about Ashura. The significance of this shift for gender activism and roles, and its relationship to notions of the pious modern, will be taken up further in chapter 6.

First, however, I want to turn to the primary vehicle through which pious Shi'i women live Ashura in their daily lives: community service. The reinterpretation of Zaynab as able to act despite her grief and the turmoil of her surroundings played an important role in inspiring hundreds

[55] For more on women's role as mothers of martyrs, see Peteet (1991) on Palestinian women and Kamalkhani (1998) on Iranian women.

of women in al-Dahiyya to volunteer their time and energy—a sacrifice of sweat—for the welfare of their community. As we will see, volunteering in a *jam'iyya* has been incorporated as a crucial aspect of public piety for Shi'i women. The next chapter takes up women's Islamic community service activities, and the ideas behind their activism. Essential among them, as this volunteer reminds us, is Ashura:

> In the *majālis* we become renewed, we are reminded. Society might be asleep, in deep sleep, and this school, these lessons enter them, and wake them up, say, "Get up, help others. Get up and see the corruption, get up and see the oppression, be mindful of your society, take care of it, become aware of it, of yourself, of other people, of your nation. See where your country is, it is occupied! See how the people of the south are suffering, how people from all sects are fleeing, are being bombed, their homes are being destroyed. What is going to be your position on this?" This is the school. This is Ashura.

CHAPTER FIVE

Community Commitment

> In the Name of God, the Most Gracious, the Most Merciful
> Have you seen the one who denies Religion [*dīn*]?
> That is the one who refuses the orphan,
> And urges not the feeding of the poor,
> So woe unto those who pray (hypocritically)
> Those who delay their prayer,
> Those who do good deeds only to be seen,
> And prevent *al-mā'ūn* [small kindnesses].
> —*Sūrat al-Mā'ūn*, The Qur'an

November 30, 2000

The traffic was insane today, though Aziza assures me this is typical of Ramadan. By the time I arrived at the Center, it was already 11 a.m. Hajjeh Huda, Dalal, and Aziza were in the front distribution area, going over paperwork, and the women in the back "kitchen"—mostly poor women helping out for modest pay or to take food home to their families—had already begun cooking today's meal. As I waved hello, a delivery truck pulled up, full of boxes of vegetables being donated by a local grocer, so Aziza and I joined in unloading and sorting the boxes in the kitchen. When we finished, I walked around to the front and greeted Hajjeh Huda and Dalal, as well as Alia, Hajjeh Rim, and Noor, who had arrived in the meantime. While Hajjeh Huda, Dalal, and Alia continued organizing paperwork, going over carefully recorded donation records, and discussing next week's meals, the rest of us divided bags of bread and sweets as they were delivered, and distributed salad greens and vegetables into plastic bags that held family-sized portions. Spirits were high today—not always a given when everyone has been fasting since before sunrise—and we chatted and joked as we worked, taking short breaks now and then. During one break, a wealthy woman walked in carrying several bags of wheat. We didn't notice her at first, until Hajjeh Huda called out, "Aziza, Lara, yalla, take the stuff from Madame!"

Gradually other volunteers joined us, each woman calling out a greeting as she jumped into whatever task was being done at that moment. A few new volunteers came, including Hajjeh Mariam and her niece, who had visited the Center for the first time yesterday. Hajjeh Huda always made a point of greeting new faces, introducing them around, and helping them find a place

5.1. Cooking at the Ramadan Center.

where they could easily join the work. As always, time flew by, and by the time the prep work was done, it was only a couple hours before *iftār*. Dalal had set up the donations table at the front entrance, and a steady stream of donors was keeping her busy. One woman, probably a first-time donor, was given a quick tour by Alia. A small group of very well-dressed women gathered near the donation table, chatting and watching the activity around them. Some were less active members of the *jam'iyya*, and others I had not seen before—but I assumed (correctly) from their inactivity and dress that they were donors or potential donors. A short while later, someone had organized these women into a circle, and given them big bags of peas to shell for the next day's meal, cleverly transforming them from spectators to participants in the project.

Meanwhile, across the Center, women (and a few men) from poor families were filling the waiting room. They registered their names with

Alia,[1] who was seated at the table that formed the "wall" between the partitioned-off waiting area and the front room. Periodically, voices would rise, and Hajjeh Huda would call for patience. Today she had brought a bag of "worry beads" that she passed out when tempers seemed short. Later, she brought bags of fresh beans and peas to the waiting room and had women there shell them to pass the time cooperatively and productively as well.

Eventually, a women from the kitchen told us that the food—today a beef and vegetable stew with rice—was ready. This is when things got hectic. We quickly formed an assembly line, some ladling food from the huge pots where it had been cooked into plastic containers, others sealing the containers and bringing them to the front. Several children ran back and forth transporting the containers, adding an element of chaos. In the front, four of us began filling *ḥuṣa*s (literally, shares), larger plastic bags that held full meals. Into each *ḥuṣa* went stew and rice, bread, sweets, salad vegetables, and a two-liter bottle of soda. We took the *ḥuṣa*s either to the distribution table where Hajjeh Huda stood with Noor, or to the Center's entrance, where a few drivers would come and pick up *ḥuṣa*s to be distributed to families unable to make the trip. As the *ḥuṣa*s were filled, Alia began calling people from the waiting room to the distribution table, where Hajjeh Huda and Noor handed them their *ifṭār* meal. Hajjeh Huda knew many of the families, so she often modified the *ḥuṣa* slightly, adding extra food for larger ones, or sweets for those with many children.

There were a few moments when rising voices filled the Center, indicating that order had been broken. Frantically running around filling *ḥuṣa*s, our only hint at this was these voices, Hajjeh Huda's above all, as she somehow managed to calm everyone's—by this time, very hungry—nerves and remedy whatever situation had arisen. Today one of these moments occurred when a group of waiting people rushed Alia all at once. At another moment a woman began complaining loudly at her bag's contents, provoking Dalal to scold her for being ungrateful. In the midst of the distribution process, another donation arrived (there is always a lot of food on Thursdays, because it's the eve of Friday): ten huge boxes of *lahm b'ajin*. We quickly began packaging it and taking it to Hajjeh Huda, who added it to the *ḥuṣa*s. Finally, just about twenty minutes before the call to prayer that would mark the end of the day's fast, all the food was distributed and the waiting room empty. Noor gave the few remaining bags of *lahm b'ajin* to a Syrian laborer who had been standing

---

[1] On a person's initial visit, her name and address were recorded, and she was asked questions about her status, financial situation, and number of people in her household. During Ramadan that year she received food every third day. After Ramadan, volunteers visited the household to assess its situation, at which point the family might become a "regularly assisted" family.

around for much of the afternoon, obviously hoping for a handout. The women working in the kitchen had long since finished washing the pots and setting up for the next day, and had taken their *ḥuṣa*s and headed home for *ifṭār*.

On most days the volunteers would have done the same, rushing home amidst the traffic, which grew more chaotic as the call to prayer approached. Today, however, was the annual fund-raising *ifṭār* for the *jamʿiyya*. Instead of hurrying home, we all changed into nicer shoes and piled into cars to brave the bumper-to-bumper route to the nearby hotel where the *ifṭār* was to be held. We arrived just as the call to prayer resounded, and made our way to the downstairs ballroom. The President of the *jamʿiyya*, along with Hajjeh Huda and Hajjeh Rim, greeted guests at the entrance. We quickly found seats at a table in the nearly full room. There were around three hundred women there, about 75 percent of them *muḥajjaba*.

As we ate, the *jamʿiyya*'s president walked to the podium on the small stage at one end of the hall, flanked by the Lebanese and *jamʿiyya* flags. After a few words of welcome, she spoke about the necessity of community service in "developing" and "raising the level" of society, and about the importance of these goals. She thanked the *jamʿiyya*'s volunteers for their time and the *ifṭār* guests in advance for their donations. She noted that Ramadan is a time when people should translate unity in fasting to unity in supporting the community. The public relations officer then described some of the *jamʿiyya*'s activities, showing a short video. She also made a point of noting the other local *jamʿiyya*s that were represented at the *ifṭār*, highlighting the cooperation among them. Then a twelve-year-old girl the *jamʿiyya* supports made a short and moving speech. In well-rehearsed formal Arabic she explained that she was an orphan and wouldn't be able to attend school if it were not for the *jamʿiyya*.

Underneath each plate was a envelope for donations, with spaces to write your name, address, amount donated, and donation type.[2] Volunteers walked among the tables throughout the evening, collecting envelopes and giving donors receipts and thank you cards. When the meal was over and the plates cleared, the male waiters and cameramen who were recording the event left the room, and a group of *mawlid* singers entered (they do not sing before men). The *mawlid* brought an amazing celebratory energy to the room, with women mingling with friends and family, dancing, and clapping along to the rhythms.

---

[2] The options that could be checked on the envelope included *tabarruʿāt* (regular charity donation) and *ḥuqūq sharʿiyya-khums* (religious tax). The latter category was then divided into: *imām* (Imam's share, given directly to the poor) and *sāda* (sayyids' share, given via the care of a sayyid). The *jamʿiyya* had permission from several major *marjiʿ*s to collect *khums*.

This was a typical day in the lives of volunteers during Ramadan. While the Center was only active during Ramadan, this *jam'iyya* was busy throughout the year. Preparations for the Center were continuous. Between Ramadan 1999 and 2000, food donations and plans were made, the Center was advertised in order to attract both donors and volunteers, the annual *iftār* was planned and invitations delivered, walls were built to partition the space in the Center more effectively, these walls were wallpapered and the Center given a general aesthetic makeover, and numerous faxes were sent and phone calls made, all to ensure that the Center would be able to provide for at least the same number of families as it had the year before, if not more. In 2000, the Center's flyers stated that it provided one thousand *iftār* meals a day, based on its 1999 activity. By the end of Ramadan 2000, the Center was providing *iftār* for over 250 families, with an average of seven members, increasing the number of people fed daily to at least 1,500.

Neither the Center, nor any of the other activities and projects of this and other *jam'iyyas* in the area would be possible without the time and energy of volunteers.[3] Volunteerism constitutes a critical thread in the social weft of the pious modern. More than humanitarian charity work, it is a *necessary* part of piety.

As Hajjeh Khadija explained in chapter 3, faith was understood as a ladder one must continually struggle to climb, in order to arrive at *taqwā*, a state of absolute faith and piety. In the conceptualization of many pious Shi'is, one of the fundamental rungs on this ladder was *mu'amalāt*, or mutual reciprocal social relations. As the vehicle through which personal piety was most clearly brought into the public realm, community service was an important component of these social relations, a component that encapsulated both the personal morality and the public expression that together constituted *iltizām*. One woman put it thus:

> Religion has two aspects. There are things with two sides, between a person and God, and there are things with three sides, between a person, God, and others in society. It is this worship that is required of us. This means a

---

[3] I use the terms "volunteerism" and "volunteer" as a translation of my interlocutors' terms *tatawu'* and *mutatawi'a*. In the Shi'i pious modern, volunteering encompassed work done for the common good for which one is not compensated monetarily. *Jam'iyya* employees who worked extra hours without compensation were considered "half-volunteers." The fact that one gained nonmonetary reward did not lesson volunteerism's status in this community, and the fact that volunteering was not necessarily "voluntary"—in the sense of being an act of absolute free will outside the constraints of social norms—did not affect these understandings.

believer's prayers are not acceptable if he does not fulfill his worship in serving others. The basis for this is in the Qur'an:[4] *fa-waylu lil-muṣallīn 'alladhīnahum 'an ṣalātihim sahūn*, meaning, those who aren't interested in their prayer; *al-ladhīnahum yur'ā'ūn*, meaning, they do things just for others to see them, not for God; *wa yamna'ūn al-mā'ūn*, meaning, those who prevent happiness for others. God will judge them, even if they pray. *Waylu lil muṣalīn* tells us that they pray, but they aren't interested in their prayers. It's not enough to pray, you have to be engaged in your prayer, and you should help others. So this is worship, worship isn't just prayer, it is those who bring these together, prayers and service to others, it is they who are living correctly.

Just as with religious practices, discourses, and commemorations, community service underwent a transformation with the Shi'i Islamic movement: during my field research there were an unprecedented number of women volunteering in *jam'iyyas* throughout al-Dahiyya. When volunteers who remember the 1960s and '70s described their histories of service, they often began with a phrase like, "Before, there was nothing here, not a single *jam'iyya*, nothing" ('*abl, ma kān fī shī hōn, wala jam'iyya, wala shī*). Their memories of volunteering before the institutionalization of the Islamic movement are testimonies to individual ingenuity and dedication, rather than organizational structure.

The establishment of networks of *jam'iyyas* accompanied the Shi'i mobilization. For many, these *jam'iyyas* represented material progress and were crucial to Shi'i "catching up" to other groups in the country. As Hajjeh Khadija noted: "The local *jam'iyyas* are a very modern idea (*fikra ktīr moderne* [Fr.]), a very necessary one, and they should have been established long ago. But the important thing is that we have arrived here now. They [the *jam'iyyas*] have a very essential role in society. . . . There is finally a framework through which we are able to help people." When Hajjeh Khadija uses "modern" here in reference to the need for Lebanese Shi'is to "catch-up" to others, she deploys a modernization-oriented discourse of progress based on material development, a discourse shared by both western and pious Shi'i ideas about being modern.

The technological modern-ness of the *jam'iyyas* was something people spent considerable time communicating to me. My first visits to *jam'iyyas* always involved tours of computer facilities, statistics offices, archival record departments, medicinal storerooms, classrooms equipped as state-of-the-art science labs—technology in all its forms. My

---

[4] The following quotation is from *Sūrat Al-Mā'ūn* [The Small Kindnesses], verses 4–7. See this chapter's epigraph.

guides always linked religion and modernization, almost as though responding to unstated accusations that the two were incompatible. An administrator at a Martyrs' Association hospital told me:

> We are trying to reflect Islam and apply it. This hospital is an attempt but our resources are limited. But as they say, to light a candle is better than to curse in darkness. Hopefully we are able to do something small here, to provide a bit of good medical treatment. I say *good* medical treatment because quality is very important to us; customer service, marketing, well-trained employees, that is what we are working on, ways to better satisfy the sick. We are hiring educated people, many of them American University of Beirut graduates, and yes, they work here because they are believers but we do not hire people because they are believers, we hire them because they are specialized. There is another saying about this, "tie your camel before you go to God." [He handed me a brochure about the hospital's technological equipment.] Look at this, you see that we also buy the latest equipment, the latest technology, but we use it in the proper path to serve people.

This statement asserts the compatibility of Islam with technology, as well as some of the other qualities associated with western modernity, like education and marketing. Yet as this man alludes, material progress was not considered sufficient.

Hajjeh Khadija's use of "modern" above also deploys the pious modern discourse of spiritual progress, as the *jam'iyyas* were believed to be a spiritually developed institutional framework for helping others. Increases in community service were linked to the authentication process and to its emphasis on participation and community betterment.

> There are some people who live traditionally; they are still affected greatly by their parents. There are others who have learned about religion and live from religious motivations, the opposite of traditional motivations. You also have people who take these religious motives that are also the motives of civilization/modernity [al-ḥaḍāra] and the motives of development [taṭawwur], and they try to make things better. So they want their country to develop, to no longer have the problems of poverty, of child labor, so they begin to give importance to community work . . .

Here Maliha clearly articulates the connection between spiritual and material progress. "Authenticated" religious motives are the motives of civilization and development that lead to the pious modern. One of the key purposes of the *jam'iyyas* was to incorporate the poor into this community. To that end, as we will see, volunteers' activities focused on both the material and spiritual "development" of the poor, as well as on their own spiritual betterment.

In the first part of this chapter, I sketch the activities of *jam'iyyas* and their volunteers, and highlight some of their underlying notions about poverty and progress, as they relate to authentication and the pious modern. Here we see that their religiosity was clearly understood as connected to the contemporary world. In the second part I turn to the volunteers themselves, to give a sense of what it was that motivated these women to contribute so much of their time and energy to those less fortunate, returning finally to the model provided by Sayyida Zaynab. Community service in al-Dahiyya was gendered in particular ways that will emerge in the subtext of this chapter—that gendering will be taken up directly in chapter 6.

TACKLING POVERTY AND "BACKWARDNESS"

Human Links between Poverty and Bureaucracy

Volunteers played an integral role in the day-to-day work, organization, and, to varying extents, administration of many *jam'iyyas* in al-Dahiyya. They planned and carried out special events, including fund-raisers,[5] trips for poor families, summer camps for orphans, and Ramadan activities like the food distribution center described above. Larger *jam'iyyas* that included schools, orphanages and hospitals counted volunteers among the staff of those institutions. Many of the paid employees of *jam'iyyas* noted that they considered themselves "part-time volunteers," as they often worked many more hours than were covered by their wages.

From among these myriad tasks and responsibilities, the area that is perhaps the most dependent on volunteer labor is that of direct welfare provision to poor families. This is also the task that best exemplifies many of the qualities of community service that are particular to the Shi'i pious modern. While exact methods varied by *jam'iyya* scale and scope, many *jam'iyyas* in al-Dahiyya, including the SAA, ICEC, and Martyrs' Association, depended on volunteers to assess families' needs and provide them with assistance. In short, volunteers provided what was viewed as the necessary human link between poor families and the bureaucracy of aid.

---

[5] Fund-raising activities included selling crafts (silk flower arrangements, baskets, candles) and going door-to-door collecting small change. At least one *jam'iyya* held all-inclusive pilgrimage trips to Iran as fund-raising events, charging slightly more than cost, so that each traveler was both visiting Shi'i holy sites and contributing to a *jam'iyya*—effectively accomplishing two pious acts simultaneously.

TACKLING POVERTY

During the (un)civil wars and Israeli invasions and occupation, al-Dahiyya absorbed numerous Shiʿi refugees from the south and from other regions of Beirut. The suburb is also home to many who were injured and/or disabled during the violence, as well as a relatively high percentage of female-headed households.[6] These factors, coupled with the dysfunctional Lebanese economy, have contributed to high rates of urban poverty in al-Dahiyya, along with its accompanying symptoms.[7] Average annual household income in the area was estimated in 1999 at US $430, while another report from 1997 cites US $410 as the per capita income, as compared with Lebanon's average of US $2,970.[8]

> We have a family with seven children. The husband works. He makes 500,000 lira [$333] a month. The rent is 250,000 [$167]. The school bus is 100,000 [$67]. We pay the children's school registration. But we have to just hope that they can continue living like this. How is that possible? No one helps them, because they are not orphans. And the father works, but how much can his salary do with seven children? The mother works too, but she is sick. And there are so few organizations to help these people. And there are so so many of them. (Hajjeh Huda)

Volunteers were highly cognizant of al-Dahiyya as materially "behind" the rest of Lebanon, and understood their work as part of the perpetual "catching up" confronting Lebanese Shiʿis. This sense of collective Shiʿi deprivation resonated with their notion of Shiʿi history as one of persecution and oppression. It was also fueled by the sheer visibility of poverty itself. There was little economic segregation in al-Dahiyya; poor and wealthy resided in the same buildings and belonged to the same extended families.[9]

---

[6] 7.9 percent of households in al-Dahiyya were female-headed (personal communication, Sayyid Abd-el-Halim Fadlullah, the Consulting Center for Studies and Documentation [CCSD]). These numbers were almost certainly underreported.

[7] Accessing accurate statistics about poverty (or anything else) by region in Lebanon was essentially impossible. The Lebanese Ministry of Social Affairs completed a survey in 1996, but unfortunately the Beirut suburbs were considered as a whole, lumping wealthy and poor neighborhoods together. The UNDP's 1997 *Profile of Sustainable Human Development in Lebanon* summarized the living conditions of the urban poor as overcrowded, with an average living space of less than ten square meters per person (the internationally accepted norm is fourteen), with a scarcity of green space, the accumulation of garbage near homes, a lack of sewer systems or the intermixing of sewerage with water distribution networks, and poorly maintained buildings, some of which were damaged during the war.

[8] The first figure was cited to me at the CCSD. Mona Fawaz reports the second set of figures, also from the CCSD (1998: 14).

[9] While there clearly were high levels of poverty in al-Dahiyya, it is debatable as to whether it was *the* poorest region in Lebanon, and it was certainly not the only poor area.

All this was exacerbated by Lebanon's general lack of government services and failing economy—factors many Lebanese take for granted as forming the backdrop for life's struggles. In some al-Dahiyya neighborhoods, this included lack of clean water and electricity, as well as problems such as unemployment, overpopulation, and unsafe buildings. *Jam'iyyas* were conscious that they were working to fill these lacunae, and volunteers frequently complained, "If there were only a government" (*iza bas kān fī dawleh*), much of the poverty and systemic and infrastructural disrepair would be alleviated.[10]

To tackle urban poverty, some *jam'iyyas* maintained programs that provided basic needs for families, including staple foods (e.g., flour, sugar, rice), clothing and shoes, and essential household items like blankets, gas for the stove, and perhaps a refrigerator. These programs often provided health assistance as well, by subsidizing medication costs and working with local doctors to provide low-cost medical attention. Above all, education was prioritized. For example, while I was in Beirut, the SAA instituted an ongoing campaign to end child labor by providing public school fees.

"VISITING" AS METHOD

The key to all these welfare provision programs is the personal contact between volunteers and poor families. When a family came to a *jam'iyya*'s attention—whether through the initiative of a family member or a volunteer—the *jam'iyya* first assessed the family's "situation" (*wada'*). At the SAA, for example, two volunteers would visit the family, recording their observations and interviewing the woman of the household, using a standard survey. They also talked with neighbors and/or relatives to cross-check and verify information. The information gathered was used to determine whether and what sort of aid the family qualified to receive. Similar processes were standard at all the *jam'iyyas* I visited.

After a *jam'iyya* "adopted" a family, regular visits continued. Generally, volunteers were assigned specific families, which then became their responsibility. During visits, they distributed money, food, and clothing; monitored economic, social, and health changes; facilitated access to health care or employment (often using personal networks); and

---

[10] Hizbullah is often accused of creating a "state within a state" in al-Dahiyya by assuming responsibilities perceived to belong to the central government (e.g., garbage collection). The party's response is that when the government provides in its place, it will cease its services. Indeed, when garbage collection was subcontracted to the Sukleen company, Hizbullah lessened its services, though according to Harik (2004), it still carries three hundred tons of garbage out of the area daily.

conducted *taw'iyya*, a combination of education and consciousness-raising, further discussed below. In essence, they functioned as liaisons between these families and the material and cultural resources managed and distributed by the *jam'iyyas*.

Through this continual contact, volunteers frequently built intense personal relationships with "their" families: "In our work here, you enter into households, you get involved with people, you live their lives and their hardships. Other work is outside the home, at centers for refugees or in schools. Here at the ICEC, we work directly with families, we visit them continuously. We feel that this work has more spirit (*rūḥ*) through our interaction with them."

As a volunteer began to feel that she was a part of the families she assisted, the emotional distance between them shrank, to the extent that volunteers sometimes began to cry when describing the situation of one of "their" families or while negotiating extra *jam'iyya* resources for a particular case. The intensity of these ties emerged in their use of the possessive to refer to these relationships: "I have four small orphans," "I have seven families." While on the one hand, these emotional ties facilitated compassionate service provision, on the other, taken to an extreme, such compassion could interfere with a volunteer's personal life.[11] In a community where anonymity was a scarce luxury, women from poor families sometimes began to reciprocate visits in order to ask volunteers for aid. When *jam'iyya* resources were not available or when a family inevitably needed more, volunteers found themselves giving more and more of their time and money. Hajjeh Umm Muhammad at the ICEC confided that she had twenty families who visited her at her home, "They come to me for everything, for any problem. If a woman is sick and needs to go to the hospital, I take her. If she needs to take a child to the hospital, she leaves her other children with me."

During a volunteers' training seminar at the SAA, Dalal cautioned us to monitor our emotional reactions:

> You have to be careful to not allow this work to take over your lives. You cannot just put your hand in your pocket each time someone asks and hand out money. It is better, in the long run, to study the case and try to help in a way that solves the larger situation, and in a way that does not affect your entire life. Hajjeh [Huda] has people at her door at 6 a.m. on most mornings. That should not have to happen.

Yet Dalal was not advocating anonymous relationships between volunteers

---

[11] No doubt the intensity of these relationships was perceived differently by and had different effects on the recipient families; however, in this study I focus solely on the perspective of the volunteers.

or *jam'iyyas* and families, she was simply advising women to set limits to the personal relationships they cultivated with "their" families. On another occasion, she expressed her fear that face-to-face service provision was fading in the area, because the growing numbers of poor who needed assistance precluded the formation of relationships with every family. In her words: "This is unfortunate, because I am afraid it will signify a lessening in concern for human dignity."

The tension between a belief in the importance of human relationships and the need to maintain boundaries between volunteers and the poor is related to a larger tension that exists between spiritual and material progress in relation to community service. A concern for the preservation of human dignity—what one administrator called "the struggle to maintain a more human and Islamic" approach to community welfare in the face of a burgeoning bureaucracy—moved many *jam'iyyas* to encourage the cultivation of these direct personal relationships between volunteers and recipient families. When volunteers talked about entering families' homes as though they belonged, they were drawing on understandings of kin relationships. Because they represented the family's provider, volunteers were parental, even paternal figures. There were, however, limits to this analogous relationship, as Dalal noted above, in the limits on demands that poor families could acceptably place on volunteers.

Kinship was also the idiom through which relationships among volunteers and employees within *jam'iyyas* worked, with women referred to as "sisters" and men as "brothers." These terms indexed their common faith and goals, while also establishing an environment where interactions between women and men could take place "appropriately." This kinship framework highlighted the difference between the impersonal bureaucracy—pictured as consisting of isolated individualized selves—that pious Shi'is associated with western notions of the modern, and their own emphasis on modern selves as embedded in social relationships. This distinction was important to *jam'iyyas*, though it also involved a continuous struggle.

Larger *jam'iyyas* in particular were constantly negotiating the tension between face-to-face relationships and an anonymous public. On the one hand, *jam'iyyas* highlighted their extensive bureaucratic structures as evidence of their "modern" efficiency and organization, deploying western discourses of modernization. On a practical level, larger organizational structures also allowed *jam'iyyas* to help more people. Yet on the other hand, beliefs about the "human" nature of "authentically Islamic" charity emphasized social relations over bureaucracy. Providing assistance through face-to-face relationships allowed *jam'iyyas* to nurture histori-cal links to notions of social welfare rooted in Islam, even as their larger structures and networks reflected their positions in the professionalizing world of international NGOs.[12] In this sense, kinlike emotional ties be-tween volunteers and recipient families provided the link that made it possible for *jam'iyyas* to position themselves—and be understood by others—as working within authentication, in keeping with the pious modern.

The tense space where these multiple notions of the modern were de-ployed, pitting authentication against efficiency, came to a head in the widespread debates among *jam'iyyas* over how to best serve the large numbers of orphans in al-Dahiyya and Lebanon. Pious Shi'is defined any child who had lost a parent as an orphan, although most orphans in Lebanon had lost their fathers. Even in those cases where an orphan has neither mother nor other extended family, adoption is not permissible in Islam. What was at issue in the community was whether it was more ap-propriate to establish orphanage-like institutions and boarding schools or to support orphans in their mothers' or relatives' homes through orphan-sponsorship programs.

Most *jam'iyyas* in al-Dahiyya preferred to support orphans in their home environments. Al-Mabarrat was the sole exception to this, with over three thousand orphans residing in their orphanages. Yet even al-Mabarrat's orphans were not fully detached from their families; they went home on weekends and holidays and during summer, essentially whenever school was not in session.

Strong feelings existed on both sides of this debate. Some volunteers felt that in order to support orphans according to authenticated Islam, it was necessary to keep them with their mothers whenever possible. The ICEC was supporting over four thousand orphans in their homes through orphan-sponsorship. This was the result of a conscious decision, made when the *jam'iyya* was founded, not to establish orphanages, so as to uphold the *sharī'a*.

The other perspective was articulated by Hajjeh Khadija, who worked, along with her husband, at an al-Mabarrat orphanage. Advo-cates of orphanages repeatedly said that poor orphans often could not be appropriately raised by their relatives, and that volunteers visiting households was not enough to break the cycle of poverty. As Hajjeh Khadija put it, "The worst thing is what these children return home to on the weekends; their mothers are poor but they are often also ignorant,

[12] While for obvious political reasons these *jam'iyyas* did not have any direct financial links to the U.S.-dominated INGO funding system, they maintained multiple transnational ties to resources, both within and outside the Muslim world.

and it is a terrible combination." She explained that al-Mabarrat held frequent workshops for mothers about hygiene, health and other issues, but that it was not enough. Rather than take on the task of reforming whole families, they attempted to break the "poverty cycle" with the new generation.

This concern with systemic poverty, and with the relationship between poverty and ignorance, was typical among volunteers. In the next section, I explore these issues, along with their importance to local understandings of development and progress. In these ideas about poverty, we will see another dimension of the uneasy and ever-negotiated relationship between the spiritual and the material in the realm of community service.

Developing the Poor

DEFINING STATUS

In order to understand how volunteers viewed the families they assisted, it is first necessary to sketch an outline of social hierarchies in al-Dahiyya, as understood by pious Shi'is. Volunteers tended to identify themselves and one another as vaguely "middle class" though they rarely spoke about anyone in class terms, using *'ādī*, "normal" or "ordinary," instead. My attempts to unravel what "ordinary" meant were usually met with puzzlement. On the surface, people made judgments based on others' homes—how fashionable their wallpaper, how new their curtains, how ornate their décor—and clothing (again with regard to fashion and fabric). Generally speaking, from the perspective of volunteers, there were three broad socioeconomic categories in their community.[13]

There were the wealthy, a very small category of people who either had "old money," dating from before the wars, or—as was usually assumed—were from among the Lebanese nouveaux riches who had made their fortunes since the 1960s through work and investment in the Gulf States, North America, or West Africa or through various black-market wartime economic activities. Wealthy women tended to patronize particular *jam'iyyas* with their financial contributions—religious taxes (*huqūq shar'iyya*) and charity donations—but rarely joined in the on-the-ground work. Many *jam'iyyas* cultivated relationships with wealthy donors through visits and fund-raisers, like the *iftār* in the opening of this chapter.

---

[13] Some people used *tabaqa*—often translated as "class"—to indicate these categories.

Later in the evening, a neighbor joined us, along with a visitor she was enter-
taining. The visitor, a local woman who lived in Dubai, was clearly very
wealthy, literally "dripping with jewels." As we continued chatting about our
work at the Center, she complained that because she lives in the Gulf, "all the
jam'iyyas have forgotten me"—alluding to how she had not received any *iftār*
invitations that year. She was immediately invited to the *jam'iyya's* upcoming
fund-raiser, and urged to come and tour the Center. (fieldnotes, December 10,
2000)

Then there were the "ordinary"—that middle category into which
every volunteer I asked placed herself. The Lebanese middle-class has
been shrinking steadily in recent decades, as war and economy have precipitated the emigration of educated professionals and young people. It
is arguable, however, that Shi'i Lebanese are an exception to this, as
their relatively late urbanization, coupled with investments in West
Africa, has contributed to an urban Shi'i "middle" or "professional"
class that did not exist in the same way several decades ago.[14] In al-
Dahiyya, this catchall group included those with college or professional
degrees, especially in younger generations, and those who owned local
businesses. These families were able to afford at least one car, though
these ranged from an old Toyota to a new 500 series BMW; they refur-
nished their multi-room, but not lavish, apartments periodically, though
they might travel to Syria to find cheaper deals on fabrics; their children
attended universities, again ranging from the public Lebanese University
to the very expensive American University of Beirut; and, crucially, they
made up the vast majority of *jam'iyya* volunteers, some of whom were
distinguishable from the wealthy only by the lack of prominent designer
labels on their silk scarves.

Here it is crucial to note that, particularly among the pious, modesty
was highly valued. As a result, many volunteers, especially those who
were motivated by religious duty, lived modestly and were generous with
their wealth. Even if others classified a woman as wealthy, she may not
have identified as such, working instead to set herself apart from the
Lebanese elite, and especially from the attitudes and values ascribed to
them, including materialism, superficiality, and "wasting time."

While I chatted with Alia at the SAA today, two other volunteers left looking
unusually dressed up. Alia rolled her eyes, "They're going to do a [fund-
raising] 'visit' [*ziyāra*] with a woman who just went on the *ḥajj* for the first

[14] Harris notes the "increased economic weight" of Shi'is in Lebanon, much of which is
due to "entrepreneurial endeavors in West Africa, North America, and the Gulf oil states"
(1997: 120).

time. You know, she'll be in the spirit of giving." I asked her why she wasn't going with them. "Oof, I've been trying to stop doing that work, I hate that part of society; they are so empty, and they only talk about each other, or about their appearances—it's all about appearances. Even though I used to live in that society, I would never want to again, I couldn't do it. I much prefer visiting the poor families; even if they don't have a place for me to sit, I feel much more comfortable with them."

For volunteers, status had to do with much more than wealth,[15] a complexity underscored by their tendency to describe themselves as "ordinary." Piety, neighborhood of residence, family reputation, and political position all converged with socioeconomic situation to form understandings of status. A woman's social status could differ from that of her husband if her family was the more prominent one. In trying to grasp these differences, I once asked two volunteers to compare two other women we all knew. Both were actively involved in *jam'iyyas* on an administrative and financial level. One was clearly wealthier than the other, and displayed her wealth more blatantly in her dress and manner. Yet both people I had cornered attributed higher status to the other woman, citing her reputation as pious and "from a good family," as well as her husband's political status.

Public piety—a visible commitment to "authenticated" Islam—was perhaps the most important element in social status in the community.[16] The way this association has contributed to new social norms for pious Shi'i women will be taken up further in the next chapter. Here I want to consider how the relationship between public piety and status impinged on volunteers' attitudes toward the poor families they assisted. Volunteers generally considered themselves more pious than the poor. But they believed that there exists a causal relationship between spiritual ignorance (and ignorance in general) and poverty. To develop the community—and to fulfill the ultimate goal of bringing the poor into the pious modern— one had to focus on both the material and the spiritual, as equally necessary to progress.

TAKHALLUF WA TAW'IYYA, BACKWARDNESS AND CONSCIOUSNESS-RAISING

The third category—the poor, or the *m'atar* (unfortunate)—included anyone who needed or might need the assistance of the *jam'iyyas*. This was perceived to be the majority of the population, those living day-to-day, month-to-month. These were households where the men, if they

---

[15] Here I follow Weber's (1946) understanding of status as involving "social estimation of honor" and the specifics of a person's lifestyle.

[16] See also White's (2002) discussion of a new Islamist elite in Turkey.

were alive and present, were un- or underemployed, as well as women-headed households, elderly couples whose children could not support them, and those that had been hit especially hard by the economic recession.

> Later, I walked over to the Abbas's house to meet eleven-year-old Hadya, who I begin tutoring next week, and her mother, whose husband left just after the youngest of their four children was born. They live in a small room on the ground floor of a building where the mother is the janitor/caretaker. The room was dark, and the electricity in the building was off. A couch filled one wall, closets lined a second, and a table and two broken televisions a third. The fourth wall held the door and the entrance to a tiny kitchenette/bathroom. Hard to believe that five people live in this tiny space during weekends, and three during the week, when the youngest two children board at an al-Mabarrat orphanage.[17] (fieldnotes, March 11, 2000)

The Abbas family was reputed in the *jam'iyyas* to be among the "good" poor families. The mother was known for her honesty, and for taking only what her children needed, and she and her daughters were all *muhajjaba* and assumed to be relatively pious. This was not the case for all poor families, some of which were seen as "working the system."

> AMANEY: Do you remember that family who removed all their furniture so we would think they were very poor? I cannot believe it but it happens. That's why we always ask the neighbors.
>
> ALIA: It all comes from *takhalluf*, this is why we need to do *taw'iyya*, so these families don't become dependent on us. This is a problem. We try to help them find work, but some women won't work outside the home; they say their husbands don't let them.
>
> AMANEY: All the lying the families sometimes do, it's a sickness in them, from the poverty. But it helps us harden our hearts.
>
> ALIA: But there are also people who have so much honor, they won't ask for help. If you offer them something, they will say that there is someone else who needs it more. These people make you want to help them even more.
>
> AMANEY: Yes, like the Abbas family, they are one of the poorest families we have, and the mother is one of the most honest people I have ever seen.
>
> ALIA: You know, she came to the office once and asked for money to buy a medicinal shot for her daughter, and when Dalal asked her how much it cost, she said 3,000 lira, so Dalal gave her a 5,000, and she said, "I'm

---

[17] In summer 2001, someone donated a bright multiroom apartment to this family through a *jam'iyya*.

sorry but I don't have the 2,000 with me to give you change." She didn't want to take more money than she needed, though God knows she could have used the change to buy bread.

Alia and Amaney's conversation highlights two key concepts in volunteers' approach to poverty: *takhalluf*, or "backwardness" and *taw'iyya*, or consciousness-raising education. Similar conversations were common at *jam'iyyas*, as volunteers exchanged anecdotes over cups of strong coffee. At first listen, their tales seemed to highlight the worst of human qualities, and the often humorous means to which people resorted in order to manipulate *jam'iyyas* for personal gain. Yet in every venting session, a voice eventually chimed in to defend the poor: "But it's not everyone, not even the majority." Volunteers appreciated the pride and honor they witnessed in some of "their" families. They remembered which poor women contributed time to *jam'iyya* activities. And they noticed who wore the *hijāb* or otherwise indicated her piety.

Honesty, pride, and piety are moral qualities; poor people who demonstrated them were viewed as having moved beyond their material conditions. This link between ignorance—spiritual or otherwise—and poverty is not about affluence indicating or contributing to piety. Rather, it is about knowledge, and an assumption that poverty limits one's access to accurate religious and other knowledge and education. In this way, poverty was believed to result in ignorance (*jahl*), which then led to *takhalluf*.[18]

> Poverty is giving birth to ignorance. Imam Ali, peace be upon him, said, *"law kān al-fuqr rajulan, faqataltuhu bisayfī"* [if poverty were a man, I would kill him with my sword]. Because poverty is behind all problems, it is the root of illiteracy, ignorance, stealing, crime, depravity. Because a poor person, when he goes from day to day like this, no matter what values he has, despite himself, he will be forced to go against those values, he will walk on the road that leads to evil. . . . I think if these people we help did not have this assistance, perhaps one of them would become a criminal, who knows? We fill his stomach so that he will be able to think, to learn, to feel that he is able to be a human being. So he will be able to grow up and see himself as a useful member of society. (Hajjeh Khadija)

The underlying premise of much of the *jam'iyyas'* work was that community progress required "developing" the poor. Sighs of *"oof, shū ha-takhalluf"* (oh, what is this backwardness) reflected volunteers' tendency

---

[18] This is a reversal of both the notion in Weber's discussion of the Protestant ethic that material prosperity indicates spiritual status, and the assumptions of development theory (discussed in Karp 2002) that underdevelopment is caused by moral "qualities."

to view poor Shi'is as representative of how "we Shi'is are not as modern" as others. More than an internalization of stereotypes and conditions, here stereotypes are displaced onto particular segments of Shi'i society, so that the (linked) material and spiritual backwardness of the poor was "holding the Shi'a back." By developing the poor, volunteers could work toward the collective progress of Shi'i Lebanese, including themselves.

A seemingly all-encompassing range of social problems fell under the rubric of *"takhalluf."* Illiteracy, ignorance about hygiene, and petty crime were due to and evidence of *"takhalluf."* A man who abandoned his wife and eight children without any financial support represented *"takhalluf."* And a woman who left her chicken pox–infected daughter at an orphanage's door in the freezing cold because her new husband had threatened to kill the child to protect his own children from the illness demonstrated (a double dose of) *"takhalluf."*

One of the largest problems the *jam'iyyas* faced was that of inadvertently creating *takhalluf* in the form of dependency, in other words, of creating a situation where poor people became entirely dependent on *jam'iyyas* for support. As one administrator put it, with a sigh: "If their toilet floods, they come here." Or, "If a man knows we will care for his children, he will be more likely to leave them." This concern with dependency distinguished the *jam'iyya* model of community service from that of "traditional" Islamic charity. Underlying charity is a notion that the poor are a permanent part of society who should be supported by the wealthy. In the pious modern conceptualization of community service, the poor hinder community progress and therefore must be "developed." Dependency means failure, of both development and progress.

To avoid such failure, the *jam'iyyas* consciously fostered independence, by trying to find ways for people to eventually support themselves. They sought employment for at least one member of each family, ran day-care centers to facilitate women's work, and provided small "business" loans to help women enter the informal economy.

Most of all, however, the *jam'iyyas* confronted *takhalluf* in all its forms through *taw'iyya*. The Arabic root for *taw'iyya* is *wa/'a/ya*, a root with a range of meaning that includes containing, remembering, knowing, cautioning, heeding, and being aware, awake, or conscious. A verbal noun from this root, *taw'iyya* is the act of calling attention to something, warning someone, or making someone conscious of something—essentially, the act of causing consciousness. Volunteers used the term liberally, in some contexts "education" is the perfect translation, while in others "consciousness-raising" is more appropriate. For the sake of simplicity, I use the term mainly in Arabic, allowing context to establish its position along the spectrum of its meaning.

The ultimate goal of *taw'iyya* was to cultivate people who were *muthaqqaf*, which literally means "educated" or "cultured." *Muthaqqaf* does not necessarily have religious overtones, and is sometimes translated as "intellectual"—with a distinct leaning toward philosophy over the arts. However, in the context of the Shi'i pious modern, to be *muthaqqaf* carried a particularly Islamic flavor. Consider the variety of offerings on the pages of the "Culture" (*thaqāfa*) section of Hizbullah's weekly newspaper: The August 3, 2001 issue includes a critique of the government for the lack of electricity during the summer heat, an analysis of the treatment of the Arab-Israeli conflict in Arab cinema, an article on a prominent community figure, and an excerpt from Khomeini's book *Patience*. In an issue published during Ashura, these pages include three pieces about different aspects of Ashura's history and meaning, a shaykh's obituary, and an article analyzing *al-taqwā*.[19]

For pious Shi'is, to be *muthaqqaf* was to be literate, well-spoken, and well-mannered, with clear knowledge of "authenticated" Islam, preferably implemented in practice. In volunteers' usage, it was also to be socially aware and responsible. In a seminar at a *jam'iyya*, a respected local principal with a Ph.D. in sociology lectured on the importance of always being critical of the social environment in order to constantly contribute to its progress and improvement. He argued that this critical ability improves as a person becomes more *muthaqqaf*. Being *muthaqqaf* meant contributing to the pious modern.

Volunteers were well aware that creating people who were *muthaqqaf* is a goal with many steps.[20] *Taw'iyya* encompassed myriad topics ranging from "proper" religious practice to how to identify tuberculosis. *Jam'iyyas* held workshops for "their" families, through which they provided what one volunteer called "modern/new/recent theories on how to raise children and on health and social topics" (*nazariyyāt hadītha 'an kīf yirabbū il-awlād w 'an mawadi' ṣaḥiyyeh w ijtimā'iyyeh*). As it aimed toward progress, *taw'iyya* drew on multiple notions of modern-ness including "authenticated" religious and contemporary scientific bodies of knowledge.

The "visiting method" was particularly conducive to effective *taw'iyya*, especially as people often could not or would not attend workshops regularly. By constantly visiting families, volunteers were able to gradually introduce new ideas into households, and track perceived improvements. Volunteers also incorporated *taw'iyya* into special events held for poor families, *mawlid*s, trips, and organized entertainment.

---

[19] *Al-Ahd/Al-Intiqād*, March 29, 2002.

[20] Indeed, in order to become part of the pious modern, poor people's sense of personhood had to change—paralleling Karp's (2002) observation that in order to become developed, poor people must become "new kinds of persons" (2002: 90).

With the spiritual a necessary element of progress, some *taw'iyya* was explicitly religious. While most *jam'iyyas* assisted women regardless of whether or not they were *muhajjaba*, volunteers often included education about the *hijāb* in their *taw'iyya*.

> I have two orphans, one is thirteen and one fifteen; they used to dress like you, pants and a sweater. So I kept after them, telling them about *shar'ī* clothes and how neat they look, and how much easier they are to wear, and how they are more comfortable. And just the other day I went, and they asked to wear *shar'ī* clothes. Their mother has been trying to convince them of this for I don't know how long, "please wear *shar'ī*, please wear *shar'ī*" and they weren't convinced, but maybe because it was from me, and they see me as a friend, they were convinced. (Tamara, from the ICEC)

Volunteers viewed the close relationships they cultivated with poor families as important for facilitating *taw'iyya*. At the most basic level, they conducted *taw'iyya* by example: "If you do something right in front of them, they begin to want to do that. If you do something wrong, then they will copy that instead."

Because volunteers were seen as role models, they themselves had to be *muthaqqaf*. *Taw'iyya* was not only considered necessary for the poor, but it was considered fundamental training for volunteers as well. I often heard an experienced volunteer say, "In order to do *taw'iyya* for others, a person should first do *taw'iyya* for herself." Care was taken by *jam'iyyas* to ensure that their volunteers were well trained and equipped to carry out their work objectively and compassionately. *Taw'iyya* for volunteers included training that was "modern" in multiple valences, in order to prepare them for the two-pronged approach to building progress. At a four-week training seminar for volunteers at the SAA in which I participated, sessions were held on a range of topics including how to identify serious illnesses, children's rights, interviewing methods and skills for needs assessment, report writing, and religious values and teachings.

Lessons on Islam served not only to ensure that volunteers taught poor women authenticated Islam correctly, but also to ensure that they understood the relationship between Islam and community service. Dealing with *takhalluf* all day long frequently taxed volunteers' patience. The ability to maintain one's patience, and to serve others with compassion and without being patronizing was understood to be a gift from God, a capacity that could—and should—be developed as part of one's personal spiritual progress.

Self-confidence and public-speaking skills are other such capacities. Speaking about a sister volunteer, one woman noted: "This work helps you to be more courageous. When Hajjeh Suad first joined us, she was shy and limited in her interactions with people. But slowly, she adapted and learned, and now she talks more and blushes less. She has much more courage than she had at first." Through *taw'iyya*, participation in community service work developed volunteers' own capacities as individuals, "strengthening" their "personalities and consciousness." Yet this self-development was about more than personal growth. Here we see the primacy of the idea that a pious modern self is socially embedded and relational, where self-development is not a private act, but one where "serving others" is its ultimate purpose.[21]

Finally, *taw'iyya* ensured that women were volunteering for the right reasons. Hajjeh Amal, a highly respected instructor who many looked to as a model of piety, brought our classroom at the SAA training seminar to a sudden hush one afternoon when she asserted that it was possible prayer might not be accepted by God. She then explained that in order for prayer to be acceptable (*maqbūla*) to God, a person must also apply the authentic principles of religion in her life by helping others "in the service of God." The handout she had prepared for the session read:

> *Al-multazimūn bi-l-ṭuqūs al-dīniyya al-tārikīn li-khidmat al-nās 'immā ghayr multafitīn li-ḥaqīqat al-dīn wa-'immā mukadhdhibīn bihi fī qarārat an-fusihim.*
>
> [People who are committed to religious practices/rituals but neglect to serve others are either not attentive to the truth of religion or are denying it in their decisions.][22]

The second part of this chapter is devoted to unpacking this "authentic" reason for serving others and exploring some of the "other" reasons women highlighted when talking about their community service activities. Along the way, we will meet a few of the volunteers and hear some of their stories.

SERVING THE COMMUNITY, SERVING GOD

Beginnings

Women of all ages participated actively in community service; mothers brought their daughters to *jam'iyyas*, and friends brought their neighbors. At the SAA, for example, grandmothers in their fifties joined younger mothers and single, widowed, or divorced women of all ages. The only lacunae were full-time university students and those with several young children.

---

[21] *Taw'iyya* is dependent on a notion of self that is responsible to God and to others; see Brenner's discussion of a new Islamic "awareness" where women's "new subjectivity" was one that required bearing responsibility for one's actions before God (1996: 684).

[22] This is essentially one of the main ideas of Sūrat al-Mā'ūn.

Women's community service histories varied by generation. Many older volunteers, like Hajjeh Umm Ali, in her fifties, expressed feeling a longstanding affinity for volunteering, that it was in their "nature" and stemmed from their "love for giving." Their volunteering often predated the *jam'iyyas*, and involved taking initiative, whether on their own or with others. Slightly younger women, particularly those who identified with the vanguard of Lebanese Shi'i mobilization—like Hajjeh Umm Hadi and Hajjeh Khadija, both in their mid-forties—frequently traced their participation to Islamic activist university groups. They often began volunteering as they became religiously committed, as an extension of their *iltizām*. Those in their late teens and early twenties (like Noor and Maliha) had the opportunity to attend the new Islamic schools in the area, which facilitated their volunteerism through school projects, for example, Ramadan food drives similar to Thanksgiving food drives in U.S. high schools. These young women were raised in a radically differ-ent environment, one where *jam'iyyas* were prevalent and provided myr-iad opportunities for community service. Their generation is also the first to come to adulthood after the Lebanese wars.

No matter when a woman began volunteering, she was usually intro-duced to a *jam'iyya* through other volunteers, usually friends or relatives who brought her along to a fund-raiser or activity, like the Ramadan Cen-ter described at the opening of this chapter. A high school teacher who was active in one *jam'iyya* inspired several of her students to join. Few women were recruited by acquaintances or women they did not know.[23] No matter what the initial inspiration, once a volunteer began to engage actively in community work, it usually became an integral part of her life and identity. Her commitment to her work was reinforced by a constant and graphic confrontation with the immediacy of poverty in al-Dahiyya.

Hajjeh Zahra's story epitomizes many of the various motivations and factors prompting women's community service activities.

HAJJEH ZAHRA'S STORY

I began community service in secondary school in the late seventies. We had a community service club at school, and we were able to use and develop many of our own ideas for service through it.[24]

---

[23] Recruitment through existing social networks worked in part through pressures of moral obligation, as will be discussed in the next chapter. But it also, importantly, guaran-teed that a woman would know with whom she would be associating, ensuring physical and social "safety" (cf. White 1996).

[24] My interviews with Hajjeh Zahra took place in a mix of English and Arabic. Al-though she was among the most educated of my interlocutors, the sentiments and experi-ences she described were echoed by many volunteers of her generation.

One of these club activities involved working with Save the Children in a rural village in the Beqaa Valley. Students implemented educational programs, painted public buildings, and planned activities for village children. This clearly made an indelible impression on Hajjeh Zahra, as it was the first time she had encountered such poverty and isolation:

> I remember one time, we took a film to the kids, and there was in this film a scene of the sea, and the children asked "What's that? What's that?" That was the first time in my life that I realized that not everyone knows the sea. I was so so surprised, and shocked really! I kept saying to myself, is it possible that there are people who don't know the sea?

Soon after, war and the first Israeli invasion catalyzed Hajjeh Zahra, and solidified her commitment to service:

> This sense that I wanted to help people, that I had to do something, it really began to be strong with the civil war. When the war started, we were living up on the mountain above Beirut; it was a very strategic location, from there we could see everywhere. So from up there I watched Beirut burn and burn and burn. It was a shock to just see Beirut burning without being able to do anything. I remember that I just wished that I could put it all in my heart, but I was too young, I was not allowed to do anything at that time.
>
> The [Israeli] invasion of 1978 was a huge shock for me. My family is from the south originally, though we are now all from Beirut; my grandfather moved to Beirut. But when people in my family die, they are buried in the south. We go home to the south at death. We go there a lot.
>
> With the invasion, hundreds of Lebanese and some Palestinians came to Beirut. And one of the buildings where the refugees were was at my school, because there were no boarders then because of the situation, so we convinced the administration to open the building for refugees. And we worked with them.

Eventually the refugees were removed from the school, but Hajjeh Zahra continued to work with them through the Red Cross and UNICEF, teaching literacy and vaccinating children:

> Wherever I was needed, I would do anything as long as it helped people. My parents did not like to let me go very far on my own; you know, it was wartime, but I went anyway, and they didn't really know where I was much of the time. They knew that I was active, but they didn't know how much or how far I went.

After graduating from high school, Hajjeh Zahra attended the American University of Beirut (AUB). Her volunteerism shifted to accommodate her studies. On campus, she worked on students rights issues. When Israel invaded again in 1982, placing Beirut under siege, many who could fled the city. But Hajjeh Zahra remained:

> The situation was unbelievable, terrible, and there were so few of us helping. We had to provide food and water for so many families. People were eating things it is unthinkable to eat. The AUB hospital was the only one functioning during the siege, and it was understaffed, so even with no medical training I would go and help there also.

Because she remained in Beirut, Hajjeh Zahra became an eyewitness to the death and horror of the Sabra and Shatila refugee camp massacres. She was in one of the first Red Cross convoys to enter the camps in the aftermath. For two weeks she buried bodies, treated the wounded, translated survivor testimonies, and filed missing person reports for the hundreds who had been "disappeared."

Afterwards, the strain prompted her to focus solely on her studies and work for several years. It was during this time that she joined the newly organizing Islamic movement on campus. She became religiously committed and chose to wear the *ḥijāb*, a decision which set her apart from her less religious family.

> Then in 1987 I decided to go on the *ḥajj*, and there I met the general manager of al-Mabarrat, but I didn't know who he was at the time. He [Sayyid Muhammad Baqir Fadlullah][25] was the guide for my group, and we spoke a lot, and I was very, very impressed by him. Very, very impressed with his humanity and how *muthaqqaf* he was, he was so full of information. I said to myself, "How is it that someone so religious has these manners, everything about him is so cultured, yet he is so religious."

At the end of the *ḥajj*, they exchanged cards, and she learned that he was both with al-Mabarrat and a chemistry professor at Lebanese University. She was even more impressed by what she perceived as a duality in harmony within him, the coexistence of education with piety.

> One month later I received a phone call from him, and he invited me to come to al-Mabarrat; it was only the orphanage in Khaldeh then. So two or three of us went and we said, this will be our project. So we began volunteering. The first thing we did was establish the same activity program that I had started in my high school program with the orphans. Eventually this led to the establishment of a women's committee for al-Mabarrat.

[25] This is Sayyid Muhammad Husayn Fadlullah's brother.

Later, in 1991, the director of al-Mabarrat contacted Hajjeh Zahra again, this time asking her to help them open a school, a move that would entail leaving a lucrative career for a field she knew little about.

> And I said, "I know nothing about schools." And then they told me, "Sayyid Muhammad Husayn wants this." And the Sayyid himself told me that my experience and personality would help me. So I decided to try it for a year, and then if I was going to stay, I would go and get my master's degree in education and do this properly.

When I interviewed her, Hajjeh Zahra had an M.A. in education from AUB and was the principal of an al-Mabarrat school, one of the largest and most successful Islamic schools in al-Dahiyya.

> I realized that the Sayyid had a point; *taklīf ilāhi* [a responsibility given by God], you know, if God gives you a gift, you have the responsibility to use it, and to use it well, to not let it be wasted. I really feel now that it was my fate somehow to go to *hajj* when I met Sayyid Muhammad Bakir. I never would have been here doing this otherwise; it all came from that fateful meeting. He is the person who really convinced me to quit my work. He said, "They don't need you; you won't be a social change agent there," which might not be a big deal for everyone, but for me, for a person who feels God's existence and knows life as eternal, it is a big deal. I know that I will always exist, but just in a different state. Knowing this makes you think differently, to have different criteria for life, to live differently and make decisions on a different scale, because you know those decisions are with you forever, and affect more than this state right now. It was a very hard decision to leave a prestigious, well-salaried job where I worked only a few hours a day, to quit that to go to where? An unknown, a mystery, a different atmosphere, a different social environment.

When I later asked her what kept her going through her long days, she replied:

> I have a sense of commitment towards *al-'amal al-sālih* [good works], because if a person believes in constant existence, you have to prepare for eternity. To tell you the truth, there are many other options for good work, options with less stress, but here there is *need*, and the Sayyid says, "When God gives you a skill, a *potential*, that is a *trust* [*amāna*], and he will ask you later how you have used that trust. Can you tell God that you wasted part of it? Do you think that we come to this life to be more relaxed? To take the easy way?" I really think that the suffering in life is nice, if there were never pain, we would never feel the blessing of not being in pain.

A brief pause and then Hajjeh Zahra continued:

Now you're going to ask me what everyone asks me, "Don't you regret it now?" And my answer is always the same, for seconds sometimes it occurs to me that I would have chosen to be a volunteer, not an essential responsible agent in this project. But it is always a fleeting thought, and then I remember the good will our God has toward us. I remember the great people in our culture and religion, like Sayyid Muhammad Husayn, our examples.

A Perfect Braid: Humanitarianism, Piety, and Politics

Hajjeh Zahra's testimony above epitomizes the entanglement of the major threads that constitute both religious and community *iltizām*, including humanitarian impulses, political sensibility, and religious faith. She also hints at the social importance of *iltizām* for women's senses of self. In what follows, I take up in detail volunteers' most common explanations for their commitment to community—reasons woven through by these threads so tightly that it is impossible to clearly separate them, reasons that illuminate the artificiality of that separation. Eventually, this fusion brings us back to Sayyida Zaynab as the ideal role model for pious Shiʻi women. She represents a woman who is pious, political, caring, and self-confident, one in whom the braid is indissoluble and complete.

"*MIN IL-INSĀNIYYEH* . . ."—"FROM HUMANITY . . ."

> *Al-insāniyya mas'ūliyya min Allah* [Humanity is a responsibility from God].
>
> —a volunteer

Perhaps the most obvious impulse motivating women to devote long hours to community service—one mentioned at least as often as faith—is simply humanitarianism. Characterized as having a "love of giving" in their nature, the words and actions of some women seemed to overflow with generosity and compassion. Hajjeh Umm Ali exemplified this, as she sacrificed time, energy, health, and sleep for her work with al-Mabarrat: "If someone doesn't care for others, he cannot be a human being. *Bithissi insāniyytik btikbar mishān ha-shughil, bithissi innik insān mishān[h]u.* You feel your humanity grows because of this work; you feel that you are a person because of it."

Humanitarian sentiment was fueled by a sense of collective Shiʻi deprivation, itself in turn fed by the sheer transparency of need. This was dramatically magnified for those who had lived through the violence of Lebanon's recent history. As one woman put it, "We saw the worst of humanity around us, so we had to do better." Lebanese writer Jean Said Makdisi described daily life during the 1982 Israeli siege of Beirut:

> Queues formed wherever the motors were running and the water being pumped; long winding queues of men, women, and children patiently standing in line carrying a colorful assortment of blue, green, orange, red, yellow plastic containers. This artesian well water was not good for drinking, but many people drank it anyway. As the siege went on and the supply of butane gas ran out, people could not even boil it—the refugees who had no stoves could not boil it in any case. The major problem with the well water, however, was that it was salty. As the supply of safe drinking water in West Beirut ended, we began to hear of babies dying because of the consumption of salt. (1990: 175)

To give voice to the countless potent and haunting testimonies of pain, terror, and resilience that remain from the wars, choking, hovering under the surface of the newly poured concrete that has paved a "rebuilt" Beirut, is another project in itself. Here I limit myself—knowing that this does not do their stories justice—to noting the links between the experience of war and the desire to help others.

> During the war, it was horrible, horrible, but we continued to work. I would take my children to the basement during the bombings. But I couldn't sit still with them like the others, drinking coffee, playing cards to pass time. When I sat like that I felt like I was dying. So whenever there was a break in the situation outside, I would go out and see what I could do to help. We would distribute drinking water to people. And whenever I found some food I would divide it into small portions and distribute it.

This woman, Hajjeh Huda, saw her brother killed during one of these water-delivery excursions. Similar stories—that highlighted both the narrator's desire to help and her loss—abounded among the women I worked with.

The postwar situation in Lebanon is also appalling, with perpetual economic downslide, a continuing refugee crisis, and infrastructural restoration that has been narrowly focused on Beirut's downtown center.[26] Today, at every turn in al-Dahiyya (as in much of Lebanon) one is confronted with poverty. While explaining why they do what they do, volunteers frequently gestured out a window to the neighborhood around them. One young woman pointed at a crumbling building across the street, fresh laundry hanging from the windows: "This is the

---

[26] See Makdisi (1997) for a critique of the rebuilding of downtown Beirut.

reality we are living in our country. It is my duty as a human being to help."

The specificity of this reality—or at least the sense of its specificity—was frequently noted by residents of al-Dahiyya. During an exhibit of community service organizations from all over the country that I attended with Amaney and Alia, Amaney exclaimed, "It's unbelievable how many of these *jam'iyyas* are from our area!" I wondered aloud why that should be, given that much of Lebanon staggered under the current economic crisis. Alia jumped in, "Because we live among them, we see the problems with our eyes, all the time. Other *jam'iyyas* are in rich areas; even in West Beirut they don't see this much poverty. They don't live next door to it."

Most, though not all, volunteers in *jam'iyyas* in al-Dahiyya lived in the area. Yet until they began volunteering, many were unaware of the severity of need that existed, in some cases, just next door. "When I first visited a poor family, I was shocked. I was shocked." As she described this home, tears welled in this volunteer's eyes and voice, "The house was in a building—what a building!—it was all broken, and the house, all of it, all of it, was perhaps the size of this hallway and a very small bathroom." Gesturing to the hallway behind us, which was perhaps five feet wide and ten or twelve feet long, she continued:

> There was no electricity, and we had to use lighters to see! Her [the woman of the household] husband had left; no one knows where he is. And she had many children, all outside playing in the street, in the dirt, because there was no place else for them. My heart broke, do you know this feeling? My heart broke. And this picture of this small, dark, dirty home and this woman trying to feed her children all by herself, it remains with me always. When I am tired and I want to say *khalas*, let me stop, it comes to my mind and allows me to keep working.

Even those to whom the nature of poverty was not unfamiliar were deeply affected by the situations of poor families, and carried their stories with them beyond the *jam'iyya* walls. The "voices" of the poor, they relayed their stories to those who preferred not to hear.

"*QURBATAN ALLAH* . . ." — "TO BE CLOSER TO GOD . . ."

Humanitarianism was inextricably linked, for many volunteers, to piety. The quotation that is the epigraph to the last section continues: "Humanity is a responsibility. God gave to humans so that we could give. In this way, volunteer work is not new work, it's not based in the Ministry of Social Affairs, or in some organization. It is based upon humanity; from the moment humanity was created, humanitarianism began."

The tangibility and omnipresence of religion in daily life extend to women's volunteerism. Fulfilling one's practical religious obligations, namely, praying and fasting, was not considered "enough" to be a pious person. Approaching *al-taqwā*, that final rung on the ladder of piety, also entailed contributing to the community. Yet this was not a unidirectional relationship. Community service itself transformed volunteers, bringing them closer to *al-taqwā*. This bidirectional relationship between the religious and community aspects of *iltizām* was often articulated as *qurbatan Allah* (becoming closer to God). One expresses and demonstrates piety by volunteering, an act pleasing to God, and at the same time, volunteering itself contributes to piety, increasing one's desire to work even harder in order to further please God.

Some women explained this process of becoming more pious as *izdiwāj*, "coupling" or "pairing" with God. The intensity of this experience for volunteers cannot be underestimated. As Hajjeh Huda told me, "We leave ourselves, we are no longer separate from this work or from God; we have entered a state of constant *izdiwāj* with it." Others drew on the notion of nourishment, explaining that rather than bringing material gain, their work nourished their souls and selves spiritually, and in doing so, brought them pleasure.

After volunteers detailed for me the long hours they devoted to *jam'iyya* work in addition to their household duties, I often asked incredulously, "Where do you get all this energy?" Without fail, their responses were either that they simply never felt tired, or that with tiredness came *liza* (pleasure), a "volunteer's high," or as one woman phrased it, "This work is morphine." The pleasure volunteering brought women cycled back into the dialectical relationship between piety and community service: "Say I'm not able to walk. The first day I walk a little, and then the second day a little more, and eventually it is possible. It is the same thing for this work. And you feel happy inside, and then you can continue without feeling tired. You feel joy! It's all from the principle of becoming closer to God" (Hajjeh Umm Ali).

I had the fortune to meet and work with Hajjeh Umm Ali and several other volunteers who were respected by their peers as women who worked for the sake of *qurbatan Allah* and had attained *izdiwāj* with God. Like the Catholic Mother Theresa, these women simply radiated the luminous serenity that often accompanies absolute faith. Each of them credited volunteering with giving her the push she needed to take a step further up the ladder of piety. Their serenity was also related to their certainty about *al-ākhira*, the afterlife. The afterlife was a common unstated assumption in conversations with the devout. As one person explained, quoting a *ḥadīth*, "The afterlife is the promise of all good things that will come in return for hardship and living correctly now. 'Idha qāmat al-qiyāma wa fī aḥadikum faskha fayaghrusha' (If Judgment Day is coming and you have a seedling in your hand, plant it)."

As noted in chapter 3, many pious Shiʿis believed that each person has an "account" (ḥisāb) with God. This "account" will be calculated on Judgment Day, determining whether a person will spend eternity in heaven or hell. Community service in this life adds 'ajr to the account. 'Ajr is divine recompense, like afterlife credits or "brownie points" that one can accumulate with God. (One volunteer used the image of a piggy-bank to explain this to me.) The more one serves others, the more 'ajr she collects, and the more certain her fate.

Implicated in these notions is the idea that all that is good is a gift from God. The way a person utilizes these gifts is crucial:

> If you need to redo your salon, redo everyone's salon. Yes, the devil will say to you, "But I worked hard for this money," but God will respond, "But who gave you the ability and opportunity and health to work?" (Hajjeh Huda)

The devout believed that a great debt was owed to God for absolutely everything. Above, Hajjeh Zahra explained this debt as a responsibility humans carry, using the concepts taklīf ilāhi and amāna. In her use of taklīf ilāhi, she conveys the idea of something that is both commanded by God, a duty, and granted by God, a responsibility. Amāna refers to a God-given trust or charge, a potential given with the understanding that one is accountable for how it is used.

Volunteering is one way pious women could fulfill their taklīf ilāhi. Taklīf ilāhi joins with the concept takāful ijtimāʿi (mutual social responsibility) in community service. Volunteers consistently used the latter phrase, takāful ijtimāʿi,[27] to convey the crux of their inspiration. This concept expresses acceptance of taklīf ilāhi specifically for the social welfare of the world—in the often cited Qurʾanic phrasing, a human being is "God's deputy on earth" (khalīfat allāh fiʾl-ʾard).

These concepts underscore the inseparability of humanitarian sentiment and religious faith, an inseparability foregrounded in the authentication process, as it consistently relates the world to the hereafter: "I think about heaven, but I work in the world. I live in fusion with the two. If I smile to another person, I make that person more comfortable, which is good in the world, and at the same time, I gain 'ajr for the afterlife. This is the beauty of it. You accomplish both at the same time" (a volunteer).

---

[27] Another phrasing of this notion is takāful al-ʿām.

For some volunteers, this relationship was a causal one, with humanitarianism inevitably stemming from religiosity. This was the subject of one session during the SAA volunteer training seminar. Hajjeh Amal taught us that humanitarianism is an innate part of humans' *fiṭra*, or natural disposition. As children grow, their *fiṭra* is corrupted by the world, and their natural tendency to do good is lost. She then emphasized that one of the most important Islamic goals of community service is *"tanmiyyat al-mashā'ir al-insāniyya"* (the development of humanitarian feelings) in the volunteers themselves. One's commitment to the community should arise from one primary source: religion. Humanitarian sentiment would then follow as natural tendencies were recouped from worldly corruption via faith. In Hajjeh Amal's words:

> Faith begins with belief in God and extends to the relationship with Creation. These are in essence the same thing. Belief in God and humanitarianism are the same thing. You cannot divide them; you must have both. To truly be religious, a person must have this relationship with Creation. A person who does not have humanitarianism is no different from one who does not believe in God. Because both serve only their own interests. One's work must serve God's interests, which are the interests of others.

For Hajjeh Amal, the necessity of community service to piety was so clearly crucial that on another occasion she suggested that helping others could replace prayer in one's afterlife account, while prayer was not sufficient to replace helping others. This statement was met with doubt, and she quickly went on to assert, "But of course this does not mean that we do not pray; we need to pray in order to keep our motivations strong." Here again we see a dialectical relationship between piety and community service.

This relationship was also implicated in the ways pious Shi'is distinguished themselves from others in Lebanon. Volunteers saw their opposite in what they considered the nonpious Lebanese elite who had no social commitment, those who seemed to spend their wealth frivolously, blind to the growing poverty in their country. One woman lamented:

> Here in Lebanon, you would say the economic situation is bad, but then you go to restaurants and you find them full. There is money in the country, but it's in private hands, and it's spent haphazardly. The problem is that those who have money don't care that there are people who sleep without food. They live in luxury, they come and go, and they say, "No, there isn't anyone hungry."

A common response to such a lament was to insist that if only the wealthy would "find" or "remember" their religion, whatever religion, and apply it correctly to life, they would lose their apathy and poverty would be alleviated.[28]

> To live with these kids makes you cry. We have one [volunteer] who works with us; she told me that the kids were invited to a restaurant. A small seven-year-old girl who has three brothers in al-Mabarrat. After they ate, the girl said to her, "What are you going to do with this chicken?" So she [the volunteer] said, "What *habībtī*, what do you want with it?" And the girl said, "Can't we take it home for our mom to eat?" So she packed it and took it to her mother.
>
> —*Hajjeh Umm Ali*

The world/afterlife fusion informs the way many volunteers cited "the orphans" as their fundamental motivation. References to orphans abounded in their daily talk, in their explanatory narratives about community service, and in the brochures and on the billboards of various *jam'iyyas*. During the most exhausting hours at the Ramadan Center, someone would often sigh, "Yalla, it's for the orphans." Brochures and billboards displayed images of poor orphans, along with a relevant Qur'anic verse or *hadīth*, for example, *"anā wa kāfil al-yatīm fi-l-janna"* (I [the Prophet] and the orphan's sponsor/supporter will be in heaven [together]).[29]

Despite this discursive and pictorial emphasis, not all *jam'iyyas* in al-Dahiyya focused on orphans. Al-Mabarrat and the Martyrs' Association are mandated to assist orphans in particular, but the ICEC and SAA are dedicated to the poor more generally. Some volunteers were critical of local emphasis on helping orphans above all others and the resulting resource allocations. Hajjeh Huda noted, "Here, an orphan has a passport that gets him help from everyone. But the poor do not." Another woman described "cases" where the father was present but the family's situation was far worse than that of some orphans. She typically sent orphan cases to organizations like al-Mabarrat in an effort to free resources for other poor people.

I asked an administrator at a non-orphan-specific *jam'iyya* why they used orphan images on their publications and he replied, "We have tried

[28]An interesting contrast to the notion that social apathy is a result of nonreligiosity is the idea I heard among a few nonreligious Lebanese friends that apathy was the only alternative to sectarianism in Lebanon, the only way to just "be a citizen."

[29]According to Bukhari's collection of *hadīth*, when the Prophet stated this, he then held his forefinger and middle finger close together, indicating closeness.

to convince people that while there are verses about helping orphans, there are also verses that discuss the importance of helping the poor, or the handicapped. But we can sit and talk for two hours and it will seem like they understand, and then, at the end, they say, 'I want to sponsor an orphan.' It is very difficult." The image of the orphan was clearly a powerful one, salient for donors and many volunteers. There are several reasons for this, beginning with the obvious point that orphans are children. The first consequence of their youth is that they are automatically more innocent than adults. Orphans cannot be held responsible for their situation, "What is their guilt/fault? (*shū zambun?*) What's the fault of the child?"

Not only can children not be blamed for their condition, but children had nothing to do with the wars. They never shot at anybody. In addition, it is indisputable that orphans *need* assistance. Many volunteers who used the phrase "for the orphans" felt that orphans were the *most* needy, because they had lost their father, who represented material support.[30] Orphans' need is also linked to ideas about the relationship of poverty to *takhalluf*. People assumed that orphans whose needs were not met were more likely to become criminals or "deviants."

The salience of the orphan as a metonym for the poor extends beyond his status as child. Orphans are allotted a special role in Islamic texts. For many pious Shi'is, part of being a good Muslim involved caring specifically for orphans. The emphasis the Prophet placed on orphans in his statements has been explained by the prevalence of war in his era. War meant the existence of widows and orphans who needed community support.

The contemporary moment in al-Dahiyya is similarly one of war widows and orphans. Shi'i Muslims bore the brunt of both the Israeli occupation and the Resistance against it. Indeed, one of the key elements involved in the iconographic salience of the orphan is the assumption that orphans are the children of Resistance martyrs. A counselor at the Martyrs' Association, where all the orphans supported actually are martyrs' children, noted that nationalist-political feelings partly inform support of their *jam'iyya*: "These children aren't just orphans, they are orphans of martyrs, and martyrs are heroes. Their fathers died fighting Israel, the enemy of the people, the land, the nation. Many people volunteer here because they have been inspired by the martyrs' self-sacrifice."

In fact, most of the orphans in al-Dahiyya were *not* the children of martyrs. Only around one-sixth of the approximately 9,500 orphans in the area (up to age twenty-one) were martyrs' children.[31] Despite this,

---

[30] The loss of one's mother represented loss of tenderness.
[31] Numbers provided by the CCSD.

people assumed a link between orphans and martyrs. Understandings of orphan images were to a certain extent dependent on a reading of those images as representing children who are poor and fatherless because their fathers made the ultimate sacrifice for the community. The image of the orphan moves from icon to symbol, from fatherless child to Islamic Resistance. For this reason, a volunteer's explanation that she exhausts herself daily "for the orphans" suggests an amalgamation that brings the political into the mix, along with the religious and humanitarian.

"BECAUSE IT IS OUR RESPONSIBILITY TO SUPPORT THE RESISTANCE AND OUR MARTYRS"

> [T]here was a private gathering a few months ago for the wives of Hizbullah fighters with Sayyid Hasan [Nasrallah]. And he said something, and I think if his words were hung in each of our homes, we would understand how large this responsibility is. He said, "Right now we are in a state of war." Israel was still occupying then. He said, "We have 1,280 martyrs. On Judgment Day each martyr will come carrying his blood on his sleeve, "I gave you my blood and sacrificed myself and left my children secure with you. Have you taken care of them?" What is going to be our response?" The blood of the martyrs is a huge responsibility that remains with us for tens and hundreds of years. It is a responsibility we have, not just to their children, but to their message.
>
> *—a volunteer*

Despite the liberation of most of Lebanon in May 2000, the emphasis on volunteering as participation in the Resistance had not subsided by July 2001. No doubt continuing disputes over the border, spurts of violence, and the Israeli occupation of Palestine contributed to this, as did the fact that people were simply inspired by the Resistance victory. Most community service work suggested a degree of support for the Resistance, but Resistance politics were most *directly* expressed in the work of the Martyrs' Association. Its volunteers and employees differentiated their *jam'iyya* from others, emphasizing that they were *not* providing charity. Rather, they considered their services "the least they could do" in supporting martyrs' families:

We do not provide assistance out of good will for the poor or average orphans. The people we help do not thank us; we do not accept thanks from them. No, it is the other way around. It is our responsibility to help them. They have given the most it is possible to give. We are their providers, since they have given the lives of their providers to the community. We are grateful to them, not the other way around.

Some volunteers came to the Association out of admiration for or a sense of indebtedness to martyrs, or because working with this particular *jam'iyya* was a direct form of participation in the Resistance. Others were themselves the widows or relatives of martyrs, women who had benefited from the Association and were now devoted to helping others in their situation:

> In 1981, Israel killed my father. We were five, and we were young. Our family came under the care of the people who later became the Martyrs' Association. At that time in Beirut, you had to stand for three, four hours to buy a loaf of bread. During this time of deprivation and destruction and war, these volunteers came to our home and secured everything for us. So my relationship with the Martyrs' Association is one of love. It took the place, to a certain extent, of my missing father. Do you know what it means to not have a father during war? Facing this, never mind doctrine ['aqīda], and never mind *iltizām*, if a *jam'iyya* raised you, of course you will feel indebted to it. We saw how the brothers and sisters were sacrificing their time to help us. They planted within us a love of giving. I grew up, and in '94 I joined the Martyrs' Association to reflect what they provided back on other families.

Many volunteers, like others in al-Dahiyya, had direct personal experiences of loss and hardship. Some lost loved ones in Israeli bombardments or to the Resistance. Others saw their homes destroyed and their families divided. They felt, or saw those close to them feel, the strains of poverty. This was not limited to Hizbullah-affiliated volunteers, but was widespread, as one woman from the SAA put it, "We have all lived suffering; we are all in this together."

In the end, for many volunteers, commitment to their community stemmed from a sense that there was something wrong with the situation in which they lived, something that could be altered for the better. Whether this was most emphatically articulated as political oppression, poverty, or the ills of the human world as opposed to the blessings of heaven, all three were laced into most of their narratives.

> We know that the situation is wrong. Not a small illness, that allows a person to say that there is no need to leave the house and tire, and to go sit in a café or on the beach instead. No, our feeling is that there is very strong injustice, and that we are oppressed.

Here, Hajjeh Umm Hadi layers references to the multifarious hardships Shi'i Lebanese have experienced. By using the language of oppression and injustice, she links current reality to the revolution of Imam Husayn, evoking a paradigmatic history of Shi'i marginalization and resistance. This history resonates in many of the role models that volunteers looked to for inspiration, and as major influences on their *iltizām*.

Models of Morality

The figures emulated by most volunteers all embody that fused triadic core that is *iltizām*. As they confronted poverty and war through embracing *takāful ijtimā'i*, most volunteers sought role models for their work in religious history. However, a few women looked to community leaders instead or in addition. These leaders were sometimes older women who had dedicated much of their lives to *jam'iyyas* and who were known for their piety (like Hajjeh Umm Ali). Religious clerics, specifically *marji'*s, were also local sources of inspiration. Many in al-Dahiyya looked to Fadlullah in this capacity, describing him as their role model on earth, a father figure, and a trusted advisor. Others, particularly older women who were among the earliest Shi'i activists, cited Musa al-Sadr or his sister as exemplary models, while younger volunteers sometimes mentioned Nasrallah. In addition to these local models, a few people mentioned examples associated with Christianity, namely, Jesus and Mother Theresa.

However, the two major sources of inspiration for the vast majority of volunteers were located at the intersections of religion and history: Ayatollah Khomeini and *'ahl al-bayt* (the family of the Prophet). The latter represent the first example, the infallibles, and the former is credited with revitalizing a connection with them.

> Studying his [Khomeini's] life and his lectures, and how he interacted with his children, and with those close to him, it is amazing; he is a leader. Every action he did had a goal, everything he did was done exactly correctly. He truly represented the role of *'ahl al-bayt* on the ground. . . . And it's true that he's not pure the way they are, but he was a human being who showed us that if we walk on their path, this is what is possible. (a volunteer)

The Islamic Revolution in Iran solidified the link between the history and values of *'ahl al-bayt*, and contemporary battles against oppression and injustice. Yet volunteers did not read Khomeini's emphasis on emulating *'ahl al-bayt* as requiring—as is commonly assumed about Islamic movements—a return to life as it was during the time of the Prophet. Instead, they understood his lesson as teaching that the principles of *'ahl al-bayt* can and should be interpreted in order to fit the contemporary world.

In keeping with this, the Prophet and *'ahl al-bayt* were important examples for volunteers. Sometimes *'ahl al-bayt* were treated as a unified whole: "We can't choose from among them! *'ahl al-bayt* are *'ahl al-bayt!*" Other times, people described specific instances of generosity. This story told by Hajjeh Umm Ja'far was a common one:

> Imam Ali, peace be upon him, and Sayyida Fatima al-Zahra, peace be upon her, they had three cases [*halāt*] that came to them, and they would cut the food from their own mouths to give to them. For three days they would deprive themselves of food, in order to give first to the orphan, then the second day to the *miskīn* [poor], and then the third day to the *'asīr*, a person who has no means and no one.

Yet even more than *'ahl al-bayt* and the Prophet, volunteers looked, almost without exception, to historical female figures in Islam as role models for devotion, strength, and *iltizām*. Some mentioned Sayyida Khadija, the Prophet's first wife and the first believer, noting that she had sacrificed her substantial self-earned material resources entirely for the sake of Islam. Others looked to Sayyida Fatima al-Zahra', for her knowledge of Islam, her abilities in teaching others, and her generosity. But by far the most common role model for pious Shi'i women was Sayyida Zaynab.[32]

In the last chapter, we saw how the interpretation of Zaynab's behavior at Karbala changed with the authentication process. It was this new activist Zaynab that volunteers emulated. They compared their contributions to society with hers, observing that they had given relatively little, and citing her as one of the most salient examples for their active participation toward their community's welfare.

> Sayyida Zaynab, after the Imam's martyrdom, she raised all the orphans. She stood by their side, and lessened their pain, even though Imam Husayn was her brother. It was her brother, and her nephews, and her children who were martyred. And she was solid in her opinions and strong in her emotions. She was able to handle all the suffering she experienced, and all the problems and pain, and at the same time she could help others. She has taught us that no matter what we experience, it will never be as much as what she bore. She is the model for our work. From her we learn to help others. (Dalal)

Sayyida Zaynab represents a woman in whom piety, humanitarian sentiment, and political awareness fuse into a perfect braid. She also epitomizes the strength and activism volunteers seek to emulate. These qualities of

---

[32] See Friedl (1997) for a discussion of both Fatima and Zaynab as role models for women in Iran. She notes that Zaynab was particularly emphasized during the Iran-Iraq war. It will be interesting to see whether the emphasis in Lebanon shifts in the years following Israeli withdrawal, away from Zaynab's direct activism toward Fatima's more stoic model.

strength and activism bleed out of the realm of community service into other aspects of their lives, and especially into their understandings of gender relations in the Shi'i pious modern. In the next chapter, the gendered aspects of public piety, community service, and the pious modern are brought center stage, as our discussion turns to women's *jihād*.

CHAPTER SIX

Public Piety as Women's *Jihād*

"THIS IS women's *jihād*." I heard that sentence over and over again, as volunteers described their community service work. The phrase "women's *jihād*" also applies to public piety more generally. This chapter is organized around unpacking that phrase and relationship, while taking a closer look at how public piety and its practices impinged on pious Shiʻi women's lives.

Although the practices of and ideas about piety based in "authenticated" Islam that have been detailed thus far involve and affect pious Shiʻis regardless of gender, they hold especial importance for women. No doubt this importance is partly constructed, the result of both the realities of field research in a highly gendered community and what one woman called "a western obsession with our women." Yet it is also an emic salience, stemming from the relationship between authentication and the greater participation of women in public life. "Women's *jihād*" captures the multifarious valences of that emic salience.

The word *jihād* has been much maligned, used either to conjure fear or inspire violence. As pious Shiʻis used it, the term meant simply a "struggle." Although it was used to refer to the Resistance, it was also used to describe personal struggles within oneself and struggles like that against poverty. "Women's *jihād*" describes the way that the work of authenticated Islam is the particular responsibility of pious Shiʻi women with regard to the markers of piety they carried and their centrality in signifying modern-ness. *Jihād* here is both a privilege and a duty.

I begin this chapter by examining the emergence of public piety as a "new" social norm with particular ramifications for women and interrogating the specifics of that newness. Public piety marked women most visibly in the pious modern via their volunteerism, their *ḥijāb*s, and the prominence of Zaynab as a model. I then turn to the relationship between public piety and women's struggles over their public participation, their "gender *jihād*." Finally, the chapter concludes by considering the implications of how women's public piety was also crucial to the community's global visibility.

A Normative Moral System with a "New" Social Norm

The reinterpreted Sayyida Zaynab provided a model of ideal comportment for pious Shi'i women and set a standard of moral behavior to which many aspired. These aspirations were manifested in daily and seasonal religious practices and in engagement with the construction of authenticated religious discourses. As we will see below, community service has also recently been incorporated as an equally crucial element in this normative moral system. The Zaynab model—essentially a model for public piety—has been emphasized to such an extent that it has had the effect of fostering elevated social expectations for women. These expectations were conveyed by family members and close friends, as well as acquaintances, neighbors, and strangers at institutions like schools and *jam'iyyas*. Many women seemed more obviously pious than their husbands, and related pleading with them to fast during Ramadan or reminding them to pray.

Self-expectations were by far the heaviest to bear. Women often compared their actions to what they imagined Zaynab would have done in their place.

> Whenever I am faced with a problem, I ask myself, am I going to act like Zaynab or not? If someone knocks at my door am I going to help him or not? Am I going to feel with others or not, am I going to give even more of myself or not, am I going to have the courage to face oppression or not? (Hajjeh Umm Ali)

Not only did this chronic comparison lead to idealized self-expectations, but it fostered pressure on other women to hold themselves to the same standard. In several *jam'iyya* meetings, a senior sister exhorted others to think about "What Zaynab would have done"—both when volunteers seemed disheartened by their never-ending work and when cooperation among them seemed to falter.

Social pressures were strongest around the most publicly visible aspects of piety—Islamic dress and volunteerism. With regard to the latter, volunteers conveyed expectations regarding participation in community service to their relatives, friends, peers, and neighbors in conversations about *jam'iyya* activities as well as outright attempts at recruitment. Relationships were cultivated with new volunteers, and expectations were reinforced through *jam'iyya* workshops and training seminars. Advocates of community service explained volunteering as a "rational" choice, clearly connected to *iltizām*, and drew on Qur'anic verses and *ḥadīth* such as "He who sleeps full while his neighbor is hungry is not a believer."[1] These quotations were included in conversations, inscribed on plaques adorning *jam'iyya* and household walls, and printed prominently on *jam'iyyas'* brochures, billboards, and invitations.

The *jam'iyyas* also contributed to the maintenance of dress norms, by either insisting or more subtly indicating that volunteers should be *muhajjaba*. One *jam'iyya* that welcomed both *muhajjaba* and non-*muhajjaba* volunteers restricted full membership and internal voting rights to the former. Defending this, Hajjeh Hala, a member of the *jam'iyya*'s administration, asserted that their members must demonstrate "good Islamic values," and therefore are required to be Muslim and *muhajjaba*. On several occasions non-*muhajjaba* volunteers argued that the *hijāb* cannot attest to a woman's character, contending that it was quite possible for a non-*muhajjaba* woman to be more pious than one who conforms to Islamic dress. While in principle Hajjeh Hala and other administrators agreed with this point, they always countered that it was crucial for the *jam'iyya* to present "an Islamic appearance," noting "people are already talking because they see non-*muhajjaba* women working with us." This final phrase indicates the extent to which not only individual women, but also *jam'iyyas* themselves are subject to judgment within the normative moral order of public piety. The reputation of the *jam'iyya* was partly dependent on the reputations of its members, resulting in pressure on its volunteers to discipline themselves within the bounds of morally acceptable behavior.

Slightly more subtle social pressures around dress took the form of comments, teasing, pointed storytelling, or praise of how beautiful a woman would look in a *hijāb*. For example, one young woman's mother, unfazed by her daughter's grimace, frequently related the story of how she (the daughter) had once worn a *hijāb* for a school play, emphasizing how lovely she had looked in the scarf.

In this context, public piety was understood as an externally visible indication of a woman's morality. Though rare, there were situations where this had serious ramifications for women's lives. One woman began both volunteering with an Islamic *jam'iyya* and wearing the *hijāb* in order to appease her in-laws after her husband's death, because she feared that if she did not publicly demonstrate her morality, they might not trust her to raise her children.[2] Unmarried women were particularly susceptible to pressure from potential spouses or self-appointed matchmakers, as many pious young men—or their families—desired visibly pious wives.

---

[1] *Man bāt shab'ānan wa jāruhu jaw'ān fa-laysa bi-muslim.*

[2] According to *sharī'a*, her husband's family would have the right to claim custody of the children after age seven for boys and nine for girls.

Community Service as a "New" Norm

The inclusion of community service within this normative moral framework is a relatively new phenomenon, and links the authentication process with its ideas about progress to women's public participation in new ways. Active volunteers were seen to embody the very qualities in Zaynab that are desired—emotional strength, outspokenness, and dedication to others. Although volunteering is only one possible way of emulating Zaynab, it has become the most commonly accepted and expected way. Taking this to an extreme, some women expressed the unorthodox conviction that community service is a religious "duty" on par with prayer, "Just as prayer and fasting are obligatory for us, now this work is too." In this community, in order to be seen as a "good" middle-class Muslim woman—barring exempting circumstances—a woman was expected to participate in at least some of the activities of at least one *jam'iyya* in addition to fulfilling her other religious obligations. In this sense, community service added a "new" element to the social norm of public piety in al-Dahiyya.

Here I qualify "new" with quotation marks because it is necessary to interrogate what exactly it is that was new about pious women's volunteerism. As we have seen, in explaining why they volunteer, women frequently drew upon concepts like *takāful ijtimā'ī* (mutual social responsibility). This is *not* a new concept; rather, it locates the roots of community service in a longstanding Islamic moral discourse about charity. Similarly, women's emulation of Zaynab connects their contemporary activities to the historical and religious past.

Yet in al-Dahiyya, volunteerism has been institutionalized into a broader public arena in ways that *are* new. Prior to the institutionalization of the Shi'i Islamic movement, pious people remembered the poor during Ramadan, and often donated food and goods, in addition to paying their *khums* and *zakāt*. Yet these charitable acts were not necessarily visible. There were people known for their generosity, but the possibility of censorship of those who did *not* contribute did not exist in the same way. The institutionalization of *takāful ijtimā'ī* in the *jam'iyyas* made giving time, as well as money, an explicitly public—and highly visible—act. As such, it became available to be commented on, praised, and encouraged by others.

This visibility has also thrust community service into a broader movement to promote the continual material and spiritual progress of the community. Women's participation was considered necessary to and indicative of this progress, raising the stakes of that participation significantly. This link between women's volunteerism and the pious modern not only constructed volunteering as a powerful normative marker of morality, but also emphasized women's public activity as a necessary component of their piety within the framework of authenticated Islam.

In striving to be pious according to this ideal, women faced what they cast as "traditional" ideas about their proper roles, ideas that needed to be left behind for the sake of both progress and piety. The next sections of this chapter look first to the ways that women's public participation via community service work fit within these traditional ideas, then to the places where it came into conflict with them, and finally, to the ways that pious Shi'i women confronted these points of conflict.

Women's Work

General consensus in al-Dahiyya held that voluntary community service was valuable and important work for women in particular.[3] This is related to the felicitous convergence of beliefs about women's "natural" nurturing proclivities with the structure and method of community work itself. Women were believed to have empathetic and emotional capacities that made them inherently suited to community work. To a certain extent, this perceived compatibility obtains from the "visiting method." Most of the tasks involved in providing aid were domestically oriented. Furthermore, in a community where a woman's—and her family's—reputation would be severely compromised if she were to receive unaccompanied male visitors in her home, household visits were impossible for male volunteers. This was compounded by the fact that many of the households assisted by *jam'iyyas* were female-headed.

An additional factor is that many women wanted to contribute in valuable ways to the Resistance, and desired access to a "door" to heaven like that provided by martyrdom. Yet military service was the only type of work for which most people believed women innately unsuited.[4] Volunteering represented an appropriate way for women to resist Israeli occupation without carrying weapons.

Community service's status as *women's* work was reflected in the spaces of the *jam'iyyas* themselves, spaces considered appropriate for pious Shi'i women, and that did not threaten the moral and social order of the community. They were also spaces where women felt comfortable,

---

[3] Most volunteers were women (e.g., only 20 of 340 ICEC volunteers were men), though many *jam'iyya* employees were men. *Jam'iyya* administrators acknowledged that this gendered division of labor was problematic but argued that it was difficult to hire women when so many men were unemployed, because in Lebanon it is men who are generally held responsible for financially supporting households.

[4] Arguments exist for women's military participation in specific situations, especially related to self-defense. See chap. 4, n. 54.

especially with regard to their relationships with other volunteers and employees.

HAJJEH SUAD: We like to come and sit here; it's our second home.

HAJJEH UMM MUHAMMAD: Even interactions with the brothers don't feel uncomfortable or strange. Here you feel like you are living within a family, with people who care about you. You feel like you are interacting with your son, your brother, your father.

The kinship idioms women used to describe their relationships with other volunteers and employees reproduce the Lebanese "kin contract"—"the ideal of family love organized within a patriarchal structure of rights and responsibilities" (Joseph 2000: 116). A dual notion of kin as representing both care and control appears in the idea that *jam'iyyas* are appropriate spaces for women because of the presence of their "brothers" and older "sisters."[5] Volunteers also entered poor households as older sisters/mothers who both support and control their "younger" relatives. In infusing these relationships with the kinship idiom, the pious modern reinforces a relational self, yet one that is viewed as different and better than the "traditional" relational self. "Traditional" people were seen as overly embedded in extended family networks to the detriment of the community. Although family is still important, the new ideal is a self in relation to *both* kin and community, with the greater good of the latter holding priority.

The spaces, relationships, and activities of the *jam'iyyas* both facilitated and circumscribed women's public participation by emphasizing its compatibility with a status quo that emphasized women's domestic nature, relationships, and responsibilities. However, despite this perceived compatibility, many pious women had to struggle in order to participate publicly, often engaging in a skilled balancing act.

Balancing the Double/Triple Shift

While some women volunteered sporadically, or exclusively during Ramadan, others took community service as seriously as employment. Between community service and *taw'iyya* for self-improvement, a volunteer's day was easily filled. Yet volunteering was undertaken in addition to household work, and sometimes employment. Pious women consciously

[5] Here volunteers used kinship idioms to describe relationships within the *jam'iyyas*. Suad Joseph argues that kin are the basis of political networks and citizenship models in Lebanon (1997c and 2000). See Joseph also on the valences of caring and control in brother-sister relationships (1994 and 1999b).

chose to take on a double or triple shift in order to contribute to their community's public welfare.[6]

All the women I worked with prioritized household responsibilities, sometimes asserting strongly that women who could not keep their households "in order" should not be involved in community service. This notion emerges from Lebanese patriarchal norms that cut across religion and class.[7] It also points to a tension among the various arguments pious Shi'i women make about their public and domestic roles.

> Doesn't Islam's emphasis, in jurisprudence and legislation [al-'aḥkām w-al-tashrī'āt], on women's femininity lead us to the conclusion that women's essential Islamic role is that of caretaker of the home/family [murabiyyat al-manzil]?
>
> . . . Does Islam force a woman to be a homemaker before and after marriage? No person has the right, whether her father, mother, brother, or any relative, to obligate a woman by the sharī'a to work in her parents' home before marriage, for housework is not required [mafrūḍan] of a woman, just as a father or mother cannot obligate a male child to do housework.
>
> Yes, she has this (role), if she chooses it voluntarily, from a sense of responsibility towards the home that raised her.
>
> And when a young woman becomes a wife, housework remains a voluntary matter, she chooses to do it or not, for the marriage contract does not obligate her from the perspective of the sharī'a to do housework, or even to raise the children, unless the two spouses included fulfilling that work as a special stipulation in the marriage contract. (Fadlullah 1997: 59–60)

Most volunteers felt that with proper "organization," women should be able to complete their housework and still have plenty of time to devote to others. Such organization required seemingly inexhaustible reserves of energy. Many women woke up extraordinarily early. Others stayed up late cooking. Hajjeh Umm Ali spent full days at al-Mabarrat, spent late afternoons and evenings with her children, grandchildren, and husband, then remained awake long after they slept, completing her housework as well as additional work for the jam'iyya: "I calculate my energy. I am able to stay up late making food. I am able to iron at night. But I don't feel tired. My energy comes from God." Faith contributed to the tirelessness of many volunteers, as energy and efficiency were viewed as gifts from God.

These capabilities were sources of pride. Hajjeh Umm Muhammad commented, "By 7:30 [a.m.] I will have turned the gas off underneath

---

[6] Some of those who took on a triple shift were employed by jam'iyyas, while others worked at businesses, banks, and schools.

[7] For discussion of patriarchal social norms in Lebanon see Joseph (1990, 1994, 1999a, 2000).

my food." Another woman responded, drily, "Truth is, she doesn't have a man in the house." As this comment indicates, for most women, husbands presented a far greater difficulty, at least in theory, than housework. General opinion held that when a man remarried, whether he divorced his first wife or not, it was often because he felt neglected. "Sometimes if a woman isn't putting her home first, of course her husband will take another wife." This followed a conversation where a neighbor told me and a friend about a very active volunteer whose husband had recently taken a second wife. My friend's initial response was, "I don't think the Hajjeh even noticed much."

More commonly, difficulties with husbands were hinted at through comments appreciating and noting those men who were supportive of their wives' public work. As Hajjeh Huda shared:

> I am lucky that my husband supports what I do. Like during Ramadan, I go to the Center from morning until after *iftār*. Some men would throw a fit, but my husband supports me. Some men just don't want their wives leaving the house. That's wrong; he should support her to go help others. When a man cannot do community work because he is busy working to feed his family, he should encourage his wife to help. He is then helping by making it easier for her to contribute.

A recent trend at some *jam'iyyas* was for young volunteers to stipulate that they be able to continue volunteering after marriage before agreeing to an engagement. Tamara had done this: "I set the condition that I continue volunteering. My husband adapted. Now he tells me, 'If I am not doing my duty, what you do should cover both of us.'" Both Hajjeh Huda and Tamara hint at another point, one often used in women's arguments for the importance of their volunteerism: that by facilitating his spouse's good works, a man is doing good himself—because facilitating good work is good work. I will return to this point below.

When I interviewed her, Tamara was several months pregnant, and expressed her intention to continue volunteering after the baby was born. Her mother had already agreed to care for the child during the day. For many women, children presented an added responsibility. Young children were often jealous of their mothers' volunteerism, particularly if they worked with orphans. The burden of teaching them to accept her absence from home fell squarely on a woman's shoulders. Hajjeh Umm Ali explained proudly that she had taught her children that there were other children out there with no mothers who needed her, so that they too now "cared for the orphans." However, most women prioritized their own children, and tried to limit their *jam'iyya* time when the children were young. For their part, the *jam'iyyas* facilitated volunteers' family commitments by providing childcare.

In addition to the balancing acts volunteers performed, they were subject to gossip and criticism from others if it was believed that their homes were being the least bit neglected. Sometimes this criticism came from "sisters"—"superwomen" who had little patience for the "less organized." Hajjeh Umm Ali was particularly strident in her criticisms, insisting: "You cannot give if there is loss in the home. The sacrifices should be personal, not placed on your family. So do less visiting, have fewer coffees with friends, limit your fun time. You have to work on yourself so that you can give without your home suffering." Here Hajjeh Umm Ali implies that through "working on yourself" women should be able to successfully manage the balancing act. The ability to do so, often through personal sacrifices, was believed to reflect upon a woman's piety.

Volunteers also confronted criticism and gossip from the larger community, and noted that this is a difficulty plaguing all women in Lebanon who wish to work in any capacity outside their homes. In the specific context of volunteerism, however, they detected a note of hypocrisy in such disapproval: "On the one hand, people are impressed if we tell them we are helping poor families. But then when they see you leaving your house, they turn around and begin talking behind your back, saying that you are neglecting your family." Such criticism stems from deeply rooted social norms that relegate "good" women to the domestic sphere. These norms, characterized by pious Shi'is either as "traditional" (taqlīdī) or sometimes "eastern" (sharqī), were understood as "inherited," and were to give way to new norms rooted in authenticated Islamic practice and discourse.[8] I now turn to the ways that pious women facilitated and actively worked toward this transformation through their "gender jihād."

Gender Jihād

Gender jihād is the work that ultimately made it possible for women to undertake the "women's jihād" of public piety.[9] In order to fully enact public piety, women had to participate in the public arena, most obvi-

---

[8] These dichotomies are both constructed and changing, for example, the idea that women should be relegated to the domicile stems from early-twentieth-century middle-class notions of modernity (Khater 2001).

[9] Abugideiri presents a useful definition of "gender jihād" as "a struggle for gender parity in Muslim society in the name of divine justice" (2001: 89). Another term that has been used in Muslim contexts in lieu of "feminist" is "gender activist" (Badran 1994 and 2002). I do not use "feminist" to refer to my interlocutors for three reasons: (1) They consciously differentiated between equality (masāwa) and equity ('adāla), understanding the former to be feminism's struggle and to mean that men and women were identical in substance and

ously through their community service activities, but also through participation in Ashura commemorations and engagement with changing religious discourses in the authentication process. As such, public participation was crucial to both their piety and the spiritual and material progress of the community as a whole—as understood emically, and as understood in relation to the importance of women's status to western ideas about what is modern.

On the one hand, pious women's presence in the public transformed understandings and definitions of that public, and reflected the porosity of public/private divisions.[10] On the other hand, women volunteers lived in a milieu where women's prolific public participation was a relatively new phenomenon. It was also, as we began to see above, not without its critics. As I weighed the different perspectives I heard regarding women's public work with volunteers' experiences, I began to ask how volunteers themselves understood the multiple and contradictory social prescriptions within which they worked, and how they responded to gender-based restrictions and exclusions, and to their critics.

Pious Shi'i women were especially aware of exclusions based on qualities that were assumed to be, or defined as, distinctly masculine.[11] These qualities included the ability to cooperate, to be organized, and to think rationally. While expounding on the importance of the SAA as a women-only *jam'iyya* one afternoon, Hajjeh Amal observed, "Men think that women can't have a *jam'iyya* that works, because they think that when women gather we just gossip or fight." Assumptions that

spirit, an equation they felt was both impossible and undesirable. They instead argued for equity—equivalent but not identical rights, and promoted interpretations emphasizing what Leila Ahmed (1992) calls the "ethical egalitarianism" of Islam. (2) The ultimate motivations underlying many of their stances were on behalf of piety, not on behalf of women's rights. (3) Much of what is connoted by "Islamic feminism" today is scholar-research based, predicated on textual reinterpretation. Most pious Shi'i women were not directly engaged in such pursuits, although they deployed religious texts in their arguments. For more on Shi'i Islam and feminism see Afshar 1998, Böttcher 2001, Mir-Hosseini 1999, Moghadam 2002.

[10] Voluntary associations are usually located in the public sphere, and, because of an assumed gendered public/private divide, particularly in studies of the Middle East/North Africa, associated with men (Joseph 1997a). Pious Shi'i women's volunteerism troubles this through both the movement of women into public spaces and the incorporation of domestic-type activities into public welfare and work. See critiques of the rigidity, ahistoricity, and gendering of the public/private distinction by Abu-Lughod 1998c, Ayubi 1995, Hale 1996, Hatem 1994, Joseph 1983 and 1997b, Nelson 1974, Reiter 1975, and Singerman 1995. See also L. Deeb 2005 and Göle 1997 on the role of women's visibility in Muslim public spheres.

[11] See Nancy Fraser's discussion of how the public sphere may be constituted in part by a gendered exclusion stemming from its definition through distinctly "masculine" discursive protocols (1999).

women are not able to cooperate "democratically and rationally" also contributed to the gendered division of labor within *jam'iyyas*, as well as to a general dearth of women in leadership positions in al-Dahiyya.[12] Another way that women's public activity was sometimes derided by men was through stereotypes about women's idleness. A male *jam'iyya* administrator once grumbled to me that all-women *jam'iyyas* promoted "the *ṣubḥiyya* model" of community work, a reference to the morning coffee visits associated with "idle" middle- and upper-class women in Lebanon.

In combating such assumptions and limitations, the women I worked with embraced gender *jihād*, actively confronting sexism and patriarchy within their community. They did so by bringing together a number of strategies that combined to form a model for gender roles and relationships based upon "authenticated" Islam, a model that includes women's public participation as a constituent aspect.

First, volunteers highlighted a distinction between themselves and the stereotype of "*ṣubḥiyya*" women, labeling the latter "traditional" (*taqlīdī*). They underscored this difference by calling upon authenticated Islam's emphasis on self-improvement and societal contribution, and their role in promoting community progress. Hajjeh Khadija characterized "women whose time is consumed by *ṣubḥiyya*s and housework" as "moving backward" and "non-useful people."

A second aspect of gender *jihād* is manifest in *jam'iyyas'* role in educating poor women and volunteers alike toward more capable public participation. Beyond this, women drew on the existence of all-women *jam'iyyas* itself as evidence of their capacities to organize in order to productively contribute to society. Hajjeh Amal underscored the role of these *jam'iyyas*, challenging the assumed masculinity of the qualities necessary for public participation: "[T]hrough the work of women's *jam'iyyas*, we provide an example of how women can work democratically and rationally, with elections and a strong organizational structure. And we work to change this image that men have of women in our society." In addition to demonstration through example, some pious women proposed explicitly conducting *taw'iyya* with pious Shi'i men. They explained that this *taw'iyya* should teach men about authenticated interpretations of Islam, so that they would, in keeping with those interpretations, facilitate their wives' public activities. Again, by helping their wives "do good," men themselves would be doing good.

This issue arose at a seminar on women's public participation held by

---

[12] There were of course exceptions to this, including the director of an al-Mabarrat school and the Chief of Staff at a Martyrs' Association hospital.

Hizbullah's Women's Committee. Someone asked whether community service—broadly defined to include such things as holding political office—was a right or a responsibility. In response, Noha, the seminar's leader, cited Khomeini to argue that it was both, but especially a responsibility. She then explained that the problem was that "the ground isn't prepared yet" because there were multiple obstacles preventing women from fulfilling this responsibility, including women's own ignorance, a lack of community support, and most crucially, men, who had to be made aware of the realities and importance of women's work and role. Another woman added that men's *taw'iyya* should also emphasize men's role in the home; teaching men to share housework and childcare with their wives.

> How is it possible to say that it is acceptable and possible for a woman to work outside the home, given men's general disinclination to help their wives with housework, considering it shameful [*mu'īb*]?
>
> The source of saying that a man working inside the home is shameful is a social culture of backwardness, not Islam. Islam has no relationship to this view, as evidenced by the story of Imam Ali (peace be upon him) with Sayyida [Fatima] al-Zahra' (pbuh). We read that Sayyida al-Zahra' and Imam Ali (pbuh) met with the Prophet to divide the work between them, because each was burdened with responsibilities. So the Prophet delegated to al-Zahra' preparing flour and bread, and he delegated to Ali sweeping the house and gathering firewood. This demonstrates that a man sharing housework is not shameful for him. (Fadlullah 1997: 79)

Pious women believed that through *taw'iyya*, men would eventually come to understand gender roles and relations from the perspective of authenticated Islam, which, as noted in this passage from Fadlullah, includes sharing housework. This model stands in contrast to ideas about the domestic responsibilities that volunteers, as women, must fulfill, and represents a key arena in which pious women struggled to facilitate their public participation. To a certain extent, it is in their emphasis on teaching men to share domestic responsibilities that Shi'i women presented the most striking challenge to "traditional" gender roles.[13]

Part of this *taw'iyya* with men involved teaching authenticated interpretations of religious texts. Throughout the Women's Committee discussion, Noha and others made constant textual references, drawing mainly on Khomeini's writings and sermons. Their consensus was that Khomeini saw women's contributions outside the home as important,

---

[13] The Sudanese Islamist women discussed by Hale (2001) provide an interesting contrast here.

but that when men read his texts, they "refuse" to see that, reading into him only what they want to read.[14]

More commonly, women drew upon Fadlullah's progressive perspectives on gender and other issues. Fadlullah was especially a source for arguments about women's abilities to interpret religious texts and debate them with men—essentially, for women's rights and capacities to participate in the authentication process.[15] Böttcher quotes a shaykh who follows Fadlallah as saying, "Women have to master theology and Shi'i law and interpret it independently. . . . [T]hey can make Islamic theology from women for women" (2001: 5). By consciously drawing on textually based argument, pious women troubled its definition as masculine and asserted that they are equitable participants in public discourse. Like women's participation in debates about religious practices, this subverted ideas about women's religious knowledge as unlearned and "traditional."

The theme of men's misinterpretation of texts—whether intentional or merely ignorant—was a common one. Many pious women stood firmly behind the notion that when Islam was interpreted, understood, and *applied* correctly many of the problems women faced because of patriarchy would dissipate.[16] To this end, gender *jihād* also deployed models of strong women in Islamic history.[17] By doing this, women were, perhaps unconsciously, invoking a long history of gender activism or feminism in Lebanon. In the 1920s, Lebanese and Syrian women looked to Muslim models—including A'isha, the Prophet's wife who led troops into battle, and Khadija, the Prophet's wife who was also a self-reliant businesswoman—while demanding full citizenship rights.[18] These are models common to Sunni Islam. For pious Shi'i women, as noted in the last chapter, it was Sayyida Fatima and, as evidenced by her

---

[14] Many Iranian feminists would disagree with my interlocutors' interpretations of Khomeini as beneficial for women. For example, Afshar (1996) argues that much of the progress made by Iranian women since the Revolution has been since Khomeini's death.

[15] In 1978, Fadlullah established the first Shi'i theological seminary for women in Lebanon, and recently, a small Islamic women's community college was founded in al-Dahiyya under his patronage (Böttcher 2001).

[16] This is the core tenet of gender *jihād*. On its relationship to Islamic feminist textual reinterpretations, see Mir-Hosseini 1999, Wadud 2000, and Barlas 2002. The gender inequities subsumed under "traditional" culture also included issues ranging from discrimination in education and employment to domestic violence to honor crimes to coercion in marriage. In a sermon given on the occasion of both Ashura and International Women's Day, Fadlullah tackled many of these issues as stemming from incorrect understandings of Islam.

[17] See ElSadda (2001) for an analysis of deployments of the Prophet's wife A'isha in this regard.

[18] See Thompson 2000: 124.

constant presence in this book, Sayyida Zaynab, who were most commonly cited.

In the context of gender *jihād*, Zaynab's outspokenness and leadership qualities were emphasized, her position as "heroine of the heroes" of Karbala. Pious women underscored her confrontation with the Caliph during her imprisonment, and her indispensable role in spreading the message of revolution after the Imam's martyrdom:

> What would have happened if Imam Husayn went to Karbala and Sayyida Zaynab wasn't there? Because the story always begins after the martyrdom. So Zaynab (peace be upon her), she went and witnessed, and she was the one who carried the truth of Karbala with her. She stood before Yazid and spoke to him, and she showed the world what happened when Imam Husayn was martyred. It was she who carried the message of revolution to others. It was she who made possible Ashura. This is the role of women. There are many women in Islamic history who have sacrificed themselves and worked hard in society, and they prove wrong all those who say that Islam tells women to only be wives and nothing else. (a volunteer)

This is the ultimate image upon which women I worked with drew to highlight the value of their public roles in their community.

The multiple elements that make up pious women's gender *jihād* together posited a model for an ideal pious modern woman, one who was educated, outspoken, strong, and visible while also being pious and committed to her faith, family, and community. This model existed in a tense relationship to ideas about western modern womanhood.[19] For some, it necessarily incorporated an appreciation for the ways "all parts of the West are working; women and men are all working together." In this view, the contributions of women were crucial to western economic and political dominance in the contemporary world. "They are working with two teams while we work with only half of that." At the same time, the pious modern ideal rejected the tenets that modern selves must be individualized and (for women) "liberated." As Saba Mahmood has argued in her work on the Egyptian mosque movement (2001, 2005), and as the preceding pages of this chapter demonstrate, it is crucial to take women's desires and motives into account without adopting the normative assumption that all women ultimately desire gender equality as defined by mainstream liberal western feminisms.

For devout Shi'i women, public participation is a necessary part of how a person is pious and moral on three levels. First, before God—where it is an element in the fulfillment of one's piety and will contribute *'ajr* to one's afterlife account. Second, before others—where it provides a

[19] See my introduction.

visible display of one's morality. And finally, before oneself—where it nourishes the continued development of one's own faith. The ultimate goal of gender *jihād* was to facilitate women's abilities to be good, moral, pious Muslims, unhindered by patriarchal social norms that limited their public participation, norms that they viewed as standing in the path of their piety. While they were confronting patriarchal norms, their major motive for doing so was not the emancipation of individualized selves but equity in the possibilities for practicing a pious and moral lifestyle.

Women as Representative of the Pious Modern

Beyond local resistance to their public activities, pious women faced stereotypes held by the West and other communities in Lebanon about Muslim women, stereotypes that depict Muslim women as backward, passive, and oppressed by their religion. Their self-conscious confrontation of these stereotypes constituted the final aspect of their *jihād* that I will discuss and framed their community-level struggles.

Pious Shi'i women and men alike expressed a keen awareness that "the West" and "others in Lebanon" had their eyes trained constantly on "their women" as a marker of their "level" of modern-ness. Women were especially aware that others wanted to know what their lives were like *as women* in particular, scrutinizing how they were "treated" and what their societal roles were. They often articulated feeling a burden of responsibility to represent Muslim women both within and outside Lebanon.

Women combated external stereotypes about themselves as nonmodern in the same ways that they confronted patriarchal norms in their community. They drew upon women's *jam'iyyas* as examples, emphasized interpretations of Islamic texts that highlight gender equity, and highlighted Zaynab's model. For example, earlier in this chapter, we saw Hajjeh Amal discuss her hope that women's *jam'iyyas* would provide evidence of women's capacities to contribute productively to society. Her intended audience was not only pious Shi'i men, but also outsiders, as she continued:

> And this fight is not only an internal one. We are also fighting the outside image of Muslim women. We admit that there are some bad images out there, of very oppressed Islamic women, but this is not authentic/true [*ḥaqīqī*] Islam. We want to represent authentic Islam and to show that *iltizām* goes along with being cultured and educated. We have no examples, because the examples are either of oppressed women or of western women who are equal to

men in everything, even in the things they should not be equal in. Instead, we have to set a new example for the world, an example of women who are Muslim but strong and educated. Our goals as women are to improve these images of Muslim women within our society that thinks that women are less than men, and to change the image of the oppressed Muslim woman that exists outside our society. This work is part of our religious duty, because woman is the example for everything. A culture is judged by the level of its women.

As Shi'i women's *jihād* takes on the work of proving to the West that Muslim women can be both pious and modern, it becomes crucial to the wider community's self-presentation as modern. Women's progress— materially and spiritually—is understood as both evidence of the larger progress of the Shi'i pious modern and necessary to it. The visibility of pious Shi'i women—marked by *muḥajjaba*s' public activities and metadiscursive voices—is crucial to the demonstration of this progress. Equally important, the constructed distinction between pious modern women and western—or westernized—modern women is necessary to this Lebanese Shi'i community's identity and self-positioning nationally and globally.

That distinction is constructed around the social and religious commitment, the *iltizām*, of the ideal pious modern woman, *iltizām* expressed in public piety. As public piety takes on meaning in the transnational context, the stakes of piety for Shi'i women are raised. Yet despite these stakes, or perhaps because of them, the relationship between personal and public piety is never constant or simple. The final chapter takes up some of these cracks and complexities in order to revisit the public piety ideal.

CHAPTER SEVEN

The Pious Modern Ideal and Its Gaps

THUS FAR, we have seen the visible manifestations of *iltizām* in the spatial and temporal cadences of al-Dahiyya, in daily religious practices and discourses, devotion to community service, Ashura commemorations, and emulation of *'ahl al-bayt* and especially of Sayyida Zaynab. We have also seen how these various textures incorporate the tight weave of piety, humanitarianism, and politics, which constitutes and reflects authentication and the pious modern. The continuing transformations of all these manifestations implicate the tensions between the personal and the performed.

The relationship between public and personal piety varied from person to person, moment to moment. While they can be conceived as separate and not necessarily complementary, they often worked to reinforce one another. Public piety reinforced the necessity and importance of personal piety among the devout, while personal piety emerged in and through their performative acts of religiosity. My aim in this closing chapter is to underscore both the processual nature of public piety as it is cultivated through authentication, and the fact that a seamless mesh between the public and the personal is an unrealized ideal and the ultimate goal for the devout. By considering briefly the gaps that linger between personal and public religiosity, the process of "becoming pious," and efforts to foster that same process in the community's youth, we will revisit the ideal of the pious modern.

GAPS AND LIMITS

At first look, public piety appeared seamless in al-Dahiyya. Those who did not perform piety could easily be located outside the boundaries of the pious modern. With time, however, and as my relationships developed, I began to see both that the boundary itself was not as sharp as I had originally believed, and that there were people who considered themselves devout Muslims who did not quite fit, those in whom there was a, sometimes rather jarring, disconnect between personal and public piety. My initial conceptualization of these disconnects as contradictions gave way to a sense that they represent tensions in the relationship between public and personal piety, not only for those who feel them intimately, but also for the broader milieu.

Gaps in the fabric of public piety ranged from the more common—such as the generational differences I will come to below—to the intensely private reflections of personal, usually concealed, struggles with faith. People could be located on the margins—whether they felt their marginality or not—in a variety of ways. Fractures sometimes appeared between public and private selves in the service of social conformity or efforts to place oneself within the bounds of normative morality, whether merely for appearances or in a heartfelt desire to become a more normatively moral person.

Undoubtedly, there were some who practiced perfect public piety that was not mirrored in their private lives. For a few people, especially those who expressed a deep reflexive awareness of their "double life," as one woman put it, this resulted from doubt and crises of faith and caused tremendous emotional strain at times. For others, this was less a crisis of faith than a disjuncture of performance. So, for example, a woman might be *muḥajjaba* and volunteer, and be held up as a perfect representation of piety by her peers, but secretly listen to popular music when no one else could hear. Many people who experienced disjunctures of performance felt confident in their faith and beliefs. They either did not agree with all the tenets of public piety but were not ready to contradict them publicly, or they hid secret "vices" that they hoped to purge themselves of someday. Underlying the latter experience was the idea that by continually practicing piety, one would naturally get "better" at it.

Another factor that must be considered is the way that the attribution of moral meaning to public piety has linked it to a particular sort of social capital, a component of status in the Shiʻi pious modern. This link distressed some women, who feared that some of their peers volunteered or wore their *ḥijāb*s "just for appearances" (*bas lil-mazhar*). It is impossible to know to what extent particular acts do or do not represent "true" piety; it is clear that for some women, public piety was motivated by intense faith, while for others, it did not *necessarily* follow from religious conviction.

Both these gaps—where people were not necessarily as pious as they appeared to be in public and where a person who did not appear to be particularly pious may have actually prayed and fasted regularly and possessed a strong sense of faith—were discussed with me from time to time. Some pious Shiʻis feared that such gaps were rampant and potentially detrimental to the pious modern, while others considered them very rare occurrences. Most people agreed, however, that most of these disjunctures were critically linked to and could be explained by generational differences in the process of becoming pious.

BECOMING PIOUS: VANGUARD VERSUS *BANNĀT* (GIRLS/DAUGHTERS)

HAJJEH KHADIJA: *Kān ballasht in-nās, ḥa'ī'atan, ballashit min 'awā'il is-sab'īnāt, ya'ni, ballashit tayyār il-islām itḥarak, kān, bi'awal ballash shway ḥarakeh, li-nās ta'rif usūl dīn(h)a* . . . [People had begun, really, beginning in the early seventies, the Islamic movement began to be active. In the beginning it was slow, to get people to know the basis of their religion . . .]

For example, I knew I was Muslim, but I didn't pray. If I fasted, I would fast because my parents did, and sometimes I would break my fast, I didn't know that was wrong. I was only Muslim on my identity card. There was no Islamic environment. There was a traditional environment, a very conservative one.

LARA: How was this different from today's environment?

HAJJEH KHADIJA: Look, for example, my parents said to me, "wear a scarf [on your head]; it is required." OK, what was that scarf I would wear? Half my hair would show and it wasn't a problem. My arms were half-showing and it wasn't a problem. Even though for us, Islamic dress covers the body. You wear long [skirts], none of your body shows, and none of your hair. This is the true Islam [*hayda il-islām l-ḥa'ī'ī*]. But the Islam our parents taught us said you should wear a scarf because it is a sign that you are Muslim.

Now, I rejected this tradition; as I told you, we were a generation of change. At first we believed that perhaps this scarf was preventing us from progressing. This was what many of the writers and politicians said, that a woman's *ḥijāb* confined her, so that she just raised children and sat at home. So at first we rejected it. But later we came to understand the truth of Islam, and we said no, Islam is preferable. A Muslim woman, she is an educated woman, an activist woman, a woman who works in society and raises her children correctly at the same time, who is able to balance the world and her family.

This passage, taken from an interview with Hajjeh Khadija, encapsulates a personal perspective on the changes depicted throughout the preceding pages. Her highlighting of the *ḥijāb* as a representative object around which both her struggle and her eventual commitment revolved is typical, as putting on the *ḥijāb* is taken to represent a woman's *iltizām*. The struggle and shift she describes is characteristic of her generation, women who came of age in a Beirut where support for leftist political parties gradually shifted to participation in the Shi'i Islamic mobilization. Indeed, the personal trajectories of many young Shi'i women mirrored that of the mobilization. As they adopted the *ḥijāb* and lengthened their skirts, young women began completing their educations and participating in the community in unprecedented numbers.

Many of these young women committed to Islam against the wills of their parents and extended families. Hajjeh Zahra described her decision to commit as "difficult, because this was something that set me apart from my family. They worried about me a great deal when I first became committed." Women like Hajjeh Khadija and Hajjeh Zahra were the vanguard of piety and had great influence in both generational directions, as daughters to an older generation and as mothers to today's youth. Eventually some of their mothers and grandmothers joined them in *iltizām*. Each person who "became religious" and embraced public piety accompanied by religious understanding contributed to the transformation of the wider environment. At the same time, these shifts in milieu encouraged further commitment and emphasized the importance of knowledge underlying practice.

In the Shi'i pious modern of contemporary al-Dahiyya, *iltizām* has become a social norm. Yet this apparent success was also a cause for concern, as today's parents work to raise pious children. On the one hand, some people believed that the new milieu, *al-bī'a*, facilitates this task. On the other hand, others feared that the normalization of public piety would contribute to a potential increase in discord between public and personal piety.

The first view was by far the dominant one. The way people casually threw the word *al-bī'a* around was reminiscent of how "culture" is sometimes used in the United States, as a catchall that connoted all those things children somehow inhale from their surroundings. Yet at the same time, *al-bī'a* involved a certain amount of very self-conscious cultivation. The *bī'a* referred to was always that in which those forms and practices specific to the pious modern dominate. It implied a normative morality.

When I asked for more clarification of *al-bī'a*, primary elements began to emerge from this blur, including, in no particular order, home, school, and all the details of public piety I have described in this book, such as visual images, prayer, Ashura, and volunteering. *Al-bī'a* also includes politics and the hardships of war and occupation, whether experienced directly or brought into children's lives via television, radio, and adult conversations, none of which make any effort to hide the realities of Israeli aggression. The extent to which the occupation factored into the worlds of many Shi'i children was highlighted for me during a visit to an Islamic school. The kindergarten's walls overflowed with drawings students had done the previous week for the "Day of Resistance and Liberation." The artwork was strongly evocative of violence, with tanks, bombs, missiles, Resistance fighters, Israeli soldiers, stones, destroyed homes, the lifeless bodies of martyrs, and so on. A teacher kept up a running commentary on the artists: "His father was killed six months ago," "She saw her house destroyed," "She has never seen her grandparents in her village."

Islamic schools formed the institutional backbone of the *bī'a* for many parents, who knew their children would receive an education that was of better quality than the notoriously shoddy public schools in al-Dahiyya while including "proper" values. The schools facilitated children's participation in the Islamic milieu, via school plays, projects, and special events. During Ashura, girls acted out the battle of Karbala and its aftermath for an audience of weeping mothers, aunts, and cousins, emphasizing the role of the young women, especially Sayyida Zaynab. Another sort of play took place in order to mark *taklīf*.

The word *taklīf*—the same term used in volunteers' phrase *taklīf ilāhi*—literally means a commissioning, charging, or commandment, usually from God. It was commonly used to refer to the *hijāb*: when a girl turns nine, the *hijāb* becomes her *taklīf*, her commission, her duty. Since the mid-1990s, schools have been holding large ceremonies, also referred to as *taklīf*, to mark these girls' "coming of age."

Today Aziza and I went to the al-Mabarrat *taklīf*, in the large auditorium underneath the major mosque in the neighborhood. A shaykh stood to one side greeting male attendees, while three women on the other side greeted women. When we entered, Hajjeh Umm Ali spotted us and sat us in the first women's row with journalists and other official looking people. . . .

After the introduction, the girls being honored walked down the side aisles to the stage, to resounding applause from the audience. They were dressed like brides (reminiscent of Catholic first communions) mostly in white, with gold garlands wrapped around their head-coverings. They sang a song, then joined the audience. Then Fadlullah's son, Sayyid Ali, spoke in his father's name. He spoke about the responsibility that comes with the *hijāb*, about how it is a cover for one's heart and morals, and about choosing the Islamic path.

Following this there was a play put on by younger and older girls from al-Mabarrat, those not being honored that day. In the play, a group of girls found a gold box. A princely figure appeared in flowing white, and they ask him to open it. He tells them that the only thing that can open the box is a secret word, which they have to discover on their own. So the girls divide into three groups to search for the word. During their wanderings, they encounter various puppets (trees, flowers, butterflies) that teach them lessons. Eventually, they reconvene at the box. One group exclaims that the secret word is *mahabat allāh* [the love of God], another group counters that it is *ma'rifa* [knowledge], while the third claims that it is *tawādu'* [modesty]. None of the words open the box. They think for a while and then one girl exclaims: "But it's all three!" and says *"al-taqwā"* [absolute piety/faith]. At this, the box opens, and a voice announces that there is a treasure inside, which turns out to be the Qur'an. After the play, a long announcement listed donors of gifts for the girls being honored, and then each girl was given a bag that Aziza speculated held prayer clothes and a Qur'an.

Over the next few weeks I asked everyone I saw about these *taklīfs*. The ceremonies had begun because school administrators felt that publicly acknowledging this transitional moment in girls' lives would mark the changes that accompanied the *ḥijāb* (such as only attending single-sex beaches) as positive, a moment of joy worthy of celebration. Yet at the same time, some feared that public *taklīfs* would create external and nonreligious motivations for girls to want to wear the *ḥijāb*, so that they would wear it in order to participate in the ceremony or fit in with their classmates. Most people felt that that was the mostly likely scenario for most nine-year-old children, but that with proper education and *al-bī'a*, they would eventually wear their scarves in earnest. The issue of how consciously committed a nine-year-old can be, coupled with the emphasis placed on choice in veiling, has led to some debate over the proper age at which a girl may become *muḥajjaba*. Several women insisted that Fadlullah had at one time contemplated raising the age of veiling to thirteen for this reason.

For girls, *taklīf* also marks the moment at which prayer, fasting, and other religious duties begin. I asked one shaykh why they do not similarly celebrate the beginning of fasting and prayer for boys—whose *taklīf* begins at age ten—and he replied that since most children of that age already pray and fast, those practices do not represent a major lifestyle change like the *ḥijāb* does. The shaykh's reply also confirmed what I had noticed during my visits to many pious households: young children often prayed and fasted alongside their parents and older siblings.

The notion that children naturally absorbed pious practices from their parents was a common one. Very few children were actively taught to pray. They usually began by imitating older household members, who then gently corrected their pronunciation and postures until they learned their prayers correctly. Children who prayed on their own at a young age were proudly praised. *"Smallah ʿalay(ha),"*[1] s/he's already praying!" Young girls who played dress-up with their mothers' scarves also garnered such praise, as did any acknowledgment on a child's part that she understood the tenets and practices of authenticated Islam.

---

[1] This phrase literally means "May God's name be upon him/her" and connotes "God bless him/her" with undertones of invoking protection from the evil eye.

Religiosity was also understood to be absorbed as children accompanied their mothers as they went about their days. During Ashura, preschool children attended *majālis* with their mothers, and often hit their chests during *nudbas* or brought Mama tissues to wipe her tears. They were also a constant presence in many *jam‘iyyas*. Some children were taught to contribute a portion of their allowance to an orphan sponsorship or put coins in *jam‘iyyas'* collection boxes. They were also given tasks like carrying a meal to a poor family or sick neighbor, enabling their participation from a young age.

Most people trusted that this Islamic milieu would be sufficient to teach their children "authenticated" Islam and public piety. They also trusted their children in ways they described as new. People bemoaned the ignorance of their own parents and invoked "the way of Islam" in child rearing with regard to everything from allowing children to dress themselves, to encouraging them to choose their own careers, to not using corporal punishment. I was frequently referred to Fadlullah's book on the subject, *World of Our Youth*, sitting on many parents' bookshelves. In a sense, this "new" process reflected larger shifts in relationality—from that which was mostly family-focused to a wider engagement with the community of the pious modern. No longer was family *necessarily* the primary source of religious knowledge and practice, but peers, institutions, and indeed, *al-bī‘a*, played a critical role.

GENERATIONAL GAPS? OR "DO OUR DAUGHTERS HAVE *ILTIZĀM?*"

This trust in *al-bī‘a* to raise pious children is somewhat surprising given that most of today's parents came to their piety via a certain amount of generational conflict. And indeed, as noted above, the Islamic milieu was a source of concern for some pious Shi‘is, who feared that the ease with which their children were integrated into a pious lifestyle belied a potential for inauthenticity in that very lifestyle. Again the question emerges: What is the relationship between public and personal piety? Or, more specifically: "Do our daughters have *iltizām?*"

> When I became committed there was a lot of talk about us. Even within my family there was talk, you know, "What's this *iltizām?*" While today, it's normal, a girl can put on the *ḥijāb* and she doesn't have a problem. She can work in a *jam‘iyya* and she doesn't have a problem. So there has been change. But we still need more *wā‘ī* [consciousness]. There is a generation growing up now that is committed, but it is a little, how can I express this? It likes to do things that don't fit exactly with *iltizām*. They don't realize that they will get

used to it. Especially because today there are more possibilities for people to be committed without being restricted.

This is the opposite of what it was like when we first became committed. Then, we had to adapt, and we did. I want to give you an example. When we became committed, of course we could no longer go to the beach. And at that time there were no women-only pools and beaches like there are today. I didn't have a problem with that. I didn't go to the beach, but I didn't have a personal crisis that "oof, I'm not going to the beach!" You see what I mean?

But now! Now my daughter is thirteen, and it causes her a crisis if I don't find a way to take her to a women-only beach! So I have to work so that she doesn't feel a religious . . . , so that she doesn't feel that religion has trapped her, because then she will mutiny against it. Maybe the difference is that I have conviction, and my daughter isn't convinced of her convictions. (Hajjeh Umm Ja'far)

Hajjeh Umm Ja'far's comparison of her generation with that of her daughter is telling. First, she reminds us that pious women of the vanguard often had to fight their elders in order to wear the *ḥijāb*, volunteer, attend religious classes, and otherwise participate in the newly forming Islamic community. The opposition they faced solidified the strength of their convictions. In contrast, as we have seen, many girls of her daughter's generation donned the *ḥijāb* at age nine as a matter of course, either because it was required by their school, or because it was the normative model of women's dress to which they had been exposed.

Hajjeh Umm Ja'far and some of her peers feared that because public piety has become the norm and institutionalized as such, it no longer requires the same strength of conviction. "I know I had conviction, I had to fight the world because of my conviction, but all of this is so normal for Lama [her daughter] I'm not certain that she understands these things," Hajjeh Huda observed. These women also worried that if the younger generation's piety did not necessarily stem from within, but instead emerged from a desire to conform to the normative moral order around them, they would be more likely to feel restricted by their religious duties.

Other people disagreed with this view, suggesting instead that the normativization of piety was a wholly positive development. Disagreement came from girls who disproved Hajjeh Umm Ja'far's fears, as well as from other women of the vanguard generation: "Today, if a girl puts on the *ḥijāb*, she doesn't face strange looks, or people asking, 'Why did you do this?' the way that we did. Now it's become the system; it's accepted, and we are the majority. Today we ask, 'Why *aren't* you *muḥajjaba*?' It is much easier" (Noha). I pushed Noha on this, asking her whether the fact that it was the "system" might not mean that more girls are *muḥajjaba* without the necessary underlying convictions. She replied that yes, that was possible, but it meant that the girl needed to "work to strengthen her conviction."

Once again, this links to debates and uncertainties within the pious modern over the relationship between public and personal piety. There were those who believe that visible display should only reflect one's inner state of piety, and find "gaps" troubling and problematic. Others, like Noha, viewed this as an ideal, emphasizing instead the dialectical relationship between the two. For them, "becoming religious" was a process by which inner states and visible display would eventually come to mirror one another. The latter perspective is one that understands public piety as a means for spiritual progress on the personal as well as the community levels.

CONCLUSION: THE IDEAL OF THE PIOUS MODERN

As we have seen, my interlocutors form a community assembled around the values of public piety. According to these values, religious practice follows from accurate knowledge; piety includes community activism and participation; commemoration of a historic-religious martyrdom fuels a contemporary fight against military occupation; and women wear the *ḥijāb* as they participate actively in the public realm for the greater good. These are among the myriad constituent elements of the pious modern.

The pious modern is an ethos, a way of being in the world, and a self-presentation. It is an ideal, hegemonic in a Gramscian sense, institutionalized for pious Shiʿis as an infrastructure, a social norm, and a desired experience. Incompletely manifested, it is a community. Its "members" draw on multiple discourses about modern-ness in order to position themselves and their community as modern/civilized in the contemporary world, and to highlight their forward movement on an axis that includes both material and spiritual progress.

Material and spiritual progress were linked causally in both directions. On the one hand, working to construct and maintain an advanced medical facility was seen as material progress that reflected public piety—in the motivations of the agents involved as well as in the implementation of principles of rationally motivated development taught by authenticated Islam. On the other hand, literacy and an improved educational system led to increased awareness in the community of authenticated Islam and its tenets, and therefore to spiritual progress. One could not be fully "modern" according to the pious modern ideal if either the material or the spiritual were missing. Spiritual development alone was not complete without the drive to improve one's situation materially, and material progress alone would lead to the empty modernity of the West—spiritually and morally vacuous, and therefore incomplete.

Throughout the preceding chapters, we have seen the ways the practices and beliefs of authenticated Islam and public piety are understood as wound up with this path of dual progress. That path is one pious Shi'is continue to forge today, as progress is a continual project of working toward the pious modern. By accepting the pious modern as a construction of modern-ness based upon a notion of progress that includes a spiritual element, we can view pious Shi'is—and many other contemporary religious communities—as trying to live an enchanted modern.

> We do not need to end up in a Star Wars world. One gets there by treating modernity as a reified and universal state of being. Modernity persists as a powerful narrative, but there are Other stories to be told. (Rofel 2002: 189)

Not quite an "Other" story, what we instead have here is an instance of multiple and ambivalently coexisting stories drawn upon by the same people in different contexts and in relation to different comparative others. For pious Shi'is, secularity and gender norms present areas where these stories interact tensely and ambivalently. These ambivalences are linked to the political stakes of being modern, as Shi'i Muslims define their place in the world in relation to others in Lebanon, Iran, Israel, and the West/United States, in addition to their own "traditional" past and contemporary instances of "tradition" within their community. The concept of modern-ness is used as a value-laden comparison, in relation to people's ideas about themselves, others, progress, and historical moments that hinge around encounters with global and local power and difference.

Deployments of multiple discourses of modern-ness are not merely abstract, nor do they have an impact only on the level of global or national politics; these deployments affect people's notions of self, faith, and morality. They imbricate people's understandings of themselves as moral persons in the world. In al-Dahiyya, as spiritual progress is included in the definition of modern-ness, public piety has emerged as both evidence and building block of the Shi'i pious modern. The visibility of piety has had ramifications for the meaning of piety itself, changing the ways pious Shi'is practice and understand religion. We have seen the effects of this on the ways that people dress, talk, pray, mourn, and express their religiosity. This is one instance of a process where the stakes and meaning of religiosity are transformed through engagements with transnational discourses, politics, and power relations. This transformation has been especially significant for pious Shi'i women's lives. Women are crucial to definitions of the modern itself, in part because of a transnational context where women, particularly Muslim women, are seen as markers of a society's status in relation to modern-ness. This linking of piety to modern-ness has added a new layer of meaning where the personal and public intersect. On a personal level, with regard to the visibility of the community as a whole, and especially in the overlaps of those arenas, the stakes of being a pious person have been transformed.

CODA

Pious Shi'is in Lebanon felt a part of a transnational Muslim community and took an active interest in "Muslim" politics around the world. The international news stories of most interest during my field research were those about Palestine, Afghanistan, Bosnia, and Chechnya, joined today by Iraq. People empathized with the struggles of other Muslims, and read them through the lense of their own struggles. These transnational links emphasized their position as Muslims in the international community, a position heavily implicated in the current context of global power relations.

In the opening passage of this book, Hajjeh Umm Zein exclaimed about the Taliban's act of cultural destruction, "This backwardness is not true Islam!" She self-consciously defended the integrity of her faith by making a distinction between Islam as she understood it, and the Taliban. That was in March 2001. In a post-9/11 world, many Muslims like Hajjeh Umm Zein are positioned as having to continuously make that strategic move of distinction.

Although a constructed opposition between an "anti-modern" Islam and a "modern" West existed long before September 11, 2001, the attacks that took place on that day served only to solidify it. Since then, the mainstream U.S. media have been replete with stories about various Islamist groups, ranging from al Qaeda to the Palestinian Hamas to the Lebanese Hizbullah—often lumped together into that same category of nonmodern other. This has been accompanied by an increase in reports about "Muslim women," as their "liberation" from the "traditions" of their religion was incorporated into the U.S. administration's justifications for attacking Afghanistan.

It should go without saying that such a constructed polarization of the world erases far more than it clarifies. In addition to erasing the differences among Muslims and various Islamic politics, it most glaringly erases the effects of U.S. policy in the Middle East and around the world. Underlying discursive oppositions—whether drawn by political and/or religious leaders, individuals, organizations, or news media—there are very real causes and effects affecting people's daily lives. The politics that are the stakes in confronting modernity are tangible.

The Shiʻi pious modern was forged in a military maelstrom where western notions of modern-ness were concretized in Apache and Black-hawk helicopters, CBU-58 cluster bombs, fighter planes, and missiles. U.S. support for Israeli military actions in Lebanon and Palestine, as well as U.S. involvement in prerevolutionary Iran, during the Iran-Iraq war, and during the first Gulf War fomented an "us" versus "them" division long before the "clash of civilizations" repercussions that multiplied after 9/11. The question then arises: what will happen as this political landscape changes?

I am often asked whether the public piety imperative has diminished since the liberation of south Lebanon in May 2000. As I write this, it has been nearly five years, yet the simple answer remains that it has not. In part, this may be related to factors extending the conflict with Israel, including the continued territorial struggle over the Shebaa Farms area, an occasionally volatile border, and the intensified violence in Palestine since the beginning of the Al-Aqsa Intifada in September 2000. And it may have to do with the recent intensification of rhetorical polarizations of the world. However, the continued importance of the intersection of piety and modernity also underscores the inseparability of religion, politics, and social responsibility in the pious modern.

This is not to say that there have not been changes in the past few years. As I finish this book, the Khiam Prison has become a museum and tourist site, with signs guiding visitors through its rooms in Arabic and English, some rooms devoted to memorials to former prisoners, Hizbullah memorabilia available for purchase, and an art/photo exhibit that includes reference to the ongoing Palestinian struggle. In a sense, Liberation has been institutionalized into the historical narrative and continuing trajectory of the Shiʻi pious modern.

To the extent that the stakes of piety on a personal level are affected by global events and dynamics, then the meanings and stakes and understandings and practices of piety will continue to be transformed. A number of possible futures could be reflected in such a continuing transformation: a just end to the Palestinian-Israeli conflict, a stable and independent Iraq and Afghanistan, economic stability and opportunity in Lebanon, political change in Iran, the potential manifestations of U.S. intentions in Syria, and the continued integration (or a new marginalization) of Hizbullah after Syrian withdrawal from Lebanon. Generational shifts add another element, especially as young people continue to leave the country for both the Arab Gulf States and the "West" in search of employment. There already exists a sense of the mutability of the pious modern. In 1998 when I visited an Islamic school, a doorman handed

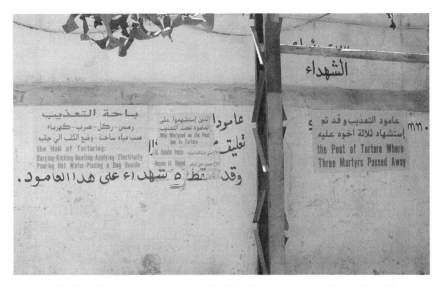

7.1. Inside the Khiam Prison Memorial. The plaque to the right reads, "The Post of Torture Where Three Martyrs Passed Away."

me an *'abāya* and *ḥijāb*; in 2001 I left my head bare upon entering the same school and no one looked twice.

As the local, national, and international political landscapes continue to change, as a global enchanting of the modern persists or diminishes, and as a generation is raised in a milieu closer to the ideals of authenticated Islam than that of their parents, it remains to be seen how the Shi'i pious modern will distill into new forms. Other moderns and other pieties remain to be imagined.

Glossary

'abāya — long black full body covering worn by Islamist women, in Iran "chador"

'ajr — divine compensation, "points" with God; literally, "remuneration" or "wages"

'aql — mind/rationality

bī'a — environment/milieu

fatwa — nonbinding religious ruling or opinion

ḥadīth — authoritative record of the Prophet's speech and actions

ḥijāb — headscarf, veil

ḥusayniyya — building for Shi'i ritual gatherings

ifṭār — the fast-breaking meal at sunset during Ramadan

ijtihād — religious interpretation

iltizām — commitment, religious/social commitment

jam'iyya — social welfare organization

jihād — a great effort

khums — a Shi'i specific religious tax, literally, "one-fifth"

laṭam — ritualized striking of the self in mourning, especially during Ashura

majlis (plural, *majālis*) — mourning gathering

marji' al-taqlīd — a religious scholar of a certain rank who is emulated with regard to religious practice; literally "source for imitation"

masīra — procession

muḥajjaba — a woman who wears the Islamic headscarf

mujtahid — one who is qualified to do *ijtihād*

nudba — elegy, lamentation

takāful ijtimā'ī — mutual social responsibility, social contract

takhalluf — backwardness

taklīf — literally a commission, charge or commandment, usually from God; also used for the ceremonies celebrating girls first wearing of the *ḥijāb*.

taqlīdī — traditional

al-taqwā — absolute faith and piety; its Qur'anic meaning also includes "fear of God"

taw'iyya — consciousness-raising, education

References

Abdul-Jabar, Faleh. 2002. The genesis and development of *marja'ism* versus the state. In *Ayatollahs, sufis and ideologues: State, religion and social movements in Iraq*, 61–89. London: Saqi Books.

Abisaab, Rula. 1999. Shi'ite beginnings and scholastic tradition in Jabal 'Amil in Lebanon. *The Muslim World* 89:1–21.

Abugideiri, Hibba. 2001. Hagar: a historical model for 'gender jihad.' In *Daughters of Abraham: Feminist thought in Judaism, Christianity and Islam*, ed. Yvonne Yazbeck Haddad and John Esposito. Gainesville: University Press of Florida.

AbuKhalil, As'ad. 1988. The Palestinian-Shiite war in Lebanon: An examination of its origins. *Third World Affairs* 10 (1):77–89.

———. 1991. Ideology and practice of Hizballah in Lebanon: Islamization of Leninist organizational principles. *Middle Eastern Studies* 27:390–403.

Abu-Lughod, Lila. 1986. *Veiled sentiments: Honor and poetry in a Bedouin society*. Berkeley: University of California Press.

———. 1993a. Finding a place for Islam: Egyptian television serials and the national interest. *Public Culture* 5:493–513.

———. 1993b. Islam and the gendered discourses of death. *International Journal of Middle East Studies* 25:187–205.

———, ed. 1998a. *Remaking women: Feminism and modernity in the Middle East*. Princeton, NJ: Princeton University Press.

———. 1998b. Introduction: Feminist longings and postcolonial conditions. In *Remaking women: Feminism and modernity in the Middle East*, 3–31. Princeton, NJ: Princeton University Press.

———. 1998c. The marriage of feminism and Islamism in Egypt: Selective repudiation as a dynamic of postcolonial cultural politics. In *Remaking women: Feminism and modernity in the Middle East*, 243–69. Princeton, NJ: Princeton University Press.

———. 2000. Modern subjects: Egyptian melodrama and postcolonial difference. In *Questions of modernity*, ed. Timothy Mitchell, 87–114. Minneapolis: University of Minnesota Press.

———. 2002. Do Muslim women really need saving? Anthropological reflections on cultural relativism and its others. *American Anthropologist* 104:783–90.

Adelkhah, Fariba. 2000. *Being modern in Iran*. New York: Columbia University Press.

Afshar, Haleh. 1996. Women and the politics of fundamentalism in Iran. In *Women and politics in the third world*, 121–41. London: Routledge.

———. 1998. *Islam and feminisms: An Iranian case study*. New York: St. Martin's Press.

Aghaie, Kamran. 2001. The Karbala narrative: Shi'i political discourse in modern Iran in the 1960s and 1970s. *Journal of Islamic Studies* 12:151–76.

Ahmed, Leila. 1992. *Women and gender in Islam: Historical roots of a modern debate*. New Haven, CT: Yale University Press.

Ajami, Fouad. 1986. *The vanished Imam: Musa al-Sadr and the Shi'a of Lebanon*. Ithaca, NY: Cornell University Press.

Alagha, Joseph. 2001. Successen Hezbollah bij 'kleine oorlog' om Shib'a [Hizbullah's successes in the 'small war' in Shib'a]. *Soera* 9 (2): 34–38.

Anderson, Benedict. 1983. *Imagined communities: Reflections on the origin and spread of nationalism*. London: Verso.

Antoun, Richard, and Mary Elaine Hegland, eds. 1987. *Religious resurgence: Contemporary cases in Islam, Christianity, and Judaism*. Syracuse, NY: Syracuse University Press.

Asad, Talal. 1986. *The idea of an anthropology of Islam*. Washington, DC: Georgetown University Center for Contemporary Arab Studies.

———. 1993. *Genealogies of religion: Discipline and reasons of power in Christianity and Islam*. Baltimore: Johns Hopkins University Press.

Avnery, Uri. 2003. Crying Wolf? *Uri Avnery's News Pages*. http://www.avnery-news.co.il/english/index.html.

Ayoub, Mahmoud. 1978. *Redemptive suffering in Islam: A study of the devotional aspects of Ashura in Twelver Shi'ism*. The Hague: Mouton Publishers.

———. 1987. Martyrdom in Christianity and Islam. In *Religious resurgence: Contemporary cases in Islam, Christianity, and Judaism*, ed. Richard Antoun and Mary Elaine Hegland, 67–77. Syracuse, NY: Syracuse University Press.

Ayubi, Nazih. 1995. Radical Islamism and civil society in the Middle East. *Contention* 4:79–105.

al-Azmeh, Aziz. 1993. *Islams and modernities*. London: Verso.

Badran, Margot. 1994. Gender activism: Feminists and Islamists in Egypt. In *Identity politics and women: Cultural reassertions and feminisms in international perspective*, ed. Valentine M. Moghadam, 202–24. Boulder, CO: Westview Press.

———. 2002. Islamic feminism: What's in a name? *Al-Ahram Weekly Online* (Cairo), no. 569, 17–23 January 2002. http://weekly.ahram.org.eg/2002/569/cu1.htm.

Barlas, Asma. 2002. *"Believing women" in Islam: Unreading patriarchal interpretations of the Qur'an*. Austin: University of Texas Press.

Barthes, Roland. 1981. *Camera lucida: Reflections on photography*. New York: Hill and Wang.

Benedict, Ruth. 1946. *The chrysanthemum and the sword*. Boston: Houghton Mifflin Company.

Berger, John. 1972. *Ways of seeing*. London: Penguin Books.

———. 1980. *About looking*. New York: Pantheon Books.

Berger, John, and Jean Mohr. 1982. *Another way of telling*. New York: Pantheon Books.

Bernal, Victoria. 1997. Islam, transnational culture, and modernity in rural Sudan. In *Gendered encounters: Challenging cultural boundaries and social hierarchies in Africa*, ed. Maria Grosz-Ngate and Omari Kokole, 131–51. New York: Routledge.

el-Bizri, Dalal. 1996. *Akhawāt al-dhul w-al-yaqīn: Islāmiyyāt bayn al-hadātha w-al-taqlīd* [Sisters of shadow and certainty: Islamist women between modernity and tradition]. Beirut: Dar an-Nahar.

———. 1999. *Islamistes, parlémentaires et Libanais: Les interventions à l'Assemblée des elus de la Jama'a Islamiyya et du Hizb Allah (1992–1996).* Centre d'études et de recherches sur le Moyen-Orient contemporain (CERMOC), Document no. 3.

Blanford, Nicholas. 2001. One way or the other, Ashura brings blood. *The Daily Star* [Beirut], May 4. http://www.dailystar.com.lb/05_04_01/art2.htm.

———. 2003. Hizballah in the firing line. *Middle East Report Online.* April 28, 2003. http://www.merip.org.

Böttcher, Annabelle. 2001. Im schatten des Ayatollahs: Schiitische feministische theologie in Libanon am anfang [In the shadow of the Ayatollah: Shi'i feminist theology in Lebanon at the beginning]. *Neue Zuericher Zeitung* [Zurich], no. 5.

Bowen, John R. 1993. *Muslims through discourse: Religion and ritual in Gayo society.* Princeton, NJ: Princeton University Press.

Brenner, Suzanne. 1996. Reconstructing self and society: Javanese Muslim women and "the veil." *American Ethnologist* 23 (4): 673–97.

Brustad, Kristen. 2000. *The syntax of spoken Arabic: A comparative study of Moroccan, Egyptian, Syrian, and Kuwaiti Dialects.* Washington, DC: Georgetown University Press.

Calvino, Italo. 1974. *Invisible cities.* New York: Harcourt Brace Jovanovich. (Orig. pub. 1972.)

Casanova, Jose. 1994. *Public religions in the modern world.* Chicago: University of Chicago Press.

Chakrabarty, Dipesh. 2000a. *Provincializing Europe.* Princeton, NJ: Princeton University Press.

———. 2000b. Witness to suffering: Domestic cruelty and the birth of the modern subject in Bengal. In *Questions of Modernity,* ed. Timothy Mitchell, 49–86. Minneapolis: University of Minnesota Press.

Chatterjee, Partha. 1993. *The nation and its fragments: Colonial and postcolonial histories.* Princeton, NJ: Princeton University Press.

Chehabi, H. E. 1997. Ardabil becomes a province: Center-periphery relations in Iran. *International Journal of Middle East Studies* 29:235–53.

———. 1990. *Iranian politics and religious modernism: The liberation movement of Iran, the Shah, and Khomeini.* Ithaca, NY: Cornell University Press.

Chelkowski, Peter J., ed. 1979a. *Ta'ziyeh: Ritual and drama in Iran.* New York: New York University Press.

———. 1979b. Ta'ziyeh: Indigenous avant-garde theater of Iran. In *Ta'ziyeh: Ritual and drama in Iran,* 1–11. New York: New York University Press.

Çinar, Alev. 2001. National history as a contested site: The conquest of Istanbul and Islamist negotiations of the nation. *Comparative Studies in Society and History* 43 (2): 364–91.

Cobban, Helena. 1985. *The making of modern Lebanon.* London: Hutchinson.

Cole, Juan. 2002. *Sacred space and holy war.* London: I. B. Tauris.

Cole, Juan, and Nikki Keddie. 1986. Introduction to *Shi'ism and social protest*, 1–29. New Haven, CT: Yale University Press.

Deeb, Lara. 2000. Lebanon: An occupation ends. *Middle East Report Online*, May 31, 2000. http://www.merip.org/mero/mero053100.html.

———. 2005. "Doing good, like Sayyida Zaynab": Lebanese Shi'i women's participation in the public sphere." In *Religion, social practice, and contested hegemonies: Reconstructing the public sphere in Muslim majority societies*, ed. Armando Salvatore and Mark LeVine, 85–108. New York: Palgrave.

Deeb, Marius. 1988. Shi'a movements in Lebanon: Their formation, ideology, social basis, and links with Iran and Syria. *Third World Quarterly* 10 (2): 683–98.

Diab, Hassan N. 1999. *Beirut: Reviving Lebanon's past*. Westport, CT: Praeger.

Donham, Donald L. 1999. *Marxist modern: An ethnographic history of the Ethiopian revolution*. Berkeley: University of California Press.

———. 2002. On being modern in a capitalist world: Some conceptual and comparative issues. In *Critically modern: Alternatives, alterities, anthropologies*, ed. Bruce Knauft, 241–57. Bloomington: Indiana University Press.

———. n.d. Murder at Cinderella: Ethnic violence and the birth of a new South Africa. Emory University, unpublished paper.

Dorraj, Manochehr. 1999. The crisis of modernity and religious revivalism: A comparative study of Islamic fundamentalism, Jewish fundamentalism, and liberation theology. *Social Compass* 46:225–40.

Eickelman, Dale F. 2000. Islam and the languages of modernity. *Daedalus*, no. 129:119–35.

Eickelman, Dale, and Jon Anderson, eds. 1999a. *New media in the Muslim world: The emerging public sphere*. Bloomington: Indiana University Press.

———. 1999b. Redefining Muslim publics. In *New media in the Muslim world: The emerging public sphere*, ed. Dale F. Eickelman and Jon W. Anderson, 1–18. Bloomington: Indiana University Press.

Eickelman, Dale F., and James Piscatori. 1996. *Muslim politics*. Princeton, NJ: Princeton University Press.

ElSadda, Hoda. 2001. Discourses on women's biographies and cultural identity: Twentieth-century representations of the life of 'A'isha Bint Abi Bakr. *Feminist Studies* 27:37–64.

Ende, Werner. 1978. The flagellations of Muharram and the Shi'ite 'ulama.' *Der Islam* 55:19–36.

Fadlullah, Ayatullah al-Sayyid Muhammad Husayn. 1996a. *Al-masā'il al-fiqhiyya* [Jurisprudence issues]. 5th ed. Beirut: Dar al-Malak.

———. 1996b. *Al-masā'il al-fiqhiyya: Al-juz' al-thāni* [Jurisprudence issues: Part two]. 5th ed. Beirut: Dar al-Malak.

———. 1997. *Dunya al-mar'a* [The world of women]. Beirut: Dar al-Malak.

———. 1998. *World of our youth*. Montreal: Organization for the Advancement of Islamic Knowledge and Humanitarian Services.

Faour, Muhammad. 1991. The demography of Lebanon: A reappraisal. *Middle Eastern Studies* 27:631–41.

Fawaz, Mona. 1998. Islam, resistance and community development: The case of the southern suburb of Beirut city. M.A. thesis, Massachusetts Institute of Technology.

Fernea, Elizabeth. 1965. *Guests of the sheik: An ethnography of an Iraqi village.* New York: Doubleday.

Fernea, Robert A., and Elizabeth W. Fernea. 1972. Variation in religious observance among Islamic women. In *Scholars, saints, and Sufis in Muslim religious institutions in the Middle East since 1500*, ed. Nikki R. Keddie, 385–401. Berkeley: University of California Press.

Fischer, Michael. 1980. *Iran: From religious dispute to revolution.* Cambridge, MA: Harvard University Press.

Fischer, Michael, and Mehdi Abedi. 1990. *Debating Muslims: Cultural dialogues in postmodernity and tradition.* Madison: University of Wisconsin Press.

Fisk, Robert. 1990. *Pity the nation: The abduction of Lebanon.* New York: Simon and Schuster.

Foucault, Michel. 1978. *The history of sexuality.* Vol. 1. New York: Vintage Books.

Fraser, Nancy. 1999. Rethinking the public sphere: A contribution to the critique of actually existing democracy. In *Habermas and the public sphere*, ed. C. Calhoun, 109–42. Cambridge, MA: MIT Press.

Friedl, Erika. 1997. Ideal womanhood in postrevolutionary Iran. In *Mixed blessings: Gender and religious fundamentalism cross-culturally*, ed. Judy Brink and Joan Mencher, 144–57. New York: Routledge.

Friedman, Jonathan. 2002. Modernity and other traditions. In *Critically modern: Alternatives, alterities, anthropologies*, ed. Bruce Knauft, 287–313. Bloomington: Indiana University Press.

Gaonkar, Dilip Parameshwar, ed. 2001. *Alternative modernities.* Durham, NC: Duke University Press.

Ghannam, Farha. 2002. *Remaking the modern: Space, relocation, and the politics of identity in a global Cairo.* Berkeley: University of California Press.

Gilsenen, Michael. 1996. *Lords of the Lebanese marches: Violence and narrative in an Arab society.* Berkeley: University of California Press.

Göle, Nilufer. 1996. *The forbidden modern: Civilization and veiling.* Ann Arbor: University of Michigan Press.

———. 1997. The gendered nature of the public sphere. *Public Culture* 10:61–81.

———. 2000. Snapshots of Islamic modernities. *Daedalus*, no. 129:91–117.

Good, Mary-Jo Delvecchio, and Byron J. Good. 1988. Ritual, the state, and the transformation of emotional discourse in Iranian society. *Culture, Medicine and Psychiatry* 12:43–63.

El Guindi, Fadwa. 1999. *Veil: modesty, privacy and resistance.* Oxford: Berg.

Haddad, Yvonne Yazbeck, and John L. Esposito, eds. 1998. *Islam, gender, and social change.* Oxford: Oxford University Press.

Haeri, Shahla. 1989. *Law of desire: Temporary marriage in Shi'i Iran.* Syracuse, NY: Syracuse University Press.

Halawi, Majed. 1992. *A Lebanon defied: Musa al-Sadr and the Shi'a community*. Boulder, CO: Westview Press.

Hale, Sondra. 1996. *Gender politics in Sudan: Islamism, socialism, and the state*. Boulder, CO: Westview Press.

———. 2001. Alienation and belonging—Women's citizenship and emancipation: Visions for Sudan's post-Islamist future. *New Political Science* 23:25–43.

Halm, Heinz. 1997. *Shi'a Islam: From religion to revolution*. Princeton, NJ: Markus Weiner Publishers. (Orig. pub. 1994.)

Hammami, Rema. 1997. From immodesty to collaboration: Hamas, the women's movement, and national identity in the Intifada. In *Political Islam: Essays from Middle East Report*, ed. J. Beinin and J. Stork, 194–210. Berkeley: University of California Press.

Hamzeh, A. Nizar. 2000a. Lebanon's Islamists and local politics: A new reality. *Third World Quarterly* 21:739–59.

———. 2000b. Myth and reality. *Index on Censorship* 29:128–30.

———. 2001. Clientalism, Lebanon: Roots and trends. *Middle Eastern Studies* 37:167–78.

Hanf, Theodore. 1993. *Coexistence in wartime Lebanon: Decline of a state and rise of a nation*. London: I. B. Tauris.

Harb el-Kak, Mona. 1996. *Politiques urbaines dans la banlieue-sud de Beyrouth: Les cahiers du CERMOC*. Beirut: Centre d'Etudes et de Recherches sur le Moyen-Orient Contemporain.

———. 1998. Transforming the site of dereliction into the urban culture of modernity: Beirut's southern suburb and Elisar project. In *Projecting Beirut: Episodes in the construction and reconstruction of a modern city*, ed. Peter Rowe and Hashim Sarkis, 173–82. Munich: Prestel.

———. 2000. Post-war Beirut: Resources, negotiations, and contestations in the Elyssar Project. *Arab World Geographer* 3:272–89.

———. 2001. Post-war Beirut: Resources, negotiations, and contestations in the Elyssar Project. In *Capital cities: Ethnographies of urban governance in the Middle East*, ed. Seteney Shami, 111–33. Toronto: University of Toronto Press.

Harding, Susan Friend. 2000. *The book of Jerry Falwell: Fundamentalist language and politics*. Princeton, NJ: Princeton University Press.

Harik, Judith Palmer. 1996. Between Islam and the system: Sources and implications of popular support for Lebanon's Hizballah. *Journal of Conflict Resolution* 40:41–67.

———. 2004. *Hezbollah: The changing face of terrorism*. London: I. B. Tauris.

Harris, William. 1997. *Faces of Lebanon: Sects, wars, and global extensions*. Princeton, NJ: Markus Wiener Publishers.

Hatem, Mervat. 1994. Do secularist and Islamist views really differ? *Middle East Journal* 48:661–76.

Hefner, Robert W. 1998. Multiple modernities: Christianity, Islam, and Hinduism in a globalizing age. *Annual Review of Anthropology* 27:83–104.

———. 2000. *Civil Islam: Muslims and democratization in Indonesia*. Princeton, NJ: Princeton University Press.

Hegland, Mary Elaine. 1983. Two images of Husain: Accommodation and revolution in an Iranian village. In *Religion and politics in Iran: Shi'ism from quietism to revolution*, ed. Nikki. R. Keddie, 218–35. New Haven, CT: Yale University Press.

———. 1987. Islamic revival or political and cultural revolution? An Iranian case study. In *Religious resurgence: Contemporary cases in Islam, Christianity, and Judaism*, ed. Richard Antoun and Mary Elaine Hegland, 194–219. Syracuse, NY: Syracuse University Press.

———. 1998a. Flagellation and fundamentalism: (Trans)forming meaning, identity, and gender through Pakistani women's rituals of mourning. *American Ethnologist* 25:240–66.

———. 1998b. The power paradox in Muslim women's *majales:* North-west Pakistani mourning rituals as sites of contestation over religious politics, ethnicity, and gender. *Signs* 23:392–428.

Henderson, Christian. 2003. Committee seeks national day to commemorate civil war: Activists say holiday would help people come to grips with painful legacy of conflict. *The Daily Star* [Beirut] www.dailystar.com.lb.

Hezbollah becomes potent anti-U.S. force. 2002. *New York Times*. www .nytimes.com.

Hijab, Nadia. 1988. *Womanpower, the Arab debate on women at work*. Cambridge: Cambridge University Press.

Hiro, Dilip. 1993. *Lebanon: Fire and embers: A history of the Lebanese civil war*. New York: St. Martin's Press.

Hirschkind, Charles. 2001. Civic virtue and religious reason: An Islamic counterpublic. *Cultural Anthropology* 16:3–34.

Hirschkind, Charles, and Saba Mahmood. 2002. Feminism, the Taliban, and politics of counter-insurgency. *Anthropological Quarterly* 75 (2): 339–54.

Höfert, Almut, and Armando Salvatore, eds. 2000a. *Between Europe and Islam: Shaping modernity in a transcultural space*. Brussels: P.I.E.-Peter Lang.

———. 2000b. Beyond the clash of civilizations: Transcultural politics between Europe and Islam. In *Between Europe and Islam: Shaping modernity in a transcultural space*, ed. Almut Höfert and Armando Salvatore, 13–35. Brussels: P.I.E.-Peter Lang.

Holmes, Douglas R. 1989. *Cultural disenchantments: Worker peasantries in Northeast Italy*. Princeton, NJ: Princeton University Press.

Holt, Maria. 1999. Lebanese Shi'i women and Islamism: A response to war. In *Women and war in Lebanon*, ed. Lamia Rustum Shehadeh, 167–94. Gainesville: University Press of Florida.

Houston, Christopher. 2001. The brewing of Islamist modernity: Tea gardens and public space in Istanbul. *Theory, Culture and Society* 18:77–97.

Humayuni, Sadeq. 1979. An analysis of a ta'ziyeh of Qasem. In *Ta'ziyeh: Ritual and drama in Iran*, ed. Peter J. Chelkowski, 12–23. New York: New York University Press.

Irvine, Judith T. 1989. When talk isn't cheap: Language and political-economy. *American Ethnologist* 16:248–67.

Jaber, Hala. 1997. *Hezbollah: Born with a vengeance*. New York: Columbia University Press.

Jafri, S. Husain M. 1979. *Origins and early development of Shi'a Islam*. London: Longman Group.

Jam'iyyat al-ma'arif al-islamiyya al-thaqafiyya. 2001. Al-hijab [A summary of

Sayyid Mutahhari's book *The Issue of the Hijab*]. N.P.: Jam'iyyat al-ma'arif al-islamiyya al-thaqafiyya.

Jay, Martin. 1996. Vision in context: Reflections and refractions. In *Vision in context: Historical and contemporary perspectives on sight*, ed. Teresa Brennan and Martin Jay, 3–12. New York: Routledge.

Joseph, Suad. 1975. *The politicization of religious sects in Borj Hammoud, Lebanon*. Ph.D. diss., Columbia University.

———. 1978. Muslim-Christian conflict in Lebanon: A perspective on the evolution of sectarianism. In *Muslim-Christian conflicts: Economic, political, and social origins*, ed. Suad Joseph and Barbara Pillsbury. Boulder, CO: Westview Press.

———. 1983. Working-class women's networks in a sectarian state: A political paradox. *American Ethnologist* 10:1–22.

———. 1990. Gender and relationality among Arab families in Lebanon. *Feminist Studies* 19:465–86.

———. 1994. Brother/sister relationships: Connectivity, love, and power in the reproduction of patriarchy in Lebanon. *American Ethnologist* 21:50–73.

———. 1997a. Gender and civil society (Interview with Joe Stork). In *Political Islam: Essays from "Middle East Report,"* ed. Joel Beinin and Joe Stork, 64–70. Berkeley: University of California Press.

———. 1997b. The public/private—The imagined boundary in the imagined nation/state/community: The Lebanese case. *Feminist Review* 57:73–92.

———. 1997c. The reproduction of political process among women activists in Lebanon: 'Shopkeepers' and feminists. In *Organizing women: Formal and informal women's groups in the Middle East*, ed. Dawn Chatty and Annika Rabo, 57–80. Oxford: Berg.

———. 1999a. Introduction: Theories and dynamics of gender, self, and identity in Arab families. In *Intimate selving in Arab families: Gender, self, and identity*, 1–17. Syracuse, NY: Syracuse University Press.

———. 1999b. Brother-sister relationships: Connectivity, love, and power in the reproduction of patriarchy in Lebanon. In *Intimate selving in Arab families: Gender, self, and identity*, 113–40. Syracuse, NY: Syracuse University Press.

———. 2000. Civic myths, citizenship, and gender in Lebanon. In *Gender and citizenship in the Middle East*, 107–36. Syracuse, NY: Syracuse University Press.

Kahan Commission. 1983. *Report of the commission of Kahan inquiry into the events at the refugee camps in Beirut*. [online]. Available from the website of Israeli Ministry of Foreign Affairs. http://www.caabu.org/press/documents/kahan-commission-contents.html.

Kamalkhani, Zahra. 1998. *Women's Islam: Religious practice among women in today's Iran*. London: Kegan Paul International.

Kapeliouk, Amnon. 1983. *Sabra and Shatila: Inquiry into a massacre*. Belmont, MA: Association of Arab-American University Graduates Press.

Karp, Ivan. 2002. Development and personhood: Tracing the contours of a moral discourse. In *Critically modern: Alternatives, alterities, anthropologies*, ed. Bruce Knauft, 82–104. Bloomington: Indiana University Press.

Keddie, Nikki R. 1995. *Iran and the Muslim world: Resistance and revolution.* New York: New York University Press.

Kelly, John D. 2002. Alternative modernities or an alternative to "modernity": Getting out of the modernist sublime. In *Critically modern: Alternatives, alterities, anthropologies,* ed. Bruce Knauft, 258–86. Bloomington: Indiana University Press.

Khalaf, Samir. 1993a. *Beirut reclaimed: Reflections on urban design and the restoration of civility.* Beirut: Dar An-Nahar.

———. 1993b. Urban design and the recovery of Beirut. In *Recovering Beirut: Urban design and post-war reconstruction,* ed. Samir Khalaf and Philip S. Khoury, 11–62. New York: Leiden.

———. 1998. Contested space and the forging of new cultural identities. In *Projecting Beirut: Episodes in the construction and reconstruction of a modern city,* ed. Peter Rowe and Hashim Sarkis, 140–64. Munich: Prestel.

———. 2001. *Cultural resistance: Global and local encounters in the Middle East.* London: Saqi Books.

———. 2002. *Civil and uncivil violence in Lebanon: A history of the internationalization of communal conflict.* New York: Columbia University Press.

Khan, Naveeda. 2001. Making sound matter: The contestation over azan (call to prayer) in Pakistan. Washington, DC: Annual Meeting of the American Anthropological Association.

Khater, Akram. 2001. *Inventing home: Emigration, gender, and the middle-class in Lebanon, 1870–1920.* Berkeley: University of California Press.

el Khazen, Farid. 2000. *The breakdown of the state in Lebanon: 1967–1976.* Cambridge, MA: Harvard University Press.

Khuri, Fuad. 1975. *From village to suburb: Order and change in Greater Beirut.* Chicago: University of Illinois Press.

Knauft, Bruce, ed. 2002a. *Critically modern: Alternatives, alterities, anthropologies.* Bloomington: Indiana University Press.

———. 2002b. Critically modern: An introduction. In *Critically modern: Alternatives, alterities, anthropologies,* 1–54. Bloomington: Indiana University Press.

Koselleck, Reinhart. 1985. *Futures past: On the semantics of historical time.* Cambridge, MA: MIT Press.

Kratz, Corinne A. 1993. "We've always done it like this . . . except for a few details": "Tradition" and "innovation" in Okiek ceremonies. *Comparative Studies in Society and History* 35:30–65.

———. 2002. *The ones that are wanted: Communication and the politics of representation in a photographic exhibition.* Berkeley: University of California Press.

Kubursi, Atif A. 1993. Reconstructing and/or reconstituting the post-war Lebanese economy: The role of infrastructural development. In *Recovering Beirut: Urban design and post-war reconstruction,* ed. Samir Khalaf and Philip S. Khoury, 167–82. New York: Leiden.

Larkin, Brian. 1997. Indian films and Nigerian lovers: Media and the creation of parallel modernities. *Africa* 67:406–40.

———. 2000. Abubaker Gumi, electronic preaching, and the transformation of religious authority in Nigeria. Seminar on African Studies, Emory University, Atlanta.

Lazreg, Marnia. 1994. *The eloquence of silence: Algerian women in question.* New York: Routledge.

Lee, Tong Soon. 1999. Technology and the production of Islamic space: The call to prayer in Singapore. *Ethnomusicology* 43:86–100.

Loeffler, Reinhold. 1988. *Islam in practice: Religious beliefs in a Persian village.* Albany: State University of New York Press.

MacBride, Sean. 1983. *Israel in Lebanon: The report of the international commission to enquire into reported violations of international law by Israel during its invasion of Lebanon.* London: Ithaca Press.

MacLeod, Arlene. 1991. *Accommodating protest: Working women, the new veiling, and change in Cairo.* New York: Columbia University Press.

Mahmood, Saba. 1998. *Women's piety and embodied discipline: The Islamic resurgence in contemporary Egypt.* Ph.D. diss., Stanford University.

———. 2001. Feminist theory, embodiment, and the docile agent: Some reflections on the Egyptian Islamic revival. *Cultural Anthropology* 16:202–36.

———. 2005. *Politics of piety: The Islamic revival and the feminist subject.* Princeton, NJ: Princeton University Press.

Makdisi, Jean Said. 1990. *Beirut fragments: A war memoir.* New York: Persea Books.

Makdisi, Saree. 1997. Laying claim to Beirut: Urban narrative and spatial identity in the age of Solidere. *Critical Inquiry* 23:661–705.

Maktabi, Rania. 1999. The Lebanese census of 1932 revisited: Who are the Lebanese? *British Journal of Middle Eastern Studies* 26:219–41.

Mallat, Chibli. 1988. *Shi'i thought from the south of Lebanon.* Oxford: Center for Lebanese Studies.

Marsden, George M. 1980. *Fundamentalism and American culture: The shaping of twentieth century evangelicalism, 1870–1925.* London: Oxford University Press.

Mazzaoui, Michel M. 1979. Shi'ism and Ashura in South Lebanon. In *Ta'ziyeh: Ritual and drama in Iran,* ed. Peter J. Chelkowski, 228–37. New York: New York University Press.

Mervin, Sabrina. 2000. *Un réformisme chiite: Ulémas et lettres du Ğabal 'Āmil de la fin de l'Empire ottoman à l'indépendance du Liban.* Paris: Karthala.

Messick, Brinkley. 1996. Media muftis: Radio fatwas in Yemen. In *Islamic legal interpretation: Muftis and their fatwas,* ed. M. K. Masud, B. Messick, and D. Powers, 310–20. Cambridge, MA: Harvard University Press.

Meyer, Birgit. 1999. *Translating the devil: Religion and modernity among the Ewe in Ghana.* Trenton, NJ: Africa World Press.

Mir-Hosseini, Ziba. 1999. *Islam and gender: The religious debate in contemporary Iran.* Princeton, NJ: Princeton University Press.

Mitchell, Timothy. 2000a. Introduction to *Questions of modernity,* xi–xxvii. Minneapolis: University of Minnesota Press.

———. 2000b. The stage of modernity. In *Questions of modernity*, 1–34. Minneapolis: University of Minnesota Press.

Moallem, Minoo. 2001. Whose fundamentalism? *Meridians: Feminism, Race, Transnationalism* 2 (2): 298–301.

Moghadam, Valentine M. 2002. Islamic feminism and its discontents: Toward a resolution of the debate. *Signs* 27:1135–71.

Momen, Moojan. 1985. *An introduction to Shi'i Islam: The history and doctrines of Twelver Shi'ism*. New Haven, CT: Yale University Press.

Mottahedeh, Roy. 1985. *The mantle of the Prophet*. New York: Simon and Schuster.

Moussavi, Ahmad. 1985. Establishment of the position of *marja'iyyt-i-taqlid* in the Twelver Shi'i community. *Iranian Studies* 18:35–51.

Munson, Henry. 2003. Islam, nationalism and resentment of foreign domination. *Middle East Policy* 10 (2): 40–54.

Mutahhari, Murtaza. n.d. *The Islamic modest dress*. Albuquerque, NM: ABJAD.

Najmabadi, Afsaneh. 1998. Feminism in an Islamic republic: "Years of hardship, years of growth." In *Islam, gender, and social change*, ed. Yvonne Yazbeck Haddad and John L. Esposito, 59–84. Oxford: Oxford University Press.

Nakash, Yitzhak. 1993. An attempt to trace the origin of the rituals of 'Ashura. *Die Welt des Islams* 33:161–81.

Nasr, Salim. 1993. New social realities and post-war Lebanon: Issues for reconstruction. In *Recovering Beirut: Urban design and post-war reconstruction*, ed. Samir Khalaf and Philip S.Khoury, 63–80. New York: Leiden.

Nelson, Cynthia. 1974. Public and private politics: Women in the Middle Eastern world. *American Ethnologist* 1:551–63.

Norton, Augustus Richard. 1987. *Amal and the Shi'a: Struggle for the soul of Lebanon*. Austin: University of Texas Press.

———. 1995. Introduction to *Civil society in the Middle East*, 1:1–25. Leiden: E. J. Brill.

———. 1999. *Hizballah of Lebanon: Extremist ideals vs. mundane politics*. New York: Council on Foreign Relations.

———. 2000. Hizballah and the Israeli withdrawal from southern Lebanon. *Journal of Palestine Studies* 30:22–35.

———. 2002. Lebanon's malaise. *Survival* 42:35–50.

Norton, Augustus Richard, and 'Ali Safa. 2000. 'Ashura in Nabatiyya. *Middle East Insight* 15:21–28.

O'Ballance, Edgar. 1998. *Civil war in Lebanon, 1975–1992*. New York: St. Martin's Press.

Ossman, Susan. 1994. *Picturing Casablanca*. Berkeley: University of California Press.

Özyürek, Esra. n.d. *Nostalgia for the Modern: Privatization of State Ideology in Turkey*. Durham, NC: Duke University Press. Forthcoming.

Peletz, Michael G. 2002. *Islamic modern: Religious courts and cultural politics in Malaysia*. Princeton, NJ: Princeton University Press.

Peteet, Julie. 1991. *Gender in crisis: Women and the Palestinian resistance movement*. New York: Columbia University Press.

———. 1997. Icons and militants: Mothering in the danger zone. *Signs: Journal of Women in Culture and Society* 23:103–29.

Peters, Emrys Lloyd. 1956. A Muslim passion play: Key to a Lebanese village. *Atlantic Monthly*, no. 198: 176–80.

Picard, Elizabeth. 1996. *Lebanon, a shattered country: Myths and realities of the wars in Lebanon*. New York: Holmes and Meier.

———. 1997. The Lebanese Shi'a and political violence in Lebanon. In *The legitimization of violence*. ed. David E. Apter, 189–233. New York: New York University Press.

Pinault, David. 1992. The Shiites: Ritual and popular piety in a Muslim community. New York: St. Martin's Press.

———. 1998. Zaynab Bint 'Ali and the place of the women of the households of the first Imams in Shi'ite devotional literature. In *Women in the medieval Islamic world: Power, patronage, and piety*. ed. Gavin R. G. Hambly, 48–57. New York: St. Martin's Press.

———. 2001. *Horse of Karbala: Muslim devotional life in India*. New York: Palgrave.

Piot, Charles. 1999. *Remotely global: Village modernity in West Africa*. Chicago: University of Chicago Press.

Raad, Walid. 1999. Missing Lebanese wars. *Public Culture* 11:i–xiv.

Rabinow, Paul. 1989. *French modern: Norms and forms of the social environment*. Chicago: University of Chicago Press.

Rahman, Fazlur. 1982. *Islam and modernity: Transformation of an intellectual tradition*. Chicago: University of Chicago Press.

Rajaee, Farhang. 1993. Islam and modernity: The reconstruction of an alternative Shi'ite worldview in Iran. In *Fundamentalisms and society*, ed. Martin E. Marty and R. Scott Appleby, 103–25. Chicago: University of Chicago Press.

Reiter, Rayna. 1975. Men and women in the south of France: Public and private domains. In *Toward an anthropology of women*. New York: Monthly Review Press.

Richard, Yann. 1995. *Shi'ite Islam*. Oxford: Blackwell. (Orig. pub. 1991.)

Riskallah, Ralph. 1997. *Yawm al-dam: mashhadiyya 'Ashura fi Jabal 'Amil: muqarabah nafsiyya wa ijtima'iyya li-maqtal al-Imam al-Husayn* [The day of blood: Ashura scenes from Jabal Amil: Comparative psychological and social analysis of the death of Imam Husayn]. Beirut: Dar al-Talabiyya lil-Tabaa'a wa al-nashar.

Rofel, Lisa. 1999. *Other modernities: Gendered yearnings in China after socialism*. Berkeley: University of California Press.

———. 2002. Modernity's masculine fantasies. In *Critically modern: Alternatives, alterities, anthropologies*, ed. Bruce Knauft, 175–93. Bloomington: Indiana University Press.

Roumani, Rhonda. 2004. Syria's last trump card. *Bitterlemons international* 36 (2). bitterlemons-international.org.

Rosiny, Stephan. 2000. *Shi'a publishing in Lebanon: With special reference to Islamic and Islamist publications*. Berlin: Verlag Das Arabische Buch.

———. 2001. "The tragedy of Fatima al-Zahra" in the debate of two Shiite theologians in Lebanon. In *The Twelver Shi'a in modern times: Religious culture and political history*, ed. Rainer Brunner and Werner Ende, 207–19. Leiden: Brill.

Rowe, Peter, and Hashim Sarkis, eds. 1998. *Projecting Beirut: Episodes in the construction and reconstruction of a modern city*. Munich: Prestel.

Ruby, Jay. 1995. *Secure the shadow: Death and photography in America*. Cambridge, MA: MIT Press.

al-Ruhaimi, Abdul-Halim. 2002. The Da'wa Islamic party: Origins, actors and ideology. In *Ayatollahs, sufis and ideologues: State, religion and social movements in Iraq*, ed. Faleh Abdul-Jabar, 149–61. London: Saqi Books.

Saad-Ghorayeb, Amal. 2002. *Hizb'ullah: Politics and religion*. London: Pluto Press.

Said, Edward W. 1979. *Orientalism*. New York: Vintage Books.

Saliba, Therese. 2002. Introduction: Gender, politics, and Islam. In *Gender, politics, and Islam*, ed. Therese Saliba, Carolyn Allen, and Judith A. Howard, 1–14. Chicago: University of Chicago Press.

Salibi, Kamal. 1976. *Crossroads to civil war: Lebanon 1958–1976*. Delmar, NY: Caravan Books.

———. 1988. *A house of many mansions: The history of Lebanon reconsidered*. Berkeley: University of California Press.

Salvatore, Armando. 1997. *Islam and the political discourse of modernity*. Reading, UK: Ithaca Press.

———. 2000a. Social differentiation, moral authority and public Islam in Egypt: The path of Mustafa Mahmud. *Anthropology Today* 16:12–15.

———. 2000b. The Islamic reform project in the emerging public sphere: The (meta-) normative redefinition of *shari'a*. In *Between Europe and Islam: Shaping modernity in a transcultural space*, ed. Almut Höfert and Armando Salvatore, 89–108. Brussels: P.I.E.-Peter Lang.

———. ed. 2001. Muslim traditions and modern techniques of power. *Yearbook of the Sociology of Islam*. Vol. 3. Munster: Lit Verlag.

Sandeen, Eric. 1995. *Picturing an exhibition: The family of man and 1950s America*. Albuquerque: University of New Mexico Press.

Sayigh, Rosemary. 1994. *Too many enemies: The Palestinian experience in Lebanon*. London: Zed Books.

Schubel, Vernon. 1991. The Muharram *majlis*: The role of a ritual in the preservation of Shi'a identity. In *Muslim families in North America*, ed. Earle Waugh, Sharon McIrvin Abu Laban, and Regula Burckhardt Qureshi, 118–31. Edmonton: University of Alberta Press.

———. 1993. *Religious performance in contemporary Islam: Shi'i devotional rituals in South Asia*. Columbia: University of South Carolina Press.

Sennett, Richard. 1993. Introduction to *Recovering Beirut: Urban design and post-war reconstruction*, ed. Samir Khalaf and Philip S. Khoury, 1–10. New York: Leiden.

Shafir, Gershon. 1989. *Land, labor, and the origins of the Israeli-Palestinian conflict, 1882–1914*. Cambridge: Cambridge University Press.

Shalom, Stephen R. 2001. The United States and the Middle East: Why do 'they' hate us? *ZNet*. http://www.zmag.org/shalomhate.htm.

Sharara, Waddah. 1968. *Transformations d'une manifestation religieuse dans un village du Liban-Sud*. Beirut: Université Libanaise Centre de Recherches.

Shryock, Andrew. 1997. *Nationalism and the genealogical imagination: Oral history and textual authority in tribal Jordan*. Berkeley: University of California Press.

Siegel, Ellen. 2001. After nineteen years: Sabra and Shatila remembered. *Middle East Policy* 8. www.mepc.org/public_asp/journal_vol8/0112_siegel.

Singerman, Diane. 1995. *Avenues of participation*. Princeton, NJ: Princeton University Press.

Soares, Benjamin F. 2002. Islam and the public signs of piety in Mali. Third Mediterranean Social and Political Research Meeting, March 20-24, Mediterranean Programme, Robert Schuman Centre for Advanced Studies, European University Institute, Florence, Italy.

Sobelman, Daniel. 2004. Still playing by the rules. *Bitterlemons International* 36 (2). bitterlemons-international.org.

Spitulnik, Debra A. 2002. Accessing "local" modernities: Reflections on the place of linguistic evidence in ethnography. In *Critically modern: Alternatives, alterities, anthropologies*, ed. Bruce Knauft, 194–19. Bloomington: Indiana University Press.

Sreberny-Mohammadi, Annabelle, and Ali Mohammadi. 1994. *Small media, big revolution: Communication, culture and the Iranian revolution*. Minneapolis: University of Minnesota Press.

Stone, Christopher. 2002. *The Rahbani nation: Musical theater and nationalism in contemporary Lebanon*. Ph.D. diss. Near Eastern Studies, Princeton University.

Sullivan, Zohreh T. 1998. Eluding the feminist, overthrowing the modern? Transformations in twentieth-century Iran. In *Remaking women: Feminism and modernity in the Middle East*, ed. Lila Abu-Lughod, 215–42. Princeton, NJ: Princeton University Press.

Tacchi, Jo. 1998. Radio texture: Between self and others. In *Material culture: Why some things matter*, ed. D. Miller, 25–45. Chicago: University of Chicago Press.

Tambiah, Stanley. 1996. *Leveling crowds: Ethnonationalist conflicts and collective violence in South Asia*. Berkeley: University of California Press.

Thaiss, Gustav. 1972. Religious symbolism and social change: The drama of Husain. In *Scholars, saints, and Sufis in Muslim religious institutions in the Middle East since 1500*, ed. Nikki R. Keddie, 349–66. Berkeley: University of California Press.

Thompson, Elizabeth. 2000. *Colonial citizens: Republican rights, paternal privilege, and gender in French Syria and Lebanon*. New York: Columbia University Press.

Tibi, Bassam. 1995. Culture and knowledge: The politics of Islamization of knowledge as a postmodern project? The fundamentalist claim to de-westernization. *Theory, Culture and Society* 12:1–24.

Torab, Azam. 1996. Piety as gendered agency: A study of *jalaseh* ritual discourse in an urban neighborhood in Iran. *Journal of the Royal Anthropological Institute* 2:235–52.

Volk, Lucia. 2001. *Missing the nation: Lebanon's post-war generation in the midst of reconstruction.* Ph.D. diss., Harvard University.

Wadud, Amina. 2000. Alternative Qur'anic interpretation and the status of Muslim women. In *Windows of faith : Muslim women scholar-activists in North America*, ed. Gisela Webb, 3–21. Syracuse, NY: Syracuse University Press.

Walzer, Michael. 1965. *The revolution of the saints: A study in the origins of radical politics.* Cambridge, MA: Harvard University Press.

Wardlow, Holly. 2002. "Hands-up"-ing buses and harvesting cheese-pops: Gendered mediation of modern disjuncture in Melanesia. In *Critically modern: Alternatives, alterities, anthropologies*, ed. Bruce Knauft, 144–72. Bloomington: Indiana University Press.

Watts, Michael. 1996. Islamic modernities? Citizenship, civil society, and Islamism in a Nigerian city. *Public Culture* 8:251–89.

Waugh, Earle H. 1977. Muharram rites: Community death and rebirth. In *Religious encounters with death: Insights from the history and anthropology of religions*, ed. Frank E. Reynolds and Earle H. Waugh, 200–13. University Park: Pennsylvania State University Press.

Weber, Max. 1946. Class, status, and party. In *Max Weber: Essays in sociology*, 180–95. Oxford: Oxford University Press.

———. 1958. *The Protestant ethic and the spirit of capitalism.* New York: Charles Scribner's Sons. (Orig. pub. 1930.)

———. 1963. *The sociology of religion.* Boston: Beacon Press. (Orig. pub. 1922.)

Wedeen, Lisa. 1999. *Ambiguities of domination: Politics, rhetoric, and symbols in contemporary Syria.* Chicago: University of Chicago Press.

White, Jenny B. 1996. Civic culture and Islam in urban Turkey. In *Civil society: Challenging western models*, ed. Chris Hann and Elizabeth Dunn, 143–54. London: Routledge.

———. 2002. *Islamist mobilization in Turkey: A study in vernacular politics.* Seattle: University of Washington Press.

Woodward, Mark R. 2002. Modernity and the disenchantment of life: A Muslim-Christian contrast. In *Islam in the era of globalization: Muslim attitudes towards modernity and identity*, ed. Johan Meuleman, 111–42. London: RoutledgeCurzon.

Yahya, Maha. 1993. Reconstituting space: The aberration of the urban in Beirut. In *Recovering Beirut: Urban design and post-war reconstruction*, ed. Samir Khalaf and Philip S. Khoury, 128–66. New York: Leiden.

Yousefi, Naghi. 1995. *Religion and revolution in the modern world: Ali Shari'ati's Islam and Persian revolution.* New York: University Press of America.

Zuhur, Sherifa. 1992. *Revealing reveiling: Islamist gender ideology in contemporary Egypt.* Albany: State University of New York Press.

Index

'abāya, 51, 51n, 111, 138, 232, 233
Abbas, 137, 144
account with God, 103, 195–96
activism, 78, 131, 149, 153–54, 158,
  163–64, 187, 201–3, 202n, 216, 220, 228
adhān, 59–61, 60n, 121, 133, 167–168
affect, 141, 147, 151
Afghanistan, 3, 230–31
afterlife, 103, 142, 162, 194–97, 217
al-Ahd, 84n, 155n, 184
'ahl al-bayt, 142, 145–49, 201–2, 220
airplanes, 231; Israeli, 44, 158–59
A'isha, 215, 215n
'ajr, 149, 151, 195, 217, 233
Ali, Imam, 11, 60–61, 64–65, 69, 117n,
  129, 134, 134n, 182, 202, 215
Amal, 47, 47n, 51, 54–55, 62, 77n, 78–79,
  78n, 82–83, 82n, 83n, 88n, 92, 135n,
  155, 162
American University of Beirut, 39, 51, 136,
  171, 179, 188–90
al-Amin, Sayyid Muhsin, 131–32, 135,
  149, 153n, 157
anonymity, 44, 57, 175
anthropologist, 34, 156n
anthropology, 21
apathy, 197, 197n
al-'aql, 21, 23, 27, 70n, 93, 114, 120, 143,
  151, 162, 233
Arab Gulf States, 19n, 25, 71, 73, 89,
  114n, 127, 178–79, 179n, 231
Asad, Talal, 21, 21n, 35n, 105, 105n
asceticism, 63, 103
Ashura, 6, 61–65, 61n, 82, 97, 102,
  105–6, 117, 127–64, 130n, 131n, 132n,
  134n, 135n, 184, 213, 217, 220,
  223–24, 226; authenticated, 133,
  137–39, 141–43, 142n, 145–54,
  156–58; discourses of, 133–56; and
  gender, 139, 139n, 148; history of, 61,
  61n, 123; and public space, 154–55,
  155n; traditional, 133, 133n, 136,
  139, 141–42, 142n, 144, 146–52,
  154, 156–58; transformation of, 7,
  131–33, 154

authenticated Islam, 6–8, 18, 20, 21n,
  22–23, 30, 33, 49, 75, 97, 102–3,
  113–14, 116–19, 124, 127–28,
  138n, 176–77, 180, 184–86, 204–5,
  208, 212, 214–15, 218, 225–26,
  228–29, 232
authentication, 8, 20, 20n, 21–22, 22n, 27,
  35, 71, 71n, 101n, 102, 118, 121–22,
  124, 127–30, 133, 149, 151, 154,
  156–59, 171–72, 177, 195, 201, 204,
  207, 213, 216, 220
authenticity, 19, 20, 21, 23n, 31, 33, 140,
  143, 156, 226
authoritative discourse, 23, 35, 124–27,
  149, 156
awareness, 19, 77, 116–17, 132, 143, 164,
  183, 186n, 201, 225–26, 228

bāb al-ijtihād, 70, 70n
backwardness, 3, 13, 16–19, 19n, 22–24,
  24n, 28n, 30, 33, 75, 113, 132,
  136, 142, 142n, 154, 158, 172, 180,
  182–83, 214–15, 218, 230. See also
  takhalluf
banners: for Ashura, 62–63, 144, 155,
  160; for the *hajj*, 65
al-Bashā'ir, 60, 126
Beirut, 12, 42, 42n, 43n, 43–45, 45n,
  48–51, 55, 60, 64–65, 67, 73, 73n, 74,
  78–81, 83, 85–86, 88, 91, 99, 132, 155,
  173, 188–89, 192–93, 200, 222
Beqaa, 47–48, 72, 72n, 73n, 79, 82, 86,
  88, 132n, 159, 188
Berri, Nabih, 55, 82n, 88n
al-bī'a, 42, 49, 61, 65, 119, 128, 222–26,
  232–33
binaries, 26, 33, 153, 230–32
blood, 131, 134, 134n, 135, 137–38, 145,
  149–50, 153, 158, 199
bombardment, Israeli, 13, 44, 48, 158,
  164, 200
born-again Christianity, 27, 28, 35. See
  also Christian fundamentalism
bureaucratization, 27, 91, 172, 176
Bush, George W., 28, 161

call to prayer, 59–61, 60n, 121, 133, 167–68
Calvinism, 22n, 36
camps, refugee, 47, 81, 189
capitalism, 14, 25, 26n, 73–74, 76
capitalists, 108
captives, Ashura, 61, 130, 138, 141–42, 145–46, 148, 159, 217
cassette tapes, 60, 60n, 126, 126n
Catholicism, 26n, 116, 224
celebration, 63–65, 86, 168, 225
census, 47n, 72, 72n
chaos, 19, 43, 86, 108, 167
charitable organization, 50, 89, 91. See also *jam'iyya*
charity, 23, 41, 88, 169, 176, 199, 207; Islamic, 183, 207
child rearing, 126, 184, 215, 223, 225–26
children, 53, 64, 90–92, 129, 135, 137–38, 144–45, 156, 159, 163, 167, 171, 173–75, 177, 181, 183, 185–86, 188, 192–93, 196, 198–99, 201, 206, 206n, 210–11, 222–26
choice, 112, 115, 205, 224–25
Christian fundamentalism, 4, 4n, 28, 29. *See also* fundamentalism
Christianity, 24n, 28, 28n, 35n, 40, 101n, 102n, 105, 119n, 131n, 201; Shi'i ideas about, 9–10
Christians, 123; Lebanese, 11, 45, 47, 47n, 48, 60n, 84n, 85; in Lebanon, 5, 72, 72n, 84, 92–93, 132n
Christmas, 65
civilization, 16–18, 76, 171, 231
civil war, 13, 24, 36, 43n, 44, 47–48, 49n, 55, 55n, 67–68, 67n, 68n, 73, 77n, 78–79, 83–84, 84n, 86, 88, 91, 151, 173, 178, 187–88, 192, 200
class, 45, 75, 110–11, 178–79, 178n, 210
clientelism, 85, 85n, 88
coexistence, 44, 55, 71n, 92, 94
colonialism, 4n, 29, 31n, 112n
commitment, to community, 31, 165, 187–88, 190–91, 196, 200, 217; religious, 34–36, 76–77, 80, 93, 102–3, 105–7, 112, 115, 121, 124, 169, 186–87, 189, 191, 194, 200–2, 205, 217–20, 222–23, 225–27, 233
common good, 34, 169, 228
communism, 75–76
Communist Party, Lebanese, 74, 77, 162

community, definitions of, 4n, 7–9, 8n, 11, 36, 48, 102, 105n, 128, 228; membership in, 105, 220, 228
community service, 7, 22, 38, 75, 125, 149, 154, 161, 163–205, 207–11, 213–15, 220, 228; as norm, 207; and piety, 194, 196, 207
community welfare, 34, 84, 87–88, 164, 169, 176–77, 195, 202, 210, 213n, 228
confessionalism, 10, 43, 53, 72–75, 84, 88, 197n
consciousness, 19, 77, 116–17, 132, 143, 164, 183, 186n, 201, 225–26, 228
consciousness-raising, 176, 180, 182–83. See also *taw'iyya*
consumerism, 25
conversion, 9–10, 37, 101, 123
conviction, 77, 113, 207, 221, 227–28. *See also* faith
corruption, 75, 85, 88, 130, 145, 164, 196
counternarrative, 75, 80
crying, 102, 131, 131n, 141–51, 159, 175, 224
cultivation of *iltizām*, 105, 105n, 115, 118, 118n, 194, 218, 220–21, 223
cultural imperialism, 24, 25, 31n
culturedness, 184–85, 189, 218

al-Dahiyya, 3, 6–8, 17, 37–38, 42–66, 42n, 55n, 68, 73, 78, 82, 82n, 86, 89–92, 94, 103, 105–8, 106n, 110–13, 117, 119–20, 119n, 125, 129, 130, 132n, 135–37, 146, 151, 154–55, 161, 164, 170, 172, 177, 178–79, 187, 190, 192–93, 197–98, 200–1, 207–8, 214, 220, 223–24, 229; description of, 7, 45–52, 45n, 47n, 48n, 59; poverty in, 19, 33, 173–74
daycare, 91, 183, 211
deprivation. See poverty.
desire, 33, 74–75, 106, 114n2, 192, 194, 207, 217, 221, 227–28
detainees, 86, 90–91, 231
development, 17–18, 19n, 73, 91, 94, 105, 168, 170–71, 178, 180, 182–83, 182n, 184n, 228–29
dialect, 145, 147
dignity, 176
dirge. See *nudba*
discipline, 206
Discourse, 119, 119n

discursive piety, 103, 118–19, 128, 158
disenchantment, 23, 26, 26n, 28
displaced persons. *See* refugees
dispossession. *See* marginalization
disruption, 22, 32; temporal, 57n
divorce, 99, 120, 186, 211
domesticity, 31n, 208–11, 215
domestic sphere, 30–31, 212, 212n
donations, blood, 135; charitable, 37, 64,
    89–91, 91n, 165–69, 168n, 178, 181n,
    207, 225; to Resistance, 85
"door of interpretation", 70, 70n
double shift, 209–10, 210n
dress, 36, 76, 103, 110, 112, 155, 166,
    178–80, 206, 225–27; Islamic, 51, 110,
    111–14, 185, 205–6, 222, 229
Druze, 72n, 100
duty, 64–65, 193, 204; household, 194,
    209–11, 215; religious, 103, 106, 124,
    128, 179, 194–95, 207, 211, 219,
    224–25, 227

the East, 24, 33
economy, 88, 88n, 173–74, 178–81, 179n,
    183, 192–93, 196, 217, 231
education, 19, 22, 23n, 38, 61–62, 74–76,
    79, 89–91, 93, 105, 111, 124, 124n,
    133, 146, 150, 171, 174, 182–83,
    185, 188–90, 214, 216n, 218–19,
    222–25, 228
Egypt, 22n, 112n, 118n, 217
elections, 49, 51, 55, 214; and Hizbullah,
    84, 85n
electricity: and desire, 108; lack of, 44,
    120, 174, 181, 184, 193; in torture, 86
elegy, 135, 138n
elites, 29, 73, 75, 92, 108, 132, 179,
    180n, 196
embodied piety, 103, 111, 117, 119,
    127–28
embodiment of Ashura, 149–50, 158–59,
    162, 201, 207
emigration: from Lebanon, 12, 48, 74n,
    126, 179, 231; and return, 31n
emotionality, 141–44, 146–47, 150–51,
    157, 175, 221
employment, 74, 91, 113n, 169n, 172,
    174, 183, 208n, 209, 210n, 216n, 231
emulation, 69, 69n, 70, 71n, 94, 104, 127,
    163, 201–2, 207, 220
enchantment, 4, 4n, 28n

enlightenment, 19
Enlightenment, 27
environment. See *al-bī'a*
equality, 30, 212n, 213n, 217–19
equity, 212n, 213n, 216, 216n, 218–19
ethnography, 5–6, 15–16, 34n, 40
Europe, 23–24, 27, 108
evangelism, 24n, 27, 124n
exhibitions, 37–38, 58, 58n, 161,
    193, 231
expatriates, 43

Fadlallah, Sayyid Ali, 115, 126, 224
Fadlallah, Sayyid Muhammad Hussein, 38,
    54–55, 60, 60n, 62, 71, 71n, 78, 78n,
    82, 89–94, 93n, 94n, 100, 104, 104n,
    113n, 114–15, 125–27, 126n, 138n,
    142, 148n, 150, 150n, 154, 162n, 189n,
    190–91, 201, 225–26; on gender
    issues, 126, 148n, 210, 215–16, 216n
faith, 5–6, 8–10, 20, 27, 34–35, 37, 40–41,
    58, 75, 77, 95, 103, 112–13, 117, 128,
    159, 161–62, 169, 176, 191, 194–96,
    210, 218, 221, 229–30. See also
    conviction
false consciousness, 40
Falwell, Jerry, 27, 35
family law, 22n
fashion, 18, 47, 99, 178
fasting, 34, 37, 64, 70, 100, 102–3, 109,
    117–18, 120–21, 120n, 165, 167–68,
    194, 205, 207, 221–22, 225
Fatima, Sayyida, 61, 64, 69, 70n, 148n,
    202, 202n, 215–16
fatwas, 93, 93n, 135, 135n, 153, 233
fear, 44–45, 53, 67, 204, 227
female-headed households, 173, 173n,
    181, 208
feminism, 30n, 212n, 213n, 216; liberal
    western, 30, 217
feminists, 29n, 212n, 216n; early
    Lebanese, 31n
fiqh, 118, 125–26
fitna, 108, 108n. See also chaos
fiṭra, 119, 196
Foucault, 25, 119
France, 68
fundamentalism, Christian, 4, 4n, 28–29;
    Islamic, 3–5, 5n, 15, 18, 22n, 26, 29n1,
    39, 48, 60n, 80, 111, 162n, 201, 230;
    religious, 3–4, 27

fundraiser, 38, 63–64, 172, 172n, 178–79, 187
fundraising, 51, 53, 64, 89–91, 91n, 168, 172n
future, 15n, 27, 143, 149, 152, 231–32

Gandhi, 27, 151
gender: and collective identity, 5n, 218–19; and modernity, 5, 26, 29–30, 29n, 204, 213, 217–19, 230; and public piety, 30–31, 204–7, 219; and the public sphere, 31, 149, 212–14, 213n; and rationality, 213–14; and visibility, 7, 34, 113, 115, 140, 149, 204–7, 213n, 217–19
gender equality, 30, 212n, 213n, 217–19
gender equity, 212n, 213n, 216, 216n, 218–19
gender roles, 22, 26, 29, 33, 94, 163, 202–3, 208, 210, 215, 217–18, 224, 229; ideal, 5, 205, 208, 215. See also womanhood: ideal
generational difference, 7, 20, 76, 116, 119n, 124, 146–47, 178–79, 187, 221–23, 226–27, 231–32
generosity, 64, 179, 191, 202, 207
gesture, 59, 192
gift from God, 185, 190, 195, 210
good deeds, 104, 165, 190, 211, 214
gossip, 212–13, 226
government, 72–73, 75, 77, 79, 83n, 85, 88, 152, 174, 174n, 184. See also state
greetings, 102, 106–9, 107n, 165, 224
grief, 56, 129, 131, 147–48, 150, 163

ḥadīth, 11, 62, 64, 70, 102, 122, 124–25, 129, 145, 194, 197, 197n, 205, 233
ḥajj, 19n, 63–64, 64n, 109, 179, 189–90
handshaking, 103, 106–11, 110n
Harakat Amal, 47, 47n, 51, 54–55, 62, 77n, 78–79, 78n, 82–83, 82n, 83n, 88n, 92, 135n, 155, 162
Harb, Shaykh Raghib, 54
ḥawza, 78, 126, 147, 160, 216n
headscarf. 10, 17, 36–37, 51, 76, 99, 102–3, 107, 109–16, 111n, 112n, 113n, 118–119, 124–25, 138, 179, 182, 185, 189, 204, 206, 221–22, 228, 232–33; literature on, 6n, 112, 112n; and piety, 113, 221–22, 224–27

health care, 18, 38, 75, 90–91, 171, 174, 178, 184
hegemony, 49, 49n, 59, 228
hell, 68
heroes, 53, 129, 158, 198, 217
Hidden Imam, 27, 64, 69, 79, 80n, 94, 152
ḥijāb, 10, 17, 36–37, 51, 76, 99, 102–3, 107, 109–16, 111n, 112n, 113n, 118–119, 124–25, 138, 179, 182, 185, 189, 204, 206, 221–22, 228, 232–33; literature on, 6n, 112, 112n; and piety, 113, 221–22, 224–27
Hijri calendar, 61, 63–65, 93
historicism, 14, 14n, 33
hit ḥaydar, 134, 134n, 135, 138n, 139n. See also laṭam
Hizb al-Daʿwa, 77–80, 82
Hizbullah, 3, 5n, 32, 34, 38–40, 39n, 45, 47, 49n, 50–51, 52n, 54–55, 60, 62, 64, 78, 84n, 85–87, 85n, 87n, 90–92, 94, 104, 106, 110–11, 113, 124, 124n, 135, 135n, 138–39, 138n, 146, 146n, 150–52, 151n, 154–55, 155n, 158–59, 161–62, 174n, 184, 200, 230–31; constituency of, 11n, 86, 85n; generalizations about, 7–8, 25; origins of, 82–84, 82n, 83n. See also the Resistance
Hizbullah Women's Committee, 38, 90, 159, 215
holiday, 36, 64–65
hospitals, 73, 89, 91, 115, 171–72, 175, 189, 214n
household responsibility, 194, 209–11, 215
humanitarianism, 7, 34–35, 169, 189, 191, 193, 195–96, 199, 202, 220; and piety, 193, 196
Husayn, Imam, 6, 61–64, 62n, 69, 106n, 123, 129–30, 134, 134n, 137–38, 142–52, 154–60, 162–63, 160n, 200, 202, 217
ḥusayniyya, 62, 62n, 91, 126, 129, 132n, 137, 144, 146, 155–57, 233

iconography, 55, 58–59, 198
identity, 12, 37, 42, 154n, 187; Arab-American, 10n; collective, 51n, 58, 60n, 103, 119n, 130n, 149, 219; crisis of, 12–13, 13n, 36; in Lebanon, 9–12, 10n, 14n; religious, 9–10, 36, 49; and sectarianism, 10–11, 10n, 13, 36, 43, 60, 222

ifṭār, 38, 64, 166–69, 178–79, 211, 233
ignorance, 19, 23, 75, 77, 116, 120, 123, 177–78, 180, 182, 215–16
ijtihād. See interpretation: religious
iltizām, 34–36, 76–77, 80, 93, 102–3, 105–7, 112, 115, 121, 124, 169, 186–87, 189, 191, 194, 200–2, 205, 217–20, 222–23, 225–27, 233
images, 49, 51, 51n, 54, 58–59, 223; Ashura, 62 (*see also* banners); critiques of, 55–58; of orphans, 49, 51–53, 53n, 57–58, 64, 197, 199; of martyrs, 49, 51–53, 52, 56–58, 57n, 140, 161; of religious leaders, 49, 51–53, 55–58, 79, 80
Imam Ali, 11, 60–61, 64–65, 69, 117n, 129, 134, 134n, 182, 202, 215
Imam Husayn, 6, 61–64, 62n, 69, 106n, 123, 129–30, 134, 134n, 137–38, 142–52, 154–60, 160n, 162–63, 200, 202, 217
Imam al-Mahdi, 27, 64, 69, 79, 80n, 94, 152
Imams, 32, 69, 70n, 102, 119, 127n
Imam al-Sadr Foundation, 88n, 92, 110
imitation, 225. *See also* emulation
individualism, 24, 30–31, 31n
individualized selves, 176, 217–18
infallibles, 70n, 201
infrastructure, 73, 85, 174, 192, 228
injustice, 133, 152, 158, 158n, 200–201
institutionalization, 27, 33, 66–67, 73, 87–88, 91, 94–95, 127, 130–31, 170, 207, 227–28, 231
institutions, 38, 44, 59, 78–79, 82–84, 87, 92, 94–95, 177, 205, 226; charitable, 23, 88–89, 91, 88n, 172; religious, 23; sectarian, 73
intercession, 142, 149n
internet, 47, 125–27, 126n, 127n
interpretation, 34, 106n; religious, 20–21, 23, 35, 70–71, 70n, 71n, 93–94, 101–2, 110, 120, 123, 125–26, 127n, 128, 149, 201, 214–16, 216n, 218, 233; of Zaynab's behavior, 130, 148–49, 162–63, 202, 205
Iran, 23n, 25, 51n, 68, 80n, 82n, 83, 84n, 90, 90n, 94n, 112n, 127n, 131n, 133, 135, 138n, 139n, 172n, 216n; Islamic revolution in, 6, 23n, 26n, 31n, 69, 71, 75, 77n, 78–80, 79n, 82, 112, 116, 150n, 151n, 201, 229, 231

Iraq, 24, 40, 51n, 68, 71, 78–79, 230–31; and Ashura, 61, 138n, 144, 147; invasion of, 161; U.S. occupation of, 24, 40, 106n, 158n
Islamic calendar, 61, 63–65, 93
Islamic Charity Emdad Committee, 38, 90, 92, 172, 175, 177, 185, 197
Islamic fundamentalism, 3, 5, 39. *See also* fundamentalism
Islamic history, 31, 61, 94, 121–23, 130–31, 143, 149, 151, 156–58, 160, 177, 201–2, 207, 216–17, 228
Islamic law, 22n, 71, 93, 102, 111–12, 177, 206n, 210
Islamic movement, 22n, 60n, 162n, 201; Lebanese Shiʻi, 6, 8, 52, 58–59, 65–68, 75, 77, 88, 91–92, 94, 102, 110, 127–28, 131, 133, 135, 153, 170, 189, 207, 222
Islamic Resistance, 8, 51, 57, 63, 83–86, 147n, 151, 155, 158–62, 161n, 198–200, 204, 208, 223; fighters in, 34, 160–62, 199; as nationalist, 159, 162; operations of, 159, 161n; support for, 12, 34, 51, 85, 85n, 199
Islamic revolution in Iran, 6, 23n, 26n, 31n, 69, 71, 75, 77n, 78–80, 79n, 82, 112, 116, 150n, 151n, 201, 229, 231
Islamism, 4, 5, 5n, 15, 18, 26, 29n, 48, 80, 111, 230
Islamization, 5
Israel, 4, 4n, 6, 24, 40n, 50, 68, 75, 79, 81, 81n, 83, 83n, 86, 85n, 87n, 90, 129, 159, 198, 200, 229; and attacks on Lebanon, 13, 44, 48, 77, 77n, 78n, 80, 82, 85, 85n, 133, 159–60, 188–89, 192, 223, 231; and occupation of Lebanon, 6, 8, 39–40, 68, 79, 82, 84, 86–87, 150, 158, 161, 163–64, 173, 198–99, 208, 223, 228; and withdrawal from Lebanon, 37, 53, 68, 84–87, 85n, 105–6, 159, 199, 223, 231
Israeli occupation forces, 81–82, 86, 162
izdiwāj, 194

Jabal ʻAmil, 72, 77n, 131–32, 132n
jamʻiyya, 37–39, 50–51, 59, 63–64, 88–92, 94–95, 99, 101, 104–6, 109, 124–25, 155, 159–60, 164, 166, 168–72, 168n, 169n, 172n, 174–87, 177n, 193–94, 197–201, 205–11, 208n, 209n, 214, 226, 233; women-only, 213–14, 218

Japan, 25, 25n, 26n
jihād, 70, 204, 233; gender, 204, 212,
212n, 214, 216–18, 216n; women's, 7,
32, 203–4, 212, 218–19
jinn, 122
Judgment Day, 27, 69, 117, 152,
195, 199

Karbala, 61, 63, 129–32, 130n, 131n,
132n, 141, 145, 147–49, 149n, 151–52,
151n, 154–60, 158n, 162, 202, 217, 224
Khadija, Sayyida, 32, 202, 216
Khamenei, Ayatollah, 54, 63, 71, 94, 94n,
125, 135n, 138, 153, 155
Khiam Prison, 86–87, 231–32
Khomeini, Ayatollah, 28, 50, 54–55, 62,
71, 80–81, 90, 94n, 116, 129, 135n,
138, 184, 201, 215, 216n
Khu'i, Sayyid, 71, 89, 94n
khums, 70, 70n, 89, 127, 168n, 207, 233.
See also religious taxes
kin relations, 176, 209, 209n
kinship idiom, 176–77, 209, 209n
knowledge, 27, 35, 60, 119n; and poverty,
182; religious, 20, 23, 30, 60, 77, 100,
103, 116–19, 121–28, 150–51, 153,
182, 184, 202, 222–26, 228; scientific,
27, 184; women's, 122, 216
Koselleck, 18n, 27

labor, 31n, 74, 89–91, 172, 208n, 214
lamentation, 129–30, 130n, 133, 138n,
141–45, 147
laṭam, 131, 131n, 132, 134–40, 134n,
135n, 138n, 139n, 149–50, 150n,
153–54, 233
laylat al-qadr, 64, 64n
Lebanese identity crisis, 12–13, 13n, 36
Lebanese Shi'i Islamic movement, 6, 8, 52,
58–59, 65–68, 75, 77, 88, 91–92, 94,
102, 110, 127–28, 131, 133, 135, 153,
170, 189, 207, 222
Lebanese Union of Muslim Students,
78, 82
lecture, Ashura, 129, 143–45
the Left, 77, 79, 80, 222; failures of, 53,
79–80, 79n
Liberation, 37, 53, 68, 84–87, 85n, 105–6,
159, 199, 223, 231
Libya, 68, 79
liturgy, 141

Al-Mabarrat Association, 38, 88–89, 92,
177, 181, 189–91, 197, 210, 214n, 224
al-Mahdi, Imam, 27, 64, 69, 79, 80n,
94, 152
majālis 'aza, 23, 37, 62, 62n, 121, 123–24,
131, 131n, 132n, 133, 135n, 137–51,
139n, 141n, 146n, 147n, 153, 155–58,
155n, 156n, 157n, 164, 226, 233
majlis. See *majālis 'aza*
al-Manār, 60, 84n, 86, 126, 159–60, 160n
mandate, French, 47, 72
marginalization, Shi'i, 13, 19, 36, 50, 52,
67, 69, 74–75, 79, 87–88, 95, 132,
201, 231
marji'iyya, 69, 69n, 70n, 71n, 94n, 127
marji' al-taqlīd, 23, 37–38, 69–71, 69n,
71n, 82, 89, 92–94, 94n, 102, 125–26,
168n, 201, 233
Maronites, 47–48, 72–73, 72n, 78
marriage, 32n, 64, 74, 111, 127n, 210–11,
216n (*see also* images); temporary, 120,
120n, 127
martyrs, 38n, 52–53, 56–58, 91, 140, 142,
145, 161–62, 161n, 224, 232; family of,
161, 163, 198–200; Resistance, 49,
53, 90, 138, 158n, 198–200; women,
162, 162n
Martyrs' Association, 38, 53n, 90–92, 115,
124, 161, 171–72, 197–200, 214n
martyrdom, 49n, 61, 69, 154, 157–58,
202, 208, 228; of Imam Husayn, 61–62,
69, 123, 130, 141, 143, 151, 156n,
162, 217
martyrdom operations, 162, 162n
masīra, 97, 105, 131, 131n, 133, 135,
135n, 137–40, 139n, 149, 155, 159, 233
massacres, 80–81, 81n, 189
materialism, 24, 30, 179
mawlid, 63–64, 168, 184
Mecca, 64
media, 25n, 43, 51n, 61, 64, 82, 106n,
114, 126, 156, 156n; Hizbullah, 38, 57,
126; U.S., 3, 24–25, 30, 162, 162n, 230
memorialization, 56–57, 106n, 161, 231
message, Ashura, 148, 151–52, 156, 158,
163, 199, 217
metadiscourse, 122, 219
middle class, 31n, 47, 85n, 88, 178–79,
207, 214
milieu, 42, 49, 61, 65, 119, 128, 222–26,
232–33

military, 24–26, 68, 73, 84, 83n, 86–87, 161–62, 231
militias, 49n, 68, 78, 80
millenarianism, 27
mind, 21, 23, 27, 70n, 93, 114, 120, 143, 151, 162, 233
mobilization, Shi'i Lebanese, 33, 68, 74–75, 78–80, 82, 95, 112, 116–17, 130, 132–33, 139, 150–51, 170, 187, 222. *See also* Lebanese Shi'i Islamic movement; women's, 138n
models. *See* role models
modernism, 19th century Islamic, 27n
modernity, alternative, 14–15, 153, 229; and Ashura, 152–53; and authenticated Islam, 23, 228; as civilized, 16–19, 25, 29, 33, 76, 80, 171, 228; critiques of, 14, 14n; discourses of, 4–5, 13–19, 15n, 22, 25, 29, 32–33, 113, 153, 153n, 170, 177, 184, 212, 218–19, 228–32; enchanted, 4–5, 28, 41, 95, 153, 228–29, 232; and gender, 5, 26, 29–30, 29n, 204, 213, 217–19, 230; Islam and, 15–16, 15n, 18, 25–26, 229; literature on, 14, 15n; nonsecular, 27, 29; plural, 14, 16; political stakes of, 5, 15, 25, 229, 231; and religion, 4, 80, 153, 171, 229, 231; salience of, 15; semantics of, 4n, 14, 15n, 16–17, 16n; and social relationships, 8, 30, 176, 186; and temporality, 18n, 152–54; western, 4n, 25, 29, 171, 176, 217, 229; western discourses of, 5, 14, 25, 25n, 26, 33, 36, 75, 153, 170, 176, 213, 230–31
modernization, 8, 19, 25–26, 33, 73–74, 93, 170–71, 176
modesty, 106, 109, 179, 224
morality, 5, 19, 22n, 23, 27, 31, 36, 75, 95, 102, 110, 115, 128, 151, 154, 169, 182, 182n, 187n, 201, 205–8, 217–18, 221, 223–24, 227, 229; normative, 206, 221, 223, 227
moral order. *See* morality
mosque, 59, 60, 62, 71, 105, 115–16, 118n, 126, 129, 134, 137, 155, 217, 224
mothers of martyrs, 163, 163n
Mother Theresa, 32, 194, 201
motivations, 76, 161–62, 213n, 217–18, 225, 228; for volunteering, 171–72, 186–87, 191, 196–97, 199, 207

mourning, 57, 59, 62, 129, 131, 142, 148–49, 149n, 155, 229
mourning gatherings, 23, 37. See also *majālis 'aza*
Movement of the Deprived, 77–78, 132
mu'amalāt, 118, 169
muhajjaba, 75–76, 99–100, 102, 107–11, 113, 113n, 115–16, 138, 168, 181, 185, 206, 219, 221, 225, 227–28, 233
Muhammad, Prophet, 6, 26–27, 28n, 32, 61, 62, 64–65, 69, 70n, 100, 114n, 117, 119, 124, 127n, 141, 145–46, 197n, 198, 201–2, 215
Muharram, 61, 61n, 62, 129–30, 133, 135, 137, 141, 144–45, 151, 155. *See also* Ashura
mujtahid, 35, 70–71, 82, 94, 107, 110n, 113n, 233. *See also* religious scholar
al-Musawi, Sayyid Abbas, 50, 54, 78n, 158–59
muthaqqaf, 184–85, 189, 218
mutual reciprocal social relations, 118, 169

Nabatieh, 82, 133, 133n, 134n, 135–37, 135n, 139n, 150, 155, 159
Najaf, 78, 132
narration, Ashura, 129, 135n, 137, 141, 143–44, 146, 148
narrative, 7, 49, 53, 58–59, 58n, 79, 130, 151n, 156–57, 229, 231; volunteers', 197, 200
Nasrallah, Sayyid Hasan, 50, 53n, 54, 71, 78, 82, 105, 138, 150, 155, 158n, 159, 199, 201
national culture, 12, 36
National Pact, 72, 84
nationalism, 33, 49n, 105n, 112n, 162, 162n, 198
nationalist movements, 139n, 163; Lebanese, 13, 13n
nation-state, 161–62; Lebanese, 13, 19, 22n, 50, 52, 59, 67, 72, 74, 77, 84n, 92, 106, 162
networks, 43n, 187n, 209n
NGOs, 177, 177n
normative moral order, 206, 221, 223, 227
normativity, 22n, 36, 205–7, 217, 221, 223, 227
normativization, 5, 127, 227
North America, 24, 24n, 178

nudba, 62, 138, 138n, 143–46, 226, 233
al-Nūr, 60, 84n

objectification: of religion, 20–21, 23n; of
    women, 24, 114
occupation: of Lebanon, 6, 8, 39–40, 68,
    79, 82, 84, 86–87, 150, 158, 161,
    163–64, 173, 198–99, 208, 223, 228; of
    Iraq, 24, 40, 106n, 158n
official discourse, 23, 35, 124–27,
    149, 156
oppression, 58, 80, 111, 151n, 152, 154,
    158, 164, 173, 200–201, 205, 218–19
orphanages, 89, 92, 172, 177, 181,
    183, 189
orphan, 49–50, 52–53, 58, 88–92, 165,
    168, 172–73, 175, 177, 185, 189,
    197–99, 202, 211; as icon, 64, 198–99.
    See also images
orphan sponsorship, 89–90, 177,
    197–98, 226
orthodoxy, 21, 21n, 105n, 122
Ottomans, 72, 72n
overpopulation, 43, 45, 47, 51, 174

Palestine, 162, 230–31
Palestinian liberation movement, 68, 74,
    77n, 139n
Palestinian resistance, 162
Palestinians, 40, 188
Parliament, 72–73, 72n, 82n, 84–85, 85n
participation of children, 224–27
passion play, 131n, 133, 134n, 135n, 151n
patriarchy, 209–10, 210n, 213–14, 216,
    218–19
performance, 36, 119n, 138, 220–21
personal piety, 103, 115, 169, 220–21,
    227–28, 231; and public piety, 23, 128,
    169, 219–21, 223, 226, 228, 230
personal status law, 22n
personhood, 184n. *See also* selfhood
Phalangists, 78, 80, 81n
photographs. *See* images
photography, 51n, 56–58, 57n; duality in,
    56–58; memorial, 56–57
piety. *See* personal piety; public piety
pilgrimage, 19n, 63–64, 64n, 109, 131n1,
    138n, 172n, 179, 189–90
planes, 231; Israeli, 44, 158–59
pleasure, 194
poetry, 129, 144, 147, 156, 161

polarizations, 26, 33, 153, 230–32
political climate, 39, 53, 106, 113
political Islam, 4
political quietism, 133, 149–50
politics, 6–7, 24, 26, 35, 42, 47–49, 51,
    54–55, 58n, 60, 66, 68–69, 75, 79, 84,
    85n, 88, 94, 94n, 106, 112–13, 128,
    146n, 191, 198–99, 215, 220, 223,
    229–32
the poor, 33–34, 65, 79, 88, 90, 92, 100,
    105, 112, 165, 171–72, 174–76,
    180–85, 184n, 193, 197–99, 202, 207,
    212, 214, 226
population density, 43, 45, 47, 51, 174
portraits. *See* images
portraiture, 57n, 58; political, 49, 51n,
    53, 56
postcolonialism, 24
poverty, 8, 45, 73–74, 90, 171–74, 173n,
    177–78, 187–88, 191–93, 196–98,
    200–1, 204; ideas about, 177–78,
    180–82; and ignorance, 180, 182
power, 15–16, 24–26, 24n, 80, 153–54,
    229–30; discursive, 5, 25
prayer, 34, 37, 59–61, 64, 70, 76, 100,
    102–6, 104n, 105n, 106n, 109, 112,
    115–19, 121, 125, 138, 144, 145n,
    165, 170, 186, 194, 196, 205, 207,
    221–23, 225
prisoners, 86, 90–91, 231. *See also* Khiam
    Prison
processions, 97, 105, 131, 131n, 133, 135,
    135n, 137–40, 139n, 149, 155, 159, 233
progress, 16–20, 18n, 22n, 24–27, 29, 33,
    52, 61, 66–67, 70–71, 75–76, 80, 87,
    94, 110, 140, 152–54, 159, 170, 172,
    178, 182–85, 207–8, 214, 219, 222,
    228–29; material, 18–19, 170–71, 176,
    178, 180, 207, 213, 219, 228–29; no-
    tions of, 5, 8; personal, 30, 118, 171,
    185–86, 209, 212, 214, 228; spiritual, 5,
    7, 18, 20, 22, 34, 42, 52, 87, 102, 113,
    117, 127–28, 143, 152–53, 171, 176,
    178, 180, 185, 207, 213, 219, 228–29
Prophet Muhammad, 6, 26–27, 28n, 32,
    61, 62, 64–65, 69, 70n, 100, 114n, 117,
    119, 124, 127n, 141, 145–46, 197n,
    198, 201–2, 215
Protestant Ethic, 28, 182n
Protestantism, 22n, 28, 35
Protestant Reformation, 27, 35

public arena, 34–35, 34n, 59, 95, 107n, 112, 156n, 207; and gender, 31, 149, 212–14, 213n

public good, 34, 164, 169, 176–77, 202, 210, 213n, 228

public participation of women, 31n, 94, 102, 113, 122, 140, 148n, 149, 156, 163, 202, 204, 207–9, 211–19, 222–23, 228; in discourse, 156–57, 205, 213, 213n, 216, 219; in military, 162, 208, 208n, 216; as progress, 207, 213–14, 219, 222–23

public piety, 35, 59, 93, 95, 102, 115, 128, 130, 158, 164, 180, 203–7, 212, 219, 221, 223, 226, 228–29, 231; and Ashura, 154, 158; definition of, 8, 34; gaps in, 220–21, 226–28; and gender, 30–31, 204–7, 219; and morality, 221; normativization of, 5, 36, 206–7, 221, 223, 227; as new, 20, 204–5, 207; and personal piety, 23, 128, 169, 219–21, 223, 226, 228, 230; and spiritual progress, 8, 18, 219, 228–29

public religiosity, 4, 26, 35, 103

public space, 6, 42, 48, 49n, 53, 112–13, 115, 154–55

public sphere, 34–35, 34n, 59, 95, 107n, 112, 156n, 207; and gender, 31, 149, 212–14, 213n

public welfare, 34, 84, 87–88, 164, 169, 176–77, 195, 202, 210, 213n, 228

purity, 71n, 118, 121, 127n

al Qaeda, 3n, 230

Qana, 13, 85, 85n

Qasim's wedding, 157, 157n

quietism, political, 133, 149–50

Qur'an, 60, 62, 64–65, 70, 76, 80, 89, 102, 114n, 117–19, 122, 127n, 129, 143, 165, 170, 170n, 186n, 195, 197, 205, 225

radio, 42n, 60–62, 64, 84n, 125–26, 126n, 156, 156n, 159, 161, 223

Ramadan, 37–38, 51, 53n, 63–65, 64n, 89–91, 100–2, 117, 120–21, 165–66, 167n, 168–69, 172, 187, 205, 207, 209, 211

Ramadan food center, 165–69, 172, 179, 187, 197, 211

rationality, 20, 22–23, 26–28, 35, 71, 93–94, 118, 205, 228; and gender, 213–14

rationalization, 22, 27, 35

reading, 123, 125–27, 141n, 215–16

reasons for volunteering, 171–72, 186–87, 191, 196–97, 199, 207

recitation, Ashura, 141–47; Qur'anic, 60, 89, 118–19

recitor, Ashura, 141–43, 141n, 145–47, 150, 152, 156

reconstruction, 43n, 192, 192n

reform, 75, 94, 116, 178, of Ashura, 131–33, 131n, 132n, 149–50, 157

refugees, 45, 79, 80–81, 88, 175, 188–89, 192; Palestinian, 47; Shi'i, 48, 81, 173

regret, 131, 149–50

reinterpretation of Zaynab's behavior, 130, 148–49, 162–63, 202, 205

relationality, 31, 31n, 186, 209, 226

religion as category of analysis, 35, 35n, 101n

religious fundamentalism. See fundamentalism

religious history, 31, 61, 94, 121–23, 130–31, 143, 149, 151, 156–58, 160, 177, 201–2, 207, 216–17, 228

religious law, 22n, 71, 93, 102, 111–12, 177, 206n, 210

religious leaders. See religious scholars

religious obligation, 103, 106, 124, 128, 179, 194–95, 207, 211, 219, 224–25, 227

religious scholars, 23, 35, 28, 69–71, 70n, 76, 78, 82, 94, 107, 110–11, 110n, 113n, 119, 125–27, 133, 135, 135n, 138, 148–50, 156–57, 201, 233. See also images

religious taxes, 70, 90, 118, 168n, 178. See also khums

representation, 53, 56–57, 141, 148, 218, 221; political, 75

reputation, 123, 180–81, 206, 208

resilience, 43–44, 114, 148, 192

resistance, 25, 106n, 150, 150n, 152, 201, 208; cultural, 15; the ḥijāb as, 111–12, 112n

the Resistance against Israeli occupation, 8, 51, 57, 63, 83–86, 147n, 151, 155, 158–62, 161n, 198–200, 204, 208, 223; fighters in, 34, 160–62, 199;

the Resistance (*continued*)
as nationalist, 159, 162; operations of, 159, 161n; support for, 12, 34, 51, 85, 85n, 199
responsibility: God-given, 190–91, 193, 195, 215; household, 194, 209–11, 215; to Resistance martyrs, 199; religious, 115, 117, 224 (*see also* duty); social, 106, 129, 144, 184, 186n, 215, 231; women's, 204, 215, 218
revolution, 76, 80, 92, 132n, 133, 143, 146n, 148–49, 151–53, 151n, 153n, 156–59, 158n, 200, 217. *See also* Iran
ritual, 34, 41, 61, 75, 105, 119, 131n, 186
role models, 26, 27, 31–32, 130, 153–54, 158, 158n, 160, 162–63, 172, 191, 201–2, 204–5, 214, 216–17; volunteers as, 185; Zaynab as, 130, 153, 156, 163, 191, 202, 202n, 204, 207, 217–18, 224

Sabra and Shatila, 80–81, 81n, 189
sacrifice, 8, 41, 49n, 57, 129, 143, 150–51, 158, 161–62, 162n, 164, 191, 198–200, 202, 212, 217
al-Sadr, Sayyid Musa, 28, 54, 55, 74, 77–80, 78n, 78n, 88, 88n, 92, 132, 132n, 138, 201; disappearance of, 79, 82n, 88
al-Sadr, Sayyida Rabab, 88n, 201
Safar, 62–63
salvation, 142, 149–51
Saudi Arabia, 25, 65, 68n
Sayyida Zaynab, 27, 32, 129–30, 138n, 142, 144–46, 148–49, 148n, 153, 156, 159, 162–63, 172, 191, 202, 202n, 204–5, 207, 217–18, 220; reinterpretation of, 130, 148–49, 162–63, 202, 205; as role model, 130, 153, 156, 163, 191, 202, 202n, 204, 207, 217–18, 224
sayyids, 28n. *See* religious scholars
school, 33, 73, 76–77, 89–91, 92, 104, 109, 115–17, 119, 119n, 143, 159, 164, 168, 172–75, 177, 187–90, 205–6, 223–25, 227, 231–32
science, 33, 89, 143, 184; and Islam, 27–28, 93
Scopes Trial, 28
scouts, 116, 138–39
seasons, 5, 22, 60–61, 63–65; of mourning, 61–63, 65
sect, 60, 73

sectarian identity, 10–11, 10n, 13, 36, 43, 60, 222
sectarianism, 10, 43, 53, 72–75, 84, 88, 197n; and space, 43, 43n, 48–49, 60
secularism, 26, 35, 113
secularists, 24n, 162; Lebanese, 10n, 11, 75–76, 78, 162, 162n
secularity, 5, 27, 29, 229
secularization, 23, 26, 29, 32
self-betterment, 30, 118, 171, 185–86, 209, 212, 214
self-consciousness, 20–22, 218, 223
self-development, 30, 118, 171, 185–86, 209, 212, 214
self-expectations, 205
self-flagellation. See *laṭam*
selfhood, 30–31, 31n, 105, 105n, 114, 118, 176, 185–86, 191, 194, 209, 217–18, 221, 229
self-improvement, 30, 118, 171, 185–86, 209, 212, 214
seminar, 38, 184, 214–15; volunteer training, 175, 185, 196, 205
seminary, 78, 126, 147, 160, 216n
September 11, 2001, 3, 4, 230–31
sermons, 60–61, 60n, 82, 113–15, 118n, 123, 125–27, 126n, 150n, 154, 215; Ashura, 141–43, 145n, 147
sexism, 214. *See also* patriarchy
Shamseddin, Shaykh Muhammad Mehdi, 78n, 88, 88n
sharī'a, 22n, 71, 93, 102, 111–12, 177, 206n, 210
Sharon, Ariel, 80, 81n
shaykhs, *See* religious scholars
Shebaa Farms, 87, 87n, 231
Shi'ism, origins of, 11n, 69–71, 69n
Sistani, Sayyid, 71, 94n
Social Advancement Association, 38, 91–92, 151, 172, 174–75, 179, 185–86, 196–97, 200, 213
social capital, 106, 106n, 221
social expectations, 11n, 113, 115, 205–7
social norms, 36, 107–8, 115, 169n, 180, 204–7, 212, 214, 218, 223, 228–29
social pressure, 11n, 113, 115, 205–7
social responsibility, 106, 129, 144, 184, 186n, 215, 231
social status, 30, 178, 180, 180n, 182n, 221

social welfare, 34, 84, 87–88, 164, 169, 176–77, 195, 202, 210, 213n, 228
solidarity, 57–59, 132, 138, 149, 153
soteriological meaning, 133, 148, 152–53
sound: public, 64, 103; sacred, 59–60
soundscape, 42n, 59–62, 64, 103
Sour, 42, 77, 88
the south, 8, 42, 47–48, 53, 72–73, 73n, 77, 77n, 79, 81–88, 82n, 90, 92, 105–6, 110, 131, 131n, 158, 164, 173, 188, 231
South Asia, 29
Southern Lebanese Army, 84–86, 86n
southern suburbs of Beirut. *See* al-Dahiyya
space, 7, 21, 47, 103, 152; claiming of, 52–53, 56, 60, 60n, 64–65; and gender, 208–9; public, 6, 42, 48, 49n, 53, 112–13, 115, 154–55; sacralization of, 59–60, 143, 145n; sectarianization of, 43, 43n, 49, 60
speech, 102, 114, 118–19, 119n
spiritual progress, 5, 7, 18, 20, 22, 34, 42, 52, 87, 102, 113, 117, 127–28, 143, 152–53, 171, 176, 178, 180, 185, 207, 213, 219, 228–29
state, 13, 22, 52, 59, 74, 77, 84, 92. *See also* government
status, 131, 230; political, 180; social, 30, 178, 180, 180n, 182n, 221; of women, 29–30, 204, 213, 218–19, 230
stereotypes, 13–14, 13n, 25n, 34n, 45, 47; about Islam, 4, 13n, 24, 32, 153; about Lebanese women, 114, 114n, 213–14; about Muslim women, 30n, 32, 111, 213–14, 218, 222, 230; about Shi'i Muslims, 13, 13n, 17, 19, 113, 136, 183; about the West, 13, 24
stigma, 11, 34n, 36, 132
subjectivity, 12, 14, 186n
suicide bombings. *See* martyrdom operations
Sunni Muslims, 13n, 61, 63, 65, 69–70, 72–73, 72n, 104n, 120–21, 120n, 132n, 216
support from men, 211, 215
Supreme Islamic Shi'i Council, 77, 78n, 79
Syria, 13n, 53n, 53, 68, 82n, 83, 84n, 85–87, 85n, 86n, 87n, 123, 179, 231
Syrian Social Nationalist Party, 74, 162

Ta'if Accord, 68, 84
takāful ijtimā'ī, 195, 195n, 201, 207, 233. *See also* social responsibility
takhalluf, 180–83, 185, 198, 233. *See also* backwardness
taklīf, 190, 195, 224, 233; of girls, 224–25
Taliban, 3, 3n, 230
taqiyya, 72
taqwā, 117, 117n, 169, 184, 194, 225, 233
taw'iyya, 175, 180–85, 233; for men, 214–15; for volunteers, 185–86, 209
tears, 129, 137, 142, 145–46, 148–50, 153–54, 158, 226
technology, 15, 17–18, 25, 91, 93, 170–71; communication, 22, 23n, 71n, 126n; and Islam, 171
television, 3, 60–62, 84n, 102, 106, 114n, 125–26, 126n, 155–56, 159, 161, 181, 223
temporality, 18n, 22n, 26–27, 147, 152–54, 154n, 220
tent, Ashura, 137, 155, 155n
territoriality, 51, 53, 55, 55n, 62, 83
terrorists, 39–40, 83, 83n
texts, 141n, 143, 153; access to, 20; religious, 21, 23, 28n, 35, 62, 102, 119, 121–22, 126, 126n, 198, 215–16, 216n, 218
textures, 42, 42n, 48–50, 61, 64, 66–67, 127, 220
time, 18, 48, 59–60, 152, 164, 201; volunteers', 168–69, 172, 191, 194, 200, 207, 210, 214; wasting, 179, 214
tiredness: lack of, 193–94, 200, 210
torture, 86
tradition, 17n, 18–23, 21n, 25, 29–31, 33, 77, 102, 112, 116–18, 123–24, 128, 131–32, 146, 153–54, 153n, 154n, 157, 212, 214, 216, 216n, 222, 229–30
traffic, 43–45, 50, 86, 165, 168
transnationality, 30n, 105n, 110, 161, 177n, 219, 229–30
Tufayli, Shaykh Subhi, 54–55, 78n
turf wars, 51, 53, 55, 55n, 62, 83
Turkey, 24, 53n, 139n, 180n
Twelfth Imam, 27, 64, 69, 79, 80n, 94, 152
Tyre, 42, 77, 88

ulama. See religious scholars
uncertainty, 35–36, 71, 228

underdevelopment, 19
underrepresentation, 72–73, 84
unemployment, 74, 174, 181, 208n
United Nations, 13, 85n
United States, 22–24, 28–29, 35, 39–40,
    49n, 65, 68, 83, 83n, 102n, 106,
    106n, 127, 161, 177n, 187, 223,
    229–31; and occupation of Iraq, 24, 40,
    106n, 158n
urbanization, 18, 47, 73–74, 132–33, 179
urban planning, 43n, 47
U.S. armed forces, 161–62
U.S. policy, 40, 230

vanguard, 116, 187, 222–23, 227
veil, 10, 17, 36–37, 51, 76, 99, 102–3,
    107, 109–16, 111n, 112n, 113n,
    118–119, 124–25, 138, 179, 182, 185,
    189, 204, 206, 221–22, 228, 232–33;
    literature on, 6n, 112, 112n; and piety,
    113, 221–22, 224–27
video, 161, 161n, 168
village, 18, 45, 47–48, 73–75, 77n, 86,
    132, 132n, 188, 224
violence, 24, 40, 48, 55n, 67, 77n, 81–82,
    86, 135n, 150, 173, 192, 199, 204,
    216n, 223, 231
visibility, 13, 34–36, 34n, 99, 106, 106n,
    127, 228; of commitment/iltizām, 180,
    204–7, 218, 228–29; and modernity, 7,
    230; of piety, 180, 204–7, 218, 228–29;
    of poverty, 173, 187, 193; of religion,
    34, 52, 67, 99, 101–3, 101n, 106, 113,
    115, 119, 122, 127, 206, 228; of Shi'a,
    34, 42, 48, 50, 102, 106, 127, 204, 228,
    230; of volunteering, 207; of women, 7,
    34, 113, 115, 140, 149, 204–7, 213n,
    217–19
visiting, 65, 105, 214; as method, 174–75,
    177, 184, 208, 212
visits: fundraising, 178–79
volunteering, 37, 91, 124, 164, 170,
    186–87, 189, 193–95, 206–9, 211, 221,
    223, 227
volunteerism, 7, 169, 169n, 187–88, 194,
    204–5, 207–8, 213n; and gender roles,
    208, 208n, 211–12; as new, 207; and
    piety, 169, 194. See also community
    service
volunteers, 7, 32, 38, 39n, 63, 89–92, 95,
    105, 117, 125, 151, 164–65, 167n,

168–71, 169n, 172–80, 182–87,
    191–201, 205–15, 208n, 224
vow, 135, 138n, 139n

Wahabi Islam, 19n
wā'ī, 19, 77, 116–17, 132, 143, 164, 183,
    186n, 201, 225–26, 228
war, 13, 24, 36, 43n, 44, 47–48, 49n, 55,
    55n, 67–68, 67n, 68n, 73, 77n, 78–79,
    83–84, 84n, 86, 88, 91, 147n, 151,
    173, 178–79, 187–88, 192, 198,
    200–201, 223
wealth, 47, 85, 89, 111, 165, 173, 178–80,
    183, 196
Weber, Max, 4, 22–23, 26n, 27–28, 35,
    182n
wedding, 62; Qasim's, 157, 157n
weeping, 102, 131, 131n, 141–51, 159,
    175, 224
welfare, community/public/social, 34, 84,
    87–88, 164, 169, 176–77, 195, 202,
    210, 213n, 228
welfare provision, 172, 174
the West, 3–4, 17, 23–27, 33, 36, 40,
    75, 80, 110–11, 153–54, 217–19,
    229–31
West Africa, 12, 178–79
westernization, 16, 24, 30, 110, 219
wilāyat al-faqīh, 69n, 80, 80n, 94
womanhood: ideal, 5, 30, 31n, 191, 205,
    214, 217–19, 222
women: discourses about, 29, 30, 204, 213,
    217–19, 222, 230; image of, 29, 213,
    218–19, 230; Islamist, 29n, 215n; public
    participation of, 31n, 94, 102, 113, 122,
    140, 148n, 149, 156–57, 162–63, 202,
    204–5, 207–9, 208n, 211–19, 213n,
    222–23, 228; status of, 29–30, 204,
    213, 218–19, 230; stereotypes about,
    30n, 32, 111, 114, 114n, 213–14, 218,
    222, 230
women-headed households, 173, 173n,
    181, 208
women's liberation, 29n, 30–33, 76,
    217–18, 230; critiques of, 30n, 76,
    217–18
women's rights, 76, 213n, 215–16
World War I, 47

Yazid, Caliph, 61, 123, 130, 138, 145–46,
    151–52, 159, 217

youth, 14n, 24, 74–75, 77–78, 91, 111, 134, 138, 150, 179, 198, 220, 223, 226, 231

zakāt, 70, 118, 207
Zaynab, Sayyida, 27, 32, 129–30, 138n, 142, 144–46, 148–49, 148n, 153, 156, 159, 162–63, 172, 191, 202, 202n, 204–5, 207, 217–18, 220; reinterpretation of, 130, 148–49, 162–63, 202, 205; as role model, 130, 153, 156, 163, 191, 202, 202n, 204, 207, 217–18, 224